PROSE MODELS
Sixth Edition

Gerald Levin
The University of Akron

HARCOURT BRACE JOVANOVICH, PUBLISHERS
San Diego   New York   Chicago   Atlanta   Washington, D.C.
London   Sydney   Toronto

ISBN: 0-15-572282-4
Library of Congress Catalog Card Number: 83-81703
Printed in the United States of America

PREFACE

As in previous editions, *Prose Models* introduces the rhetoric and logic of the essay through analysis of single and multiple paragraphs and complete essays. Although the essential plan and philosophy of the book are the same as before, the Sixth Edition has at least six new features that will further help students learn to write through reading, analyzing, and writing.

Headnotes that accompany each selection give brief information about the author and the selection itself. Where necessary, I have explained the context of excerpts, discussing the point of view and central ideas of the source. The discussions in each of the 36 sections now introduce the selections instead of following the first in each group.

I have also revised and reorganized several sections. The combined treatment of parallelism and balance in the new edition explains sentence balance as an aspect of parallelism instead of as a separate topic. In the material on the sentence, climax now immediately follows loose and periodic sentences in a natural continuation. I have also reorganized the section on the logic of the essay. The discussion of inductive reasoning now precedes that of deductive reasoning. "Interpretation of Evidence" now appears under "Argument and Persuasion," following the presentation of inductive and deductive reasoning. I have revised most of the discussions with simpler, less formal language. In addition, the greater number of reading selections and complete essays gives students and teachers even more choices than did earlier editions.

Although this new edition is a substantial revision, users of previous editions will find in it the features they have found useful in teaching composition. They will recognize the movement from part to whole and from shorter to longer selections. The discussion of paragraph development prepares the student for discussion of the same topics in the sentence and the expository essay. Later sections build on earlier ones, though each section is self-contained. The large number of complete essays are on topics of interest to the freshman student. Of the 109 selections, 49 are complete essays or self-contained sections of books.

The book provides teachers and students with theoretical and practical materials and abundant models. I offer a detailed treatment of the elements of sentence and paragraph development in the context of particular styles and subject matter. The selections illustrate the many kinds of sentence and paragraph arrangements available to the student writer.

The detailed discussion of the logic of the essay gives students guidance on this important topic, too. My presentation of inductive and deductive reasoning offers ample illustrations, and the final section gives attention to some important persuasive devices in argumentative writing. In addition, an apparatus for studying the essays in each section provides students with a discussion of the topic, with questions, and with suggestions for writing.

The book contains a representative selection of contemporary writing styles, with examples from some of the major essayists and writers of the twentieth century, including George Orwell, Eudora Welty, Mary McCarthy, Winston S. Churchill, E. B. White, James Thurber, and Norman Mailer. Also included are examples of writing by John Updike, Ernest Hemingway, Shirley Jackson, James Baldwin, Rachel Carson, Tom Wolfe, Russell Baker, William Zinsser, John Ciardi, Norman Cousins, Brooks Atkinson, H. L. Mencken, George Bernard Shaw, and W. S. Merwin. And minority writers and women are well represented.

The philosophy of the Sixth Edition of *Prose Models* has not changed from that of previous editions. To quote James Sledd, "Nobody ever learned to write without reading." Student writers need to understand the methods of prose composition; but these methods cannot serve alone to teach them the skills developed in the composition course. Students need to see these methods in practice. They need to see how writers use these methods in different ways and with different effects. Although examination of the writing process and exercises in invention can enhance writing skills, nothing can substitute for the close analysis of a large number of readings such as this book provides. While learning to generate ideas is a good place to begin, reading *Prose Models* gives students options for strategies to develop those ideas, as well as a sense of how a finished essay reads.

In choosing reading selections, I have looked for those of special interest to freshman students. I am not referring to selections concerned with sports or popular culture generally, though some do concern these. My own experience in teaching composition for almost thirty years has taught me that freshmen have wider interests and a greater capacity (and desire) to do abstract thinking than some teachers (and writers of textbooks) recognize. By the time they enter college, they are young adults—eager to consider the important issues of their society and concerned with learning how to think, read, and write about these issues.

In the belief that discussion and writing develop out of concrete experience and observation, I have organized the book so that students progress in their reading and writing in this way. Thus the experiences described concretely in earlier sections occur again in abstract and theoretical discussions later in the book. For example, many of the selections—those by Sally Carrighar, Maxine Hong Kingston, Mary E.

CONTENTS

Mebane, Winston Churchill—describe learning experiences in childhood and adolescence. A number of later selections—notably those of John Holt, Margaret Mead and Rhoda Metraux, Nancy K. Hill, and Liane Ellison Norman—discuss the problem of learning and the goal of education in a theoretical way. The thematic table of contents indicates these connections, and I have discussed them in the suggestions for teaching the selections in the Instructor's Manual.

My hope is that teachers and students will find the materials in this book exciting to read and to discuss.

In preparing this Sixth Edition, I owe particular thanks to Alan Hart, University of Akron, for his help in revising the discussions of logic. I owe thanks also to the following colleagues at the University of Akron who made suggestions for this edition: William Francis, Bruce Holland, Robert Holland, Julia Hull, David L. Jones, Walter Lehrman, Alice Mac-Donald, Lisa McFarren, Cheryl Pastor, John S. Phillipson, Sally K. Slocum, David Sowd, Linda Weiner, and Helen E. Woodman. I wish to thank the following for their suggestions also: Nancy Bent, State University of New York at Cortland; Linda Elden, California State University at Los Angeles; Robert Garner, Central Texas College; Jay Grover-Rogoff, Lemoyne College; Theodore L. Johnson, Northern Arizona University; Mark G. Roberts, Lemoyne College; Louise H. Strecker, San Diego State University.

Previous editions owe much to my earlier editors, especially Eben Ludlow and Natalie Bowen. I owe special thanks to the editors of this Sixth Edition, Marlane Agriesti and Gene Carter Lettau, for the same invaluable judgment and advice; to the designer, Ann Smith, for her creative efforts; and also to my production editor, Catherine Fauver, and production supervisor, Lynn Edwards, for their hard work. As always, I owe much to my wife, Lillian Levin, who assisted at each stage of this and previous editions.

Gerald Levin

Contents

PART TWO
THE WHOLE ESSAY

PART ONE

THE
ELEMENTS
OF THE ESSAY

THE PARAGRAPH: ORGANIZATION

Topic Sentence

In this first section of Part One we will consider how to organize and develop single paragraphs. In reading an essay, we usually depend on the opening sentences of paragraphs to show us the direction the essay is taking. Most paragraphs give us this direction by telling us what the paragraph will be about—that is, by stating its subject or topic—and sometimes giving us a full statement of the central idea. Here are examples of such topic sentences from an essay by Eric Sevareid describing his hometown in North Dakota:

> Consolidation [*one-word topic sentence stating the subject*]. The nearby hamlets of Sawyer and Logan and Voltaire had their own separate banks and papers and schools in my days of dusty buggies and Model Ts marooned in the snowdrifts. Now these hamlets are dying. . . .
> Sights have changed [*topic sentence stating the central idea*]: there is a new precision about street and home, a clearing away of chicken yards, cow barns, pigeon-crested cupolas, weed lots and coulees, the dim and secret adult-free rendezvous of boys. An intricate metal "jungle gym" is a common backyard sight, the sack swing uncommon. . . .

The topic sentence also may ask a question, to be answered in the paragraph. A later paragraph in Sevareid's essay opens: "But now I must ask myself: Are they nearer to one another?" The topic sentence, as these examples show, is usually the broadest statement of the paragraph, a generalization which details and other ideas develop. As such it may appear later, perhaps at the end of the paragraph, with a series of details or ideas building to it. The paragraph is said to have an implied topic sentence when the details alone make the point, the generalization remaining unstated.

EDWIN WAY TEALE

EDWIN WAY TEALE *(1899–1980) wrote much about nature in numerous articles and books and was also a distinguished photographer. His discussion of country superstitions appears in his book,* Wandering Through Winter, *for which Teale received the Pulitzer Prize in 1965. The book is one in a series of describing the seasons of the year in North America. In his paragraph Teale develops a single idea through a series of unusual examples.*

Country Superstitions

[1]In the folklore of the country, numerous superstitions relate to winter weather. [2]Back-country farmers examine their corn husks—the thicker the husk, the colder the winter. [3]They watch the acorn crop—the more acorns, the more severe the season. [4]They observe where white-faced hornets place their paper nests—the higher they are, the deeper will be the snow. [5]They examine the size and shape and color of the spleens of butchered hogs for clues to the severity of the season. [6]They keep track of the blooming of dogwood in the spring—the more abundant the blooms, the more bitter the cold in January. [7]When chipmunks carry their tails high and squirrels have heavier fur and mice come into country houses early in the fall, the superstitious gird themselves for

Topic Sentence   5

a long, hard winter. [8]Without any scientific basis, a wider-than-usual black band on a woolly-bear caterpillar is accepted as a sign that winter will arrive early and stay late. [9]Even the way a cat sits beside the stove carries its message to the credulous. [10]According to a belief once widely held in the Ozarks, a cat sitting with its tail to the fire indicates very cold weather is on the way.

QUESTIONS

1. How do sentences 2–10 illustrate the topic sentence of the paragraph?
2. How does Teale remind us of his topic idea in later sentences?
3. What do these illustrations tell us about country life?

WRITING ASSIGNMENTS

1. Describe a series of superstitions related to another season or to a particular activity. Build your paragraph to a conclusion about these superstitions.
2. Use one of the following statements as the topic sentence of a paragraph of your own. Develop it through a series of illustrations:
   a. Winter or summer, sports make special demands on participants or spectators.
   b. Riding the subway (or a similar activity) requires special skills.
   c. People have different driving habits.

MARSHALL McLUHAN

MARSHALL McLUHAN *(1911–1980) taught English and directed the Center for Culture and Technology at the University of Toronto. He is best known for his theory*

*that media shape the way we think and feel because
they are, in their different ways, extensions of our
senses. McLuhan was particularly interested in what
happens when new media like television and the press
displace an older medium like books. In this passage
from his book* Understanding Media, *he shows how a
"non-stop" medium like the newspaper generates an
experience different from the private experience of
reading a book. "The owners of media," McLuhan says
later, "always endeavor to give the public what it wants,
because they sense that their power is in the* medium
and not in the message *or the program."*

The Nonstop Use of Media

The first items in the press to which all men turn are the
ones about which they already know. If we have witnessed
some event, whether a ball game or a stock crash or a
snowstorm, we turn to the report of that happening, first.
Why? The answer is central to any understanding of media.
Why does a child like to chatter about the events of its day,
however jerkily? Why do we prefer novels and movies about
familiar scenes and characters? Because for rational beings
to see or re-cognize their experience in a new material form
is an unbought grace of life. Experience translated into a
new medium literally bestows a delightful playback of earlier awareness. The press repeats the excitement we have in
using our wits, and by using our wits we can translate the
outer world into the fabric of our own beings. This excitement of translation explains why people quite naturally
wish to use their senses all the time. Those external extensions of sense and faculty that we call media we use as
constantly as we do our eyes and ears, and from the same
motives. On the other hand, the book-oriented man considers this nonstop use of media as debased; it is unfamiliar to
him in the book-world.

QUESTIONS

1. Does the opening sentence—the topic sentence of the paragraph merely state the subject or instead give a full statement of the central idea?
2. What is the central idea of the paragraph, and how does McLuhan develop it?
3. How do the details help to explain what McLuhan means by *media*? What is the defining quality according to sentence 10?
4. What is the difference between reading a book and reading a newspaper according to McLuhan? Do you recognize such a difference in your own reading of newspapers and books?

WRITING ASSIGNMENTS

1. In a well-developed paragraph describe how you read a newspaper—what you turn to first, and what else you habitually read, and in what order. In a second paragraph discuss whether or not your experience confirms McLuhan's theory of media.
2. In two or more well-developed paragraphs discuss how well McLuhan explains your preference in books or movies.

JAMES STEVENSON

JAMES STEVENSON *has written a series of articles and profiles for* The New Yorker Magazine. *His description of a steep road in Los Angeles—from one of these profiles—introduces us to a contemporary director of horror films, John Carpenter. Notice how Stevenson creates a feeling of suspense in his selection of details and building of the paragraph.*

Loma Vista Drive

Partway down the long, very steep slope of Loma Vista
Drive, descending through Beverly Hills, with the city of Los
Angeles spread out far below the houses of sparkling opu-
lence on either side, there is a sign warning "Use Lowest
Gear" and, shortly after that, a sign that says "Runaway
Vehicle Escape Lane 600 Feet Ahead." Just before Loma
Vista crosses Doheny Road, it expands on the right into a
third lane, composed of a succession of low, uneven piles of
loose gravel nestled against cement block set in an embankment. The operator of a runaway vehicle is apparently
expected to steer his car into this soft and receptive lane and
come to a halt like a baseball player sliding into third. It
seems a perfectly reasonable solution; the unsettling aspect
is the underlying assumption that automobiles will so frequently go berserk hereabouts that some accommodation
must be made for them. Similarly, along the heavily popu-
lated canyon roads of Beverly Hills there are signs forbidding cigarettes and matches: these dry hills may burst into
flame at any time. The houses above Sunset Boulevard are
stuck in the nearly vertical slopes like cloves in a ham; how
they stay there is mysterious. It seems likely that, if they do
not catch fire first, a good rain will send them tumbling
down the mountain; already, earth has slid out from under
retaining walls, terraces, swimming pools, driveways, even
roads. In some places, tons of concrete have been poured
like icing over a section of hillside to hold it back—and the
concrete has even been painted green—but the earth has
begun to slip away beneath that, too, leaving edges of concrete sticking out against the sky. In addition, of course, the
entire area sits close to the quiescent but menacing San
Andreas Fault. Gazing up the perilous roads at the plucky,
high-risk homes perched in the tinderlike hills near the
great rift, a visitor feels that this may be a community where
desire and imagination automatically take precedence over
danger, and even over reality.

QUESTIONS

1. Stevenson builds to his central idea instead of starting the paragraph with it. How does the opening topic sentence introduce the subject and prepare the reader for the details that follow?
2. How do the details develop the central idea, stated in the final sentence?
3. Did Stevenson need to state the central idea, or could he have depended on the details to state it implicitly?
4. How is the paragraph appropriate as an introduction?

WRITING ASSIGNMENTS

1. Use Stevenson's paragraph as a model for a description of a street you know well. Describe it for someone who has not seen it—building through a series of details to the central idea as Stevenson does.
2. Write a second paragraph describing the street from the point of view of a person seeing it for the first time. Let your details develop an idea; do not state it explicitly. Your details should be vivid enough and well enough organized to make the idea clear to your reader.

Main and Subordinate Ideas

An author may develop the main or central idea of the paragraph through a series of subordinate ideas. Consider the opening sentences of Teale's paragraph on country superstitions. The first sentence is the main idea; the second sentence, a subordinate idea that develops it through illustration:

> In the folklore of the country, numerous superstitions relate to winter weather.
>> Back-country farmers examine their corn husks—
>>> the thicker the husk, the colder the winter.

We have indented to show the levels of subordination in these sentences. Notice that the third sentence has the same importance as the second in developing the main idea:

> They watch the acorn crop—
>> the more acorns, the more severe the season.

Of course, in writing paragraphs we do not indent in this way to show the relative importance of our ideas. But we do in writing essays: the break for a new paragraph—through an indentation—tells the reader that we are introducing a new idea or topic. Within the paragraph we need ways of substituting for the indentations shown above. One of these ways is the use of parallel phrasing to show that ideas have the same importance:

> They watch the acorn crop. . . .
> They observe. . . .
> They examine. . . .

We will consider later in this section other devices that show the relative importance of ideas—among them transitional words and phrases (for example, the phrase *of equal importance*).

In longer paragraphs, the main idea may be distinguished by repeating or restating it at the end. We will see later in the book

that the beginning and ending are usually the most emphatic parts
of sentences because of their prominence. The same is true of
paragraphs and essays.

SALLY CARRIGHAR

The writer and naturalist SALLY CARRIGHAR *was born
in Cleveland, Ohio, the scene of the introduction to her
autobiography,* Home to the Wilderness, *reprinted here.
After graduation from Wellesley College she wrote for
radio and the movies; discovering an interest in birds
and animals, she decided to become a nature writer:
"There could be no finer subject than woods and fields,
streams, lakes, and mountainsides and the creatures
who live in that world. It would be a subject of inex-
haustible interest," she writes. For nine years she lived
in an isolated Alaskan village, studying Eskimo life and
the animals of the Arctic region. She has written about
this experience and about wildlife generally in*
Icebound Summer, Wild Voice of the North, Wild Heritage, *and other books. In the passage that follows, Carrighar describes experiences and people that awakened
her imagination and curiosity about life.*

The Blast Furnace

We were a father and his first-born, a four-year-old girl, 1
setting out every Sunday afternoon to see the industrial
marvels of Cleveland, Ohio. The young man had grown up
in a smaller Canadian town and he was delighted with
Cleveland, which hummed and clanged with the vast new
developments steel had made possible. In temperament he
was anything but an engineer; here however he was excited

to feel that he had jumped into the very heart of the torrent of progress.

Most often we walked on the banks of the Cuyahoga 2 River to see the drawbridge come apart and rise up, like giant black jaws taking a bite of the sky, so that boats could go through: the long freighters that brought iron ore from Lake Superior, other large and small freighters, fishing boats, passenger steamers. My father's eyes never tired of watching them make their smooth way up and down the river. His father, born in Amsterdam of a seagoing family, had been a skipper on the Great Lakes. Perhaps my father too should have been a sailor, but he was something nearly as satisfying—he worked for a railroad.

And so we went to the roundhouse where the steam 3 engines stood when they were not pulling trains. They had all entered through the same door but inside their tracks spread apart, as gracefully as the ribs of a lady's fan. My father knew a great deal about engines, he knew the names of some of these and he walked among them with pride.

On our way to the roundhouse we passed through the 4 freight yards where long trains of boxcars lay on their sidings. My father said that the cars belonged to different railroads and came from various parts of the country, being coupled together here because all those in one train were bound for the same destination. This was getting too complicated but there was nothing complicated about my father's emotion when he said, "Working for a railroad is like living everywhere in the country at once!" A characteristic enchantment came into his eyes and voice, a contagious exhilaration which meant that anything it attached to was good. Living everywhere was something that even a child could grasp vaguely and pleasantly.

My father and I made other trips and best were the 5 ones to the blast furnaces. He explained how the iron ore from the boats was mixed with coal and carried in little cars to the top of the chimney above the furnace. It was dumped in, and as it fell down "a special kind of very hot air" was blown into it. The coal and iron ore caught fire, and below they fell into great tubs as melting metal, a pinkish gold liquid, incandescent as the sun is when it is starting to set. The man and child were allowed to go rather near the vats, to feel the scorching heat and to drown their gaze in the glowing boil. All the rest of the building was dark; the silhouettes of the men who worked at the vats were black shadows. Wearing long leather aprons, they moved about the vats ladling off the slag. That was very skilled work, my father said; the men had to know just how much of the worthless slag to remove. For years afterwards, when we could no longer spend Sunday afternoons on these expeditions, we used to go out of our house at night to see the pink reflections from the blast furnaces on the clouds over Cleveland. We could remember that we had watched the vatfuls of heavily moving gold, and those events from the past were an unspoken bond between us.

Someone once said, "Your father must have been trying 6 to turn you into a boy. He'd probably wanted his first child to be a son." Perhaps; but it was not strange to him to show a girl the achievements of men. He thought of women as human beings and assumed that they, even one very young, would be interested in anything that was interesting to him. He had absorbed that attitude from the women he'd grown up with, his mother and her four sisters, all of whom led adventurous lives. His favorite Aunt Chris had married a clipper captain and sailed with him all her life. When they retired, having seen the entire world, they chose to settle in Burma. Another aunt married one of the Morgan family, who established the famous breed of Morgan horses, and took up a homestead in Manitoba. Aunt Mary, a physician's wife, went with him out to San Francisco during the Gold Rush and stayed there. The fourth aunt had married the inspector of ships' chronometers at Quebec; and my father's mother, of course, had married her skipper from Holland. In the winter when he was not on his ship he ran a factory for making barrel staves that he had established in western Kentucky—all this and the fathering of five children by the time he was twenty-eight, when he lost his life in a notorious Lake Erie storm. His wife, a musician, brought up her five without complaint, just as her mother, also an early widow, had reared her five gallant girls. With his memories of women like these it was not surprising that my father would wish, even somewhat prematurely, to show his daughter the things that were thrilling to him. I did not comprehend all his family history at four but I did absorb the impression that girls and women reached out for life eagerly and that it was natural for them to be interested in absolutely everything.

QUESTIONS

1. In paragraph 1 Carrighar develops her opening sentence—the main idea of the paragraph—with specific detail about her father. What is the main idea of paragraph 2, and how does she use the detail of the paragraph to develop it?

2. Paragraph 4 moves from specific detail to the main idea. What is that idea, and how does the author give it prominence?

3. Which of the subordinate ideas in paragraph 5 are in turn illustrated or developed?

4. Paragraphs 1–5 are subordinate to paragraph 6, which draws a conclusion from the experiences described, and develops this conclusion through details of a different sort. What is this conclusion, and what new details develop it? How is this conclusion—the main idea of the paragraph—restated later in the paragraph and made prominent?

WRITING ASSIGNMENTS

1. Write several paragraphs describing childhood experiences with a parent or relative that taught you something about the adult world and about yourself. Begin with these truths, or build the paragraphs to them, as Carrighar does.

2. Write several paragraphs about the impressions you received as a child about girls and women from information you received or impressions you developed about women in your

family. If you wish, contrast these impressions with those you received about boys and men.

3. Discuss how particular childhood experiences with friends led you to discoveries about yourself and the world that conflicted with values and ideas held by your parents and teachers. Use this discussion to draw a conclusion about growing up.

MAXINE HONG KINGSTON

After her graduation from the University of California, Berkeley, in 1962, MAXINE HONG KINGSTON *taught English in high school and college in California and Hawaii. In her autobiography,* The Woman Warrior, *from which the passage reprinted below is taken, she describes the special experience of Chinese-Americans: ". . . when you try to understand what things in you are Chinese, how do you separate what is peculiar to childhood, to poverty, insanities, one family, your mother who marked your growing with stories, from what is Chinese? What is Chinese and what is the movies?" Kingston provides an answer in the story of the woman warrior. She is concerned, like Carrighar, with childhood experiences that shape our imagination and values.*

The Woman Warrior

When we Chinese girls listened to the adults talking-story, 1 we learned that we failed if we grew up to be but wives or slaves. We could be heroines, swordswomen. Even if she had to rage across all China, a swordswoman got even with anybody who hurt her family. Perhaps women were once so dangerous that they had to have their feet bound. It was a woman who invented white crane boxing only two hundred years ago. She was already an expert pole fighter, daughter of a teacher trained at the Shao-lin temple, where there lived an order of fighting monks. She was combing her hair one morning when a white crane alighted outside her window. She teased it with her pole, which it pushed aside with a soft brush of its wing. Amazed, she dashed outside and tried to knock the crane off its perch. It snapped her pole in two. Recognizing the presence of great power, she asked the spirit of the white crane if it would teach her to fight. It answered with a cry that white crane boxers imitate today. Later the bird returned as an old man, and he guided her boxing for many years. Thus she gave the world a new martial art.

This was one of the tamer, more modern stories, mere 2
introduction. My mother told others that followed swordswomen through woods and palaces for years. Night after night my mother would talk-story until we fell asleep. I couldn't tell where the stories left off and the dreams began, her voice the voice of the heroines in my sleep. And on Sundays, from noon to midnight, we went to the movies at the Confucius Church. We saw swordswomen jump over houses from a standstill; they didn't even need a running start.

At last I saw that I too had been in the presence of great 3
power, my mother talking-story. After I grew up, I heard the chant of Fa Mu Lan, the girl who took her father's place in battle. Instantly I remembered that as a child I had followed my mother about the house, the two of us singing about how Fa Mu Lan fought gloriously and returned alive from war to settle in the village. I had forgotten this chant that was once mine, given me by my mother, who may not have known its power to remind. She said I would grow up a wife and a slave, but she taught me the song of the warrior woman, Fa Mu Lan. I would have to grow up a warrior woman.

The call would come from a bird that flew over our roof. 4
In the brush drawings it looks like the ideograph for "human," two black wings. The bird would cross the sun and lift

into the mountains (which look like the ideograph "mountain"), there parting the mist briefly that swirled opaque again. I would be a little girl of seven the day I followed the bird away into the mountains. The brambles would tear off my shoes and the rocks cut my feet and fingers, but I would keep climbing, eyes upward to follow the bird. We would go around and around the tallest mountain, climbing ever upward. I would drink from the river, which I would meet again and again. We would go so high the plants would change, and the river that flows past the village would become a waterfall. At the height where the bird used to disappear, the clouds would gray the world like an ink wash.

Even when I got used to that gray, I would only see 5 peaks as if shaded in pencil, rocks like charcoal rubbings, everything so murky. There would be just two black strokes—the bird. Inside the clouds—inside the dragon's breath—I would not know how many hours or days passed. Suddenly, without noise, I would break clear into a yellow, warm world. New trees would lean toward me at mountain angles, but when I looked for the village, it would have vanished under the clouds.

The bird, now gold so close to the sun, would come to 6 rest on the thatch of a hut, which, until the bird's two feet touched it, was camouflaged as part of the mountainside.

QUESTIONS

1. The topic sentence of paragraph 1 states the central idea: ". . . we learned that we failed if we grew up to be but wives or slaves." The second sentence develops this idea—"We could be heroines, swordswomen." How is this idea in turn developed by the third and fourth sentences? Do the remaining sentences describing the inventor of a new martial art develop a preceding idea or introduce a new one?

2. Paragraphs 2 and 3 build to a more important idea than any of the preceding. What is that idea, and how does Kingston show us its importance? How do paragraphs 4–6 develop it?

3. The parentheses in the second sentence of paragraph 4 tell us

that the information about the ideograph is a less important idea. Why does the information about the clouds in the third sentence of paragraph 5 appear inside dashes instead of parentheses?

4. These paragraphs open a book about the growing up of a Chinese-American girl in San Francisco. What do they suggest about the personality and view of life of the writer and about the themes of the book?

WRITING ASSIGNMENTS

1. Carrighar and Kingston develop the same idea in different ways. In a well-developed paragraph or two state this idea, then discuss the differences in how they develop it.

2. Kingston describes the importance of talking-stories in her growing up. In a well-developed paragraph or two discuss the effect of a similar story on your values and view of yourself.

Unity

A unified paragraph develops one idea at a time, instead of jumping from one to another. We will keep it unified if we have in mind the order in which we want to present our ideas and details. Sometimes the subject of the paragraph and sometimes the audience we have in mind—and sometimes both—determine the order. For example, a paragraph on parallel parking, written for people learning to drive, will best present each step as it occurs. But a paragraph written for driving instructors might present these steps in the order of their difficulty, to single out those needing most practice.

An account of a process, or a narrative, is usually chronological. A description of a scene is spatial in organization—the details presented as the eye sees them, moving from one part of what is seen to another. You can also order the details or ideas in other ways—for example

- from the easy to the difficult as in the paragraph written for driving instructors;
- from the less to the more important;
- from the less to the more interesting or exciting;
- from the general to the specific—from the theory of combustion to the details of the process;
- from the specific to the general—from simple effects of gravity, like falling off a bike, to complex effects, like the "black hole."

A paragraph may follow more than one order. The paragraph written for driving instructors may move from the easy to the difficult steps of parallel parking and, at the same time, from the less to the more important or even interesting.

EUDORA WELTY

One of America's most distinguished writers of fiction,
EUDORA WELTY *was born and raised in Jackson, Missis-*
sippi. After college she worked at a number of jobs
before beginning her career as a photographer and wri-
ter about Mississippi life. She is the author of numerous
short stories, novels and essays; her novel The Op-
timist's Daughter *won the Pulitzer Prize for fiction in*
1973. Her description of a corner store, taken from a
essay about her childhood in Jackson, reveals what one
writer describes as her "camera-like eye" which "sees
and records with precision the surface reality, then, by
the inclusion of lights and shadows . . . the poetic depths
which underlie and surround the human condition."

The Corner Store

Our Little Store rose right up from the sidewalk; standing in 1
a street of family houses, it alone hadn't any yard in front,
any tree or flower bed. It was a plain frame building covered
over with brick. Above the door, a little railed porch ran
across on an upstairs level and four windows with shades
were looking out. But I didn't catch on to those.

Running in out of the sun, you met what seemed total 2
obscurity inside. There were almost tangible smells—
licorice recently sucked in a child's cheek, dill pickle brine
that had leaked through a paper sack in a fresh trail across
the wooden floor, ammonia-loaded ice that had been
hoisted from wet croker sacks and slammed into the icebox
with its sweet butter at the door, and perhaps the smell of
still untrapped mice.

Then through the motes of cracker dust, cornmeal dust, 3
the Gold Dust of the Gold Dust Twins that the floor had
been swept out with, the realities emerged. Shelves climbed
to high reach all the way around, set out with not too much

of any one thing but a lot of things—lard, molasses, vinegar, starch, matches, kerosine, Octagon soap (about a year's worth of octagon-shaped coupons cut out and saved brought a signet ring addressed to you in the mail). It was up to you to remember what you came for, while your eye traveled from cans of sardines to tin whistles to ice cream salt to harmonicas to flypaper (over your head, batting around on a thread beneath the blades of the ceiling fan, stuck with its testimonial catch).

Its confusion may have been in the eye of its beholder. 4 Enchantment is cast upon you by all those things you weren't supposed to have need for, to lure you close to wooden tops you'd outgrown, boy's marbles and agates in little net pouches, small rubber balls that wouldn't bounce straight, frail, frazzly kite string, clay bubble pipes that would snap off in your teeth, the stiffest scissors. You could contemplate those long narrow boxes of sparklers gathering dust while you waited for it to be the Fourth of July or Christmas, and noisemakers in the shape of tin frogs for somebody's birthday party you hadn't been invited to yet, and see that they were all marvelous.

You might not have even looked for Mr. Sessions when 5 he came around his store cheese (as big as a doll's house) and in front of the counter looking for you. When you'd finally asked him for, and received from him in its paper bag, whatever single thing it was that you had been sent for, the nickel that was left over was yours to spend.

Down at a child's eye level, inside those glass jars with 6 mouths in their sides through which the grocer could run his scoop or a child's hand might be invited to reach for a choice, were wineballs, all-day suckers, gumdrops, peppermints. Making a row under the glass of a counter were the Tootsie Rolls, Hershey bars, Goo Goo Clusters, Baby Ruths. And whatever was the name of those pastilles that came stacked in a cardboard cylinder with a cardboard lid? They were thin and dry, about the size of tiddledy-winks, and in the shape of twisted rosettes. A kind of chocolate dust came out with them when you shook them out in your hand. Were they chocolate? I'd say, rather, they were brown. They didn't taste of anything at all, unless it was wood. Their attraction was the number you got for a nickel.

Making up your mind, you circled the store around and 7 around, around the pickle barrel, around the tower of Crackerjack boxes; Mr. Sessons had built it for us himself on top of a packing case like a house of cards.

If it seemed too hot for Crackerjacks, I might get a cold 8 drink. Mr. Sessions might have already stationed himself by the cold-drinks barrel, like a mind reader. Deep in ice water that looked black as ink, murky shapes—that would come up as Coca-Colas, Orange Crushes, and various flavors of pop—were all swimming around together. When you gave the word, Mr. Sessions plunged his bare arm in to the elbow and fished out your choice, first try. I favored a locally bottled concoction called Lake's Celery. (What else could it be called? It was made by a Mr. Lake out of celery. It was a popular drink here for years but was not known universally, as I found out when I arrived in New York and ordered one in the Astor bar.) You drank on the premises, with feet set wide apart to miss the drip, and gave him back his bottle and your nickel.

But he didn't hurry you off. A standing scales was by 9 the door, with a stack of iron weights and a brass slide on the balance arm, that would weigh you up to three hundred pounds. Mr. Sessions, whose hands were gentle and smelled of carbolic, would lift you up and set your feet on the platform, hold your loaf of bread for you, and, taking his time while you stood still for him, he would make certain of what you weighed today. He could even remember what you weighed the last time, so you could subtract and announce how much you'd gained. That was goodbye.

QUESTIONS

1. Welty orders her description chronologically and spatially. Which parts does she present chronologically—in the order of time—and which parts does she present spatially?

2. What is the main idea of paragraph 8? How are subordinate ideas distinguished from the main idea?

3. What overall impression do you get of the story? Does Welty state the impression directly, or does she let it emerge from the details? Which contribute most to this impression?

4. Does Welty present each feature of the store and her experiences one at a time without repetition, or does she return to earlier features or details?

WRITING ASSIGNMENTS

1. Describe a store you remember from childhood. Decide on a dominant impression and choose details that develop it. Then decide on an order of details appropriate to your purpose. Remember that, although your reader has not seen the store, you need not give all of its details to develop an impression of it.

2. Welty states in paragraph 4: "Its confusion may have been in the eye of its beholder." Write a description of an institution like a government office or room in a school to show how your feelings and attitude determine what you notice and consider important.

MARY McCARTHY

"I was born in Seattle in 1912, the first of four children," the novelist and essayist MARY McCARTHY *tells us in her autobiography,* Memories of a Catholic Girlhood. *Following the death of her parents in the influenza epidemic of 1918, she and her three brothers lived for a short time with "Uncle Myers, "a fat man of forty-two,"* who had recently married their great-aunt, and later with various relatives in Minneapolis and Seattle. "Uncle Myers was our White Whale,"* she tells us in the preface. "Anyone who came near us found they had shipped for the voyage."* We discover why in this amazing description of an eccentric man.*

Uncle Myers

And here was another strange thing about Myers. He not only did nothing for a living but he appeared to have no history. He came from Elkhart, Indiana, but beyond this fact nobody seemed to know anything about him—not even how he had met my aunt Margaret. Reconstructed from his conversation, a picture of Elkhart emerged for us that showed it as a flat place consisting chiefly of ball parks, poolrooms, and hardware stores. Aunt Margaret came from Chicago, which consisted of the Loop, Marshall Field's, assorted priests and monsignors, and the black-and-white problem. How had these two worlds impinged? Where our family spoke freely of its relations, real and imaginary, Myers spoke of no one, not even a parent. At the very beginning, when my father's old touring car, which had been shipped on, still remained in our garage, Myers had certain seedy cronies whom he took riding in it or who simply sat in it in our driveway, as if anchored in a house-boat; but when the car went, they went or were banished. Uncle Myers and Aunt Margaret had no friends, no couples with whom they exchanged visits—only a middle-aged, black-haired, small, emaciated woman with a German name and a yellowed skin whom we were taken to see one after-noon because she was dying of cancer. This protracted death had the aspect of a public execution, which was doubt-less why Myers took us to it; that is, it was a spectacle and it was free, and it inspired restlessness and depression. Myers was the perfect type of rootless or municipalized man who finds his pleasures in the handouts or overflow of an indus-trial civilization. He enjoyed standing on a curbstone, watch-ing parades, the more nondescript the better, the Labor Day parade being his favorite, and next to that a military pa-rade, followed by the commercial parades with floats and girls dressed in costumes; he would even go to Lake Cal-houn or Lake Harriet for doll carriage parades and compe-titions of children dressed as Indians. He liked bandstands, band concerts, public parks devoid of grass; sky writing attracted him; he was quick to hear of a department-store demonstration where colored bubbles were blown, advertising a soap, to the tune of "I'm Forever Blowing Bubbles," sung by a mellifluous soprano. He collected coupons and tinfoil, bundles of newspaper for the old rag-and-bone man (thus interfering seriously with our school paper drives), free samples of cheese at Donaldson's, free tickets given out by a neighborhood movie house to the first installment of a serial—in all the years we lived with him, we never saw a full-length movie but only those truncated beginnings. He was also fond of streetcar rides (could the system have been municipally owned?), soldiers' monuments, cemeteries, big, coarse flowers like cannas and cockscombs set in beds by city gardeners. Museums did not appeal to him, though we did go one night with a large crowd to see Marshal Foch on the steps of the Art Institute. He was always weighing himself on penny weighing machines. He seldom left the house except on one of these purposeless errands, or else to go to a ball game, by himself. In the winter, he spent the days at home in the den, or in the kitchen, making candy. He often had enormous tin trays of decorated fondants cooling in the cellar, which leads my brother Kevin to think today that at one time in Myers' life he must have been a pastry cook or a confectioner. He also liked to fashion those little figures made of pipe cleaners that were just then coming in as favors in the better candy shops, but Myers used *old* pipe cleaners, stained yellow and brown. The bonbons, with their pecan or almond topping, that he laid out in such perfect rows were for his own use; we were permitted to watch him set them out, but never—and my brother Kevin confirms this—did we taste a single one.

QUESTIONS

1. At the beginning of the paragraph Mary McCarthy discusses Uncle Myers' history and proceeds to his friendships and interests. What are these interests?

2. Why does she save the information about the pipe cleaners and the candy for the end of the paragraph? How would the impression of Uncle Myers have been changed if the paragraph ended with the details of his cronies and his collections?

3. The paragraph is unified because McCarthy discusses one thing at a time, without returning haphazardly to earlier considerations. What is the order of details in the whole paragraph? What does she gain by not dividing the paragraph into several shorter ones?

4. Does McCarthy directly state her attitude toward Uncle Myers, or does she let it emerge through what she shows about him? What is that attitude?

5. How else might McCarthy have organized the paragraph to develop a different idea or impression?

6. Does Uncle Myers seem monstrous to you, or does McCarthy show his human side or give some explanation for his character?

WRITING ASSIGNMENTS

1. Build a paragraph around a central impression of an unusual person, selecting details from different areas of experience. Do not state your attitude toward the person; let your details reveal it.

2. Rewrite the paragraph on Uncle Myers, presenting the details in a different order and providing a new topic sentence. In a short second paragraph explain your reasons for organizing the new paragraph as you did.

Transitions

Transitional words and phrases help us show how we connect ideas and details in our paragraphs and essays. We especially need them when we change the subject or course of discussion, as in the following sentence by Stevenson:

> In some places, tons of concrete have been poured like icing over a section of hillside to hold it back—and the concrete has even been painted green—but the earth has begun to slip away beneath that, too, leaving edges of concrete sticking out against the sky.

The transitional words *even* and *too* show us the course of Stevenson's thinking in the sentence: *even* tells us he is adding a detail to intensify his description of the street; *too* shows he is comparing the slipping earth to other sections of the road.

Words like *after* and *since* express relationships of time; words like *above* and *below*, relationships of space. Here are some important transitions that show the relationship of ideas:

- qualification: *however, nevertheless, nonetheless*
- illustration and explanation: *for example, so, thus*
- comparison: *similarly, in the same way, by comparison, likewise*
- contrast: *by contrast, on the one hand, on the other hand*
- consequence: *thus, as a result, consequently, therefore*
- concession: *admittedly, nevertheless, however*
- amplification: *moreover, furthermore, also, in addition, indeed*
- summation: *in conclusion, to sum up, all in all, finally*

Punctuation also shows us how ideas are related. A colon tells us that an expansion, explanation or illustration follows; a semicolon, that the ideas joined are closely related or of the same importance.

MARY E. MEBANE

*Born in 1933 in Durham, North Carolina, MARY E.
MEBANE grew up on a farm—the world she describes in
her autobiography,* Mary, *published in 1981. Following
her graduation from college in Durham, she taught in
public schools and took graduate degrees at the University of North Carolina. She has taught at the University
of South Carolina since 1974. Like Kingston and Carrighar, Mebane shows us the influence of an unusual
parent on a girl growing into womanhood; like Carrighar, Welty and McCarthy she immerses us in the
sights, sounds, and smells of the childhood world she
remembers so well.*

Nonnie

Nonnie led a structured, orderly existence. Before six o'clock   1
in the morning, she was up, starting her day. First she
turned on WPTF and listened to the news and the weather
and the music. Later, when WDNC in Durham hired
Norfleet Whitted, the first black announcer in the area, she
listened first to one station, then to the other. Some mornings it would be "They Traced Her Little Footprints in the
Snow," and other mornings it would be black gospel-singing
and rhythm-and-blues. Then she would make a fire in the
wood stove and start her breakfast. She prepared some
meat—fried liver pudding or fatback, or a streak-of-fat
streak-of-lean—and made a hoecake of bread on top of the
stove, which she ate with either Karo syrup or homemade
blackberry preserves, occasionally with store-bought strawberry preserves, or sometimes with homemade water-
melon-rind preserves that she had canned in the summer.
Then she would drink her coffee, call me to get up, and leave
the house in her blue uniform, blue apron, and blue cap—it
would still be dark when she left on winter mornings—and

go to catch her ride to the tobacco factory (with Mr. Ralph Baldwin at first, and then, when he retired, with Mr. James Yergan). When Miss Delilah still lived in Wildwood, before she and Mr. Leroy separated, she would come by and call from the road and the two of them would walk together to the end of the road near the highway and wait for Mr. Ralph there.

My job after she was left was to see that the fire didn't 2 go out in the wood stove, to see that the pots sitting on the back didn't burn—for in them was our supper, often pinto beans or black-eyed peas or collard greens or turnip salad. Occasionally there was kale or mustard greens or cressy salad. The other pot would have the meat, which most often was neck bones or pig feet or pig ears, and sometimes spareribs. These would cook until it was time for me to go to school; then I would let the fire die down, only to relight it when I came home to let the pots finish cooking.

After Nonnie left, I also had the task of getting Ruf 3 Junior up so that he could get to school on time. This presented no problem to me until Ruf Junior was in high school and started playing basketball. Often he would travel with the team to schools in distant towns, sometimes getting home after midnight, and the next morning he would be tired and sleepy and wouldn't want to get up. I sympathized, but I had my job to do. If I let him oversleep, I knew that Nonnie would fuss when she got home. But on the other hand, no matter how often I called to him, he would murmur sleepily, "All right, all right," then go back to sleep. I solved this problem one bitter-cold winter morning. I jerked all the covers off his bed and ran. I knew that the only place he could get warm again would be in the kitchen. (The only fire was in the wood stove.) The fire was already out, so he'd have to make one. After that, I didn't have such a hard time getting him up.

My mother worked as a cutter, clipping the hard ends 4 of each bundle of tobacco before it was shredded to make cigarettes. At noon she ate the lunch she had brought from home in a brown paper bag: a biscuit with meat in it and a sweet potato or a piece of pie or cake. Some of the women ate in the cafeteria, but in her thirty years at the Liggett and Myers factory, she never once did. She always took her lunch. Then she worked on until closing time, caught her ride back to Wildwood, and started on the evening's activities. First she had supper, which I had finished preparing from the morning. After I got older we sometimes had meat other than what had to be prepared in a "pot." It would be my duty to fry chicken or prepare ham bits and gravy.

After supper, she'd read the Durham *Sun* and see to it 5 that we did the chores if we hadn't done them already: slop the hogs, feed the chickens, get in the wood for the next day. Then we were free. She'd get her blue uniform ready for the next day, then listen to the radio. No later than nine o'clock, she would be in bed. In the morning she would get up, turn on the radio, and start frying some fatback. Another day would have started.

Saturdays were work days, too, the time for washing, 6 ironing, going to the garden, preparing Sunday dinner (no one was supposed to work on the Sabbath, so we ran the chicken down in the yard and Nonnie wrung its neck or chopped its head off with the ax). Sometimes we went to town on Saturday but not often, for Nonnie went to town every day. Sometimes, at lunchtime, she'd go down to Belk's, and always on Friday she went to the A&P on Mangum Street and bought her groceries; then she'd stop at the Big Star in Little Five Points if she had heard that there was a particularly good buy on something. So the Saturday-in-town ritual that is so much a part of the lives of most country children was not mine at all. I myself sometimes went to Brookstown several times a week when my father was alive, because that is where he went to get trash, sell vegetables, and visit his relatives.

Sunday afternoons she would go to see her friends or 7 they would come to see her. She would say, "I believe I'll go up to Miss Angeline's a little while." Or it would be Miss

Pauline's or Claudia's. And she would stay until about dusk and come home, listen to the radio, then go to bed, ready to start Monday morning again.

In the spring and summer after work, my mother would [8] plant in her garden: tomatoes, string beans, okra, and she'd sow a turnip patch. Then, every day after work, she'd go over to the garden on the hill to see how it was doing. On Saturdays she'd get her buckets if it was time for us to go berrypicking. And on hot summer evenings, if the peaches man had been around, she'd can them after work because they wouldn't keep until Saturday, the day she did most of her canning.

This was her routine—fixed, without change, unvary- [9] ing. And she accepted it. She more than accepted it, she embraced it; it gave meaning to her life, it was what she had been put here on this earth to do. It was not to be questioned.

To Nonnie this life was ideal; she saw nothing wrong [10] with it. And she wondered in baffled rage why her daughter didn't value it but rather sought something else, some other rhythm, a more meaningful pattern to human life.

Nonnie Mebane was not political. However, a special [11] awe would come into her voice when she said, "And Lee *surrendered.*" She was from Virginia, and I realize now that she probably would have been imbued with Virginia history in her eight years of schooling there. I myself never heard Robert E. Lee's name mentioned in any class at Wildwood School. But my mother loved to say, "And Lee *surrendered.*" She also liked to say sometimes that the Yankee soldiers rode up and said, "Come on out. Ya'll are free this morning."

The way she said it, I could see the men on horse- [12] back—the Yankees—coming around to the fields and to the cabins and saying to the blacks who had been slaves for centuries, "Come on out. Ya'll are free this morning." That was a magical moment. I used to get cold chills when she said it, for, I now realize, in her voice I heard the voice of my mother's mother as she told Nonnie and her other children how the Yankees came early one morning and what they had said. My mother's grandmother had heard them.

Nonnie was a good plain cook, but she couldn't sew very 13 well, couldn't fix hair—her own or her daughter's—and, though dutiful, was an indifferent housekeeper. She was thrifty and paid all of her bills on time. Work at the tobacco factory was her life.

QUESTIONS

1. How does the opening sentence—"Nonnie led a structured, orderly existence"—organize the paragraphs that follow?

2. Many of the transitional words are chronological, showing how the events of the day were connected in time. What examples of such transitions do you find in paragraphs 1, 4, and 8?

3. What transitional ideas do *often, but,* and *on the other hand* express in paragraph 3? What about *too* and *so* in paragraph 6, *however* in paragraph 11, and *for* in paragraph 12? Might Mebane have omitted any of these without loss of coherence— that is, without losing the sense of connection between ideas?

4. Does Mebane imply more about her mother's life than she states? What does she reveal about her own feelings or attitudes?

WRITING ASSIGNMENTS

1. Mebane describes the work she performed as a member of the family. Describe jobs that you similarly performed, and use this description to say something about the general attitude in your family toward everyday life or the role of children in the family.

2. Mebane refers in paragraph 10 to "some other rhythm, a more meaningful pattern to human life." She is suggesting here the different values that children sometimes discover they possess. Discuss a conflict in values that developed between yourself and another member of your family and the origin of this conflict as you see it.

RENÉ DUBOS

RENÉ DUBOS *(1901–1982), one of the world's leading bacteriologists, was associated most of his life with Rockefeller University for Medical Research in New York City and made important contributions to the treatment of tuberculosis and the development of commercial antibiotics. In later years, he wrote much about the environment and the social consequences of advances in medicine and technology. His many books include* Only on Earth *(written with Barbara Ward), and* So Human an Animal—*awarded the Pulitzer Prize in 1969. In his book* Man Adapting, *Dubos argues that advances in medical care have led people increasingly to neglect one important means of dealing with the world, the development of human "adaptive resources"—which he illustrates in the passage reprinted here. But he warns that this adaptability can be dangerous because "it implies so often a passive acceptance of conditions which really are not desirable for mankind. The lowest common denominators of existence tend to become the accepted criteria, merely for the sake of gray and anonymous peace or tranquility."*

Fitness in the Modern World

¹There is no such thing as fitness per se with regard to military service, because fitness must always be defined in terms of a particular combat situation. ²In consequence, the armed forces find it necessary to revise the physical standards of health at frequent intervals, in order to keep them in tune with the changing requirements of military service. ³With propeller-driven aircraft, for example, there were many situations in which survival depended on strength of arm and limb. ⁴Moreover, the pilot of a fighter airplane in World War II had to watch for enemies in the sky by direct visual perception. ⁵His head swiveled from side to side look-

ing to the rear, and for this reason calisthenics to develop neck muscles were part of training.

[6]Today, power controls have lessened physical requirements of the aircraft operator, and with electronic vision the fighter pilot never needs to look to the rear. [7]In any case, direct vision would be of little help in modern air combat because of the terrific speeds at which aircraft approach each other. [8]At 600 miles per hour, and this is now moderate speed, half a mile means little more than a second, clearly not enough time for the pilot to see, to react, and to change the direction of his aircraft. [9]As a result, keenness of distant vision no longer means the difference between life and death for the fighter pilot; this attribute has been superseded by keenness in ability to detect slight changes on electronic dials and gauges. [10]More generally, strenuous physical conditioning programs are no longer as directly relevant to performance in the armed forces as they used to be. [11]And in fact, recent tests indicate that pilots at the peak of physical form do not score any better in difficult operations than do those of comparable groups who are less well endowed physically.

[12]The changes in relevance of physical prowess to military performance have many counterparts in civilian life. [13]Effectiveness in modern technology depends to a large extent on dial-watching and on reading printed matter. [14]Whereas physical stamina and distant vision were once extremely important, muscles are now called into play chiefly during leisure time, and nearsightedness has become almost an asset in several professions. [15]The present trends of life seem to provide justification for the child who does not want to walk because he considers it old-fashioned and for his mother who dissuades him from engaging in physical exertion or exposing himself to inclemencies because modern existence is and will increasingly become air-conditioned and effortless. [16]And yet this attitude may have unfavorable consequences in the long run. [17]A state of adaptedness to the conditions of today is no guarantee of adaptability to the challenges of tomorrow.

QUESTIONS

1. What transitional words and phrases do you find in sentences 2–4? What relationships do these establish?
2. What relationships do the transitions in the second paragraph express? Could any of these transitions be omitted without loss of coherence or clarity?
3. What other transitions might the author have substituted for those in sentences 2, 4, 9, and 11?
4. How does the whole discussion illustrate sentence 17—the thesis statement or main idea of the three paragraphs?

WRITING ASSIGNMENTS

1. Write a paragraph from your own experience that develops one of the following ideas. Restate the idea, qualifying or disagreeing with it, if you wish. Use transitional words and phrases where appropriate.
   a. What we learn in school often is obsolete by the time we are ready to use it.
   b. Adults do not always tell us the whole truth about the world.
2. Illustrate sentence 17 from your own experience. You might show how physical capabilities once important in childhood are no longer important to you. Use transitional words and phrases where needed for coherence.

Climax

One order of ideas, we saw earlier, is from the less to the more important. Since the sense of importance is usually our own, we need to show this to the reader, perhaps through a simple transition like *more importantly*. We can dispense with such transitions when the sense of rising importance is expressed directly, as in the famous statement of Julius Caesar—"I came, I saw, I conquered"—or in the details themselves:

> A furious gale attacks hims like a personal enemy, tries to grasp his limbs, fastens upon his mind, seeks to rout his very spirit out of him.—Joseph Conrad, *Typhoon*

As in this sentence, climax can be achieved by making one idea seem to anticipate another, and by giving weight to the final idea (in Conrad's sentence, through the word *very*). The terminal position in a sentence or paragraph is a position of natural emphasis because of its prominence—a fact which we can take advantage of in giving weight to ideas or details.

LYTTON STRACHEY

LYTTON STRACHEY *(1880–1932), one of England's great biographers, was particularly interested in revered figures of the nineteenth century, whose human qualities he wanted to discover. In these studies Strachey looked at both the strengths and failings of his subjects, joining fact with the imagined creation of their inner life. We see this method in his portrait of Queen Victoria. Born in 1819, Victoria became queen in 1837 at the age of eighteen, and in 1840 married a first cousin her own age, the German prince Albert of Saxe-Coburg. When Albert died of a sudden illness in 1861, at the age of 42, she entered a long period of private mourning, for*

*the remainder of her life preserving her physical sur-
roundings as they had existed in his lifetime. Strachey
shows how little needs to be said when the right details
are chosen and organized carefully.*

Queen Victoria at the End
of Her Life

[1]She gave orders that nothing should be thrown away—and
nothing was. [2]There, in drawer after drawer, in wardrobe
after wardrobe, reposed the dresses of seventy years. [3]But
not only the dresses—the furs and the mantles and subsidi-
ary frills and the muffs and the parasols and the bonnets—all were ranged in chronological order, dated and
complete. [4]A great cupboard was devoted to the dolls; in the
china room at Windsor a special table held the mugs of her
childhood, and her children's mugs as well. [5]Mementoes of
the past surrounded her in serried accumulations. [6]In every
room the tables were powdered thick with the photographs
of relatives; their portraits, revealing them at all ages,
covered the walls; their figures, in solid marble, rose up
from pedestals, or gleamed from brackets in the form of
gold and silver statuettes. [7]The dead, in every shape—in
miniatures, in porcelain, in enormous life-size oil-paint-
ings—were perpetually about her. [8]John Brown stood upon
her writing-table in solid gold.* [9]Her favorite horses and
dogs, endowed with a new durability, crowded round her
footsteps. [10]Sharp, in silver gilt, dominated the dinner table;
Boy and Boz lay together among unfading flowers, in
bronze. [11]And it was not enough that each particle of the
past should be given the stability of metal or of marble: the
whole collection, in its arrangement, no less than its entity,
should be immutably fixed. [12]There might be additions, but

---

*John Brown (1826–1883) was the Scottish attendant to Victoria's husband, Prince
Albert, and after the death of the Prince in 1861, to the Queen herself. Ed.

there might never be alterations. [13]No chintz might change, no carpet, no curtain, be replaced by another; or, if long use at last made it necessary, the stuffs and the patterns must be so identically reproduced that the keenest eye might not detect the difference. [14]No new picture could be hung upon the walls at Windsor, for those already there had been put in their places by Albert, whose decisions were eternal. [15]So, indeed, were Victoria's. [16]To ensure that they should be the aid of the camera was called in. [17]Every single article in the Queen's possession was photographed from several points of view. [18]These photographs were submitted to Her Majesty, and when, after careful inspection, she had approved of them, they were placed in a series of albums, richly bound. [19]Then, opposite each photograph, an entry was made, indicating the number of the article, the number of the room in which it was kept, its exact position in the room and all its principal characteristics. [20]The fate of every object which had undergone this process was henceforth irrevocably sealed. [21]The whole multitude, once and for all, took up its steadfast station. [22]And Victoria, with a gigantic volume or two of the endless catalogue always beside her, to look through, to ponder upon, to expatiate over, could feel, with a double contentment, that the transitoriness of this world had been arrested by the amplitude of her might.

QUESTIONS

1. In this portrait of Victoria in her old age, Strachey develops and illustrates several major ideas that build to his thesis idea. What are these ideas?

2. Strachey states in sentence 2 that Victoria saved the dresses of seventy years; in sentence 3, that she saved her furs and bonnets, as well as other articles of clothing—and arranged and dated them chronologically. How does the formal transition between these sentences help to show that Strachey is moving from one surprising, even astonishing, fact to an even more surprising one?

3. Compare sentences 11 and 12 with those that follow. How does Strachey indicate that he is building the paragraph to even more surprising details?
4. What contributes to the climactic effect of the final sentence of the paragraph?
5. Has Strachey made Queen Victoria human to you? Or is she merely an eccentric?

WRITING ASSIGNMENTS

1. Write a character sketch of an unusual relative, friend, or teacher, centering on a dominant trait and presenting related traits as Strachey does. Present these related traits in the order of rising importance—as illustrations of the dominant trait.
2. Rewrite Strachey's paragraph, beginning with his concluding sentence, and achieving a sense of climax in your reordering of ideas and details.

GEORGE PLIMPTON

As a student at Harvard, GEORGE PLIMPTON *edited the humor magazine, the* Harvard Lampoon, *and later founded the* Paris Review, *which he still edits. He is best known for his articles and books describing his training with professional athletes in a number of sports. He describes his baseball experiences in* Out of My League *(1961), and his experiences with the Detroit Lions in his most famous book,* Paper Lion *(1966). Plimpton trained and practiced with the Lions in 1963, participating briefly in exhibition games. In the following paragraphs from the book, he describes his practice with the blocking sleds. Roger Brown was a lineman on the team; Aldo Forte and Les Bingaman, former players, were assistant coaches. Plimpton is especially gifted in constructing sentences that express the action described.*

Blocking Sleds

I never tried playing any of the big interior lineman posi-   1
tions, such as Brown's—either on defense or offense. Down
on the field I tried their drills. I tried the blocking sleds, and
also tackling the big leather dummy that hung above a
sawdust pit from chains and pulleys attached to a steel
support like a playground structure. The team stood in line
and sprinted off one by one, and the structure would creak
and the pulleys shriek as the dummy was hit. The trick was
to use the shoulders rather than the arms, and to keep on
driving through the pit and let the bag slide off the shoulders and back. If you wrapped your arms around the tackling dummy, and hung on and tried to wrestle it down, as I
did the first time, the bag turned over and one sagged
ignominiously to the sawdust pit, the bag on top, somewhat
the way one is turned by a rubber seahorse in a swimming
pool. Aldo Forte would yell, "Keep your head up, keep to
your feet, drive, drive, drive—when your head is down, you
fall down, head up, up, up!"

The blocking sleds, off in a far corner of the field, had   2
curved padded supports to contain the simultaneous rush of
seven linemen, their shoulders to the pads, their legs driving, and the sled, with Bingaman standing on it, would
sweep across the grass. It seemed simple enough to try, like
pushing a car, except that I found it difficult to spring off the
three-point stance with the astonishing drive and timing of
the regular linemen. Bingaman would announce the hike
number, and then call the quarterback's cadence *"Hut*-one
hut-two *hut*-three," and the line would push off at the "hut"
of whatever the hike number was, getting that fraction of a
second's advantage, and the sled would spring away without my getting a shoulder to it—and I would lunge forward
after it, almost toppling forward, like trying to catch an
animal running low to the ground, until my shoulder would
fetch up against the pads. Sometimes on the blocking sleds
the players would gag around, and at the hike number I

would be the only one to drive forward at the sled, the others holding up on some secret signal, and without the others to help, and with Bingaman's weight, it was like jarring a shoulder into a wall. The players all stood up, grinning, and Forte yelled, "Keep to your feet, drive, drive, drive, head up, up, up."

QUESTIONS

1. Plimpton builds his two paragraphs to a climax—Forte's barked commands. Which of the paragraphs conveys a greater sense of rising climax, and why do you think so?

2. Which details in the first paragraph create suspense? Which details in the second paragraph do so?

3. What impression do you get of the players and coaches from the episode? What are Plimpton's feelings? Is his account of the episode intended to be humorous?

WRITING ASSIGNMENTS

1. Describe a similar learning experience in a sport you play or in some other activity. Build your details to a climax as Plimpton does, using transitions where necessary.

2. Describe a similar embarrassing episode, explaining the circumstances as Plimpton does and building to a climax in the same way. Draw a conclusion from what happened.

Point of View

In a descriptive paragraph or essay we must be careful to specify the place where the author makes the observation. Indeed, we may need to specify the angle of observation. Notice how carefully James Stevenson does so in his description of Loma Vista Drive:

> Partway down the long, very steep slope of Loma Vista Drive, descending through Beverly Hills, with the city of Los Angeles spread out far below the houses of sparkling opulence on either side, there is a sign warning "Use Lowest Gear" and, shortly after that, a sign that says "Runaway Vehicle Escape Lane 600 Feet Ahead."

Something more than the physical point of view is suggested in this opening sentence: a dominant mood or attitude. The author often conveys this psychological point of view by the details of the description.

If we fail to clarify the point of view from which we make the observation, or fail to clarify a change in position, details will seem blurred. Abrupt or unexpected shifts in mood or attitude can also be confusing. Brief transitions that bridge these changes or shifts are the remedy.

GEOFFREY MOORHOUSE

The English journalist and writer GEOFFREY MOORHOUSE *has written about his travels in more than thirty countries for periodicals in England and other countries. In his book* The Fearful Void *(1974), Moorhouse describes a two thousand mile crossing of the Sahara Desert he made by camel. In his book on the Indian city of Calcutta, published in 1971, he describes the problems created by an immense population crowded into a small area. As the passage reprinted here shows, Moorhouse selects his details for an audience unfamiliar with the Asian city.*

Calcutta

When the international and jet-propelled traveler disem- 1
barks at Dum Dum he finds, if he has come by the right
airline, that a highly polished limousine awaits his pleasure.
It will be 6.30 or thereabouts in the morning, and the atmosphere will already be faintly sticky with heat and so unmis-
takably sweetened with a compound of mainly vegetable
odors that the visitor can almost taste it. He need fear no
discomfort at this stage, however, for he is to be transported
into the city in air-conditioned splendor behind delicately
tinted windows. From this smooth and relaxing position he
can begin to observe how the other half of humanity lives.
From the outset he notices some things which are reassur-
ingly familiar. Along the first mile of this wide and tar-
macadamed airport road are spaced the very same collection of gaudy hoardings that signal the way in and out of
Heathrow or J. F. Kennedy or Fiumicino; "Try a Little VC-
10derness", says one—and some untidy idiot seems to have
thrown up a collection of chicken coops in the shade of
BOAC. Beside these homely reference points, however, the
peculiarities of India are to be seen. The road is bordered by
ditches and ponds, all brimming with water, in which
women even at this hour are flogging garments clean, in
which men are taking the first bath of the day. Beyond the
spindle-elegant sodium lights, with buzzards and vultures
perched on top, stand thickets of bamboo-and-thatch huts
among avenues of palm. Along a canal, a large black barge
top-heavy with hay is being poled inches at a time through a
mass of pretty but choking mauve water hyacinth. And in
the distance, lurking on the horizon, a range of tall factory
chimneys is beginning to smoke.

Calcutta is announced with a pothole or two. Then a bus 2
is overtaken, such a vehicle as the traveler has never seen
before; its bodywork is battered with a thousand dents, as
though an army of commuters had once tried to kick it to
bits, and it is not only crammed with people, it has a score or

so hanging off the platform and around the back like a cluster of grapes. It is lumbering and steaming into a sub-urban wasteland, stippled with blocks of dilapidated flats; and maybe Bishop Heber's imagery was not so far-fetched after all, for these are not at all unlike some of the homes for the workers you can see in Moscow today, though there they are not colored pink and they certainly haven't been deco-rated with the hammer and sickle in crude whitewash on the walls.* Swiftly, the outer Calcutta of these revolutionary symbols now coagulates into the inner Calcutta which is unlike anywhere else on earth. The limousine now lurches and rolls, for there are too many potholes to avoid. It rocks down cobblestoned roads lined with high factory walls which have an air of South Lancashire about them. It begins to thread its way through traffic along thoroughfares that have something of Bishopsgate or Holborn in their buildings.

It is the traffic that makes it all unique. A traffic in trams grinding round corners, a traffic in approximately London buses whose radiators seem ready to burst, in gypsy-green lorries with 'Ta-ta and By-by' and other slo-gans painted on the back, in taxis swerving all over the road with much blowing of horns, in rickshaws springing unex-pectedly out of sidestreets, in bullock carts swaying pon-derously along to the impediment of everyone, in sacred Brahmani cows and bulls nonchalantly strolling down the middle of the tram-tracks munching breakfast as they go. A traffic, too, in people who are hanging on to all forms of public transport, who are squatting cross-legged upon the counters of their shops, who are darting in and out of the roadways between the vehicles, who are staggering under enormous loads, who are walking briskly with briefcases, who are lying like dead things on the pavements, who are drenching themselves with muddy water in the gutters, who

---

*Reginald Heber (1783–1826), who became bishop of Calcutta in 1823, compared the city to Moscow. He commented also on the large Greek-style houses and the city's hospitality. Ed.

are arguing, laughing, gesticulating, defecating, and who are sometimes just standing still as though wondering what to do. There never were so many people in a city at seven o'clock in the morning. Patiently the driver of the limousine steers his passage between and around them, while they pause in mid-stride to let him through, or leap to get out of his way, or stare at him blankly, or curse him roundly, or occasionally spit in the path of his highly polished Cadillac. Presently, and quite remarkably, he comes to the end of the journey without collision and deposits the traveler and his luggage upon the pavement in front of an hotel. And here the traveler has his first encounter with a beggar. He had better make the best of it, for beggary is to be with him until the end of his days in Calcutta.

QUESTIONS

1. The traveler to India might see Calcutta for the first time from a taxi or bus rather than from "a highly polished limousine." What is gained by seeing the city from the physical angle Moorhouse chooses?

2. The reference to the "very same collection of gaudy hoardings" leading in and out of Heathrow, J. F. Kennedy, and Fiumicino (the international airports of London, New York, and Rome, respectively) suggests that the traveler will at first think he is in a familiar world. He soon discovers that he is moving into an unfamiliar one. What other contrasts of this sort does Moorhouse imply?

3. How does Moorhouse reveal the feelings of the typical traveler at the end of his journey to the hotel? Does he establish his own attitude toward Calcutta?

4. The reference to Bishopsgate and Holborn shows that Moorhouse is writing with a British audience in mind, people familiar with the architecture of these areas of London. What other statements call for knowledge of this kind?

5. Does Moorhouse succeed in capturing your attention and interest? Why or why not?

WRITING ASSIGNMENT

Use Moorhouse's description of Calcutta as a model for a description of a section of a college town or your home town. You may wish to describe the town as seen from a limousine, a Volkswagen, or a bicycle, but be careful to make the angle of vision contribute to the overall impression and the revelation of an attitude. Do not specify this attitude; let your selection of details reveal it.

WINSTON S. CHURCHILL

SIR WINSTON CHURCHILL *(1874–1965) had a long and distinguished career in politics before serving Great Britain as prime minister during World War Two and later from 1951 to 1955. Churchill was also a historian, and one of the most gifted speakers and writers of English. His account of his first day at an English public school (a private school in the United States) occurs at the beginning of his autobiography* My Early Life, *published in 1930. Churchill tells us that he looked forward to going to school, though "I was perfectly helpless. Irresistible tides drew me swiftly forward. I was no more consulted about leaving home than I had been about coming into the world." Churchill was at this time seven years old. "How I hated this school, and what a life of anxiety I lived there for more than two years," he tells us. Like Lytton Strachey and Mary McCarthy, Churchill has an eye for details that give us the sense of place as well as of people.*

My First Introduction to the Classics

The school my parents had selected for my education was   1
one of the most fashionable and expensive in the country. It

modeled itself upon Eton and aimed at being preparatory for that Public School above all others. It was supposed to be the very last thing in schools. Only ten boys in a class; electric light (then a wonder); a swimming pond; spacious football and cricket grounds; two or three school treats, or "expeditions" as they were called, every term; the masters all M.A.'s in gowns and mortar-boards; a chapel of its own; no hampers allowed; everything provided by the authorities. It was a dark November afternoon when we arrived at this establishment. We had tea with the Headmaster, with whom my mother conversed in the most easy manner. I was preoccupied with the fear of spilling my cup and so making "a bad start." I was also miserable at the idea of being left alone among all these strangers in this great, fierce, formidable place. After all I was only seven, and I had been so happy in my nursery with all my toys. I had such wonderful toys: a real steam engine, a magic lantern, and a collection of soldiers already nearly a thousand strong. Now it was to be all lessons. Seven or eight hours of lessons every day except half-holidays, and football or cricket in addition.

When the last sound of my mother's departing wheels 2 had died away, the Headmaster invited me to hand over any money I had in my possession. I produced my three half-crowns which were duly entered in a book, and I was told that from time to time there would be a "shop" at the school with all sorts of things which one would like to have, and that I could choose what I liked up to the limit of the seven and sixpence. Then we quitted the Headmaster's parlor and the comfortable private side of the house, and entered the more bleak apartments reserved for the instruction and accommodation of the pupils. I was taken into a Form Room and told to sit at a desk. All the other boys were out of doors, and I was alone with the Form Master. He produced a thin greeny-brown-covered book filled with words in different types of print.

"You have never done any Latin before, have you?" 3 he said.

"No sir." 4

"This is a Latin grammar." He opened it at a well- 5

thumbed page. "You must learn this," he said, pointing to a number of words in a frame of lines. "I will come back in half an hour and see what you know."

Behold me then on a gloomy evening, with an aching 6 heart, seated in front of the First Declension.

Mensa	a table
Mensa	O table
Mensam	a table
Mensae	of a table
Mensae	to or for a table
Mensa	by, with or from a table

What on earth did it mean? Where was the sense of it? 7 It seemed absolute rigmarole to me. However, there was one thing I could always do: I could learn by heart. And I thereupon proceeded, as far as my private sorrows would allow, to memorize the acrostic-looking task which had been set me.

In due course the Master returned.   8

"Have you learnt it?" he asked.   9

"I think I can *say* it, sir," I replied; and I gabbled it off. 10

He seemed so satisfied with this that I was emboldened 11 to ask a question.

"What does it mean, sir?"   12

"It means what it says, Mensa, a table. Mensa is a noun 13 of the First Declension. There are five declensions. You have learnt the singular of the First Declension."

"But," I repeated, "what does it mean?"   14

"Mensa means a table," he answered.   15

"Then why does mensa also mean O table," I enquired, 16 "and what does O table mean?"

"Mensa, O table, is the vocative case," he replied.   17

"But why O table?" I persisted in genuine curiosity.   18

"O table,—you would use that in addressing a table, in 19 invoking a table." And then seeing he was not carrying me with him, "You would use it in speaking to a table."

"But I never do," I blurted out in honest amazement.   20
"If you are impertinent you will be punished, and pun- 21
ished, let me tell you, very severely," was his conclusive
rejoinder.

QUESTIONS

1. How important is the description of the school to your appreciation of Churchill's feelings about it? How careful is he to
   specify the physical point of view following his mother's
   departure?
2. What exactly were his feelings? Does he state them for us or
   instead imply them in the telling of the episode?
3. What point do you think Churchill is making in the whole
   account? What in particular does the exchange with the form
   master contribute?
4. Would you say that Churchill finds humor in the episode?
   Notice the difference between what Churchill, the man, sees,
   and what Churchill, the boy, felt. Is the psychological point of
   view that of the boy or that of the man—or is it possibly both?

WRITING ASSIGNMENTS

1. Write a characterization of Winston Churchill on the basis of
   what he reveals about himself in the telling of this episode.
   Consider what he chooses to emphasize as well as his selection
   of details.
2. Write a narrative of a similar experience of your own—your
   first day in a new school, your own first introduction to a
   forbidding subject, or your discovery that adults could be different from what you had known them to be. Clarify both the
   physical and psychological point of view for your reader.

THE PARAGRAPH:
METHODS
OF DEVELOPMENT

Definition

There are many ways of defining something, and the way we choose depends on our purpose. If we are in a store that sells "Hero Sandwiches" and a visitor asks what these are, we can point to one on the counter. But pointing may not be enough: we may have to explain or "denote" what a hero sandwich is—that is, single the "hero" out from all other things like it. Now in a denotative definition we can start with a very broad class of things like food and single the hero out from all kinds. But since the visitor knows a hero is something to eat, we can limit our class to sandwiches, for our visitor knows what these are. A dictionary definition usually gives us a denotative definition of this sort—identifying first the class or genus of objects to which the word belongs and then distinguishing the word by its specific difference. As we noted, the class or genus may be broad (*food*) or it may be narrow (*sandwich*). The following dictionary definition of *hero* chooses a narrow genus:

> *hero* U.S. A sandwich [*genus*] made with a loaf of bread cut lengthwise [*specific difference*].—*Standard College Dictionary*

Sometimes we want to do more than merely name or identify an object: we want to present ideas and impressions, the emotional aura we associate with it. The word *rose* has a precise denotation—a particular flower with describable properties. It also has a range of connotations or associations. Thus roses are often associated with success or happiness, and we recognize this association in the popular expression "a rosy future." Connotations may be positive in their implication, or negative. Though the words *inexpensive* and *cheap* both mean low in price, *cheap* usually carries the connotation of poor quality or of something contemptible. *Inexpensive* is an emotionally neutral word; *cheap* is not. Notice that some connotations seem to be inherent in the word, as in *cheap*; others, like *rosy*—to mean promising success—are not.

Denotative and connotative definitions tell us how words are used currently. Sometimes we find it helpful to give the original meaning or etymology to clarify the current meaning—for example, to explain that the word *gravity* comes from the Latin *gravitas* meaning weight or heaviness. But we must be careful not to assume that a current word possesses, or should possess, its original meaning. The word *sinister* originally referred to the left, but this meaning is rare today, and we would certainly be misunderstood if we used *sinister* to refer to a left-handed person. But notice how the etymology of sinister helps to explain an expression like a left-handed compliment.

TIME

> *The following discussion on euphemism is the first of a number of selections in this book concerned with misuses of language. George Orwell, in the essay on the political uses of language which appears later in this book, discusses the consequences of the "wholesale corruption of the language" illustrated here. Notice how* Time *combines etymological with other kinds of definition to explain what euphemism is.*

Euphemism

From a Greek word meaning "to use words of good omen," 1
euphemism is the substitution of a pleasant term for a blunt

one—telling it like it isn't. Euphemism has probably existed since the beginning of language. As long as there have been things of which men thought the less said the better, there have been better ways of saying less. In everyday conversation the euphemism is, at worst, a necessary evil; at its best, it is a handy verbal tool to avoid making enemies needlessly, or shocking friends. Language purists and the blunt-spoken may wince when a young woman at a party coyly asks for direction to "the powder room," but to most people this kind of familiar euphemism is probably no more harmful or annoying than, say, a split infinitive.

On a larger scale, though, the persistent growth of 2 euphemism in a language represents a danger to thought and action, since its fundamental intent is to deceive. As linguist Benjamin Lee Whorf has pointed out, the structure of a given language determines, in part, how the society that speaks it views reality. If "substandard housing" makes rotting slums appear more livable or inevitable to some people, then their view of American cities has been distorted and their ability to assess the significance of poverty has been reduced. Perhaps the most chilling example of euphemism's destructive power took place in Hitler's Germany. The wholesale corruption of the language under Nazism, notes critic George Steiner, is symbolized by the phrase *endgültige Lösung* (final solution), which "came to signify the death of 6,000,000 human beings in gas ovens."

QUESTIONS

1. The *Time* essay includes the etymology of *euphemism* in the first sentence. What help does the etymology give you in understanding its present meaning? What present meanings are not contained in the etymology?

2. What denotative definition of *euphemism* does the author of the essay give? How similar is this definition to the one in your dictionary?

3. What examples of negative connotations of the word does the author give? Does the word have a positive connotation, and is there an example of it?

4. How do the examples in the second paragraph help you understand Whorf's idea that "the structure of a given language determines, in part, how the society that speaks it views reality"?

WRITING ASSIGNMENTS

1. Write a paragraph illustrating the positive uses of euphemism. Distinguish these uses carefully through various examples, drawing them from several areas of experience.

2. Write a paragraph illustrating the negative uses of euphemism. Distinguish these uses, and vary your examples.

3. Illustrate Whorf's statement about language and reality through euphemisms relating to death or some other experience. Be careful to state what your examples reveal about the people who use them.

4. Use the *Oxford English Dictionary* and other reference books to investigate the etymology and properties of one of the following, and write an account of the word:
   a. gyroscope   d. sergeant
   b. alcohol   e. schooner
   c. cotton gin   f. vaccine

5. Use the *Oxford English Dictionary* and other reference books to show how etymology sheds light on the current meanings of one of the words below. Indicate the extent to which original meanings of the word have been retained in current usage.
   a. silly   d. jargon
   b. humorous   e. nice
   c. foolish   f. mediocre

WILLIAM ZINSSER

WILLIAM ZINSSER *considers euphemism from a broader perspective than does* Time—*analyzing euphemism as one kind of faulty language, with qualities similar to the*

laborious phrase, corporate language, and the in-
teroffice memo. Zinsser has had wide opportunity to
study cluttered language as a journalist and teacher. His
long career includes experience as a film critic, a feature
writer for The New York Herald Tribune, *and colum-*
nist for Life *Magazine and* The New York Times, *and*
he has published several collections of essays on life in
America. He also taught writing at Yale for a number of
years, and gives valuable advice on the subject in his
book On Writing Well, *from which his discussion of*
clutter is reprinted.

Clutter

Clutter is the laborious phrase which has pushed out the   1
short word that means the same thing. These locutions are a
drag on energy and momentum. Even before John Dean
gave us "at this point in time," people had stopped saying
"now." They were saying "at the present time," or "currently," or "presently" (which means "soon"). Yet the idea
can always be expressed by "now" to mean the immediate
moment ("now I can see him"), or by "today" to mean the
historical present ("today prices are high"), or simply by the
verb "to be" ("it is raining"). There is no need to say "at the
present time we are experiencing precipitation."

Speaking of which, we are experiencing considerable   2
difficulty getting *that* word out of the language now that it
has lumbered in. Even your dentist will ask if you are experiencing any pain. If he were asking one of his own children
he would say, "Does it hurt?" He would, in short, be himself.
By using a more pompous phrase in his professional role he
not only sounds more important; he blunts the painful edge
of truth. It is the language of the airline stewardess demonstrating the oxygen mask that will drop down if the plane
should somehow run out of air. "In the extremely unlikely
possibility that the aircraft should experience such an even-

tuality," she begins—a phrase so oxygen-depriving in itself that we are prepared for any disaster, and even gasping death shall lose its sting.

Clutter is the ponderous euphemism that turns a slum 3 into a depressed socioeconomic area, a salesman into a marketing representative, a dumb kid into an underachiever and a bad kid into a pre-delinquent. (The Albuquerque public schools announced a program for "delinquent and pre-delinquent boys.")

Clutter is the official language used by the American 4 corporation—in the news release and the annual report—to hide its mistakes. When a big company recently announced that it was "decentralizing its organizational structure into major profit-centered businesses" and that "corporate staff services will be aligned under two senior vice-presidents" it meant that it had had a lousy year.

Clutter is the language of the interoffice memo ("the 5 trend to mosaic communication is reducing the meaningfulness of concern about whether or not demographic segments differ in their tolerance of periodicity") and the language of computers ("we are offering functional digital programming options that have built-in parallel reciprocal capabilities with compatible third-generation contingencies and hardware").

QUESTIONS

1. In paragraph 1 Zinsser defines *clutter denotatively*. What is the genus and the specific difference of the definition?

2. Zinsser identifies clutter with various qualities of language, suggested in paragraphs 1–3 by the words *laborious, pompous*, and *ponderous*. Which of these words describe the language of the corporation and the interoffice memo quoted in paragraphs 4-5?

WRITING ASSIGNMENTS

1. Write a short paragraph in simple, clear language. Rewrite the paragraph in cluttered language. In a third paragraph explain

why your second paragraph is cluttered and your first paragraph is not.

2. Write an analysis of the following passage, discussing first what you think it says, then analyzing its success or failure in expressing the idea clearly:

> Objective consideration of contemporary phenomena compels the conclusion that success or failure in competitive activities exhibits no tendency to be commensurate with innate capacity, but that a considerable element of the unpredictable must invariably be taken into account.

PAUL FUSSELL

PAUL FUSSELL, *a professor of English at Rutgers University, has written numerous books on poetry and the social aspects of literature, including* The Great War and Modern Memory, *for which he received the National Book Award in 1976. Fussell writes in this book about the poets of the First World War and also about changes in modern warfare—including the life in the trenches described in the following passage. Trench warfare began with the First Battle of the Marne in September, 1914; after this battle the German and Allied armies were dug into trenches until the German offensive in the spring of 1918, and the Allied counteroffensive that followed. War was never again to be fought as it had been before the trenches.*

World War One Trenches

The two main British sectors duplicated each other also in   1
their almost symbolic road systems. Each had a staging
town behind: for Ypres it was Poperinghe (to the men,
"Pop"); for the Somme, Amiens. From these towns troops

proceeded with augmenting but usually well-concealed terror up a sinister road to the town of operations, either Ypres
itself or Albert. And running into the enemy lines out of
Ypres and Albert were the most sinister roads of all, one
leading to Menin, the other to Bapaume, both in enemy
territory. These roads defined the direction of ultimate attack and the hoped-for breakout. They were the goals of the
bizarre inverse quest on which the soldiers were ironically
embarked.

But most of the time they were not questing. They were 2
sitting or lying or squatting in place below the level of the
ground. "When all is said and done," Sassoon notes, "the
war was mainly a matter of holes and ditches."[1] And in
these holes and ditches extending for ninety miles, continually, even in the quietest times, some 7000 British men and
officers were killed and wounded daily, just as a matter of
course. "Wastage," the Staff called it.

There were normally three lines of trenches. The front- 3
line trench was anywhere from fifty yards or so to a mile
from its enemy counterpart. Several hundred yards behind
it was the support trench line. And several hundred yards
behind that was the reserve line. There were three kinds of
trenches: firing trenches, like these; communication
trenches, running roughly perpendicular to the line and
connecting the three lines; and "saps," shallower ditches
thrust out into No Man's Land, providing access to forward
observation posts, listening posts, grenade-throwing posts,
and machine gun positions. The end of a sap was usually not
manned all the time: night was the favorite time for going
out. Coming up from the rear, one reached the trenches by
following a communication trench sometimes a mile or more
long. It often began in a town and gradually deepened. By
the time pedestrians reached the reserve line, they were well
below ground level.

A firing trench was supposed to be six to eight feet deep 4
and four or five feet wide. On the enemy side a parapet of

---

[1]Siegfried Sassoon, *Memoirs of an Infantry Officer* (1930; New York, 1937), p. 228.

earth or sandbags rose about two or three feet above the ground. A corresponding "parados" a foot or so high was often found on top of the friendly side. Into the sides of trenches were dug one- or two-man holes ("funk-holes"), and there were deeper dugouts, reached by dirt stairs, for use as command posts and officers' quarters. On the enemy side of a trench was a fire-step two feet high on which the defenders were supposed to stand, firing and throwing grenades, when repelling attack. A well-built trench did not run straight for any distance: that would have been to invite enfilade fire. Every few yards a good trench zig-zagged. It had frequent traverses designed to contain damage within a limited space. Moving along a trench thus involved a great deal of weaving and turning. The floor of a proper trench was covered with wooden duckboards, beneath which were sumps a few feet deep designed to collect water. The walls, perpetually crumbling, were supported by sandbags, corrugated iron, or bundles of sticks or rushes. Except at night and in half-light, there was of course no looking over the top except through periscopes, which could be purchased in the "Trench Requisites" section of the main London department stores. The few snipers on duty during the day observed No Man's Land through loopholes cut in sheets of armor plate.

The entanglements of barbed wire had to be positioned 5 far enough out in front of the trench to keep the enemy from sneaking up to grenade-throwing distance. Interestingly, the two novelties that contributed most to the personal menace of the war could be said to be American inventions. Barbed wire had first appeared on the American frontier in the late nineteenth century for use in restraining animals. And the machine gun was the brainchild of Hiram Stevens Maxim (1840–1916), an American who, disillusioned with native patent law, established his Maxim Gun Company in England and began manufacturing his guns in 1889. He was finally knighted for his efforts. At first the British regard for barbed wire was on a par with Sir Douglas Haig's understanding of the machine gun. In the autumn of 1914, the first wire Private Frank Richards saw emplaced before the British positions was a single strand of agricultural wire found in the vicinity.[2] Only later did the manufactured article begin to arrive from England in sufficient quantity to create the thickets of mock-organic rusty brown that helped give a look of eternal autumn to the front.

The whole British line was numbered by sections, 6 neatly, from right to left. A section, normally occupied by a company, was roughly 300 yards wide. One might be occupying front-line trench section 51; or support trench S 51, behind it; or reserve trench SS 51, behind both. But a less formal way of identifying sections of trench was by place or street names with a distinctly London flavor. *Piccadilly* was a favorite; popular also were *Regent Street* and *Strand*; junctions were *Hyde Park Corner* and *Marble Arch*. Greater wit—and deeper homesickness—sometimes surfaced in the naming of the German trenches opposite. Sassoon remembers "Durley" 's account of the attack at Delville Wood in September, 1916: "Our objective was Pint Trench, taking Bitter and Beer and clearing Ale and Vat, and also Pilsen Lane."[3] Directional and traffic control signs were everywhere in the trenches, giving the whole system the air of a parody modern city, although one literally "underground."

QUESTIONS

1. Here is one dictionary definition of the word *trench:*

> A long, irregular ditch, lined with a parapet of the excavated earth, to protect troops.—*Standard College Dictionary*

How much of this information does Fussell include in his extended definition of the World War One trench? Can you think of any other information you need to visualize or understand trenches?

---

[2]Frank Richards, *Old Soldiers Never Die* (1933), pp. 44–45.
[3]*Memoirs of an Infantry Officer*, p. 51.

2. What points is Fussell making about the trenches through the details that define them?

3. Why does Fussell mention the names of the trench sections? Is this information essential to our understanding of what trenches are?

4. What details if any surprised you, and why? In general, what does Fussell tell you about the nature of trench warfare?

WRITING ASSIGNMENT

Write a definition of one of the following. Relate the details of your definition to the uses of the object:

a. an expressway interchange
b. the playing of a game like Monopoly
c. the instrument panel of a video game
d. part of a musical instrument (trumpet keys, violin strings)
e. bicycle chain
f. lawn mower blade

Other Uses of Definition

We can use definition to fix words that have become indefinite or confused in popular usage. We sometimes call this kind of definition *precising*. Another use of definition is to stipulate or propose a name or term for a newly discovered phenomenon so that we can refer to it. An example is the term *quasar*, proposed in the 1960s for newly discovered "quasi-stellar" sources of light in the sky that seemed not to be stars. Stipulative definitions are proposed with the understanding that the term may change later as more is discovered. By contrast, theoretical definitions propose an explanation or theory of the phenomenon: they do not merely propose a term for discussion and further research. Most textbook definitions of democracy and similar ideas are theoretical. In giving definitions, we should be clear about the use we are making of them. It will matter to the reader whether we are trying to make a commonly used word more exact in its usage or proposing a definition without claiming to know the truth about it or proposing a definition that does make such a claim.

MARCIA SELIGSON

MARCIA SELIGSON *has written much about American customs in magazine articles and in two books,* Options *and* The Eternal Bliss Machine, *which contains the following definition of the American wedding. Seligson tells us in the introduction:* "Whatever it is about weddings that makes people go a little bananas—construct ships out of chopped liver or dye mashed potatoes pink to match the bridesmaids' dresses—it transcends ethnic division and crosses state lines." *Her view is a humorous one, but as in much humor she has a serious point to make.*

The American Wedding

Every culture, in every time throughout history, has com- 1
memorated the transition of a human being from one state
in life to another. Birth, the emergence into manhood,
graduation from school at various levels, birthdays, marriage, death—each of these outstanding steps is acknowledged by a ceremony of some sort, always public, the guests
in effect becoming witnesses to the statement of life's ongo-
ingness, of the natural order of history. To insure the special
significance of the rite of passage, its apartness from any
other event of the day, these rituals usually require pag-
eantry, costumed adornment, and are accompanied by
gift-bearing and feasting. We wear black to funerals, bring
presents to christenings and birthday parties, get loaded at
wakes, eat ourselves sick at bar mitzvahs. Birth, marriage
and death, to be sure, are the most elemental and major
steps, and as there is only one of those ritual commemora-
tions for which we are *actually*, fully present, the wedding
becomes, for mankind, its most vital rite of passage. And
for this reason it is anchored at the very core of civilization.

For the rites of passage the ceremony itself is organic to 2
the society for which the individual is being groomed, in his
journey from one state to the next. In African hunting
societies, for example, a boy at puberty is thrown naked into
the jungle and required to kill a lion. His value as a man will
be judged by how successful he can be in meeting the demands of his culture. In America, newlyweds are being
prepared for their roles in a consumer society, so it is surely
appropriate that all of the dynamics of wedding hoo-hah
testify to these commercial, mercantile terms. Gifts are purchased not only by the "witnesses" but by bride for groom,
groom for bride, bride for attendants, attendants for bride.
Prenuptial parties, bachelor dinners, showers. The ever-
mushrooming splash and flash circuses of the wedding
itself. The American wedding is a ritual event of ferocious,

gluttonous consuming, a debauch of intensified buying, never again to be repeated in the life of an American couple.

QUESTIONS

1. The first paragraph defines *rite of passage* denotatively. What theory of social reality does Seligson present in the second paragraph?

2. What is the order of ideas in the first paragraph? Does the author develop the second paragraph in the same way?

3. Has Seligson exaggerated her characterization of the American wedding, or has she described it as it is?

WRITING ASSIGNMENTS

1. Describe a ceremony of high-school or college life—June graduation, the class play, the senior dance—and discuss the extent to which it is "organic" to the society of the institution.

2. Examine advertisements in magazines and newspapers that depict brides and festivities associated with weddings (bridal showers, the wedding ceremony, receptions, and the like). In a short essay describe these advertisements and discuss whether or not they support Seligson's statement that the American wedding is "a ritual event of ferocious, gluttonous consuming, a debauch of intensified buying."

JOSEPH WOOD KRUTCH

A distinguished drama critic and teacher of English, JOSEPH WOOD KRUTCH *(1893–1970) taught at Columbia until 1950. He spent the remainder of his life writing about nature, conservation, and American life and values in a series of books, including* The Desert World, If You Don't Mind My Saying So, *and* Human Nature and the Human Condition, *in which his definition of "nor-*

mal" appears. As his definition suggests, Krutch was opposed to "adjustment" as the measure of good and happiness. "If men are nothing but the product of their society," he writes, "if what is called 'human nature' is actually determined by the existing system of production and distribution, then man will become more and more merely that creature whose desires and convictions and acts are best 'adjusted' to his external condition." Krutch had an unusual gift for writing about complex ideas in plain language—free of clutter and fashionable jargon.

The Meaning of "Normal"

The words we choose to define or suggest what we believe to 1
be important facts exert a very powerful influence upon civilization. A mere name can persuade us to approve or disapprove, as it does, for example, when we describe certain attitudes as "cynical" on the one hand or "realistic" on the other. No one wants to be "unrealistic" and no one wants to be "snarling." Therefore his attitude toward the thing described may very well depend upon which designation is current among his contemporaries; and the less critical his mind, the more influential the most commonly used vocabulary will be.

It is for this reason that, even as a mere verbal confu- 2
sion, the use of "normal" to designate what ought to be called "average" is of tremendous importance and serves not only to indicate but actually to reinforce the belief that average ability, refinement, intellectuality, or even virtue is an ideal to be aimed at. Since we cannot do anything to the purpose until we think straight and since we cannot think straight without properly defined words, it may be that the very first step toward an emancipation from the tyranny of "conformity" should be the attempt to substitute for "normal," as commonly used, a genuine synonym for "average."

Fortunately, such a genuine and familiar synonym does ₃ exist. That which is "average" is also properly described as "mediocre." And if we were accustomed to call the average man, not "the common man" or still less "the normal man," but "the mediocre man" we should not be so easily hypnotized into believing that mediocrity is an ideal to be aimed at.

A second step in the same direction would be to return ₄ to the word "normal" its original meaning. According to the Shorter Oxford Dictionary it derives from the Latin "norma," which has been Anglicized as "norm" and is, in turn, thus defined: "A rule or authoritative standard." The adjective "normative" is not commonly misused—no doubt because it is not part of that "vocabulary of the average man" by which educators now set so much store. It still generally means "establishing a norm or standard." But "normal" seldom means, as it should, "corresponding to the standard by which a thing is to be judged." If it did, "a normal man" would again mean, not what the average man *is* but what, in its fullest significance, the word "man" should imply, even "what a man *ought* to be." And that is a very different thing from the "average" or "mediocre" man whom we have so perversely accustomed ourselves to regard as most worthy of admiration.

Only by defining and then attempting to reach up to- ₅ ward the "normal" as properly defined can a democratic society save itself from those defects which the enemies of democracy have always maintained were the necessary consequences of such a society. Until "preparation for life" rather than "familiarity with the best that has been thought and said" became the aim of education every schoolboy knew that Emerson had bid us hitch our wagons to a star. We now hitch them to a mediocrity instead.

Unless, then, normal is a useless and confusing ₆ synonym for average, it should mean what the word normative suggests, namely, a *concept of what ought to be* rather than a *description of what is*. It should mean what at times it has meant—the fullest possible realization of what the human being is capable of—the complete, not the aborted human being. It is an *entelechy*, not a mean; something excellent, not something mediocre; something rare, not common; not what the majority are, but what few, if any, actually measure up to.

Where, it will be asked, do we get this norm, upon what basis does it rest? Upon the answer to that question depends what a civilization will be like and especially in what direction it will move. At various times religion, philosophy, law, and custom have contributed to it in varying degrees. When none of these is available poetry and literature may do so. But unless we can say in one way or another, "I have some idea of what men ought to be as well as some knowledge of what they are," then civilization is lost.

QUESTIONS

1. Krutch's definition of *normal* is a precising definition: he is seeking to make an uncommon meaning of *normal* its common one. How does Krutch try to persuade us of the need for this definition?

2. How does Krutch account for the present differences in the connotations of *normative* and *normal*, which derive from the same word? Does he state or imply why *normal* came to mean *average*?

3. Can the meaning of *entelechy* be determined from its context? What help does the etymology of the word provide?

4. Use the synonym listings in your dictionary to determine the exact difference in meaning between the following pairs of words. Write sentences using ten of the italicized words to reflect their precise dictionary meanings.
   a. *essential;* necessary
   b. *predict;* prophesy
   c. *mimic;* mock
   d. sinister; *portentous*
   e. fortitude; *forbearance*
   f. phase; *facet*
   g. agent; *factor*

   h. recumbent; *prone*
   i. adroit; *deft*
   j. *dextrous;* handy
   k. blended; *mingled*
   l. *perturbed;* agitated

WRITING ASSIGNMENTS

1. Define one of the following words by stating what it is not as well as what it is. Comment on the significance of its etymology.
   a. tolerance   c. barbecue
   b. stinginess   d. soccer

2. Discuss the different meanings of one of the following words, illustrating these meanings by your use of them.
   a. funny   d. crazy
   b. average   e. tacky
   c. cool   f. weird

Classification and Division

In definition, our purpose is to explain what a word means—to show how an object or idea is different from others like it. But there are times when we want to show how the object or idea relates to others, or how various objects relate to one another. We may, for example, want to show the range of cars manufactured in the United States to illustrate the importance of cars in our lives. To do so, we engage in the process of classification—the grouping of objects, persons or ideas that share significant qualities. For example, we can classify Chevrolets with Dodges, Fords, and other American automobiles, and if we want to illustrate the importance of General Motors in the manufacture of cars, we can classify Chevrolets with Buicks, Oldsmobiles, and other GM cars. The number of classes to which an object can be fitted is obviously great.

Instead of relating an object to others like it, we may want to show its various types. We call this process of analysis division. Chevrolets, for example, come in various models—Citation and Chevette, to name two. Notice that we have divided according to the model and name. But we might divide Chevrolets in other ways—for example, by engine or body size or fuel economy. Again the basis or principle of division we choose depends on the purpose of our analysis. To carry the process of division further, having distinguished various Chevrolet models, we might divide one of them—Citation—on the basis of its transmission. Here is an example of division in a scientific discussion of meteorites:

purpose of analysis For the investigator of meteorites the basic challenge is deducing the history of the *meteorites* from a bewildering abundance of evidence. The richness of the problem is indicated by the sheer variety of *types* of meteorite. The two

division
  according to
  constituent material
  first type: stony
  second type: iron

main classes are the *stony meteorites* and the *iron meteorites.* The stony meteorites consist mainly of silicates, with an admixture of nickel and iron. The iron meteorites consist mainly of *third type: stony-iron* nickel and iron in various proportions. A smaller class is the stony-iron meteorites, which are intermediate in composition between the other two. Stony meteorites are in turn divided into two groups: the chondrites and the achondrites, according to whether or not they contain chondrules, spherical aggregates of iron-magnesium silicate. Within each group there are further subdivisions based on mineralogical and chemical composition.

subdivision of stony meteorites according to presence or absence of chrondules

further subdivisions

—I. R. Cameron,
"Meteorites and Cosmic Radiation"
(italics added)

JOSEPH G. ROSA

JOSEPH G. ROSA, *who lives and works in England, has interpreted the old American West for a British audience in numerous periodicals, in radio commentaries for the British Broadcasting Company, and in his books* They Called Him Wild Bill *(on William Hickock) and* The Gunfighter. *Notice that Rosa associates the qualities of the gunfighter with "desirable characteristics of the Victorian era"—qualities likely to be familiar to many British readers—and corrects misconceptions that his audience may have about the West.*

The Gunfighter

Descriptions of a legendary gunfighter's personal character   1
follow a pattern. Almost without exception they were

generous to a fault, chivalrous, and fond of children. It is possible that certain individuals among the actual gunfighters possessed these qualities. But it is important to remember that these qualities were high on the list of desirable characteristics of the Victorian era and that the legend makers would naturally endow their heroes with them. Thus it is easy to understand why such scoundrels as Billy the Kid were included in the good-bad category by misguided admirers.

Believers in and perpetrators of the Western myth also 2 contend that the gunfighters shared certain physical characteristics. Great attention has been paid to the color of their eyes and hair and to fancied similarities in physical appearance. One modern writer has devoted a whole book to the subject,[1] claiming also to list all the facets that went into making a typical bad man. Nevertheless, there was only one personality trait they all shared: the disposition to kill when provoked. In physical attributes they were as individual as any random group of men. In the few available photographs of members of the gunfighting fraternity, their expressions reveal varying degrees of intelligence. The legendary "sadness" to be seen in their eyes was probably eyestrain caused by the length of time they had to sit unblinking for an early-day portrait.

The so-called "Western Code" never really existed. 3 Men bent on killing did so in the most efficient and expeditious way they knew. Jesse James was shot in the back by Bob Ford as he stood on a chair adjusting a picture. Ben Thompson was led into a trap in a theater and shot down with his friend King Fisher. Billy the Kid died as he entered a darkened room. Wild Bill Hickok was shot from behind while he was playing poker. In each case the victim had no chance to defend himself.

It has been pointed out that the gunfighters—especially 4 those who allied themselves with some aspect of law

---

[1]George David Hendricks, *The Bad Men of the West* (San Antonio: Naylor, 1941).

enforcement—were accepted by the society on whose fringes they lived. Another factor in a gunfighter's acceptance was whether or not he was regularly employed. If he was out of a job, he was likely to be arrested for "vagrancy," a catchall charge that served to discourage potential troublemakers from staying in town. Even Hickok was not immune to such charges. On June 17, 1875, Wild Bill was charged with vagrancy in Cheyenne, Wyoming Territory, and a warrant for his arrest was issued the same day. A $200 bail bond was ordered and was returned and filed on June 18 and approved on June 22. By August 4 the charge had cost the county $5.25 in expenses. In November, however, when the case was to be tried, Bill had disappeared, and a continuance was ordered. On June 12, 1876, Hickok had still not been apprehended, although he was known to be in town or nearby preparing for his trip to the Black Hills. The case was again continued to the next term. When Hickok was murdered, a clerk wrote across the docket entry, "Deft dead. Dismissed."[2]

Contemporary reports of his death hinted that the town 5 marshal was afraid to bring in Wild Bill, a suggestion the marshal angrily denied. No one seemed to know why Hickok had been charged in the first place. As one historian commented, "Bill was always classed as a law and order man."[3] The explanation appears to be that Hickok was believed to be potentially dangerous, and the vagrancy charge was the easiest means of safeguarding the town against trouble.

No discussion of the gunfighter as a man would be 6 complete without mentioning the men in official positions who used their offices to act on the wrong side of the law. Their activities have provided the basis for innumerable plots in Western books, movies, and television shows, in

---

[2]Laramie County Clerk of Court Criminal Appearance Docket, Book II, 230, June 17, 1875–June 12, 1876, copy supplied by the Wyoming State Archives, Cheyenne, Wyoming.

[3]Russell Thorp to the author, October 14, 1960.

which the crooked banker or sheriff has become a familiar figure. One of the most notorious of such men was Henry Newton Brown, marshal of Caldwell Kansas. Believed to have been a former associate of Billy the Kid, Brown had served briefly as assistant marshal of Caldwell early in 1882, and on December 21 of that year was appointed marshal. His effective policing of the town was appreciated by the citizens, who presented him with a fine, handsomely engraved Winchester rifle. As far as the townspeople were concerned, Marshal Brown and his assistant, Ben Wheeler, were ideal peace officers.

QUESTIONS

1. Rosa is examining the basis on which those who created the myth of the West put certain people into the class of gunfighters. What were the qualities attributed to the gunfighter?
2. Does Rosa show that all those identified as gunfighters actually possessed these qualities? Did Wild Bill Hickok?
3. Would those considered scoundrels have been identified or classified as gunfighters? Was Henry Newton Brown considered a scoundrel?
4. What does Rosa's classification tell us about the values and needs of people living in the West?

WRITING ASSIGNMENTS

1. Discuss the qualities you believe are generally attributed to people in your city or part of the country. Then discuss the extent to which your personal experience confirms these qualities.
2. Do the same to test the stereotype of a racial or ethnic group or the stereotype of those engaged in a particular sport or occupation.

ALLAN NEVINS

*One of America's most important historians, ALLAN
NEVINS (1890–1971) taught at Columbia and was associated with the Huntington Library in California for
many years. Nevins wrote important biographies of
many famous Americans, including John D. Rockefeller
and Henry Ford, and won Pulitzer Prizes in 1933 and
1937 for his lives of Grover Cleveland and Hamilton
Fish. His discussion of newspapers shows one important
use of division in exposition and also tells us something
important about the interpretation of evidence—a subject we will consider later in this book.*

The Newspaper

Obviously, it is futile to talk of accuracy or inaccuracy, au-   1
thority or lack of authority, with reference to the newspaper
as a whole. The newspaper cannot be dismissed with either
a blanket endorsement or a blanket condemnation. It cannot be used as if all its parts had equal value or authenticity.
The first duty of the historical student of the newspaper is to
discriminate. He must weigh every separate department,
every article, every writer, for what the department or article or writer seems to be worth. Clearly, a great part of what
is printed in every newspaper is from official sources, and
hence may be relied upon to be perfectly accurate. The
weather report is accurate; so are court notices, election
notices, building permits, lists of marriage licenses, bank-
ruptcy lists. Though unofficial, other classes of news are
almost totally free from error. The most complete precautions are taken to keep the stock market quotations minutely
accurate, both by stock exchange authorities and by the
newspaper staffs. An error in stock quotations may have
the most disastrous consequences, and mistakes are hence

excluded by every means within human power. So with shipping news, news of deaths, and a considerable body of similar matter—sports records, registers of Congressional or legislative votes, and so on.

Thus one great division of material in newspapers can 2 be treated as completely authentic. There is another large division which may in general be treated as trustworthy and authoritative. This is the news which is prepared by experts under conditions exempt from hurry and favorable to the gathering of all the significant facts. The weekly review of a real estate expert is a case in point. The sporting news of the best newspapers, prepared by experts under conditions which make for accuracy, is singularly uniform, and this uniformity is the best evidence that it is truthful and well proportioned. Society news, industrial news, and similar intelligence, especially when it appears in the form of weekly surveys written by known specialists, is worthy of the utmost reliance.

But in dealing with news which contains a large subjec- 3 tive element, and which is prepared under conditions of hurry and strain, the critical faculty must be kept constantly alert. Every conscientious correspondent at an inauguration, or a battle, or a political rally, or in an interview, tries to report the facts. But not one of them can help reporting, in addition to the facts, the impression that he has personally received of them. The most honest and careful observer ordinarily sees a little of what he wishes to see. It is through failure to make critical allowance for this fact that the historical student of newspapers is most likely to be led astray. Beveridge in his life of Lincoln remarks upon the striking difference between the Democratic reports and the Republican reports of the Lincoln-Douglas debates. At Ottawa, Illinois, for example, these two great leaders held their first joint debate on August 21, 1858. Lincoln came on a special train of fourteen cars crowded with shouting Republicans. It arrived at Ottawa at noon and, according to the Republican papers, when Lincoln alighted a shout went up from a dense and enthusiastic crowd which made the bluffs of the Illinois River and the woods along it ring and ring again. Lincoln entered a carriage; according to the *Chicago Tribune* men with evergreens, mottoes, fair young ladies, bands of music, military companies, and a dense mass of cheering humanity followed him through the streets in a scene of tumultuous excitement. But according to the *Philadelphia Press* and other Douglas papers, Lincoln had only a chilly and lackadaisical reception. "As his procession passed," stated the *Philadelphia Press,* "scarcely a cheer went up. They marched along silently and sorrowfully, as if it were a funeral cortege following him to the grave." On the other hand, the Democratic papers declared that the reception of Douglas was perfectly tremendous; the cheers were so thundering, said the *Philadelphia Press*, that they seemed to rend the very air. But the *Chicago Tribune* said that Douglas had no reception of consequence; that the only cheers he got came from the Irish Catholics. Yet both reports were probably fairly honest. They saw what they wished to see.

QUESTIONS

1. On what basis does Nevins divide newspapers? What are the three divisions he distinguishes?

2. What point is he making through these divisions?

3. In referring to the "large subjective element" of certain newspaper accounts, is Nevins referring to bias or prejudice? What does his example of the Lincoln-Douglas debates show?

4. What is the order of ideas in the three paragraphs? Why does Nevins save "news which contains a large subjective element" for last?

5. How many classes can you think of for newspapers?

WRITING ASSIGNMENTS

1. Divide materials in newspapers by another principle of division and use your division to make a point, as Nevins does.

2. Analyze the front-page stories of an issue of a newspaper according to the degree of their reliability. Discuss the "subjective element" of one of the stories, as Nevins discusses the account of the Lincoln-Douglas debates.

JOHN HOLT

JOHN HOLT *widely influenced ideas on the teaching of children in the 1960s and 1970s—through such books as* How Children Fail, How Children Learn, *and* Freedom from Beyond. *Basing his ideas on his experience as a high school teacher in Colorado and Massachusetts, Holt stresses the idea that teachers do their job best when they help students teach themselves. His later essay in this book argues one of his most controversial ideas—that students should control their own learning. The assumptions that underlie Holt's thinking on education are stated in his discussion of the various disciplines that guide our learning.*

Kinds of Discipline

A child, in growing up, may meet and learn from three different kinds of disciplines. The first and most important is what we might call the Discipline of Nature or of Reality. When he is trying to do something real, if he does the wrong thing or doesn't do the right one, he doesn't get the result he wants. If he doesn't pile one block right on top of another, or tries to build on a slanting surface, his tower falls down. If he hits the wrong key, he hears the wrong note. If he doesn't hit the nail squarely on the head, it bends, and he has to pull it out and start with another. If he doesn't measure properly what he is trying to build, it won't open, close, fit, stand up, fly, float, whistle, or do whatever he wants it to do. If he closes his eyes when he swings, he doesn't hit the ball. A child meets this kind of discipline every time he tries to *do* something, which is why it is so important in school to give children more chances to do things, instead of just reading or listening to someone talk (or pretending to). This discipline is a great teacher. The learner never has to wait long for his answer; it usually comes quickly, often instantly. Also it is clear, and very often points toward the needed correction; from what happened he can not only see that what he did was wrong, but also why, and what he needs to do instead. Finally, and most important, the giver of the answer, call it Nature, is impersonal, impartial, and indifferent. She does not give opinions, or make judgments; she cannot be wheedled, bullied, or fooled; she does not get angry or disappointed; she does not praise or blame; she does not remember past failures or hold grudges; with her one always gets a fresh start, this time is the one that counts.

The next discipline we might call the Discipline of Culture, of Society, of What People Really Do. Man is a social, a cultural animal. Children sense around them this culture, this network of agreements, customs, habits, and rules binding the adults together. They want to understand it and be a part of it. They watch very carefully what people around them are doing and want to do the same. They want to do right, unless they become convinced they can't do right. Thus children rarely misbehave seriously in church, but sit as quietly as they can. The example of all those grownups is contagious. Some mysterious ritual is going on, and children, who like rituals, want to be part of it. In the same way, the little children that I see at concerts or operas, though they may fidget a little, or perhaps take a nap now and then, rarely make any disturbance. With all those grownups sitting there, neither moving nor talking, it is the most natural thing in the world to imitate them. Children who live among adults who are habitually courteous to each other, and to them, will soon learn to be courteous. Children who live surrounded by people who speak a certain way will speak that way, however much we may try to tell them that speaking that way is bad or wrong.

The third discipline is the one most people mean when they speak of discipline—the Discipline of Superior Force, of sergeant to private, of "you do what I tell you or I'll make you wish you had." There is bound to be some of this in a child's life. Living as we do surrounded by things that can hurt children, or that children can hurt, we cannot avoid it. We can't afford to let a small child find out from experience the danger of playing in a busy street, or of fooling with the pots on the top of a stove, or of eating up the pills in the medicine cabinet. So, along with other precautions, we say to him, "Don't play in the street, or touch things on the stove, or go into the medicine cabinet, or I'll punish you." Between him and the danger too great for him to imagine we put a lesser danger, but one he can imagine and maybe therefore want to avoid. He can have no idea of what it would be like to be hit by a car, but he can imagine being shouted at, or spanked, or sent to his room. He avoids these substitutes for the greater danger until he can understand it and avoid it for its own sake. But we ought to use this discipline only when it is necessary to protect the life, health, safety, or well-being of people or other living creatures, or to prevent destruction of things that people care about. We ought not to assume too long, as we usually do, that a child cannot understand the real nature of the danger from which we want to protect him. The sooner he avoids the danger, not to escape our punishment, but as a matter of good sense, the better. He can learn that faster than we think. In Mexico, for example, where people drive their cars with a good deal of spirit, I saw many children no older than five or four walking unattended on the streets. They understood about cars, they knew what to do. A child whose life is full of the threat and fear of punishment is locked into babyhood.

There is no way for him to grow up, to learn to take responsibility for his life and acts. Most important of all, we should not assume that having to yield to the threat of our superior force is good for the child's character. It is never good for *anyone's* character. To bow to superior force makes us feel impotent and cowardly for not having had the strength or courage to resist. Worse, it makes us resentful and vengeful. We can hardly wait to make someone pay for our humiliation, yield to us as we were once made to yield. No, if we cannot always avoid using the Discipline of Superior Force, we should at least use it as seldom as we can.

There are places where all three disciplines overlap. 4 Any very demanding human activity combines in it the disciplines of Superior Force, of Culture, and of Nature. The novice will be told, "Do it this way, never mind asking why, just do it that way, that is the way we always do it." But it probably *is* just the way they always do it, and usually for the very good reason that it is a way that has been found to work. Think, for example, of ballet training. The student in a class is told to do this exercise, or that; to stand so; to do this or that with his head, arms, shoulders, abdomen, hips, legs, feet. He is constantly corrected. There is no argument. But behind these seemingly autocratic demands by the teacher lie many decades of custom and tradition, and behind that, the necessities of dancing itself. You cannot make the moves of classical ballet unless over many years you have acquired, and renewed every day, the needed strength and suppleness in scores of muscles and joints. Nor can you do the difficult motions, making them look easy, unless you have learned hundreds of easier ones first. Dance teachers may not always agree on all the details of teaching these strengths and skills. But no novice could learn them all by himself. You could not go for a night or two to watch the ballet and then, without any other knowledge at all, teach yourself how to do it. In the same way, you would be unlikely to learn any complicated and difficult human activity without drawing heavily on the experience of those who know it better. But the point is that the authority of these experts or teachers stems from, grows out of their greater competence and experience, the fact that what they do *works*, not the fact that they happen to be the teacher and as such have the power to kick a student out of the class. And the further point is that children are always and everywhere attracted to that competence, and ready and eager to submit themselves to a discipline that grows out of it. We hear constantly that children will never do anything unless compelled to by bribes or threats. But in their private lives, or in extracurricular activities in school, in sports, music, drama, art, running a newspaper, and so on, they often submit themselves willingly and wholeheartedly to very intense disciplines, simply because they want to learn to do a given thing well. Our Little-Napoleon football coaches, of whom we have too many and hear far too much, blind us to the fact that millions of children work hard every year getting better at sports and games without coaches barking and yelling at them.

QUESTIONS

1. Does Holt divide discipline according to source or to the uses of discipline in education—or according to some other principle?
2. Is Holt's division exhaustive?
3. Holt states in paragraph 4 that the kinds of discipline distinguished overlap. How do they?
4. The principle of division might have been the effects of discipline on the personality of the young person. Is Holt concerned with effects in the course of his discussion?
5. How else might discipline be analyzed in a discussion of it, and to what purpose?
6. Do you agree with Holt that people learn best when they are not coerced? Do you agree with him about football coaches?

WRITING ASSIGNMENTS

1. Divide discipline according to a principle different from Holt's. Make your divisions exclusive of one another and indicate how exhaustive you think they are.

2. Write an essay on jobs or hobbies, developing the topic by division. If you divide by more than one principle, keep each breakdown and discussion separate and consistent.

Comparison and Contrast

Comparison shows the similarities between two people or things; contrast shows the differences. The word comparison sometimes refers to both kinds of analysis. Here is a paragraph that compares and contrasts the personality and behavior of President Franklin Roosevelt with the same in Great Britain's wartime prime minister, Winston Churchill:

> Roosevelt, as a public personality, was a spontaneous, optimistic, pleasure-loving ruler who dismayed his assistants by the gay and apparently heedless abandon with which he seemed to delight in pursuing two or more totally incompatible policies, and astonished them even more by the swiftness and ease with which he managed to throw off the cares of office during the darkest and most dangerous moments. Churchill too loves pleasure, and he too lacks neither gaiety nor a capacity for exuberant self-expression, together with the habit of blithely cutting Gordian knots in a manner which often upset his experts; but he is not a frivolous man. His nature possesses a dimension of depth—and a corresponding sense of tragic possibilities—which Roosevelt's light-hearted genius instinctively passed by.—Sir Isaiah Berlin

The paragraph presents a comparison of wholes—first the details about Roosevelt, then the details about Churchill. The author compares the two wartime leaders point by point:

> Roosevelt played the game of politics with virtuosity, and both his successes and his failures were carried off in splendid style; his performance seemed to flow with effortless skill. Churchill is acquainted with darkness as well as light. Like all inhabitants and even transient visitors of inner worlds, he gives evidence of seasons of agonized brooding and slow recovery. Roosevelt might have spoken of sweat and blood, but when Churchill offered his people tears, he spoke a word which might have been uttered by Lincoln or Mazzini or Cromwell, but not by Roosevelt, greathearted, generous and perceptive as he was.

Notice that the comparison builds from similarities to differences in both paragraphs. Were the similarities more important, the author would probably have built to them. Notice also the purpose of the comparison—to arrive at a relative estimate of the two men as leaders. We discover the qualities of Roosevelt through Churchill, and those of Churchill through Roosevelt. This kind of estimate is usually the purpose of comparison and contrast.

MARIE WINN

MARIE WINN *is the author of numerous articles and books on parents and children. Her book on children and television,* The Plug-In Drug *(1977), is based on interviews with parents and children, social workers, teachers, and child psychologists conducted in Denver and New York City. Like Marshall McLuhan, Winn is concerned about our experience with television and about what happens to children when it takes the place of reading. Winn believes that years of television viewing, particularly in children who read little, "has influenced adversely viewers' ability to concentrate, to read, to write clearly—in short, to demonstrate any of the verbal skills a literate society requires." Her comparison between reading and television viewing tells us why.*

Reading and Television

A comparison between reading and viewing may be made 1 in respect to the pace of each experience, and the relative control a person has over that pace, for the pace may influence the ways one uses the material received in each experience. In addition, the pace of each experience may determine how much it intrudes upon other aspects of one's life.

The pace of reading, clearly, depends entirely upon the 2
reader. He may read as slowly or as rapidly as he can or
wishes to read. If he does not understand something, he
may stop and reread it, or go in search of elucidation before
continuing. The reader can accelerate his pace when the
material is easy or less than interesting, and slow down
when it is difficult or enthralling. If what he reads is moving,
he can put down the book for a few moments and cope with
his emotions without fear of losing anything.

The pace of the television experience cannot be con- 3
trolled by the viewer; only its beginning and end are within
his control as he clicks the knob on and off. He cannot slow
down a delightful program or speed up a dreary one. He
cannot "turn back" if a word or phrase is not understood.
The program moves inexorably forward, and what is lost or
misunderstood remains so.

Nor can the television viewer readily transform the ma- 4
terial he receives into a form that might suit his particular
emotional needs, as he invariably does with material he
reads. The images move too quickly. He cannot use his own
imagination to invest the people and events portrayed on
television with the personal meanings that would help him
understand and resolve relationships and conflicts in his
own life; he is under the power of the imagination of the
show's creators. In the television experience the eyes and
ears are overwhelmed with the immediacy of sights and
sounds. They flash from the television set just fast enough
for the eyes and ears to take them in before moving on
quickly to the new pictures and sounds . . . so as *not to lose
the thread.*

Not to lose the thread . . . it is this need, occasioned by 5
the irreversible direction and relentless velocity of the television experience, that not only limits the workings of the
viewer's imagination, but also causes television to intrude
into human affairs far more than reading experiences can
ever do. If someone enters the room while one is watching
television—a friend, a relative, a child, someone, perhaps,

one has not seen for some time—one must continue to watch or one will lose the thread. The greetings must wait, for the television program will not. A book, of course, can be set aside, with a pang of regret, perhaps, but with no sense of permanent loss.

QUESTIONS

1. What is the purpose of the comparison, according to paragraph 1?

2. What are the differences? In what order does she present them?

3. Does Winn say that we should give up television, or is she making no recommendation?

4. Do you agree with her description of reading and watching television? Is reading ever as compelling an experience as television for you?

5. Is the experience of watching a sports event on television much the same as watching the news or a movie? If not, what are the differences? Do these similarities give support to Winn, or do they provide contrary evidence?

WRITING ASSIGNMENTS

1. In a few well-developed paragraphs, develop a comparison between one of the following pairs. State the purpose of your comparison somewhere in your essay, and draw conclusions as you discuss the similarities or differences.
   a. playing baseball (or another sport) and watching baseball
   b. listening to a particular kind of music and dancing to it
   c. reading a book and seeing the movie made from it
   d. riding a bicycle and driving a car on a busy highway

2. Compare the experience of reading a newspaper or newsmagazine with that of reading a novel or a textbook. Draw conclusions from your comparison at the end of your discussion.

3. Several writers in this book describe learning experiences in childhood. Choose two of the writers, and compare and contrast these experiences. Use your comparison to make a point:
   a. Sally Carrighar
   b. Maxine Hong Kingston
   c. Mary E. Mebane
   d. Winston S. Churchill

4. Compare a learning experience of your own with one of those described by Carrighar, Kingston, Mebane, or Churchill.

5. The following activities require similar skills. First discuss these similarities, and then discuss the different skills also required:
   a. parallel parking and backing into a garage
   b. pruning a hedge and pruning a tree
   c. learning to ride a bike and learning to drive
   d. painting a chair and painting a room

J. BRONOWSKI

A distinguished mathematician and scientist, JACOB BRONOWSKI *(1908–1974) was born in Poland and educated in England. Coming to the United States in 1964, he taught at various universities and did scientific research at the Salk Institute of Biological Studies in San Diego. Bronowski sought in him many books to bridge the sciences and the humanities. In his book (and television series)* The Ascent of Man *he says, "We are a scientific civilization; that means, a civilization in which knowledge and its integrity are crucial. Science is only a Latin work for knowledge." Science does not exist independent of values, nor can we afford to be ignorant of or unconcerned about these values. "Knowledge is not a loose-leaf notebook of facts. Above all, it is a responsibility for the integrity of what we are, primarily of what we are as ethical creatures." Bronowski's*

comparison of the athlete and the gazelle, taken from
The Ascent of Man, *illustrates how facts of nature can
help us understand ourselves as human beings.*

The Athlete and the Gazelle

Every human action goes back in some part to our animal 1
origins; we should be cold and lonely creatures if we were
cut off from that blood-stream of life. Nevertheless, it is
right to ask for a distinction: What are the physical gifts that
man must share with the animals, and what are the gifts
that make him different? Consider any example, the more
straightforward the better—say, the simple action of an
athlete when running or jumping. When he hears the gun,
the starting response of the runner is the same as the flight
response of the gazelle. He seems all animal in action. The
heartbeat goes up; when he sprints at top speed the heart is
pumping five times as much blood as normal, and ninety per
cent of it is for the muscles. He needs twenty gallons of air a
minute now to aerate his blood with the oxygen that it must
carry to the muscles.

The violent coursing of the blood and intake of air can 2
be made visible, for they show up as heat on infra-red films
which are sensitive to such radiation. (The blue or light
zones are hottest; the red or dark zones are cooler.) The
flush that we see and that the infra-red camera analyses is a
by-product that signals the limit of muscular action. For the
main chemical action is to get energy for the muscles by
burning sugar there; but three-quarters of that is lost as
heat. And there is another limit, on the runner and the
gazelle equally, which is more severe. At this speed, the
chemical burn-up in the muscles is too fast to be complete.
The waste products of incomplete burning, chiefly lactic
acid, now foul up the blood. This is what causes fatigue, and
blocks the muscle action until the blood can be cleansed with
fresh oxygen.

So far, there is nothing to distinguish the athlete from the gazelle—all that, in one way or another, is the normal metabolism of an animal in flight. But there is a cardinal difference: the runner was not in flight. The shot that set him off was the starter's pistol, and what he was experiencing, deliberately, was not fear but exaltation. The runner is like a child at play; his actions are an adventure in freedom, and the only purpose of his breathless chemistry was to explore the limits of his own strength. 3

Naturally there are physical differences between man and the other animals, even between man and the apes. In the act of vaulting, the athlete grasps his pole, for example, with an exact grip that no ape can quite match. Yet such differences are secondary by comparison with the overriding difference, which is that the athlete is an adult whose behavior is not driven by his immediate environment, as animal actions are. In themselves, his actions make no practical sense at all; they are an exercise that is not directed to the present. The athlete's mind is fixed ahead of him, building up his skill; and he vaults in imagination into the future. 4

Poised for that leap, the pole-vaulter is a capsule of human abilities: the grasp of the hand, the arch of the foot, the muscles of the shoulder and pelvis—the pole itself, in which energy is stored and released like a bow firing an arrow. The radical character in that complex is the sense of foresight, that is, the ability to fix an objective ahead and rigorously hold his attention on it. The athlete's performance unfolds a continuous plan; from one extreme to the other, it is the invention of the pole, the concentration of the mind at the moment before leaping, which give it the stamp of humanity. 5

QUESTIONS

1. What similarities between humans and animals does Bronowski develop through his example?

2. What are the differences between the pole vaulter and the gazelle and other animals discussed?

3. In general, what are the physical traits that humans share with animals, and what gifts make humans different?

4. What other comparison between humans and animals could Bronowski have used to distinguish human from animal qualities?

WRITING ASSIGNMENTS

1. Compare and contrast one of the following pairs of activities to arrive at a relative estimate of them and to make a point:
   a. softball and hardball
   b. football and touch football
   c. jogging and running
   d. tennis and badminton
   e. checkers and chess

2. Do the same for one of the following pairs of activities:
   a. studying for examinations in different subjects
   b. repairing or changing an automobile and a bicycle tire
   c. driving in a small town and in a large city

HANNAH ARENDT

HANNAH ARENDT *(1906–1975) was one of the great political philosophers of the twentieth century. Raised and educated in Germany, she witnessed the rise of Hitler and the beginnings of the Nazi state. Leaving Germany after Hitler came to power, she did social work in Paris for six years before coming to the United States in 1941. Arendt taught at various universities, including Princeton, Chicago, and the New School for Social Research. Her most famous and influential book is* The Origins of Totalitarianism, *from which the following paragraph is taken. Arendt tells us that "totalitarian movements are mass organizations of atomized, iso-lated individuals." The purpose of the concentration camp was to reduce the inmate to this condition.*

The Concentration-Camp Inmate

Forced labor as a punishment is limited as to time and intensity. The convict retains his rights over his body; he is not absolutely tortured, and he is not absolutely dominated. Banishment banishes only from one part of the world to another part of the world, also inhabited by human beings; it does not exclude from the human world altogether. Throughout history slavery has been an institution within a social order; slaves were not, like concentration-camp inmates, withdrawn from the sight and hence the protection of their fellow-men; as instruments of labor they had a definite price and as property a definite value. The concentration-camp inmate has no price, because he can always be replaced; nobody knows to whom he belongs, because he is never seen. From the point of view of normal society he is absolutely superfluous, although in times of acute labor shortage, as in Russia and in Germany during the war, he is used for work.

QUESTIONS

1. Arendt might simply have described the typical existence of the concentration-camp inmate. Instead she defines that existence through contrast with other forms of imprisonment and ser-vitude: through a relative estimate. What is the advantage of this procedure—defining by means of contrast—over other methods?

2. What accounts for the order of ideas? Are they presented in the order of their importance?

3. What does the paragraph tell us about the values of a society in which concentration camps exist?

WRITING ASSIGNMENTS

1. Make a list of significant similarities and differences between one of the following pairs and use it to write a paragraph. Use your comparison and contrast to arrive at a relative esti-mate—which is better or worse?—and to make a definite point.
   a. streetcar or bus nuisance and back-seat driver
   b. silent bore and talkative bore
   c. classroom comic and dormitory comic
   d. expectations of high-school and college English teachers

Analogy

Illustrative *analogy* is a special kind of example, a comparison between two quite different things or activities for the purpose of explanation—a child growing like a tender plant and needing sun, water, and a receptive soil as well as proper care from a skilled gardener. The comparison may be point by point. But there are differences also, and if there is danger of the analogy being carried too far (children are not so tender that they need as much protection as plants from the hazards of living), the writer may state these differences to limit the inferences readers may draw. He or she has chosen the analogy for the sake of vivid illustration and nothing more. We will see later that analogy is often used in argument: children *should* be fully protected from various hazards because they are tender plants. The argument will stand or fall depending on how convinced we are of the similarities and of the unimportance of the differences.

Analogy is often used in explanations of scientific ideas. One of the most famous is Fred Hoyle's analogy between the moving apart of the galaxies in the universe and an expanding raisin cake:

> Suppose the cake swells uniformly as it cooks, but the raisins themselves remain of the same size. Let each raisin represent a cluster of galaxies, and imagine yourself inside one of them. As the cake swells, you will observe that all the other raisins move away from you. Moreover, the farther away the raisin, the faster it will seem to move. When the cake has swollen to twice its initial dimensions, the distance between all the raisins will have doubled itself—two raisins that were initially an inch apart will now be two inches apart; two raisins that were a foot apart will have moved two feet apart. Since the entire action takes place within the same time interval, obviously the more distant raisins must move apart faster than those close at hand. So it happens with the clusters of galaxies.

And Hoyle draws a further conclusion from his analogy:

> No matter which raisin you happen to be inside, the others will always move away from you. Hence the fact that we observe all the other galaxies to be moving away from us does not mean that we

are situated at the center of the universe. Indeed, it seems certain
that the universe has no center. A cake may be said to have a center
only because it has a boundary. We must imagine the cake to extend
outward without any boundary, an infinite cake, so to speak, which
means that however much cake we care to consider there is always
more.

Hoyle points out the limits of the analogy in these final sentences.
One advantage of the raisin analogy is the disparity of size between a raisin and a galaxy—a system of sometimes billions of
stars occupying an enormous amount of space. The disparity in
size provides a relative estimate of size in the universe.

J. ANTHONY LUKAS

J. ANTHONY LUKAS *has written for the* Baltimore Sun
and New York Times *during his career as a journalist.
In 1968 he won the Pulitzer Prize for local reporting.
Lukas has written much about American youth in the
1960s—notably in* Don't Shout: We Are Your Children!
*In his essay "The Inner Game of Pinball," which ap-
peared in* The Atlantic Monthly *in 1979, Lukas explains
why pinball—unlike baseball, chess and poker—is his
game. He says later in his essay, "I suppose it was inevitable, but I regret the sanitization of pinball. Part of
its attraction was always its raffishness. There was simply no redeeming social value in the game; it was an
utter waste of time. . . ."*

Pinball

Pinball is a metaphor for life, pitting man's skill, nerve,   1
persistence, and luck against the perverse machinery of
human existence. The playfield is rich with rewards: targets
that bring huge scores, bright lights, chiming bells, free
balls, and extra games. But it is replete with perils, too:

culs-de-sac, traps, gutters, and gobble holes down which the ball may disappear forever.

Each pull of the plunger launches the ball into a minia- 2 ture universe of incalculable possibilities. As the steel sphere hurtles into the ellipse at the top of the playfield, it hangs for a moment in exquisite tension between triumph and disaster. Down one lane lies a hole worth thousands, down another a sickening lurch to oblivion. The ball trembles on the lip, seeming to lean first one way, then the other.

A player is not powerless to control the ball's wild 3 flight, any more than man is powerless to control his own life. He may nudge the machine with hands, arms, or hips, jogging it just enough to change the angle of the ball's descent. And he is armed with "flippers" which can propel the ball back up the playfield, aiming at the targets with the richest payoffs. But, just as man's boldest strokes and bravest ventures often boomerang, so an ill-timed flip can ricochet the ball straight down "death alley," and a too vigorous nudge will send the machine into "tilt." Winning pinball, like rewarding life, requires delicate touch, fine calibrations, careful discrimination between boldness and folly.

QUESTIONS

1. What are the points of similarity between pinball and life?
2. In what order does Lukas present these points of similarity?
3. Given the purpose of the analogy, need Lukas have presented any points of dissimilarity between pinball and life? Can you think of any that would weaken the analogy or qualify it?
4. To what extent would tennis or basketball or football present an analogy to a rewarding life?
5. Do you find the analogy to pinball effective?

WRITING ASSIGNMENTS

1. Describe a rewarding life through the analogy of another game or activity that presents a sufficient number of similarities. If

there are significant points of dissimilarity that qualify or weaken the analogy, discuss these also.

2. Describe an unrewarding life through the analogy of another game or activity. Then contrast the points you have made with those Lukas makes about a rewarding life.

NIGEL CALDER

Born in London and educated at Cambridge, NIGEL CALDER *worked as a research physicist before becoming a science writer—one of the finest writing today. Calder has written several distinguished science documentaries for television and numerous books including* The Violent Universe, The Restless Earth, The Key to the Universe, *and* Einstein's Universe, *from which his explanation of black holes is taken. Like Bronowski, Calder is particularly skilled in explaining complex scientific ideas in plain words and through extraordinary analogies.*

The Black Hole

The idea of extracting a little energy from objects falling 1 under gravity is familiar enough. For instance, nations well endowed with mountains generate a good deal of electricity from waterfalls. River water rushing down a mountainside drives the turbines of a hydro-electric power station. The greater the "head" of water, from the start of its fall to the turbines, the more energy you can win from it. The water of most rivers does not drop any farther than the sea-level. But you could run water into a deep depression, as in the Dead Sea or the Qattara Depression in the Middle East, and so gain more energy from it.

What is the limit to that process? Imagine a mad engi- 2
neer who is dissatisfied with the "head" of water that he is
given to work with. He proposes to perfect his hydro-electric
scheme by digging a very deep tube well in the ground, right
down to the center of the Earth. In principle the engineer
could gain a lot by dropping his water all that way, but not
as much as he might expect. As he digs deeper, the rocks
above begin to neutralize the gravity of the rocks and the
iron core beneath. At the center of the Earth, gravity is zero.
That restricts the amount of energy he can obtain by this
strategy.

In his cosmic madness, our engineer will see what he 3
has to do: compress the rocks of the Earth into a very small
volume, while keeping his supply of water in orbit, ready to
feed the ultimate waterfall. Let the practical difficulties
speak for themselves; we talk of cosmic principles. If he
devises suitable hoops for squeezing the Earth from a diam-
eter of 8000 miles to less than an inch, its gravity will be
sustained for a much longer drop, and it will become extremely strong in the vicinity of the miniaturized Earth. In
fact the engineer has created a black hole, where the grip of
gravity becomes so great that even light cannot escape from
it. Now if he drops his water in, the engineer's efforts will be
rewarded: each drop of water will accelerate to almost the
speed of light. Recovering most or all of the rest-energy is
now a possibility, and every drop of water becomes equivalent to a hundred tons of high-explosive.

QUESTIONS

1. The black hole, one of the most amazing objects in space if they
exist, is extremely difficult to describe. The journalist Walter
Sullivan describes black holes as

> . . . the remnants of stars that, having exhausted their nuclear fuel,
> have collapsed to an ultimate extreme of density. Such an object
> would generate gravity so strong that nothing could escape it or
> pass close by, not even light waves.

The collapsing star must be much more massive than our sun to collapse to such an extreme. What features of the black hole is Calder trying to explain through his analogy?

2. What processes in our world does he use to explain these features?

3. What are the differences between the things being compared in the analogy? How do these differences heighten your sense of the unfamiliar and amazing qualities of black holes?

4. How does the analogy explain why gravity is so strong in the black hole? Do you understand why light cannot escape from it?

WRITING ASSIGNMENT

Use an analogy to explain the sensation of being alone in a car in heavy traffic or a storm or of traveling away from home for the first time. At some point in your explanation, comment on the differences between the things you are comparing.

Example

The word *example* originally referred to a sample or typical instance. The word still has this meaning, and for many writers it is an outstanding instance—even one essential to the idea under discussion, as in the following explanation of right and left-handedness in the world:

> The world is full of things whose right-hand version is different from the left-hand version: a right-handed corkscrew as against a left-handed, a right snail as against a left one. Above all, the two hands; they can be mirrored one in the other, but they cannot be turned in such a way that the right hand and the left hand become interchangeable. That was known in Pasteur's time to be true also of some crystals, whose facets are so arranged that there are right-hand versions and left-hand versions.—J. Bronowski, *The Ascent of Man*

Examples are essential when we are presenting ideas. Those that seem clear to us may not be clear to our readers. Concrete instances will help to make our ideas understood.

E. B. WHITE

E. B. WHITE *is one of America's most distinguished writers—an essayist, poet, and writer of fiction. His association with* The New Yorker *magazine began in 1926, and he had a long association also with* Harper's *magazine, for which he wrote a column titled "One Man's Meat." His essays from that column were published in a book of the same title in 1942, and other of his essays are collected in* The Second Tree From the Corner, The Points of My Compass, *and* Essays of E. B. White. *White has written much about Maine, where he lives, and also about New York City, as in this paragraph from a profile of the city first published in* Holiday *magazine.*

New York

It is a miracle that New York works at all. The whole thing is implausible. Every time the residents brush their teeth, millions of gallons of water must be drawn from the Catskills and the hills of Westchester. When a young man in Manhattan writes a letter to his girl in Brooklyn, the love message gets blown to her through a pneumatic tube—*pfft*—just like that. The subterranean system of telephone cables, power lines, steam pipes, gas mains and sewer pipes is reason enough to abandon the island to the gods and the weevils. Every time an incision is made in the pavement, the noisy surgeons expose ganglia that are tangled beyond belief. By rights New York should have destroyed itself long ago, from panic or fire or rioting or failure of some vital supply line in its circulatory system or from some deep labyrinthine short circuit. Long ago the city should have experienced an insoluble traffic snarl at some impossible bottleneck. It should have perished of hunger when food lines failed for a few days. It should have been wiped out by a plague starting in its slums or carried in by ships' rats. It should have been overwhelmed by the sea that licks at it on every side. The workers in its myriad cells should have succumbed to nerves, from the fearful pall of smoke-fog that drifts over every few days from Jersey, blotting out all light at noon and leaving the high offices suspended, men groping and depressed, and the sense of world's end. It should have been touched in the head by the August heat and gone off its rocker.

QUESTIONS

1. What examples does White give to show that "the whole thing is implausible"?
2. White explicitly compares New York City to a human being.

Example **101**

What are the similarities, and how does the comparison help to emphasize the "miracle" he is describing?

3. What is the tone of the paragraph, and how does White achieve it?

WRITING ASSIGNMENTS

1. In a well-developed paragraph state an idea about your hometown or city and develop it by a series of short examples. Make your examples vivid and lively.

2. Develop one of the following statements by example:
   a. "The insupportable labor of doing nothing."—Sir Richard Steele
   b. "The first blow is half the battle."—Oliver Goldsmith
   c. "Ask yourself whether you are happy, and you cease to be so."—John Stuart Mill
   d. "Parentage is a very important profession; but no test of fitness for it is ever imposed in the interest of the children."—George Bernard Shaw

TOM WOLFE

TOM WOLFE *has written much about American life in the 1960s and 1970s, particularly about the "youth culture" of this period. Wolfe has documented this world in a large number of articles published in such periodicals as the* New York Herald Tribune, New York *magazine, and* Esquire *magazine. These have been collected in a number of books, including* The Electric Kool-Aid Acid Test *and* The Pump House Gang. *Wolfe's ironic view of urban life is no better illustrated than in his portrait of New York teenagers at a subway station at rush hour. Wolfe here develops one of his favorite themes, the "generation gap"—shown graphically—in addition to saying something about New York life generally.*

Thursday Morning in a
New York Subway Station

Love! Attar of libido in the air! It is 8:45 A.M. Thursday 1
morning in the IRT subway station at 50th Street and
Broadway and already two kids are hung up in a kind of
herringbone weave of arms and legs, which proves, one has
to admit, that love is not *confined* to Sunday in New York.
Still, the odds! All the faces come popping in clots out of the
Seventh Avenue local, past the King Size Ice Cream machine, and the turnstiles start whacking away as if the world
were breaking up on the reefs. Four steps past the turnstiles
everybody is already backed up haunch to paunch for the
climb up the ramp and the stairs to the surface, a great
funnel of flesh, wool, felt, leather, rubber and steaming
alumicron, with the blood squeezing through everybody's
old sclerotic arteries in hopped-up spurts from too much
coffee and the effort of surfacing from the subway at the
rush hour. Yet there on the landing are a boy and a girl, both
about eighteen, in one of those utter, My Sin, backbreaking
embraces.

He envelops her not only with his arms but with his 2
chest, which has the American teen-ager concave shape to
it. She has her head cocked at a 90-degree angle and they
both have their eyes pressed shut for all they are worth and
some incredibly feverish action going with each other's
mouths. All round them, ten, scores, it seems like hundreds,
of faces and bodies are perspiring, trooping and bellying up
the stairs with arteriosclerotic grimaces past a showcase full
of such novel items as Joy Buzzers, Squirting Nickels, Finger
Rats, Scary Tarantulas and spoons with realistic dead flies
on them, past Fred's barbershop, which is just off the landing and has glossy photographs of young men with the kind
of baroque haircuts one can get in there, and up onto 50th
Street into a madhouse of traffic and shops with weird
lingerie and gray hair-dyeing displays in the windows, signs

Example
103

for free teacup readings and a pool-playing match between the Playboy Bunnies and Downey's Showgirls, and then everybody pounds on toward the Time-Life Building, the Brill Building or NBC.

The boy and the girl just keep on writhing in their embroilment. Her hand is sliding up the back of his neck, which he turns when her fingers wander into the intricate formal gardens of his Chicago Boxcar hairdo at the base of the skull. The turn causes his face to start to mash in the ciliated hull of her beehive hairdo, and so she rolls her head 180 degrees to the other side, using their mouths for the pivot. But aside from good hair grooming, they are oblivious to everything but each other. Everybody gives them a once-over. Disgusting! Amusing! How touching! A few kids pass by and say things like "Swing it, baby." But the great majority in that heaving funnel up the stairs seem to be as much astounded as anything else. The vision of love at rush hour cannot strike anyone exactly as romance. It is a feat, like a fat man crossing the English Channel in a barrel. It is an earnest accomplishment against the tide. It is a piece of slightly gross heroics, after the manner of those knobby, varicose old men who come out from some place in baggy shorts every year and run through the streets of Boston in the Marathon race. And somehow that is the gaffe against love all week long in New York, for everybody, not just two kids writhing under their coiffures in the 50th Street subway station; too hurried, too crowded, too hard, and no time for dalliance.

QUESTIONS

1. Wolfe illustrates "the gaffe against love all week long in New York." What precisely is the "gaffe"? What do the details suggest about the Thursday morning mood of New Yorkers?
2. What does the description of the showcase and of 50th Street imply about the world of the lovers? Would they seem comical in any setting?

3. How similar is Wolfe's view of New York to White's, in the quality of life or its pace?

WRITING ASSIGNMENTS

1. Every piece of writing suggests something about the personality, interests, and ideas of the author, even when he or she speaks to us through a narrator. Discuss the impression you receive of the author of this selection.

2. Describe one or two people in a situation made comical by the setting. Allow your reader to visualize the setting as well as the situation through your choice of examples.

Process

A process is a series of connected actions, each developing from the preceding one, and leading to a result of some kind: a product, an effect, even a decision. Mechanical processes are probably the kind we deal with the most, and two of the examples in this section are of these—one the simple process of sharpening a knife, the other the complex process of preparing to walk in space. A mechanical process is one that we create. By contrast, a natural process such as Bronowski describes in his description of the athlete is one we may initiate but do not create:

> He seems all animal in action. The heartbeat goes up; when he sprints at top speed the heart is pumping five times as much blood as normal, and ninety per cent of it is for the muscles.

Both mechanical and natural processes are repeatable. A particular historical process—the events that led to Pearl Harbor or produce an economic depression—is not, though the general circumstances may repeat themselves at another time.

Though we are committed in describing a process to present the steps chronologically—in the order they occur—we may interrupt the account to discuss the implications or details of a particular stage. In describing a complex process, we need to distinguish the main stages and the steps and procedures each of these contain. Process and causal analysis, discussed in the next section, are closely related and are often combined.

FLORENCE H. PETTIT

A designer and professional craftswoman, FLORENCE PETTIT *has written much about the craft arts. Her description of how to sharpen a knife, from her book* How to Make Whirligigs and Whimmy Diddles, *shows how important the consideration of audience is in exposi-*

tion: Pettit selects her details with beginners in mind, and is careful to define her tools and equipment, focusing on the difficult steps of the process.

How to Sharpen Your Knife

If you have never done any whittling or wood carving before, the first skill to learn is how to sharpen your knife. You may be surprised to learn that even a brand-new knife needs sharpening. Knives are never sold honed (finely sharpened), although some gouges and chisels are. It is essential to learn the firm stroke on the stone that will keep your blades sharp. The sharpening stone must be fixed in place on the table, so that it will not move around. You can do this by placing a piece of rubber inner tube or a thin piece of foam rubber under it. Or you can tack four strips of wood, if you have a rough worktable, to frame the stone and hold it in place. Put a generous puddle of oil on the stone— this will soon disappear into the surface of a new stone, and you will need to keep adding more oil. Press the knife blade flat against the stone in the puddle of oil, using your index finger. Whichever way the cutting edge of the knife faces is the side of the blade that should get a little more pressure. Move the blade around three or four times in a narrow oval about the size of your fingernail, going *counterclockwise* when the sharp edge is facing right. Now turn the blade over in the same spot on the stone, press hard, and move it around the small oval *clockwise,* with more pressure on the cutting edge that faces left. Repeat the ovals, flipping the knife blade over six or seven times, and applying lighter pressure to the blade the last two times. Wipe the blade clean with a piece of rag or tissue and rub it flat on the piece of leather strop at least twice on each side. Stroke *away* from the cutting edge to remove the little burr of metal that may be left on the blade.

QUESTIONS

1. What details help the reader to visualize the mechanical process described in the paragraph?
2. Are the stages of the process presented chronologically? If not, why not?
3. Are any terms defined in context—that is, in the description of how to sharpen a knife?

WRITING ASSIGNMENTS

1. Describe a mechanical process comparable to sharpening a knife—for example, sharpening the blades of a hand mower or pruning a tree or painting the exterior of a house.
2. Rewrite the paragraph on how to sharpen a knife, explaining the process to a child who is just beginning to learn how to carve wood.

HENRY S. B. COOPER, JR.

A New Yorker *staff writer since 1958,* HENRY S. B. COOPER, JR. *has written numerous articles on space and lunar exploration. His books on the subject include* Moon Rocks *(1970) and* Thirteen: The Flight That Failed *(1973). Cooper shares the views of Jacob Bronowski on science writing. "I proceed on the assumption," he says, "that there is no basic division between the sciences and the humanities, and accordingly I try to treat science (in particular space science) as though it were simply another branch of human thought—like poetry or art." Like Florence Pettit, Cooper writes with an eye to a specific audience— interested in space exploration but also unfamiliar with the special terms, equipment, and ideas of the enterprise.*

The Space Walk

As long as everything is going all right, the mission spe- 1
cialist can remain comfortably inside the orbiter, manipulat-
ing the satellite and its modules from the rear window; if,
however, there is any foul-up—perhaps the satellite's
ground controllers at Goddard are unable to bring it to
heel—he may have to put his space suit on and go out and
take a hand himself. He will be a lot quicker getting into his
space suit than astronauts used to be; they sometimes spent
half an hour wriggling into their suits, which were clumsy
one-piece affairs with elaborate zippers. The shuttle astronauts have two-piece suits, which go on more easily. The
torso is a single hard shell, like a turtle's. The arms of the
suit, which, of course, are flexible, are attached to the shell;
the pants, which are not, snap to a pressure-sealed metal
ring around the waist of the shell. The mission specialist
won't have to struggle with a backpack, for his life-support
system is incorporated into the hard shell; as a result, he is
also freed from wrestling with the hoses and other connections that used to make astronauts look like soldiers laden
with equipment for battle. The suits may not fit as well as
the old ones did, however, for they were tailor-made for
each astronaut—an expensive proposition. Because so
many people will be going into space now, the new suits are
put together from a number of parts that come in different
sizes—five sizes of torso, nine sizes of gloves, and different
lengths of upper arms, lower arms, thighs, calves, and feet.
The helmet comes in only one size.

The pressure inside the orbiter is fourteen and seven- 2
tenths pounds per square inch, the same as the pressure at
sea level on earth, but the pressure inside the suit, which
would be too rigid at that figure, will be about four pounds
per square inch. If the astronauts don't adjust slowly to the
change, ridding their body tissues of nitrogen, they could get
the bends—something that could never have happened in
the old days, when the cabin atmosphere was pure oxygen

(thus insuring that the astronauts' bodies would be nitrogen-free) and cabin pressure was already at about a third that on the ground. NASA wanted the orbiter's atmosphere to be as earthlike as possible, because of the number of people who will be travelling aboard it, many of whom will not be professional astronauts; besides being easier to get used to, an atmosphere with nitrogen in it is not flammable, like a pure-oxygen one, and its greater density means that, for the first time in a NASA spacecraft, electronic equipment can be air-cooled.

Before the mission specialist can go outside, the entire ₃ craft will be depressurized to nine pounds per square inch, the point at which body tissues begin ridding themselves of nitrogen; twelve hours later, he will enter the air lock, put on his space suit and helmet, and pump oxygen through them, until he is breathing ninety per cent oxygen. The air lock will be depressurized, causing the suit to inflate; then, when the pressure in the air lock nears zero, the astronaut will open the hatch and float out into the cargo bay, being careful not to bump into any of the delicate equipment there. He can pull himself along on a series of handholds at the hinge line of the cargo-bay doors. Then, in order to get out to the wayward satellite, he may have to grab a handhold on the end of the manipulator arm; the arm will swing him out and capture it for him. Or, if the satellite has drifted more than fifty feet away, beyond the arm's reach, he may hop aboard the manned maneuvering unit (M.M.U.)—a chair with thrusters, which the Skylab astronauts tested as a sort of space bicycle, and which is latched to the forward bulkhead of the cargo bay. Either way, he is not allowed to pursue the satellite underneath the orbiter, lest the arm or the chair bump into the thermal tiles and break some. (The only time an astronaut might have to go underneath would be to inspect the craft's underbelly. He would go down in the M.M.U., and if the inspection revealed any broken tiles he would make repairs, with a spray-on silicone carbide or an epoxy foam currently under development. If fuel left over from the launch, passing through a pipe between the external tank and the main engines in the orbiter, has leaked out and frozen open a hatch in the tiles, he will have to chop away the ice so that the hatch can close for entry.) If, after the mission specialist reaches the satellite, he finds that it is still spinning, he has to wrestle it to a stop; then he slowly floats it over to the cradle, which is sticking up out of the cargo bay to receive it, and clamps it on. The men in Houston who designed the space suit do not believe that any fancy automated equipment will ever replace a suited astronaut, and they think his work will not stop there. Very likely, they believe, he will have to make all the repairs himself— removing the satellite's old modules and inserting the new ones—and will possibly conclude by tightening a screw in the manipulator arm and one in the exchange module as well.

QUESTIONS

1. What are the main stages of the process Cooper describes?
2. Which of these stages contains steps or procedures that Cooper needs also to describe? Might any of these subordinate steps or procedures have been omitted from the description without loss?
3. To what audience is Cooper writing, and how do you know?
4. What physical and mental qualities fit the astronaut for the job he does? How does Cooper illustrate these?

WRITING ASSIGNMENT

1. Each of the following processes contains several main stages; one or more of these stages contain steps or procedures. Give an analysis of one of them, or do so for a comparable process you know well. Distinguish the main and subordinate stages and procedures carefully, as Cooper does:
   a. replacing or repairing a flat tire
   b. cutting down a dead tree
   c. painting the outside of a house
   d. parking on a hill
   e. writing an essay

MARK TWAIN

MARK TWAIN *(1835–1910) is known to every reader in America. His many stories, sketches, essays and novels contain the humor, comedy, and wit that he distinguishes at the beginning of his description of how to tell a story. Twain shows once again how indispensable examples are in explaining an idea like humor. We see, too, how essential audience and point of view are in an effective definition and illustration. We have reprinted here part of a longer essay.*

How to Tell a Story

1   I do not claim that I can tell a story as it ought to be told. I only claim to know how a story ought to be told, for I have been almost daily in the company of the most expert storytellers for many years.

2   There are several kinds of stories, but only one difficult kind—the humorous. I will talk mainly about that one. The humorous story is American, the comic story is English, the witty story is French. The humorous story depends for its effect upon the *manner* of the telling; the comic story and the witty story upon the *matter.*

3   The humorous story may be spun out to great length, and may wander around as much as it pleases, and arrive nowhere in particular; but the comic and witty stories must be brief and end with a point. The humorous story bubbles gently along, the others burst.

4   The humorous story is strictly a work of art—high and delicate art—and only an artist can tell it; but no art is necessary in telling the comic and the witty story; anybody can do it. The art of telling a humorous story—understand, I mean by word of mouth, not print—was created in America, and has remained at home.

5   The humorous story is told gravely; the teller does his best to conceal the fact that he even dimly suspects that

there is anything funny about it; but the teller of the comic story tells you beforehand that it is one of the funniest things he has ever heard, then tells it with eager delight, and is the first person to laugh when he gets through. And sometimes, if he has had good success, he is so glad and happy that he will repeat the "nub" of it and glance around from face to face, collecting applause, and then repeat it again. It is a pathetic thing to see.

Very often, of course, the rambling and disjointed 6 humorous story finishes with a nub, point, snapper, or whatever you like to call it. Then the listener must be alert, for in many cases the teller will divert attention from that nub by dropping it in a carefully casual and indifferent way, with the pretence that he does not know it is a nub.

Artemus Ward used that trick a good deal; then when 7 the belated audience presently caught the joke he would look up with innocent surprise, as if wondering what they had found to laugh at. Dan Setchell used it before him, Nye and Riley and others use it to-day.

But the teller of the comic story does not slur the nub; 8 he shouts it at you—every time. And when he prints it, in England, France, Germany, and Italy, he italicizes it, puts some whooping exclamation-points after it, and sometimes explains it in a parenthesis. All of which is very depressing, and makes one want to renounce joking and lead a better life.

Let me set down an instance of the comic method, using 9 an anecdote which has been popular all over the world for twelve or fifteen hundred years. The teller tells it in this way:

THE WOUNDED SOLDIER.

In the course of a certain battle a soldier whose leg had 10 been shot off appealed to another soldier who was hurrying by to carry him to the rear, informing him at the same time of the loss which he had sustained; whereupon the generous son of Mars, shouldering the unfortunate, proceeded to carry out his desire. The bullets and cannon-balls were flying in all directions, and presently one of the latter took the wounded man's head off—without, however, his deliverer being aware of it. In no long time he was hailed by an officer, who said:

"Where are you going with that carcass?"

"To the rear, sir—he's lost his leg!"

"His leg, forsooth?" responded the astonished officer; "you mean his head, you booby."

Whereupon the soldier dispossessed himself of his bur- 11 den, and stood looking down upon it in great perplexity. At length he said:

"It is true, sir, just as you have said." Then after a pause he added, *"But he* TOLD *me* IT WAS HIS LEG! ! ! ! !"

Here the narrator bursts into explosion after explo- 12 sion of thunderous horse-laughter, repeating that nub from time to time through his gaspings and shriekings and suffocatings.

QUESTIONS

1. On what basis does Twain divide stories into three groups— comic, witty, humorous?

2. Is he saying that there is only one way to tell a humorous story, or is he describing one of many ways? How do you know?

3. What are the essential stages in the process he describes? To which does he give the most attention, and why?

4. Would his definition of the comic story have been clear to you without the example? Would the process have been clear without the details Twain gives us?

WRITING ASSIGNMENTS

1. Describe the process in which you or a friend or relative tells a humorous story. Noting significant similarities and differences, compare this process with that described by Twain.

2. Twain tells us that the comic story depends for its effect upon the content or matter. Analyze a comic story by Twain or another humorist or a comic strip to show what in the content and in the telling provokes laughter.

Cause and Effect

Unlike process analysis, there is not just one kind of causal analysis. The kind of explanation that satisfies the ordinary person—the reason for a cold, for example—will usually not satisfy a scientist. Later in this book we shall consider this more demanding kind of causal explanation. Usually we look for an event prior to the one we are trying to explain; but often there are many—some close to the event, some remote in time. For example, failure to study for an important exam may lead to a student's eventual failure in a course, and a subsequent drop in grade point average. The course failure—the immediate cause of the drop in the average—will probably be of most concern to college officials considering a scholarship renewal; the remote cause, the failure to study, probably will be of more concern to the student in seeking to improve. In writing about such events, which of them we discuss as the "cause" depends on the purpose of our analysis.

Objects, too, have more than one cause. One useful kind of analysis here distinguishes four related ones. Consider a dictionary. Its material cause is the paper, ink, and other materials used in its manufacture. The formal cause is its shape—the alphabetic arrangement of words, and the arrangement of definitions according to a plan. The efficient cause is the dictionary writer, and the final cause, the use intended for the dictionary. The analysis of a chemical compound is more rigorous, demanding an account of substances that form the compound and the process by which the formation occurs. Process analysis ("how") often combines with causal analysis ("why") because we are interested in both the how and why of objects and of events.

JOHN BROOKS

JOHN BROOKS *was a contributing editor of* Time *magazine, and has been on the staff of* The New Yorker *magazine for many years, writing about American business. His books include* The Go-Go Years *(1973) and*

The Telephone (1976), a history of A. T. and T., from which these paragraphs are reprinted. Toward the end of the paragraphs, Brooks refers to the ideas of Marshall McLuhan, summarized earlier in this book. He illustrates for us McLuhan's idea that the telephone is a "cool" medium—one requiring full participation since, unlike print, it is empty of content. The user supplies this content, unlike the reader of a book. Brooks says later in his book: "In the uneasy postwar world, people seemed to be coming to associate the telephone with their frustrations, their fears, and their sense of powerlessness against technology."

The Telephone

What has the telephone done to us, or for us, in the hundred 1 years of its existence? A few effects suggest themselves at once. It has saved lives by getting rapid word of illness, injury, or famine from remote places. By joining with the elevator to make possible the multistory residence or office building, it has made possible—for better or worse—the modern city. By bringing about a quantum leap in the speed and ease with which information moves from place to place, it has greatly accelerated the rate of scientific and technological change and growth in industry. Beyond doubt it has crippled if not killed the ancient art of letter writing. It has made living alone possible for persons with normal social impulses; by so doing, it has played a role in one of the greatest social changes of this century, the breakup of the multigenerational household. It has made the waging of war chillingly more efficient than formerly. Perhaps (though not provably) it has prevented wars that might have arisen out of international misunderstanding caused by written communication. Or perhaps—again not provably—by magnifying and extending irrational personal conflicts based on voice contact, it has caused wars. Certainly it has extended the scope of human conflicts, since it impartially disseminates the useful knowledge of scientists and the babble of bores, the affection of the affectionate and the malice of the malicious.

But the question remains unanswered. The obvious ef- 2 fects just cited seem inadequate, mechanistic; they only scratch the surface. Perhaps the crucial effects are evanescent and unmeasurable. Use of the telephone involves personal risk because it involves exposure; for some, to be "hung up on" is among the worst of fears; others dream of a ringing telephone and wake up with a pounding heart. The telephone's actual ring—more, perhaps, than any other sound in our daily lives—evokes hope, relief, fear, anxiety, joy, according to our expectations. The telephone is our nerve-end to society.

In some ways it is in itself a thing of paradox. In one 3 sense a metaphor for the times it helped create, in another sense the telephone is their polar opposite. It is small and gentle—relying on low voltages and miniature parts—in times of hugeness and violence. It is basically simple in times of complexity. It is so nearly human, recreating voices so faithfully that friends or lovers need not identify themselves by name even when talking across oceans, that to ask its effects on human life may seem hardly more fruitful than to ask the effect of the hand or the foot. The Canadian philosopher Marshall McLuhan—one of the few who have addressed themselves to these questions—was perhaps not far from the mark when he spoke of the telephone creating "a kind of extra-sensory perception."

QUESTIONS

1. Why does Brooks consider the effects he discusses in paragraph 1 less significant than those in paragraph 2? What does he mean by the statement, "Perhaps the crucial effects are evanescent and unmeasurable"?

2. In what ways is the telephone a paradox? Does the author show it to be a paradox in paragraphs 1 and 2?

3. Has Brooks stated all the effects of the telephone, or has he identified only a few? What central point is he making?

WRITING ASSIGNMENTS

1. Develop one of the ideas in the essay from your personal experience. You might discuss your own positive and negative attitudes toward the telephone, and the reasons for them, or you might develop the statement, "In some ways it is in itself a thing of paradox."
2. Write an essay describing what it would be like to live without a telephone.
3. Discuss the impact of the telephone on life in your home. Distinguish the various uses and effects of the telephone for various members of your family.

MARVIN HARRIS

> MARVIN HARRIS, *who teaches anthropology at the University of Florida, writes about American life from the point of view of the anthropologist in* Cannibals and Kings *(1977) and* America Now *(1981), from which the selection reprinted below is taken. Harris gives us an interesting illustration of Murphy's Law without trying to explain it. Notice that he combines many of the types of exposition discussed in this section of the book, including definition, process, and example.*

Why Nothing Works

According to a law attributed to the savant known only as 1
Murphy, "if anything can go wrong, it will." Corollaries to
Murphy's Law suggest themselves as clues to the shoddy
goods problem: If anything can break down, it will; if anything can fall apart, it will; if anything can stop running, it
will. While Murphy's Law can never be wholly defeated, its
effects can usually be postponed. Much of human existence

consists of efforts aimed at making sure that things don't go wrong, fall apart, break down, or stop running until a decent interval has elapsed after their manufacture. Forestalling Murphy's Law as applied to products demands intelligence, skill, and commitment. If these human inputs are assisted by special quality-control instruments, machines, and scientific sampling procedures, so much the better. But gadgets and sampling alone will never do the trick since these items are also subject to Murphy's Law. Quality-control instruments need maintenance; gauges go out of order; X rays and laser beams need adjustments. No matter how advanced the technology, quality demands intelligent, motivated human thought and action.

Some reflection about the material culture of prehistoric   2
and preindustrial peoples may help to show what I mean. A single visit to a museum which displays artifacts used by simple preindustrial societies is sufficient to dispel the notion that quality is dependent on technology. Artifacts may be of simple, even primitive design, and yet be built to serve their intended purpose in a realiable manner during a lifetime of use. We acknowledge this when we honor the label "handmade" and pay extra for the jewelry, sweaters, and handbags turned out by the dwindling breeds of modern-day craftspeople.

What is the source of quality that one finds, let us say, in   3
a Pomo Indian basket so tightly woven that it was used to hold boiling water and never leaked a drop, or in an Eskimo skin boat with its matchless combination of lightness, strength, and seaworthiness? Was it merely the fact that these items were handmade? I don't think so. In unskilled or uncaring hands a handmade basket or boat can fall apart as quickly as baskets or boats made by machines. I rather think that the reason we honor the label "handmade" is because it evokes not a technological relationship between producer and product but a social relationship between producer and consumer. Throughout prehistory it was the fact that producers and consumers were either one and the same individuals or close kin that guaranteed the highest

degree of reliability and durability in manufactured items. Men made their own spears, bows and arrows, and projectile points; women wove their own baskets and carrying nets, fashioned their own clothing from animal skins, bark, or fiber. Later, as technology advanced and material culture grew more complex, different members of the band or village adopted craft specialties such as pottery-making, basket-weaving, or canoe-building. Although many items were obtained through barter and trade, the connection between producer and consumer still remained intimate, permanent, and caring.

A man is not likely to fashion a spear for himself whose 4 point will fall off in midflight; nor is a woman who weaves her own basket likely to make it out of rotted straw. Similarly, if one is sewing a parka for a husband who is about to go hunting for the family with the temperature at sixty below, all stitches will be perfect. And when the men who make boats are the uncles and fathers of those who sail them, they will be as seaworthy as the state of the art permits.

In contrast, it is very hard for people to care about 5 strangers or about products to be used by strangers. In our era of industrial mass production and mass marketing, quality is a constant problem because the intimate sentimental and personal bonds which once made us responsible to each other and to our products have withered away and been replaced by money relationships. Not only are the producers and consumers strangers but the women and men involved in various stages of production and distribution—management, the worker on the factory floor, the office help, the salespeople—are also strangers to each other. In larger companies there may be hundreds of thousands of people all working on the same product who can never meet face-to-face or learn one another's names. The larger the company and the more complex its division of labor, the greater the sum of uncaring relationships and hence the greater the effect of Murphy's Law. Growth adds layer on layer of executives, foremen, engineers, production workers, and sales specialists to the payroll. Since each new employee contributes a diminished share to the overall production process, alienation from the company and its product are likely to increase along with the neglect or even purposeful sabotage of quality standards.

QUESTIONS

1. What role does Murphy's Law play in Harris's explanation of why nothing works? Does he say or imply that the law is irreversible and that things inevitably break down?

2. How does Harris prove that quality is not dependent on technology? Has he provided enough evidence to establish this point?

3. Does Harris provide the same kind of evidence for his explanation of the source of quality in the handmade products he discusses in paragraphs 3–5? Does he claim that his evidence is certain?

4. We can test the evidence Harris presents in paragraph 2 by examining the museum objects discussed. Can you think of a way to test the explanation in paragraphs 3–5 if the evidence cannot be tested directly? How convincing do you find his explanation in these paragraphs?

WRITING ASSIGNMENTS

1. Write your own explanation of why something you own does not work. In the course of your analysis, discuss the extent to which the ideas of Harris offer an explanation.

2. Write an essay on one of the following topics using causal analysis and examples to develop a thesis. The more limited your focus and discussion, the stronger your thesis will be.
   a. cheating in high school
   b. driving habits of teenagers
   c. family arguments or rivalries
   d. choosing a college

THE SENTENCE

Addition and Modification

As a paragraph usually begins with a topic sentence that states the subject or central idea, so the sentence may begin with a main clause that performs a similar job. Here is a sentence from Jane Jacobs' description of a New York street scene in the essay that follows:

> *Character dancers come on,*
> *a strange old man* with strings of old shoes over his shoulders,
> *motor-scooter riders* with big beards and girl friends who bounce on the back of the scooters and wear their hair long in front of their faces as well as behind,
> *drunks* who follow the advice of the Hat Council and are always turned out in hats,
> but not hats the Council would approve.

The three additions—*strange old man, motor-scooter riders, drunks*—make the main clause specific: they name the character dancers. Notice that these *appositives* (adjacent words or phrases that explain or identify another word) are considerably longer than the main clause. Notice, too, that the third appositive is itself modified. English sentences can be modified endlessly. They are not, however, because the reader would soon lose sight of the central idea. The length of a sentence often depends on how many ideas and details a reader can grasp.

JANE JACOBS

Hudson Street

Under the seeming disorder of the old city, wherever the old   1
city is working successfully, is a marvelous order for maintaining the safety of the streets and the freedom of the city.
It is a complex order. Its essence is intricacy of sidewalk use,
bringing with it a constant succession of eyes. This order is
all composed of movement and change, and although it is
life, not art, we may fancifully call it the art form of the city
and liken it to the dance—not to a simple-minded precision
dance with everyone kicking up at the same time, twirling in
unison and bowing off en masse, but to an intricate ballet in
which the individual dancers and ensembles all have distinctive parts which miraculously reinforce each other and com-
pose an orderly whole. The ballet of the good city sidewalk

never repeats itself from place to place, and in any one place is always replete with new improvisations.

The stretch of Hudson Street where I live is each day the 2
scene of an intricate sidewalk ballet. I make my own first entrance into it a little after eight when I put out the garbage can, surely a prosaic occupation, but I enjoy my part, my little clang, as the droves of junior high school students walk by the center of the stage dropping candy wrappers. (How do they eat so much candy so early in the morning?)

While I sweep up the wrappers I watch the other rituals 3
of morning: Mr. Halpert unlocking the laundry's handcart from its mooring to a cellar door, Joe Cornacchia's son-in-law stacking out the empty crates from the delicatessen, the barber bringing out his sidewalk folding chair, Mr. Goldstein arranging the coils of wire which proclaim the hardware store is open, the wife of the tenement's superin-tendent depositing her chunky three-year-old with a toy mandolin on the stoop, the vantage point from which he is learning the English his mother cannot speak. Now the primary children, heading for St. Luke's, dribble through to the south; the children for St. Veronica's cross, heading to the west, and the children for P.S. 41, heading toward the east. Two new entrances are being made from the wings: well-dressed and even elegant women and men with brief cases emerge from doorways and side streets. Most of these are heading for the bus and subways, but some hover on the curbs, stopping taxis which have miraculously appeared at the right moment, for the taxis are part of a wider morning ritual: having dropped passengers from midtown in the downtown financial district, they are now bringing down-towners up to midtown. Simultaneously, numbers of women in housedresses have emerged and as they crisscross with one another they pause for quick conversations that sound with either laughter or joint indignation, never, it seems, anything between. It is time for me to hurry to work too, and I exchange my ritual farewell with Mr. Lofaro, the short, thick-bodied, white-aproned fruit man who stands outside his doorway a little up the street, his arms folded, his feet

planted, looking solid as earth itself. We nod; we each glance quickly up and down the street, then look back to each other and smile. We have done this many a morning for more than ten years, and we both know what it means: All is well.

The heart-of-the-day ballet I seldom see, because part 4 of the nature of it is that working people who live there, like me, are mostly gone, filling the roles of strangers on other sidewalks. But from days off, I know enough of it to know that it becomes more and more intricate. Longshoremen who are not working that day gather at the White Horse or the Ideal or the International for beer and conversation. The executives and business lunchers from the industries just to the west throng the Dorgene restaurant and the Lion's Head coffee house; meat-market workers and communications scientists fill the bakery lunchroom. Character dancers come on, a strange old man with strings of old shoes over his shoulders, motor-scooter riders with big beards and girl friends who bounce on the back of the scooters and wear their hair long in front of their faces as well as behind, drunks who follow the advice of the Hat Council and are always turned out in hats, but not hats the Council would approve. Mr. Lacey, the locksmith, shuts up his shop for a while and goes to exchange the time of day with Mr. Slube at the cigar store. Mr. Koochagian, the tailor, waters the luxuriant jungle of plants in his window, gives them a critical look from the outside, accepts a compliment on them from two passersby, fingers the leaves on the plane tree in front of our house with a thoughtful gardener's appraisal, and crosses the street for a bite at the Ideal where he can keep an eye on customers and wigwag across the message that he is coming. The baby carriages come out, and clusters of everyone from toddlers with dolls to teenagers with homework gather at the stoops.

When I get home after work, the ballet is reaching its 5 crescendo. This is the time of roller skates and stilts and tricycles, and games in the lee of the stoop with bottletops and plastic cowboys; this is the time of bundles and packages, zigzagging from the drug store to the fruit stand and back over to the butcher's; this is the time when teenagers, all dressed up, are pausing to ask if their slips show or their collars look right; this is the time when beautiful girls get out of MG's; this is the time when the fire engines go through; this is the time when anybody you know around Hudson Street will go by.

As darkness thickens and Mr. Halpert moors the laun-   6
dry cart to the cellar door again, the ballet goes on under lights, eddying back and forth but intensifying at the bright spotlight pools of Joe's sidewalk pizza dispensary, the bars, the delicatessen, the restaurant and the drug store. The night workers stop now at the delicatessen, to pick up salami and a container of milk. Things have settled down for the evening but the street and its ballet have not come to a stop.

I know the deep night ballet and its season best from   7
waking long after midnight to tend a baby and, sitting in the dark, seeing the shadows and hearing the sounds of the sidewalk. Mostly it is a sound like infinitely patterning snatches of party conversation and, about three in the morning, singing, very good singing. Sometimes there is sharpness and anger or sad, sad weeping, or a flurry of search for a string of beads broken. One night a young man came roaring along, bellowing terrible language at two girls whom he had apparently picked up and who were disappointing him. Doors opened, a wary semicircle formed around him, not too close, until the police came. Out came the heads, too, along Hudson Street, offering opinion, "Drunk . . . Crazy . . . A wild kid from the suburbs."*

Deep in the night, I am almost unaware how many   8
people are on the street unless something calls them together, like the bagpipe. Who the piper was and why he favored our street I have no idea. The bagpipe just skirled out in the February night, and as if it were a signal the random, dwindled movements of the sidewalk took on di-

---

*He turned out to be a wild kid from the suburbs. Sometimes, on Hudson Street, we are tempted to believe the suburbs must be a difficult place to bring up children.

rection. Swiftly, quietly, almost magically a little crowd was there, a crowd that evolved into a circle with a Highland fling inside it. The crowd could be seen on the shadowy sidewalk, the dancers could be seen, but the bagpiper himself was almost invisible because his bravura was all in his music. He was a very little man in a plain brown overcoat. When he finished and vanished, the dancers and watchers applauded, and applause came from the galleries too, half a dozen of the hundred windows on Hudson Street. Then the windows closed, and the little crowd dissolved into the random movements of the night street.

The strangers on Hudson Street, the allies whose eyes   9 help us natives keep the peace of the street, are so many that they always seem to be different people from one day to the next. That does not matter. Whether they are so many always-different people as they seem to be, I do not know. Likely they are. When Jimmy Rogan fell through a plate-glass window (he was separating some scufflng friends) and almost lost his arm, a stranger in an old T shirt emerged from the Ideal bar, swiftly applied an expert tourniquet and, according to the hospital's emergency staff, saved Jimmy's life. Nobody remembered seeing the man before and no one has seen him since. The hospital was called in this way: a woman sitting on the steps next to the accident ran over to the bus stop, wordlessly snatched the dime from the hand of a stranger who was waiting with his fifteen-cent fare ready, and raced into the Ideal's phone booth. The stranger raced after her to offer the nickel too. Nobody remembered seeing him before, and no one has seen him since. When you see the same stranger three or four times on Hudson Street, you begin to nod. This is almost getting to be an acquaintance, a public acquaintance, of course.

I have made the daily ballet of Hudson Street sound 10 more frenetic than it is, because writing it telescopes it. In real life, it is not that way. In real life, to be sure, something is always going on, the ballet is never at a halt, but the general effect is peaceful and the general tenor even leisurely. People who know well such animated city streets will know how it is. I am afraid people who do not will always have it a little wrong in their heads—like the old prints of rhinoceroses made from travelers' descriptions of rhinoceroses.

On Hudson Street, the same as in the North End of 11 Boston or in any other animated neighborhoods of great cities, we are not innately more competent at keeping the sidewalks safe than are the people who try to live off the hostile truce of Turf in a blind-eyed city. We are the lucky possessors of a city order that makes it relatively simple to keep the peace because there are plenty of eyes on the street. But there is nothing simple about that order itself, or the bewildering number of components that go into it. Most of those components are specialized in one way or another. They unite in their joint effect upon the sidewalk, which is not specialized in the least. That is its strength.

QUESTIONS

1. The main clause in the first sentence of paragraph 3 is followed by a series of appositives explaining the *rituals of morning.* How many appositives do you find? Which of them is modified?

2. The colon in the following sentence introduces an addition that explains the main clause:

    > Two new entrances are being made from the wings: well-dressed and even elegant women and men with brief cases emerge from doorways and side streets.

    Does the colon in the succeeding sentences, in paragraph 3, serve the same purpose? What about the colon in the concluding sentence of the paragraph?

3. The second sentence of paragraph 5 might have been divided into four separate sentences. What is gained by joining the main clauses through semicolons? Are the semicolons in paragraph 3 used in the same way?

4. Notice that the main clause of the first sentence of paragraph 6 is modified by the opening subordinate clause and by the

phrases that follow, beginning with *eddying*. Try rewriting the sentence, beginning with *eddying*. Try rewriting the sentence, beginning with the main clause. Can the opening subordinate clause be put elsewhere in the sentence without obscuring the meaning?

5. What point is Jacobs making about the "daily ballet" of Hudson Street? How do the various details illustrate her point?

6. Jacobs is defining what makes a New York street a neighborhood. How different is this neighborhood from yours?

WRITING ASSIGNMENTS

1. Explain why the specialization in each of the "bewildering number of components" that make up the street is the source of its strength. Show how Jacobs illustrates this strength.

2. Develop the following main clauses through addition. Use colons and semicolons if you wish:
   a. "Deep in the night, I am almost unaware how many people are on the street . . ."
   b. "The crowd could be seen on the shadowy sidewalk . . ."
   c. "People who know well such animated city streets will know how it is . . ."

3. Develop the following main clauses through appositives that explain the italicized word:
   a. "This is the time of roller skates and stilts and *tricycles* . . ."
   b. "The night workers stop now at the delicatessen, to pick up salami and a container of *milk* . . ."
   c. "He was a very little man in a plain brown *overcoat* . . ."

Emphasis

In speaking, we vary our sentences without much if any thought—interrupting the flow of ideas to emphasize a word or phrase, or to repeat an idea. The speaker of the following sentence, a witness before a congressional committee, repeats certain phrases and qualifies his ideas in a typical way:

> My experience is that we hold people sometimes in jail, young people in jail, for days at a time with a complete lack of concern of the parents, if they do live in homes where parents live together, a complete lack of concern in many instances on the part of the community or other agencies as to where these young people are or what they are doing.

Sentences as complex and disjointed as this one seems when transcribed can be understood easily when they are spoken because the speaker is able to vary the vocal inflection to stress key words and phrases. Written punctuation can sometimes clarify the points of emphasis but in a limited way. In writing, we cannot depend directly on vocal inflection for clarity and emphasis; we can suggest these inflections by shaping the sentence in accord with ordinary speech patterns. Clear written sentences stay close to these patterns.

The core of English sentences, we saw, can be expanded, and at length, if each modifier is clearly connected to what precedes it. To achieve special emphasis the writer may vary the sentence even more, perhaps by making special use of the end of the sentence—the position that in English tends to be the most emphatic:

> The cold passed reluctantly from the earth, and the retiring fogs revealed an army stretched out on the hills, *resting.*—Stephen Crane, *The Red Badge of Courage*

Or the writer may break up the sentence so that individual ideas and experiences receive separate emphasis:

> The youth stopped. He was transfixed by this terrific medley of all noises. It was as if worlds were being rended. There was the ripping sound of musketry and the breaking crash of the artillery.—Crane

The relation of subordinate clauses to other elements in a sentence is controlled largely by the requirements of English word order. The position of subordinate clauses that serve as nouns or adjectives (sometimes called noun clauses and adjective clauses) is rather fixed; the position of subordinate clauses that serve as adverbs (sometimes called adverb clauses) is not. The position of the adverb clause depends on its importance as an idea and on its length:

> I majored in zoology *because I like working with animals.*
>
> *Because I like working with animals,* I majored in zoology.

The position of the subordinate clause determines what information is stressed: In the first sentence the subordinate clause seems to express the more important idea because it follows the main clause. In the second sentence, the main clause receives the emphasis. But the end of the sentence will not take the thrust of meaning if ideas appearing toward the beginning are given special emphasis.

Our informal spoken sentences show the least variation and depend heavily on coordination. The so-called *run-on sentence* in writing—a series of ideas strung together with *and* and other conjunctions—is a heavily coordinated sentence without the usual vocal markers. The sentence *fragment* sometimes derives from the clipped sentences and phrases common in speech.

MARK TWAIN

Born and raised in Hannibal, Missouri, on the Mississippi River, SAMUEL CLEMENS *worked as a river pilot from 1857 to 1861. He wrote about these experiences in* Life on the Mississippi, *published in 1883. The influence of the boy Twain describes in the passage reprinted below was momentous: "Boy after boy managed to get on the river. The minister's son became an engineer. The doctor's and the postmaster's sons became 'mud clerks'. . . ." Twain, too, ran away, but without immediate success: "Months afterward the hope within me struggled to a reluctant death, and I found myself without an ambition. But I was ashamed to go home." Eventually he did become a cub pilot on a river boat. Later, working as a newspaper reporter, he adopted the pen name "Mark Twain," the term of leadsmen on river boats for "two fathoms deep."*

The Steamboatman

¹My father was a justice of the peace and I supposed he possessed the power of life and death over all men and could hang anybody that offended him. ²This was distinction enough for me as a general thing, but the desire to be a steamboatman kept intruding nevertheless. ³I first wanted to be a cabin-boy, so that I could come out with a white apron on and shake a table-cloth over the side, where all my old comrades could see me; later I thought I would rather be the deck-hand who stood on the end of the stage-plank with the coil of rope in his hand, because he was particularly conspicuous. ⁴But these were only day-dreams—they were too heavenly to be contemplated as real possibilities. ⁵By and by one of our boys went away. ⁶He was not heard of for a long time. ⁷At last he turned up as apprentice engineer or "striker" on a steamboat. ⁸This thing shook the bottom out of all my Sunday-school teachings. ⁹That boy had been notoriously worldly and I just the reverse; yet he was exalted to this eminence and I left in obscurity and misery. ¹⁰There was nothing generous about this fellow in his greatness. ¹¹He would always manage to have a rusty bolt to scrub while his boat tarried at our town, and he would sit on the inside guard and scrub it, where we all could see him and envy him and loathe him. ¹²And whenever his boat was laid up he would come home and swell around the town in his blackest and greasiest clothes, so that nobody could help remembering that he was a steamboatman; and he used all

sorts of steamboat technicalities in his talk, as if he were so used to them that he forgot common people could not understand them. [13]He would speak of the "labboard" side of a horse in an easy, natural way that would make one wish he was dead. [14]And he was always talking about "St. Looy" like an old citizen; he would refer casually to occasions when he was "coming down Fourth Street," or when he was "passing by the Planter's House," or when there was a fire and he took a turn on the brakes of "the old Big Missouri"; and then he would go on and lie about how many towns the size of ours were burned down there that day. [15]Two or three of the boys had long been persons of consideration among us because they had been to St. Louis once and had a vague general knowledge of its wonders, but the day of their glory was over now. [16]They lapsed into a humble silence and learned to disappear when the ruthless "cub"-engineer approached. [17]This fellow had money, too, and hair-oil. [18]Also an ignorant silver watch and a showy brass watch-chain. [19]He wore a leather belt and used no suspenders. [20]If ever a youth was cordially admired and hated by his comrades, this one was. [21]No girl could withstand his charms. [22]He "cut out" every boy in the village. [23]When his boat blew up at last, it diffused a tranquil contentment among us such as we had not known for months. [24]But when he came home the next week, alive, renowned, and appeared in church all battered up and bandaged, a shining hero, stared at and wondered over by everybody, it seemed to us that the partiality of Providence for an undeserving reptile had reached a point where it was open to criticism.

QUESTIONS

1. Rewrite Twain's first sentence, subordinating one of the clauses. How does the revision affect the emphasis of ideas in the original sentence?

2. Combine sentences 17, 18, and 19 into a single sentence. What is gained or lost in emphasis in your revision?

3. How are coordinate conjunctions used for emphasis in sentences 23 and 24?

4. What emotions does Twain convey, and how does the sentence construction help him to convey them and create a mood?

5. How well has Twain conveyed the sense of childhood aspiration and frustration?

WRITING ASSIGNMENTS

1. Rewrite Twain's paragraph, giving different emphasis to his ideas through a different coordination and subordination of sentence elements. You need not revise all of the sentences.

2. Twain says in his autobiography: "The truth is a person's memory has no more sense than his conscience and no appreciation whatever of values and proportions." Develop this idea from your own experience.

CARL SANDBURG

Born in Galesburg, Illinois, CARL SANDBURG *(1878– 1967) began his career as a newspaper reporter in Chicago and Milwaukee. After winning a poetry prize in 1914, he increasingly gave his time to verse— publishing collections of his poems, beginning with* Chicago Poems *in the same year. His* Collected Poems *was awarded the Pulitzer Prize in 1951. Sandburg was also a distinguished biographer, his book* Abraham Lincoln—The War Years *earning the Pulitzer Prize for history in 1939. In his autobiography,* Always the Young Strangers, *Sandburg describes an incident from his youth in Galesburg—the funeral of General Grant, in 1885, under unusual circumstances, as Sandburg explains.*

The Funeral of General Grant

¹The Galesburg Marine Band marched past, men walking and their mouths blowing into their horns as they walked. ²One man had a big horn that seemed to be wrapped around him and I was puzzled how he got into it. ³They had on blue coats and pants and the stripe down the sides of the pants was either red or yellow and looked pretty. ⁴Their music was slow and sad. ⁵General Grant was dead and this was part of his funeral and the music should be sad. ⁶It was only twenty years since the war ended and General Grant was the greatest general in the war and they wanted to show they were sad because he was dead. ⁷That was the feeling I had and I could see there were many others had this same feeling. ⁸Marching past came men wearing dark-blue coats and big black hats tied round with a little cord of what looked like gold with a knot and a little tassel. ⁹They were the G.A.R., the Grand Army of the Republic, and I heard that some of these men had seen General Grant and had been in the war with him and could tell how he looked on a horse and what made him a great general. ¹⁰Eight or ten of these G.A.R. men walked along the sides of a long black box on some kind of a black car pulled by eight black horses. ¹¹The body of General Grant wasn't in the box, but somewhere far away General Grant was being buried in a box like this one. ¹²I could see everybody around was more quiet when this part of the parade passed.

QUESTIONS

1. What words does Sandburg repeat in sentences 4–6? How does this repetition help establish a dominant mood?

2. Sentences 2–7 are mainly simple and compound—mostly main clauses, with almost no variation. How does this evenness also help establish a dominant mood?

3. What other repetitions do you notice in the paragraph, and what do they contribute to the dominant mood?

4. Is the point of view that of a child or of an adult remembering a childhood experience? How do you know?

WRITING ASSIGNMENTS

1. Rewrite Sandburg's paragraph, subordinating clauses wherever possible. Then discuss the effect of the changes you made on the original paragraph.
2. Describe a parade or celebration, and construct your sentences so that they convey the mood of the event.

NORMAN MAILER

Born in New Jersey and raised in Brooklyn, NORMAN MAILER *attended Harvard University where he made the decision to become a writer. After serving in the Pacific in World War Two, he wrote a novel,* The Naked and the Dead, *that established his reputation as an important American writer. Mailer has maintained that reputation through a series of controversial novels about postwar America, and also through his journalism on a wide range of topics—from boxing to "hip" culture, lunar exploration, and American politics. A remarkable example is his eyewitness account of the knockout of Benny Paret in the twelfth round of a world championship welterweight bout at Madison Square Garden on March 25, 1962. Paret died on April 3, at the age of 24. Norman Cousins, later in this book, discusses the cause of Paret's death.*

The Death of Benny Paret

¹Paret was a Cuban, a proud club fighter who had become welterweight champion because of his unusual ability to take a punch. ²His style of fighting was to take

three punches to the head in order to give back two. ³At the end of ten rounds, he would still be bouncing, his opponent would have a headache. ⁴But in the last two years, over the fifteen-round fights, he had started to take some bad maulings.

⁵This fight had its turns. ⁶Griffith won most of the early rounds, but Paret knocked Griffith down in the sixth. ⁷Griffith had trouble getting up, but made it, came alive and was dominating Paret again before the round was over. ⁸Then Paret began to wilt. ⁹In the middle of the eighth round, after a clubbing punch had turned his back to Griffith, Paret walked three disgusted steps away, showing his hindquarters. ¹⁰For a champion, he took much too long to turn back around. ¹¹It was the first hint of weakness Paret had ever shown, and it must have inspired a particular shame, because he fought the rest of the fight as if he were seeking to demonstrate that he could take more punishment than any man alive. ¹²In the twelfth, Griffith caught him. ¹³Paret got trapped in a corner. ¹⁴Trying to duck away, his left arm and his head became tangled on the wrong side of the top rope. ¹⁵Griffith was in like a cat ready to rip the life out of a huge boxed rat. ¹⁶He hit him eighteen right hands in a row, an act which took perhaps three or four seconds, Griffith making a pent-up whimpering sound all the while he attacked, the right hand whipping like a piston rod which has broken through the crankcase, or like a baseball bat demolishing a pumpkin. ¹⁷I was sitting in the second row of that corner—they were not ten feet away from me, and like everybody else, I was hypnotized. ¹⁸I had never seen one man hit another so hard and so many times. ¹⁹Over the referee's face came a look of woe as if some spasm had passed its way through him, and then he leaped on Griffith to pull him away. ²⁰It was the act of a brave man. ²¹Griffith was uncontrollable. ²²His trainer leaped into the ring, his manager, his cut man, there were four people holding Griffith, but he was off on an orgy, he had left the Garden, he was back on a hoodlum's street. ²³If he had been able to

break loose from his handlers and the referee, he would have jumped Paret to the floor and whaled on him there.

²⁴And Paret? ²⁵Paret died on his feet. ²⁶As he took those eighteen punches something happened to everyone who was in psychic range of the event. ²⁷Some part of his death reached out to us. ²⁸One felt it hover in the air. ²⁹He was still standing in the ropes, trapped as he had been before, he gave some little half-smile of regret, as if he were saying, "I didn't know I was going to die just yet," and then, his head leaning back but still erect, his death came to breathe about him. ³⁰He began to pass away. ³¹As he passed, so his limbs descended beneath him, and he sank slowly to the floor. ³²He went down more slowly than any fighter had ever gone down, he went down like a large ship which turns on end and slides second by second into its grave. ³³As he went down, the sound of Griffith's punches echoed in the mind like a heavy ax in the distance chopping into a wet log.

QUESTIONS

1. Each sentence in the second paragraph focuses on a distinct moment of the action. Could any of the sentences be combined without blurring the action?

2. Sentence 22 joins a number of actions occurring simultaneously. How does the sentence convey the jarring confusion of the moment?

3. Does sentence 29 describe a continuous action? Would the mood of the paragraph be changed if Mailer broke the sentence into segments or punctuated it differently?

4. How does repetition in sentence 32 reinforce the feeling conveyed in the final paragraph?

5. Mailer's sentences are closer to spoken patterns than those of others we have been studying. In how many of his sentences does he depart from the normal subject-verb-object pattern—and to what effect?

6. Is Mailer concerned only with Paret, or is he making a statement about boxing as a sport? (See "Who Killed Benny Paret?" by Norman Cousins for another view of Paret's death in the ring.)

WRITING ASSIGNMENTS

1. Discuss the implications of the passage, including what it tells you about Mailer's attitude toward the death of Paret. Explain how Mailer conveys these ideas and attitudes.

2. Revise the following sentences to give increased emphasis to the italicized words:

    a. "*Paret was a Cuban*, a proud club fighter who had become welterweight champion because of his unusual ability to take a punch."

    b. "At the end of ten rounds, *he would still be bouncing*, his opponent would have a headache."

    c. "*For a champion*, he took much too long to turn back around."

    d. "I was sitting in the second row of that corner—*they were not ten feet away from me*, and like everybody else, I was hypnotized."

Loose and Periodic Sentences

Sentences are sometimes classified as loose or periodic to distinguish two important kinds of emphasis: the use made of the beginning or the end of the sentence. The loose sentence begins with the core idea, explanatory and qualifying phrases and clauses trailing behind:

> It was not a screeching noise, only an intermittent hump-hump, as if the bird had to recall his grievance each time before he repeated it.—Flannery O'Connor

If the ideas that follow the core are afterthoughts, or inessential details, the sentence will seem "loose"—easy and relaxed in its movement, perhaps even plodding if the content of the sentence permits:

> His eyes glittered like open pits of light as he moved across the sand, dragging his crushed shadow behind him.—O'Connor

A subordinate element will not seem unemphatic or plodding, however, if it expressed a strong action or idea:

> He beat louder and louder, bamming at the same time with his free fist until he felt he was shaking the house.—O'Connor

Opening with modifiers or with a series of appositives, the periodic sentence ends with the core:

> Living this way by the creek, where the light appears and vanishes on the water, where muskrats surface and dive, and redwings scatter, I have come to know a special side of nature.—Annie Dillard

The strongly periodic sentence is usually reserved for unusually strong emphasis:

> To believe your own thought, to believe that what is true for you in your private heart is true for all men—that is *genius.*—Ralph Waldo Emerson

Most contemporary English sentences fall between the extremely loose and the extremely periodic. Compound sentences seem loose when succeeding clauses serve as afterthoughts or qualifications rather than as ideas equal in importance to the opening idea:

> I was very conscious of the crowds at first, almost despairing to have to perform in front of them, and I never got used to it.—George Plimpton

Periodic sentences are used sparingly, with a distribution of emphasis more often through the whole sentence, as in Dillard's sentence above. Sometimes two moderately periodic sentences will be coordinated, with a corresponding distribution of emphasis:

> Though reliable narration is by no means the only way of conveying to the audience the facts on which dramatic irony is based, it is a useful way, and in some works, works in which no one but the author can conceivably know what needs to be known, it may be indispensable.—Wayne C. Booth

JOHN STEINBECK

JOHN STEINBECK *(1902–1968) was born in the Salinas Valley of California, the setting of many of his stories and novels. In 1962 he received the Nobel Prize for Literature—a testimony to the great reputation of his fiction throughout the world. His greatest work is undoubtedly* The Grapes of Wrath—*an account of the Joad family that, dispossessed of their Oklahoma farm during the Great Depression, make an arduous journey to California. Steinbeck's account of depression poverty and the exploitation of migrant workers—awarded the Pulitzer Prize in 1939—remains a powerful one. Toward the beginning of the novel, Steinbeck describes a turtle making its own difficult journey—a hint of what*

is to follow. Steinbeck's sentences are notable for the
various ways they convey the movement of the turtle up
the embankment.

The Turtle

[1]The sun lay on the grass and warmed it, and in the
shade under the grass the insects moved, ants and ant lions
to set traps for them, grasshoppers to jump into the air and
flick their yellow wings for a second, sow bugs like little
armadillos, plodding restlessly on many tender feet. [2]And
over the grass at the roadside a land turtle crawled, turning
aside for nothing, dragging his highdomed shell over the
grass. [3]His hard legs and yellow-nailed feet threshed slowly
through the grass, not really walking, but boosting and
dragging his shell along. [4]The barley beards slid off his
shell, and the clover blurs fell on him and rolled to the
ground. [5]His horny beak was partly open, and his fierce,
humorous eyes, under brows like fingernails, stared straight
ahead. [6]He came over the grass leaving a beaten trail behind him, and the hill, which was the highway embankment,
reared up ahead of him. [7]For a moment he stopped, his
head held high. [8]He blinked and looked up and down. [9]At
last he started to climb the embankment. [10]Front clawed
feet reached forward but did not touch. [11]The hind feet
kicked his shell along, and it scraped on the grass, and on
the gravel. [12]As the embankment grew steeper and steeper,
the more frantic were the efforts of the land turtle. [13]Push-
ing hind legs strained and slipped, boosting the shell along,
and the horny head protruded as far as the neck could
stretch. [14]Little by little the shell slid up the embankment
until at last a parapet cut straight across its line of march,
the shoulder of the road, a concrete wall four inches high.
[15]As though they worked independently the hind legs
pushed the shell against the wall. [16]The head upraised and

peered over the wall to the broad smooth plain of cement.
[17]Now the hands, braced on top of the wall, strained and
lifted, and the shell came slowly up and rested its front end
on the wall. [18]For a moment the turtle rested. [19]A red ant
ran into the shell, into the soft skin inside the shell, and
suddenly head and legs snapped in, and the armored tail
clamped in sideways. [20]The red ant was crushed between
body and legs. [21]And one head of wild oats was clamped
into the shell by a front leg. [22]For a long moment the turtle
lay still, and then the neck crept out and the old humorous
frowning eyes looked about and the legs and tail came out.
[23]The back legs went to work, straining like elephant legs,
and the shell tipped to an angle so that the front legs could
not reach the level cement plain. [24]But higher and higher the
hind legs boosted it, until at last the center of balance was
reached, the front tipped down, the front legs scratched at
the pavement, and it was up. [25]But the head of wild oats was
held by its stem around the front legs.

QUESTIONS

1. The base idea in sentence 2 is *a land turtle crawled.* If this
   clause were moved to the end of the sentence what change
   would occur in focus or meaning?
2. How does the structure of sentence 3 help us visualize the
   movement of the turtle? Is the sentence loose or periodic?
3. Consider this revision of sentence 7:

   His head held high, he stopped for a moment.

   Is the meaning of the original sentence changed?
4. Combine sentences 7, 8 and 9 into one sentence. What change
   in meaning, focus, or emphasis occurs?
5. Consider this revision of sentence 11:

   The hind feet kicking his shell along, it scraped on the grass and on
   the gravel.

   What is gained or lost in meaning or effect by the revision?

6. Sentences 11 and 12 both describe the action of the turtle—moving on the grass at the edge of the embankment, then moving up the steep part. What difference do you see in the structure of these sentences? How does each structure convey the action in a different way?

7. How does the coordinate structure of sentence 23 show that the movement of the legs and tipping of the shell are not happening at the same time? How could Steinbeck change the structure of the sentence if he wanted to show the two actions occurring at the same time?

8. How does the structure of sentence 24 help us to visualize the action here?

WRITING ASSIGNMENT

Steinbeck's turtle seems to many readers symbolic of the Joad family in *The Grapes of Wrath*, the novel in which this description of the turtle appears. Dispossessed of their Oklahoma farm during the Great Depression of the 1930s, they make an arduous journey to California. Discuss the qualities or attitudes that Steinbeck might be symbolizing in the turtle.

PHILIPPE COUSTEAU

The photographer and oceanographer PHILIPPE COUSTEAU, *born in 1940, worked with his father, Jacques-Yves Cousteau, aboard their famous boat,* Calypso. *Together with a large crew they explored the ocean bed throughout the world. Philippe directed the film company that produced numerous television and film documentaries. In 1979 he died in a seaplane accident in Portugal. His description of sharks in his book on them reveals the curiosity and love of the ocean and its inhabitants revealed in his films.*

Sharks

¹In the Mediterranean, sharks are rare and cause few accidents. But their very rarity confers a peculiar solemnity on each encounter. ²My "first" sharks, at Djerba, were Mediterranean and impressed me unduly, because I had not expected to see them. ³On the other hand, in the Red Sea, where it is practically impossible to dive among the reefs of the open sea without being surrounded by sharks, coexistence was inevitable and my companions and I very soon became imprudent, almost unaware of their presence. ⁴I even sensed in our team the beginnings of a certain affectation of disdain for these inoffensive prowlers, a tendency to feign ignorance of them, to speak of them only in jest. ⁵I argued against this form of snobbishness because it could become dangerous, but I was vulnerable to it myself. ⁶It is intoxicating for an awkward and vulnerable creature, such as a diver becomes the instant he drops beneath the surface of the water, to imagine himself stronger than a creature far better armed than he. ⁷It was in this climate of excessive vanity and confidence in the early years that I dived myself and allowed others to dive, without protection, in the most dangerous waters. ⁸On the reef of João Valente, in the Cape Verde Islands, we jostled or pulled on the tails of animals over twelve feet in length, incomparably more powerful and competent than we awkward intruders with steel bottles on our backs, our field of vision limited by the masks we wore, and caricatures of fins on our feet. ⁹The day at João Valente when Dumas and I glimpsed in the distance the pale silhouette of a great white shark (the species that all specialists qualify as a man-eater), we were frozen with terror and instinctively drew closer together. ¹⁰We had seen him before he saw us. But as soon as he became aware of our presence, it was he who was seized with panic; emptying out his intestines, he disappeared with a single flick of his tail. ¹¹Later, in the Indian Ocean, the same incident occurred on two separate occasions. ¹²And each time, the violent emo-

tion brought on in us by the appearance of the great white shark gave way to an unjustified sensation of triumph when he fled at the mere sight of us. [13]Each of these unusual encounters provoked great excitement among us, and with it an excessive confidence in ourselves and a consequent relaxation of security measures.

[14]Deep-sea diving with self-contained breathing equipment brings with it a kind of narcosis, which we christened "intoxication of the depths": it becomes evident anywhere around a depth of a hundred and thirty feet and becomes annoying and even dangerous at depths below two hundred feet. [15]The "intoxication" manifests itself in a sort of euphoria, then in a quickening of some of the senses—the hearing in particular. [16]The sense of reality is reduced, and consequently the instinct of self-preservation. [17]All these symptoms disappear, as if by magic, during the period of return to the surface. [18]It is therefore logical that the depth to which one dives, since it can bring about such psychic upheavals, can also influence the reactions of a diver confronted with sharks. [19]Once, in mid-Atlantic, on board the *Elie Monnier*, we encountered large schools of dolphins, so we brought the ship to a halt while we dived among them, as far down as a hundred to a hundred and fifty feet. [20]The dolphins disappeared within a matter of minutes, but we could still see schools of yellow-finned tuna and great ocean sharks, a hundred or so feet below us. [21]I can remember now the eerie sensations of these insane dives. [22]At about one hundred and fifty feet the surface had practically disappeared and the area of water surrounding me was strangely somber, a blue that was almost black; the intoxication of the depths was there, flooding my entire being, but it seemed to me to be controllable, like the first puff of opium. [23]Mad with liberty, weightless, and completely removed from the world, listening to the beating of my heart in this pelagic silence, I was ready to commit any kind of imprudence. [24]And today I realize that I committed all of them.

[25]Far from the surface, where the sun perhaps was shining, but still more than two miles from the bottom of the

sea, lost in water which was black as ink and yet incredibly transparent, because light passed through it without inter- ference, I lost all notion of horizontal and vertical. ²⁶I could no longer distinguish between up and down. ²⁷I had only one reference with which to orient myself: the bubbles of air escaping from the pressure tanks on my back. ²⁸What I felt in the course of these giddy dives was perhaps stranger, even more disconcerting than the impressions felt by the first "space walkers." ²⁹The astronauts, leaving their capsule, can clearly see the familiar stars and planets, while I felt myself lost in immensity, with no landmarks to guide me. ³⁰The only reassuring existence in my realm was a somewhat remote one; the boat which I knew—or thought—to be above me, carefully following the traces left on the surface by my air bubbles. ³¹It was in this extraordi- nary atmosphere that sharks made their most dramatic appearance. ³²I still knew little of these sharks of the high seas and I was fascinated by their majesty. ³³They were generally much larger than those of the reefs. ³⁴There were species of them, at that time, which I was unable to identify. ³⁵The majority had sharper noses and more clearly defined silhouettes than, for example, the tiger shark. ³⁶They seemed to be following the schools of dolphins, but main- taining a certain distance from them. ³⁷When they appeared out of nowhere they made no effort to approach me, but instead changed their course when they were about fifty feet away, as if to keep me in sight. ³⁸The first time I found myself in this situation, the sighting of the first shark was a violent emotional shock. ³⁹Framed in light in the darkness of the water, he stood out clearly, in an unreal, terrifying man- ner. ⁴⁰And, certainly as a result of the intoxication caused by the one-hundred-fifty-foot depth at which I was swimming, the admiration and fear I experienced were abruptly trans- formed into an unreasoning sense of exultation. ⁴¹I swam straight toward the great shark, armed only with my cam- era, but he drew away from me, keeping the same distance between us. ⁴²I went on swimming through the blue-black depths, pursuing a silhouette which finally disappeared, diving far down below me; I was alone now, breathing hard, lost, my temples throbbing, my mind disturbed, realizing confusedly that my conduct had been idiotic, but proud of thinking myself capable of putting such a formidable creature to flight. [43]In an element which was not naturally mine, which put out traps for me at every flick of my rubber fins, I felt the vanity of having conducted myself as a conqueror, a master. [44]I had put—we had put—the great ocean sharks to flight; man was invincible, beneath the water as well as on earth. [45]The legend of man-eating sharks collapsed around me.

QUESTIONS

1. Sentences 1–8 are predominantly loose and coordinate; sentence 9 and the two parts of sentence 10, periodic. Does their content justify the increased tightening of sentences 9 and 10—with an increase of suspense?

2. How does Cousteau construct sentence 15 to emphasize the quickened sense of hearing in deep-sea diving? How does he emphasize the color of the water in the first part of sentence 22?

3. Tighten sentence 19 by subordinating the first part of it (the first main clause and its modifiers) to the second part (beginning with the words "we brought"). Does the content justify the increased emphasis given to this second part?

4. Rewrite sentences 23, 25, 39 and 40 as loose sentences. What do you gain or lose in emphasis and effect with your revisions?

5. Rewrite the two parts of sentence 42 as periodic sentences. What do you gain or lose with these revisions?

6. Is the periodic structure of sentence 43 appropriate to the ideas expressed?

7. What is gained by coordinating the two parts of sentence 44 (through the semicolon) instead of making them separate sentences?

8. Notice that each of the three paragraphs builds to a climax. Is there a built-in climax through the whole passage?

WRITING ASSIGNMENT

Cousteau shows us how he made an unexpected discovery about himself and a creature of nature he had feared: "I had put—we had put—the great ocean sharks to flight; man was invincible, beneath the water as well as on earth. The legend of man-eating sharks collapsed around me." Describe a similar experience in the world of nature that brought you to an unexpected discovery about yourself and perhaps about the world of nature or one of its creatures.

Climax

Our discussion of periodic sentences indicates one important way to achieve climax—by delaying the main idea or the completion of the main idea until the end of the sentence. We saw also that, even in loose or coordinated sentences, modifying or qualifying phrases and clauses that follow the main idea can be arranged in the order of rising importance—as in *I came, I saw, I conquered*. A necessary condition of climax is a sense of anticipation, promoted chiefly through the ideas themselves. Obviously anticlimax will result if we make the culminating idea less significant than what has gone before. The letdown that results may be deliberately comic, as in this sentence by Thomas De Quincey:

> If once a man indulges himself in murder, very soon he comes to think little of robbery; and from robbing he next comes to drinking and Sabbath-breaking, and from that to incivility and procrastination.

PETER MATTHIESSEN

Born in New York City in 1927, PETER MATTHIESSEN *was educated at the Sorbonne in Paris, France, and at Yale University. He worked for a time as a commercial fisherman, and later was a member of various scientific expeditions to Alaska, the Canadian Northwest Territory, Peru, and New Guinea. He has described these experiences and his exploration of other parts of the world in a series of remarkable books, including* The Cloud Forest *and* The Snow Leopard. *He is also a widely read novelist. Matthiessen is unsurpassed in his ability to convey the excitement and beauty of ocean life. In* Blue Meridian: The Search for the Great White Shark, *he shows us a darker side in the killing of a whale, witnessed aboard a whale-catcher off the coast of South Africa, in 1969.*

The Killing of the Whale

¹9:48. ²On the bow, the Gunner's heavy form rises and falls, breaking the line of the horizon. ³The harpoon gun swings from port to starboard, searching for the biggest whale, but these close groups are composed of cows under thirty-three feet; he finds no target. ⁴The bow cuts the pod in half, and the whale shapes, fleeing to the side, slide like cloud shadows beneath the sea. ⁵In moments, they rise, surging and blowing, and the ship rides down on them. ⁶The Gunner raises one hand almost casually to point; he bends to his gun again as the ship surges. ⁷A loud thump on the wind, muffled and ear-stunning—the mate runs forward along the catwalk to reload the gun.

⁸Oddly, the shot has missed; the Gunner sits down heavily as the mate reloads. ⁹A sailor lugs a slotted red harpoon from the foredeck and with the help of the mate jams it into the muzzle. ¹⁰Inside the four flights of the point, the harpoon, four feet long, weighs 185 pounds. ¹¹The mate sets the explosive grenade that detonates in the whale's body three seconds after impact, and with a few turns of light lanyard secures the harpoon against sliding out of the tilted muzzle. ¹²Then the human silhouettes retire from the bow, all but the form of the seated Gunner, as black as the gun itself on the sparkling sea. ¹³Less than three minutes have elapsed, and already W-29 is circling in on another pod of whales, so close that one can see the distinct forward angle of the sperm-whale spout that issues from a hole just to the left of the center line of the head. ¹⁴(The Gunner says that this hole is closed when a sea washes over it and that sometimes a whale in flight will try to spout underwater.) ¹⁵Ploughing and blowing, the whales leave a white wake in the blue, backs gleaming like smooth boulders of obsidian in a swift torrent; as W-29 comes down on them, they sound. ¹⁶One black back arches into a curve, and a huge fluke rises in slow motion from the sparkling ocean. ¹⁷Water cascading from its fluke, the whale slides down in silence into the sea.

¹⁸At 10:15, as the ship heels into position, the whole pod broaches in one mighty burst of mist and spray. ¹⁹The ship rides herd on the black backs, the harpoon point still seeking a big whale. ²⁰At 10:19, a series of explosions: the shot, the muffled boom in the whale's body, and the jolt of a huge spring belowdecks. ²¹The nylon harpoon line, with a breaking strength of twenty-four long tons, is reeved through chocks under the gun platform, then up over a heavy pulley under the crow's-nest, high on the mainmast, then down again to heavy winches at the aft end of the foredeck, under the superstructure; the pulley is rigged to enormous springs under the foredeck that take the main impact of the whale's first thrash.

²²The whole ship quakes. ²³The dying whale has veered away to starboard, and the harpoon line shivers spray as it snaps taut; the white of the cachalot's toothed lower mandible flashes in the light as the beast rolls, and the first well of its blood spreads on the surface. ²⁴With her winch, the ship is warped alongside, and the mate puts a killer harpoon—a grenade-carrier with no line attached, known to the Norwegians as the flea—into the thrashing hulk as the crewmen jump to dodge the wall of spray. ²⁵Now the whale is still; only the pectorals twitch a little as the last life ebbs out of her. ²⁶Already a long pole has been used to jam a hose tube into the carcass, and air is pumped in to make sure the whale will float. ²⁷At the same time, the sailors rig a heavy noose around the base of the fluke, which in turn is secured to the big float of the marker buoy. ²⁸With a flensing knife lashed to the end of a long pole, the mate, doubled up over the gunwale, cuts the harpoon line where it is spliced to the imbedded missiles, and the ship backs off from the buoyed whale. ²⁹The harpoon gun has already been reloaded, and a new line spliced to the harpoon. ³⁰Eleven minutes have passed from the moment the first iron struck the life out of the whale until the whale-catcher reverses her screws and backs away.

³¹The inflated whale lies on her side, washed by red waves of her own blood. ³²Already the bright stain on the

bright sea is huge and thick, as if it would never wash away. [33]The blood spurting from the wounds is a deep mammalian red, but on the surface of the sea it turns red red, as vivid as a dye, and the amount of it is awful.

QUESTIONS

1. We saw earlier that building a sentence to the main clause or base idea increases the emphasis given it. Not all sentences constructed in this way convey suspense or climax: this effect depends on the content of the sentence—on what the sentence expresses or shows. How much does the construction of the two parts of sentence 15 convey the suspense or climax? How much suspense does the content create?

2. Which sentence is more suspenseful or climactic—18 or 19? How do you explain the difference in effect?

3. Which paragraph conveys the greater suspense or climax—the fourth paragraph or the last—and why do you think so?

4. How does Matthiessen construct the final sentence of the passage—sentence 33—to give emphasis to his feelings about what he has seen?

5. Has Matthiessen selected details merely to describe how whales are killed, or has he an additional purpose in mind? Do you think he is trying to make a point or argue a thesis?

WRITING ASSIGNMENTS

1. Compare the attitudes toward sharks and whales you find stated or implied in Cousteau and Matthiessen. Then discuss the different means each uses to convey his attitude.

2. Compare the attitude toward the killing of an animal stated or implied in Matthiessen with the attitude you find in one of the following selections in this book:
   a. Hemingway, "The Shooting of the Buffalo"
   b. Woiwode, "Killing a Deer"
   c. Orwell, "Shooting an Elephant"

JOHN UPDIKE

Born in Shillington, Pennsylvania in 1932, JOHN UP-
DIKE *began his long association with* The New Yorker
*magazine early in his career and has published many of
his poems, stories, and essays in that magazine. His
collection of stories,* The Music School, *won the O.
Henry Award in 1966, and he received the National
Book Award in 1963 for his novel* The Centaur. *The
speaker in one of Updike's stories is describing his
grandmother as he remembers her from his youth. He
says about her: "At the time I was married, she was in
her late seventies, crippled and enfeebled. She had
fought a long battle with Parkinson's disease; in my
earliest memories of her she is touched with it. Her
fingers and back are bent; there is a tremble about her
as she moves about through the dark, odd-shaped rooms
of our house in the town where I was born." His
thoughts turn in this passage to happier days.*

My Grandmother

¹When we were all still alive, the five of us in that
kerosene-lit house, on Friday and Saturday nights, at an
hour when in the spring and summer there was still abundant light in the air, I would set out in my father's car for
town, where my friends lived. ²I had, by moving ten miles
away, at last acquired friends: an illustration of that strange
law whereby, like Orpheus leading Eurydice, we achieve our
desire by turning our back on it. ³I had even gained a girl, so
that the vibrations were as sexual as social that made me
jangle with anticipation as I clowned in front of the mirror
in our kitchen, shaving from a basin of stove-heated water,
combing my hair with a dripping comb, adjusting my reflection in the mirror until I had achieved just that electric angle
from which my face seemed beautiful and everlastingly, by
the very volumes of air and sky and grass that lay mutely
banked about our home, beloved. ⁴My grandmother would

hover near me, watching fearfully, as she had when I was a child, afraid that I would fall from a tree. [5]Delirious, humming, I would swoop and lift her, lift her like a child, crooking one arm under her knees and cupping the other behind her back. [6]Exultant in my height, my strength, I would lift that frail brittle body weighing perhaps a hundred pounds and twirl with it my arms while the rest of the family watched with startled smiles of alarm. [7]Had I stumbled, or dropped her, I might have broken her back, but my joy always proved a secure cradle. [8]And whatever irony was in the impulse, whatever implicit contrast between this ancient husk, scarcely female, and the pliant, warm girl I would embrace before the evening was done, direct delight flooded away: I was carrying her who had carried me, I was giving my past a dance, I had lifted the anxious caretaker of my childhood from the floor, I was bringing her with my boldness to the edge of danger, from which she had always sought to guard me.

QUESTIONS

1. In the Updike, how does the ending of sentence 3 vary the normal sentence pattern to take advantage of the strong terminal position? Does the context justify the double emphasis given to *beloved*?

2. Sentence 3 develops through an accumulation of detail. Does the sentence develop a single idea? Could Updike break it up without interrupting the meaning or disturbing the effect?

3. What technique aids in achieving the climax in sentences 5 and 8? Does the same kind of sentence construction achieve it?

WRITING ASSIGNMENTS

1. Describe an episode or a series of incidents involving a close relative or friend. Let your details reveal your attitude toward him or her; do not state the attitude directly.

2. Discuss how sentence climax conveys the sense of anticipation built into Updike's paragraph.

Parallelism

The italicized words in the following sentence are parallel in structure, that is, they perform the same grammatical function in the sentence and, as infinitives, are the same in form:

> So long as I remain alive and well I shall continue *to feel* strongly about prose style, *to love* the surface of the earth, and *to take* a pleasure in solid objects and scraps of useless information.—George Orwell, *Why I Write*

In speaking and writing, we make elements such as these infinitives parallel naturally. No matter how many words separate them, we continue the pattern we start. Indeed, our "sentence sense" tells us when a pattern has been interrupted. We know something is wrong when we read

> I shall continue to feel strongly about prose style, to love the surface of the earth, and taking pleasure in solid objects and scraps of useless information.

Parallelism is an important means to concision and focus in sentences. It also allows us to make additions to the sentence without loss of clarity.

A special use of parallelism is the balancing of similar ideas in a sentence for special emphasis:

> The savage bows down to idols of wood and stone: the civilized man to idols of flesh and blood.—George Bernard Shaw

Notice that the parallel phrases here are of the same weight and length. Writers can balance clauses and occasionally whole sentences in the same way as President Franklin Roosevelt does in his First Inaugural Address:

> Yet our distress comes from no failure of substance. We are stricken by no plague of locusts. Compared with the perils which our forefathers conquered because they believed and were not afraid, we have still much to be thankful for. Nature still offers her bounty and human efforts have multiplied it. Plenty is at our doorstep, but a generous use of it languishes in the very sight of the supply.

The marked rhythm of these sentences creates a highly formal effect by slowing the tempo. Such exact balance interrupts the natural flow of the sentence, giving emphasis to most or all of its parts. For this reason it is exceptional to find sentences as studied and formal as these in modern writing. But we do find a moderate balance used to give a greater emphasis to similar ideas than ordinary parallelism provides.

JOHN A. WILLIAMS

> JOHN A. WILLIAMS, *who teaches English at Rutgers University, has written much about black people in America in his newspaper and magazine articles, memoirs, novels, and biography of Martin Luther King, Jr. His description of driving in a snowstorm is taken from his book on his travels through America,* This Is My Country Too. *Like Steinbeck, William conveys the physical sensation through the structure of his sentences.*

Driving Through Snowstorms

[1]Driving through snowstorms on icy roads for long distances is a most nerve-racking experience. [2]It is a paradox that the snow, coming down gently, blowing gleefully in a high wind, all the while lays down a treacherous carpet, freezes the windows, blocks the view. [3]The might of automated man is muted. [4]The horses, the powerful electrical systems, the deep-tread tires, all go for nothing. [5]One minute the road feels firm, and the next the driver is sliding over it, light as a feather, in a panic, wondering what the heavy trailer trucks coming up from the rear are going to do. [6]The trucks are like giants when you have to pass them, not at sixty or seventy as you do when the road is dry, but at

twenty-five and thirty. [7]Then their engines sound unnaturally loud. [8]Snow, slush and chips of ice spray from beneath the wheels, obscure the windshield, and rattle off your car. [9]Beneath the wheels there is plenty of room for you to skid and get mashed to a pulp. [10]Inch by inch you move up, past the rear wheels, the center wheels, the cab, the front wheels, all sliding too slowly by. [11]Straight ahead you continue, for to cut over sharply would send you into a skid, right in front of the vehicle. [12]At last, there is distance enough, and you creep back over, in front of the truck now, but with the sound of its engine still thundering in your ears.

QUESTIONS

1. What phrases does Williams make parallel in sentence 2 to emphasize similar ideas?
2. What other sentences contain a similar use of parallelism?
3. How does the structure of sentence 10 imitate the action described?
4. The following sentences contain errors in parallelism. Revise them to correct the errors. The original sentences are from Joseph Conrad's story "Youth":
   a. And while we pumped the ship was going from us piecemeal: the bulwarks went, torn out were the stanchions, the ventilators smashed, burst in was the cabin door.
   b. We forgot the day of the week, the name of the month, forgetting what year it was, and forgot whether we had ever been ashore.
   c. O youth! It has strength, the faith of it, youth has imagination!
   d. I think of her with pleasure, with affection, and think of her with regret.

WRITING ASSIGNMENT

Describe an experience you have had driving or walking on icy or wet streets or sidewalks. Then contrast this experience with that of Williams.

ERNESTO GALARZA

ERNESTO GALARZA, the American labor leader, teacher and writer, was born in Mexico, and came to the United States when he was six. He went to school in Sacramento and later studied at Occidental College and Stanford and Columbia Universities where he received his doctorate in 1944. Galarza's youthful experience as a farm and cannery worker prepared him for his life's work organizing agricultural workers. He has taught at various universities, has been Regents Professor at the University of California, San Diego, and has written a number of books including the autobiography Barrio Boy, *which describes his childhood in California.*

Boyhood in a Sacramento Barrio

Our family conversations always occurred on our own   1
kitchen porch, away from the gringos. One or the other of
the adults would begin: *Se han fijado?* Had we noticed—
that the Americans do not ask permission to leave the
room; that they had no respectful way of addressing an
elderly person; that they spit brown over the railing of the
porch into the yard; that when they laughed they roared;
that they never brought *saludos* to everyone in your family
from everyone in their family when they visited; that *General Delibree* was only a clerk; that *zopilotes* were not allowed on the streets to collect garbage; that the policemen
did not carry lanterns at night; that Americans didn't keep
their feet on the floor when they were sitting; that there was
a special automobile for going to jail; that a rancho was not
a rancho at all but a very small hacienda; that the saloons
served their customers free eggs, pickles, and sandwiches;
that instead of bullfighting, the gringos for sport tried to kill
each other with gloves?

I did not have nearly the strong feelings on these mat- 2
ters that Doña Henriqueta expressed. I felt a vague admiration for the way Mr. Brien could spit brown. Wayne, my
classmate, laughed much better than the Mexicans, because
he opened his big mouth wide and brayed like a donkey so
he could be heard a block away. But it was the kind of
laughter that made my mother tremble, and it was not
permitted in our house.

Rules were laid down to keep me, as far as possible, *un* 3
muchacho bien educado. If I had to spit I was to do it
privately, or if in public, by the curb, with my head down
and my back to people. I was never to wear my cap in the
house and I was to take it off even on the porch if ladies or
elderly gentlemen were sitting. If I wanted to scratch, under
no circumstances was I to do it right then and there, in
company, like the Americans, but I was to excuse myself. If
Catfish or Russell yelled to me from across the street I was
not to shout back. I was never to ask for tips for my errands
or other services to the tenants of 418 L, for these were
atenciones expected of me.

Above all I was never to fail in *respeto* to grownups, no 4
matter who they were. It was an inflexible rule; I addressed
myself to *Señor* Big Singh, *Señor* Big Ernie, *Señora* Dodson,
Señor Cho-ree Lopez.

My standing in the family, but especially with my 5
mother depended on my keeping these rules. I was not
punished for breaking them. She simply reminded me that it
gave her acute *vergüenza* to see me act thus, and that I
would never grow up to be a correct *jefe de familia* if I did
not know how to be a correct boy. I knew what *vergüenza*
was from feeling it time and again; and the notion of growing up to keep a tight rein over a family of my own was
somehow satisfying.

In our musty apartment in the basement of 418 L, ours 6
remained a Mexican family. I never lost the sense that we
were the same, from Jalco to Sacramento. There was the
polished cedar box, taken out now and then from the closet
to display our heirlooms. I had lost the rifle shells of the

revolution, and Tío Tonche, too, was gone. But there was the butterfly sarape, the one I had worn through the Battle of Puebla; a black lace mantilla Doña Henriqueta modeled for us; bits of embroidery and lace she had made; the tin pictures of my grandparents; my report card signed by Señorita Bustamante and Don Salvador; letters from Aunt Esther; and the card with the address of the lady who had kept the Ajax for us. When our mementos were laid out on the bed I plunged my head into the empty box and took deep breaths of the aroma of *puro cedro*, pure Jalcocotán mixed with camphor.

We could have hung on the door of our apartment a sign like those we read in some store windows—*Aquí se habla español.* We not only spoke Spanish, we read it. From the *Librería Española,* two blocks up the street, Gustavo and I bought novels for my mother, like *Genoveva de Brabante,* a paperback with the poems of Amado Nervo and a handbook of the history of Mexico. The novels were never read aloud, the poems and the handbook were. Nervo was the famous poet from Tepic, close enough to Jalcocotán to make him our own. And in the history book I learned to read for myself, after many repetitions by my mother, about the deeds of the great Mexicans Don Salvador had recited so vividly to the class in Mazatlán. She refused to decide for me whether Abraham Lincoln was as great as Benito Juárez, or George Washington braver than the priest Don Miguel Hidalgo. At school there was no opportunity to settle these questions because nobody seemed to know about Juárez or Hidalgo; at least they were never mentioned and there were no pictures of them on the walls.

The family talk I listened to with the greatest interest was about Jalco. Wherever the conversation began it always turned to the pueblo, our neighbors, anecdotes that were funny or sad, the folk tales and the witchcraft, and our kinfolk, who were still there. I usually lay on the floor those winter evenings, with my feet toward the kerosene heater, watching on the ceiling the flickering patterns of the light filtered through the scrollwork of the chimney. As I listened once again I chased the *zopilote* away from Coronel, or

7

8

watched José take Nerón into the forest in a sack. Certain things became clear about the *rurales* and why the young men were taken away to kill Yaqui Indians, and about the Germans, the Englishmen, the Frenchmen, the Spaniards, and the Americans who owned the haciendas, the railroads, the ships, the big stores, the breweries. They owned Mexico because President Porfirio Díaz had let them steal it, José explained as I listened. Now Don Francisco Madero had been assassinated for trying to get it back. On such threads of family talk I followed my own recollection of the years from Jalco—the attack on Mazatlán, the captain of Acaponeta, the camp at El Nanchi and the arrival at Nogales on the flatcar.

Only when we ventured uptown did we feel like aliens 9 in a foreign land. Within the *barrio* we heard Spanish on the streets and in the alleys. On the railroad tracks, in the canneries, and along the riverfront there were more Mexicans than any other nationality. And except for the foremen, the work talk was in our language. In the secondhand shops, where the *barrio* people sold and bought furniture and clothing, there were Mexican clerks who knew the Mexican ways of making a sale. Families doubled up in decaying houses, cramping themselves so they could rent an extra room to *chicano* boarders, who accented the brown quality of our Mexican *colonia.*

VOCABULARY

barrio:	neighborhood
Se jan fijado?:	Did you notice?
saludos:	greetings
zopilotes:	vultures, buzzards
un muchacho bien educado:	a well-bred boy
atenciones:	duties
respeto:	respect
vergüenza:	shame, embarrassment
jefe de familia:	head of the family
puro cedro:	pure cedar
Aqui se habla español:	Spanish spoken here

Librería Española:	Spanish Bookstore
rurales:	rural mounted police
chicano:	American of Mexican descent
colonia:	colony

QUESTIONS

1. How does the author use parallelism in the third sentence of paragraph 1 to give equal emphasis to the various ideas?
2. How is the same use made of parallelism in paragraph 6?
3. Whole sentences can be parallel to one another. How much parallelism of this kind do you find in paragraph 3?
4. In general, how loose or how strict do you find the parallelism of Galarza's sentences? How formal an effect do his sentences create?
5. How do you believe children are best taught to respect people different from them culturally? How different from Galarza's was your training in manners?

WRITING ASSIGNMENTS

1. Galarza uses his account to say something about Mexican and American folkways and the changes brought about in moving from one world to another. Discuss what Galarza is saying, and comment on his attitude toward the changes he experiences.
2. Discuss the increased importance manners have when you find yourself in a new environment, perhaps in a new school or neighborhood. You might want to discuss changes in speech habits as well as changes in behavior.

MAX LERNER

In his long career as teacher, editor, and writer, MAX LERNER *has been concerned with American law, politics, and culture. He has been a magazine editor, for many years has written a column for the* New York Post, *and has taught at several universities, including Brandeis from 1949 to 1973 as Professor of American Civilization. His discussion of American sports is taken from* America as a Civilization, *published in 1957.*

Sports in America

The psychic basis of American mass sports is tribal and 1
feudal. Baseball is a good example of the modern totem
symbols (Cubs, Tigers, Indians, Pirates, Dodgers, and
Braves) and of sustained tribal animosities. The spectator is
not *on* the team, but he can be *for* the team; he identifies
himself with one team, sometimes with one player who
becomes a jousting champion wearing his colors in a
medieval tournament. Hence the hero symbolism in American sports and the impassioned hero worship which makes
gods of mortals mediocre in every other respect, and gives
them the place among the "Immortals" that the French
reserve for their Academy intellectuals.

There is a stylized relation of artist to mass audience in 2
the sports, especially in baseball. Each player develops a
style of his own—the swagger as he steps to the plate, the
unique windup a pitcher has, the clean-swinging and hard-
driving hits, the precision quickness and grace of infield and
outfield, the sense of surplus power behind whatever is
done. There is the style of the spectator also: he becomes
expert in the ritual of insult, provocation, and braggadocio;
he boasts of the exaggerated prowess of his team and cries
down the skill and courage of the other; he develops sustained feuds, carrying on a guerrilla war with the umpires
and an organized badinage with the players, while he con-
sumes mountains of ritual hot dogs and drinks oceans of
ritual soda pop.

Each sport develops its own legendry, woven around 3
the "stars" who become folk heroes. The figures in
baseball's Hall of Fame have their sagas told and retold in
newspapers and biographies, and the Plutarchs who re-

count exploits become themselves notable figures in the culture. Some of these sports writers later become political columnists, perhaps on the assumption that politics itself is only a sport riddled with greater hypocrisy and that it takes a salty and hard-hitting sports writer to expose the politicians. The sports heroes become national possessions, like the Grand Canyon and the gold in Fort Knox. It is hard for a people who in their childhood have treasured the sports legendry as a cherished illusion to surrender it when they grow up.

QUESTIONS

1. The longer the phrases that are parallel in structure and meaning, the greater the sense of balance in sentences and paragraphs. How does Lerner vary the length of phrases and clauses balanced in the second and third sentences of paragraph 2? How does this variation in length prevent the sentences from sounding too formal?

2. Is the balance of phrases in paragraph 1 tighter than in paragraph 2? How does this balance of phrases give emphasis to key ideas and promote concision?

3. How exactly are sentences balanced in paragraph 3?

4. Could Lerner's analysis be extended to country or rock music or some other area of American life?

WRITING ASSIGNMENT

1. Discuss another American sport in light of one of the following statements:
   a. "The psychic basis of American mass sports is tribal and feudal."
   b. "There is a stylized relation of artist to mass audience in the sports."
   c. "Each sport develops its own legendry, woven around the 'stars' who become folk heroes."

Antithesis

When contrasting ideas are balanced in sentences and paragraphs, they are said to be in antithesis:

> History proves that dictatorships do not grow out of strong and successful governments, but out of weak and helpless ones.—Franklin D. Roosevelt

This moderate balancing to heighten the contrast of ideas is found often in modern writing, though usually in formal discussions. Like the exact balance of similar ideas, the balancing of sentences containing antithetical phrases is exceptional today. The following passage is the climax of a long book on the history of Roman society:

> Rome did not invent education, but she developed it on a scale unknown before, gave it state support, and formed the curriculum that persisted till our harassed youth. She did not invent the arch, the vault, or the dome, but she used them with such audacity and magnificence that in some fields her architecture has remained unequaled.—Will Durant, *Caesar and Christ*

CASEY MILLER AND KATE SWIFT

CASEY MILLER *has worked in publishing and as a free-lance writer and editor.* KATE SWIFT *is also a free-lance writer and editor and has been a science writer for the American Museum of Natural History, and a news director for the Yale School of Medicine. The discussion reprinted here is taken from* Words and Women *(1976)—a book concerned with the influence of language on the lives of women.*

"Manly" and "Womanly"

Webster's Third New International Dictionary (1966) de-   1
fines *manly* as "having qualities appropriate to a man: not
effeminate or timorous; bold, resolute, open in conduct or
bearing." The definition goes on to include "belonging or
appropriate in character to a man" (illustrated by "manly
sports" and "beer is a manly drink"), "of undaunted courage: gallant, brave." The same dictionary's definition of
womanly is less specific, relying heavily on phrases like
"marked by qualities characteristic of a woman"; "possessed of the character or behavior befitting a grown woman"; "characteristic of, belonging to, or suitable to a woman's nature and attitudes rather than to a man's." Two of
the examples provided are more informative: "convinced
that drawing was a waste of time, if not downright womanly
. . ." and "her usual womanly volubility."

In its definition of *manly* the Random House Dictionary   2
of the English Language (1967) supplies the words "strong,
brave, honorable, resolute, virile" as "qualities usually considered desirable in a man" and cites "feminine; weak,
cowardly," as antonyms. Its definitions of *womanly* are "like
or befitting a woman; feminine; not masculine or girlish"
and "in the manner of, or befitting, a woman." The same
dictionary's synonym essays for these words are worth quot-
ing in full because of the contrasts they provide:

> MANLY, MANFUL, MANNISH mean possessing the qual-
> ities of a man. MANLY implies possession of the most valu-
> able or desirable qualities a man can have, as dignity, hon-
> esty, directness, etc., in opposition to servility, insincerity,
> underhandedness, etc.: *A manly foe is better than a weak
> friend.* It also connotes courage, strength, and fortitude:
> *manly determination to face what comes.* MANFUL stresses
> the reference to courage, strength, and industry: *manful
> resistance.* MANNISH applies to that which resembles man: *a
> boy with a mannish voice.* Applied to a woman, the term is

derogatory, suggesting the aberrant possession of masculine characteristics: *a mannish girl; a mannish stride.*

WOMANLY, WOMANLIKE, WOMANISH, mean resembling a woman. WOMANLY implies resemblance in appropriate, fitting ways: *womanly decorum, modesty.* WOMANLIKE, a neutral synonym, may suggest mild disapproval or, more rarely, disgust: *Womanlike, she (he) burst into tears.* WOM-ANISH usually implies an inappropriate resemblance and suggests weakness or effeminacy: *womanish petulance.*

What are these parallel essays saying? That we perceive 3 males in terms of human qualities, females in terms of qualities—often negative—assigned to them as females. The qualities males possess may be good or bad, but those that come to mind when we consider what makes "a man" are positive. Women are defined circularly, through characteristics seen to be appropriate or inappropriate to women—not to human beings. In fact, when women exhibit positive attributes considered typical of men—dignity, honesty, courage, strength, or fortitude—they are thought of as aberrant. A person who is "womanlike" may (although the term is said to be "neutral") prompt a feeling of disgust.

The broad range of positive characteristics used to 4 define males could be used to define females too, of course, but they are not. The characteristics of women—weakness is among the most frequently cited—are something apart. At its entry for *woman* Webster's Third provides this list of "qualities considered distinctive of womanhood": "Gentleness, affection, and domesticity or on the other hand fickleness, superficiality, and folly." Among the "qualities considered distinctive of manhood" listed in the entry for *man*, no negative attributes detract from the "courage, strength, and vigor" the definers associate with males. According to this dictionary, *womanish* means "unsuitable to a man or to a strong character of either sex."

Lexicographers do not make up definitions out of thin 5 air. Their task is to record how words are used, it is not to say how they should be used. The examples they choose to illustrate meanings can therefore be especially revealing of cultural expectations. The American Heritage Dictionary (1969), which provides "manly courage" and "masculine charm," also gives us "Woman is fickle," "brought out the woman in him," "womanly virtue," "feminine allure," "feminine wiles," and "womanish tears." The same dictionary defines *effeminate*, which comes from the Latin *effeminare*, meaning "to make a woman out of," as "having the qualities associated with women; not characteristic of a man; unmanly" and "characterized by softness, weakness, or lack of force; not dynamic or vigorous." For synonyms one is referred to feminine.

Brother and *sister* and their derivatives have acquired   6
similar features. A columnist who wrote that "the political operatives known as 'Kennedy men' and 'Nixon men' have been sisters under their skins" could not possibly have called those adversaries "brothers," with all the mutual respect and loyalty that word implies. As the writer explained, "Like the colonel's lady and Judy O'Grady, their styles were different but their unwavering determination to win was strikingly similar." Other kinds of sisters for whom no comparable male siblings exist include the sob sister, the weak sister, and the plain ordinary sissy, whose counterpart in the brotherhood is the buddy, a real pal. Like *effeminate*, these female-related words and phrases are applied to males when a cutting insult is intended.

Masculine, manly, manlike, and other male-associated   7
words used to compliment men are frequently also considered complimentary when applied to women: thus a woman may be said to have manly determination, to have a masculine mind, to take adversity like a man, or to struggle manfully against overwhelming odds. The one male-associated word sometimes used to insult her is mannish, which may suggest she is too strong or aggressive to be a true woman, or that she is homosexually oriented, in which case mannish can become a code word.

Female-associated words, on the other hand, must be   8
hedged, as in "He has almost feminine intuition," if they are

used to describe a man without insulting him. He may be praised for admirable qualities defined as peculiar to women, but he cannot be said to have womanly compassion or womanlike tenderness. In exceptions to this rule—for example, when a medic on the battlefield or a sports figure in some postgame situation of unusual drama is said to be "as gentle as a woman"—the life-and-death quality of the circumstances makes its own ironic and terrible commentary on the standards of "masculinity" ordinarily expected of men.

The role expectations compressed into our male-positive-important and female-negative-trivial words are extremely damaging, as we are beginning to find out. The female stereotypes they convey are obvious, but the harm doesn't stop there. The inflexible demands made on males, which allow neither for variation nor for human frailty, are dehumanizing. They put a premium on a kind of perfection that can be achieved only through strength, courage, industry, and fortitude. These are admirable qualities, but if they are associated only with males, and their opposites are associated only with females, they become sex-related demands that few individuals can fulfill.

9

QUESTIONS

1. The Miller-Swift essay illustrates the use of moderate antithesis in ordinary exposition—antithesis arising naturally from a contrast of ideas. In how many ways do the writers contrast words and attitudes relating to assumed masculine and feminine qualities?

2. What elements in the second sentence of paragraph 3 are antithetical? What elements in later sentences of the same paragraph are also antithetical?

3. Identify antithetical phrases or clauses in the following:
   a. paragraph 5, sentence 2
   b. paragraph 6, sentence 3
   c. paragraph 8, sentence 2
   d. paragraph 9, sentence 1

How does the antithesis sharpen the contrast of ideas in these sentences?

4. Do you agree that language today makes "sex-related demands that few individuals can fulfill"? Do movies and television make similar demands?

WRITING ASSIGNMENTS

1. Discuss the extent to which the attitudes toward men and women contained in the dictionary definitions discussed are reflected in prevailing attitudes toward work or recreation. Draw on your own experience for examples. Disagree with Miller and Swift if your experience suggests attitudes different from those they identify.

2. Analyze your own conception of manliness and womanliness, contrasting ideas where possible and using moderate antithesis in some of your sentences.

MARTIN LUTHER KING, JR.

Born in 1929, MARTIN LUTHER KING, JR. *was ordained in 1947 in the Atlanta church where his father is still the pastor. He graduated from Morehouse College the following year and received his Ph.D. from Boston University in 1953. In 1955 he rose to prominence in America and throughout the world as leader of the Montgomery, Alabama, bus boycott, and he continued as one of the leaders of the Civil Rights Movement until his assassination at Memphis on April 4, 1968. "From my Christian background I gained my ideals, and from Gandhi my technique," King said. It is the technique of passive resistance that he describes here. King's style of writing reflects the cadences of his speeches — influenced strongly by the style of the Old Testament prophetic books, to name just one of many sources.*

Nonviolent Resistance

Oppressed people deal with their oppression in three characteristic ways. One way is acquiescence: the oppressed resign themselves to their doom. They tacitly adjust themselves to oppression, and thereby become conditioned to it. In every movement toward freedom some of the oppressed prefer to remain oppressed. Almost 2800 years ago Moses set out to lead the children of Israel from the slavery of Egypt to the freedom of the promised land. He soon discovered that slaves do not always welcome their deliverers. They become accustomed to being slaves. They would rather bear those ills they have, as Shakespeare pointed out, than flee to others that they know not of. They prefer the "fleshpots of Egypt" to the ordeals of emancipation.

There is such a thing as the freedom of exhaustion. Some people are so worn down by the yoke of oppression that they give up. A few years ago in the slum areas of Atlanta, a Negro guitarist used to sing almost daily: "Ben down so long that down don't bother me." This is the type of negative freedom and resignation that often engulfs the life of the oppressed.

But this is not the way out. To accept passively an unjust system is to cooperate with that system; thereby the oppressed become as evil as the oppressor. Noncooperation with evil is as much a moral obligation as is cooperation with good. The oppressed must never allow the conscience of the oppressor to slumber. Religion reminds every man that he is his brother's keeper. To accept injustice or segregation passively is to say to the oppressor that his actions are morally right. It is a way of allowing his conscience to fall asleep. At this moment the oppressed fails to be his brother's keeper. So acquiescence—while often the easier way—is not the moral way. It is the way of the coward. The Negro cannot win the respect of his oppressor by acquiescing; he merely increases the oppressor's arrogance and contempt. Acquiescence is interpreted as proof of the Negro's inferiority.

The Negro cannot win the respect of the white people of the South or the peoples of the world if he is willing to sell the future of his children for his personal and immediate comfort and safety.

A second way that oppressed people sometimes deal 4 with oppression is to resort to physical violence and corroding hatred. Violence often brings about momentary results. Nations have frequently won their independence in battle. But in spite of temporary victories, violence never brings permanent peace. It solves no social problem; it merely creates new and more complicated ones.

Violence as a way of achieving racial justice is both 5 impractical and immoral. It is impractical because it is a descending spiral ending in destruction for all. The old law of an eye for an eye leaves everybody blind. It is immoral because it seeks to humiliate the opponent rather than win his understanding; it seeks to annihilate rather than to convert. Violence is immoral because it thrives on hatred rather than love. It destroys community and makes brotherhood impossible. It leaves society in monologue rather than dialogue. Violence ends by defeating itself. It creates bitterness in the survivors and brutality in the destroyers. A voice echoes through time saying to every potential Peter, "Put up your sword." History is cluttered with the wreckage of nations that failed to follow this command.

If the American Negro and other victims of oppression 6 succumb to the temptation of using violence in the struggle for freedom, future generations will be the recipients of a desolate night of bitterness, and our chief legacy to them will be an endless reign of meaningless chaos. Violence is not the way.

The third way open to oppressed people in their quest 7 for freedom is the way of nonviolent resistance. Like the synthesis in Hegelian philosophy, the principle of nonviolent resistance seeks to reconcile the truths of two opposites— acquiescence and violence—while avoiding the extremes and immoralities of both. The nonviolent resister agrees with the person who acquiesces that one should not be physically aggressive toward his opponent; but he balances the equation by agreeing with the person of violence that evil must be resisted. He avoids the nonresistance of the former and the violent resistance of the latter. With nonviolent resistance, no individual or group need submit to any wrong, nor need anyone resort to violence in order to right a wrong.

8   It seems to me that this is the method that must guide the actions of the Negro in the present crisis in race relations. Through nonviolent resistance the Negro will be able to rise to the noble height of opposing the unjust system while loving the perpetrators of the system. The Negro must work passionately and unrelentingly for full stature as a citizen, but he must not use inferior methods to gain it. He must never come to terms with falsehood, malice, hate, or destruction.

9   Nonviolent resistance makes it possible for the Negro to remain in the South and struggle for his rights. The Negro's problem will not be solved by running away. He cannot listen to the glib suggestion of those who would urge him to migrate en masse to other sections of the country. By grasping his great opportunity in the South he can make a lasting contribution to the moral strength of the nation and set a sublime example of courage for generations yet unborn.

10   By nonviolent resistance, the Negro can also enlist all men of good will in his struggle for equality. The problem is not a purely racial one, with Negroes set against whites. In the end, it is not a struggle between people at all, but a tension between justice and injustice. Nonviolent resistance is not aimed against oppressors but against oppression. Under its banner consciences, not racial groups, are enlisted.

11   If the Negro is to achieve the goal of integration, he must organize himself into a militant and nonviolent mass movement. All three elements are indispensable. The movement for equality and justice can only be a success if it

has both a mass and militant character; the barriers to be overcome require both. Nonviolence is an imperative in order to bring about ultimate community.

A mass movement of militant quality that is not at the 12 same time committed to nonviolence tends to generate conflict, which in turn breeds anarchy. The support of the participants and the sympathy of the uncommitted are both inhibited by the threat that bloodshed will engulf the community. This reaction in turn encourages the opposition to threaten and resort to force. When, however, the mass movement repudiates violence while moving resolutely toward its goal, its opponents are revealed as the instigators and practitioners of violence if it occurs. Then public support is magnetically attracted to the advocates of nonviolence, while those who employ violence are literally disarmed by overwhelming sentiment against their stand.

QUESTIONS

1. Note the sentences that conclude paragraph 1:

> They would rather *bear those ills they have,* as Shakespeare pointed out,
>> than *flee to others that they know not of.*

> They prefer *the "fleshpots of Egypt"*
>> to *the ordeals of emancipation.*

What sentences in paragraph 5 contain antithetical elements? How exact is the antithesis? How many of these sentences are balanced to emphasize similar ideas?

2. How exact is the antithesis of ideas in paragraphs 8 and 10?

3. One way to moderate the tension of a passage containing considerable balance and antithesis is to vary the length of clauses or sentences. To what extent are the sentences of paragraphs 5, 8, and 10 varied in their length?

WRITING ASSIGNMENTS

1. Compare King's sentence style with that of another of his writings, for example, "Letter from Birmingham Jail." Discuss how the relative exactness of sentence balance and antithesis is used to moderate or increase the tension of the writing.

2. Compare a letter by Saint Paul in the King James version of the Bible with the rendering of the same letter in the Revised Standard Version. Comment on the differences you notice in the use of balance or antithesis.

Length

There is nothing inherently effective or ineffective, superior or inferior about short or long sentences, just as there is nothing inherently effective in a single note of the scale. How effective a sentence is depends on what it does in a paragraph or essay. The very short, disconnected sentences in a story by Ernest Hemingway effectively express the monotony a young war veteran feels on his return home, but would probably create a feeling of monotony in a piece of writing on another subject:

> He did not want any consequences. He did not want any consequences ever again. He wanted to live alone without consequences. Besides he did not really need a girl. The army had taught him that. It was all right to pose as though you had to have a girl. Nearly everybody did that. But it wasn't true. You did not need a girl. That was the funny thing.—"Soldier's Home"

Ordinary exposition, as we have seen, often starts with the main idea and develops it:

> She was a spirited-looking young woman, with dark curly hair cropped and parted on the side, a short oval face with straight eyebrows, and a large curved mouth.—Katherine Anne Porter

How much detail a writer can provide depends on how prominent the main ideas are—whether in a sentence consisting of a single core idea, followed by a series of modifiers as in Porter, or in one consisting of a series of connected core ideas or main clauses, modified as in this sentence:

> Morrall would duck his head in the huddle and if it was feasible he would call a play which took the ball laterally across the field—a pitchout, perhaps, and the play would eat up ground toward the girls, the ball carrier sprinting for the sidelines, with his running guards in front of him, running low, and behind them the linemen coming too, so that twenty-two men were converging on them at a fair clip.—George Plimpton

Plimpton is here depicting one connected action: a series of short sentences would have been inappropriate. Sentences longer and more modified than Plimpton's are uncommon in modern prose, mainly because of the difficulty in achieving clarity.

ERNEST HEMINGWAY

ERNEST HEMINGWAY (1899–1961), the American novelist and short story writer, as a young man discovered the values of the hunter in the northern Michigan woods where he spent much time with his physician father. He knew war from his experience as an ambulance corpsman in the First World War and later as a journalist observing the Spanish Civil War; he also observed the world of bullfighting, and traveled and hunted in Africa—experiences that shaped his interest in the codes through which the soldier, bullfighter, and hunter try to create a heroic ideal in a world where people create their own values. The title character in his story "The Short Happy Life of Francis Macomber," on an African hunting expedition with his wife and a guide, Robert Wilson, acts cowardly but later redeems himself in the hunting of a water buffalo. Hemingway's description of the encounter is notable for the continuous action shown in a single remarkable sentence.

The Shooting of the Buffalo

[1]The car was going a wild forty-five miles an hour across the open and as Macomber watched, the buffalo got bigger and bigger until he could see the gray, hairless, scabby look of one huge bull and how his neck was a part of

his shoulders and the shiny black of his horns as he gal-
loped a little behind the others that were strung out in that
steady plunging gait; and then, the car swaying as though it
had just jumped a road, they drew up close and he could see
the plunging hugeness of the bull, and the dust in his
sparsely haired hide, the wide boss of horn and his out-
stretched, wide-nostrilled muzzle, and he was raising his
rifle when Wilson shouted, "Not from the car, you fool!"
and he had no fear, only hatred of Wilson, while the brakes
clamped on and the car skidded, plowing sideways to an
almost stop and Wilson was out on one side and he on the
other, stumbling as his feet hit the still speeding-by of the
earth, and then he was shooting at the bull as he moved
away, hearing the bullets whunk into him, emptying his rifle
at him as he moved steadily away, finally remembering to
get his shots forward into the shoulder, and as he fumbled
to re-load, he saw the bull was down. ²Down on his knees,
his big head tossing, and seeing the other two still galloping
he shot at the leader and hit him. ³He shot again and missed
and he heard the *carawonging* roar as Wilson shot and saw
the leading bull slide forward onto his nose.

QUESTIONS

1. Read aloud the first sentence, noting the main clauses. In light
   of the considerable length of the sentence, how are these
   clauses given emphasis? Read the sentence aloud again, this
   time breaking it into shorter sentences. What change in effect
   do you notice? Is there an *equivalence* between the original
   sentence, particularly in its length, and the experience
   described?

2. Why does Hemingway end the sentence with *he saw the bull
   was down*?

3. Change the subordinate elements in sentence 2 into main
   clauses and the first two main clauses of sentence 3 into subordinate clauses. How do these changes affect the passage?

4. Use your dictionary to determine whether there are synonyms
   for the following words: *scabby, plunging, hugeness, speeding-*

by, whunk, carawonging. Would any synonyms you found be more suitable than Hemingway's words? How do you explain the absence of some of these words in the dictionary?

WRITING ASSIGNMENT

Rewrite the entire passage by breaking it into shorter sentences. In a second paragraph discuss the ways in which the revision alters the mood.

SHIRLEY JACKSON

SHIRLEY JACKSON *(1919–1965) gained immediate re-known in 1948 with the publication of her story "The Lottery." The remarkable stories, essays, and novels that followed established her as one of the finest postwar writers in America—particularly of the "cryptic, haunted tale." As the* New York Times *noted following her early death, there were two Shirley Jacksons—one of them capable of writing about the abnormal as if it were the everyday world, the other capable of describing "delights and turmoils of ordinary domestic life with detached hilarity." It is this second Shirley Jackson that we discover in this description of an ordinary domestic happening.*

The Night We All Had Grippe

My husband caught the grippe first, on a Friday, and snarled and shivered and complained until I prevailed upon him to go to bed. By Friday night both Laurie and the baby were feverish, and on Saturday Jannie and I began to cough and sniffle. In our family we take ill in different manners;

my husband is extremely annoyed at the whole procedure, and is convinced that his being sick is somebody else's fault, Laurie tends to become a little lightheaded and strew handkerchiefs around his room, Jannie coughs and coughs and coughs, the baby turns bright red, and I suffer in stoical silence, so long as everyone knows clearly that I am sick. We are each of us privately convinced that our own ailment is far more severe than anyone else's. At any rate, on Saturday night I put all the children into their beds, gave each of them half an aspirin and the usual fruit juice, covered them warmly, and then settled my husband down for the night with his glass of water and his cigarettes and matches and ash tray; he had decided to sleep in the guest room because it was warmer. At about ten o'clock I checked to see that all the children were covered and asleep and that Toby was in his place on the bottom half of the double-decker. I then took two sleeping pills and went to sleep in my own bed in my own room. Because my husband was in the guest room I slept on his side of the bed, next to the bed table. I put my cigarettes and matches on the end table next to the ash tray, along with a small glass of brandy, which I find more efficacious than cough medicine.

I woke up some time later to find Jannie standing be- 2 side the bed. "Can't sleep," she said. "Want to come in *your* bed."

"Come along," I said. "Bring your own pillow." 3

She went and got her pillow and her small pink blanket 4 and her glass of fruit juice, which she put on the floor next to the bed, since she had gotten the side without any end table. She put her pillow down, rolled herself in her pink blanket, and fell asleep. I went back to sleep, but some time later the baby came in, asking sleepily, "Where's Jannie?"

"She's here," I said. "Are you coming in bed with us?" 5

"Yes," said the baby. 6

"Go and get your pillow, then," I said. She returned 7 with her pillow, her books, her doll, her suitcase, and her fruit juice, which she put on the floor next to Jannie's. Then she crowded in comfortably next to Jannie and fell asleep. Eventually the pressure of the two of them began to force me uneasily toward the edge of the bed, so I rolled out wearily, took my pillow and my small glass of brandy and my cigarettes and matches and my ash tray and went into the guest room, where my husband was asleep. I pushed at him and he snarled, but finally moved over to the side next to the wall, and I put my cigarettes and matches and my brandy and my ash tray on the end table next to *his* cigarettes and matches and ash tray and tin glass of water and put my pillow on the bed and fell asleep. Shortly after this he woke me and asked me to let him get out of the bed, since it was too hot in the room to sleep and he was going back to his own bed.

He took his pillow and his cigarettes and matches and 8 his ash try and his tin glass of water and went padding off down the hall. In a few minutes Laurie came into the guest room where I had just fallen asleep again; he was carrying his pillow and his glass of fruit juice. "Too cold in my room," he said, and I moved out of the way and let him get into the bed on the side next to the wall. After a few minutes the dog came in, whining nervously, and came up onto the bed and curled himself up around Laurie, and I had to get out or be smothered. I gathered together what of my possessions I could, and made my way into my own room, where my husband was asleep with Jannie on one side and the baby on the other. Jannie woke up when I came in and said, "Own bed," so I helped her carry her pillow and her fruit juice and her pink blanket back to her own bed.

The minute Jannie got out of our bed the baby rolled 9 over and turned sideways, so there was no room for me. I could not get into the crib and I could not climb into the top half of the double-decker so since the dog was in the guest room I went and took the blanket off the crib and got into the bottom half of the double-decker, setting my brandy and my cigarettes and matches and my ash tray on the floor next to the bed. Shortly after that Jannie, who apparently felt left out, came in with her pillow and her pink blanket and her fruit juice and got up into the top half of the double-decker, leaving her fruit juice on the floor next to my brandy.

At about six in the morning the dog wanted to get out, 10 or else he wanted his bed back, because he came and stood next to me and howled. I got up and went downstairs, sneezing, and let him out, and then decided that since it had been so cold anyway in the bottom half of the double-decker I might as well stay downstairs and heat up some coffee and have that much warmth, at least. While I was waiting for the coffee to heat, Jannie came to the top of the stairs and asked if I would bring *her* something hot, and I heard Laurie stirring in the guest room, so I heated some milk and put it into a jug and decided that while I was at it I might just as well give everybody something hot, so I set out enough cups for everyone and brought out a coffeecake and put it on the tray and added some onion rolls for my husband, who does not eat coffeecake. When I brought the tray upstairs Laurie and Jannie were both in the guest room, giggling, so I put the tray down in there and heard Baby waking from our room in the front. I went to get her and she was sitting up in the bed talking to her father, who was only very slightly awake. "Play card?" she was asking brightly, and she opened her suitcase and dealt him onto the pillow next to his nose four diamonds to the ace jack and the seven of clubs.

I asked my husband if he would like some coffee and he 11 said it was terribly cold. I suggested that he come down into the guest room, where it was warmer. He and the baby followed me down to the guest room and my husband and Laurie got into the bed and the rest of us sat on the foot of the bed and I poured the coffee and the hot milk and gave the children coffeecake and my husband the onion rolls. Jannie decided to take her milk and coffeecake back into her own bed and since she had mislaid her pillow she took one from the guest room bed. Baby of course followed her, going first back into our room to pick up *her* pillow. My husband fell asleep again while I was pouring his coffee, and Laurie set his hot milk precariously on the headboard of the bed and asked me to get his pillow from wherever it was, so I went into the double-decker and got him the pillow from the top, which turned out to be Jannie's, and her pink blanket was with it.

I took my coffeecake and my coffee into my own bed 12 and had just settled down when Laurie came in to say cloudily that Daddy had kicked him out of bed and could he stay in here? I said of course and he said he would get a pillow and he came back in a minute with the one from the bottom half of the double-decker, which was mine. He went to sleep right away, and then the baby came in to get her books and her suitcase and decided to stay with her milk and her coffeecake so I left and went into the guest room and made my husband move over and sat *there* and had my coffee. Meanwhile Jannie had moved into the top half of the double-decker, looking for her pillow, and had taken instead the pillow from baby's bed and my glass of brandy and had settled down there to listen to Laurie's radio. I went downstairs to let the dog in and he came upstairs and got into his bed on the bottom half of the double-decker and while I was gone my husband had moved back over onto the accessible side of the guest-room bed so I went into Jannie's bed, which is rather too short, and I brought a pillow from the guest room, and my coffee.

At about nine o'clock the Sunday papers came and I 13 went down to get them, and at about nine-thirty everyone woke up. My husband had moved back into his own bed when Laurie and Baby vacated it for their own beds, Laurie driving Jannie into the guest room when he took back the top half of the double-decker, and my husband woke up at nine-thirty and found himself wrapped in Jannie's pink blanket, sleeping on Laurie's green pillow and with a piece of coffeecake and Baby's fruit-juice glass, not to mention the four diamonds to the ace jack and the seven of clubs. Laurie in the top half of the double-decker had my glass of brandy and my cigarettes and matches and the baby's pink pillow. The dog had my white pillow and my ash tray. Jannie in the guest room had one white pillow and one blue pillow and

two glasses of fruit juice and my husband's cigarettes and
matches and ash tray and Laurie's hot milk, besides her
own hot milk and coffeecake and her father's onion rolls.
The baby in her crib had her father's tin glass of water and
her suitcase and books and doll and a blue pillow from the
guest room, but no blanket.

The puzzle, is, of course, what became of the blanket 14
from Baby's bed? I took it off her crib and put it on the
bottom half of the double-decker, but the dog did not have it
when he woke up, and neither did any of the other beds. It
was a blue-patterned patchwork blanket, and has not been
seen since, and I would most particularly like to know where
it got to. As I say, we are very short of blankets.

QUESTIONS

1. Many of Jackson's sentences are exceptionally long because
   of the very large number of details they contain. Here is an
   example:

   > I pushed at him and he snarled, but finally moved over to the side
   > next to the wall, and I put my cigarettes and matches and my
   > brandy and my ashtray on the end table next to *his* cigarettes and
   > matches and ashtray and tin glass of water and put my pillow on
   > the bed and fell asleep [paragraph 7].

   What is gained in meaning or effect by the repetition and heavy
   coordination? Would the sentence be as effective if Jackson
   had broken it into segments?

2. Notice that Jackson repeats these details in the following sentence:

   > He took his pillow and his cigarettes and matches and his ash tray
   > and his tin glass of water and went padding off down the hall.

   Why are these details repeated? And what is gained by telling
   us what the other children brought into bed?

3. Jackson also depends heavily on coordination throughout the
   selection. What is the overall effect of this coordination and the

repetition of details? And how do they help Jackson convey her feelings? Does she show that the rest of the family felt the same?

4. Why does Jackson end with the statement, ". . . we are very short of blankets"?

5. Is Jackson making a point, or merely describing a humorous incident?

WRITING ASSIGNMENTS

1. Mark Twain finds humor in the manner in which a story is told. First discuss how Jackson's manner in telling her story creates humor. Then compare her manner with that of another humorist in this book—for example, Art Buchwald, Russell Baker, or Calvin Trillin.

2. Describe how you behave when you have a cold or the flu. Let the details of the experience reveal the qualities you display.

3. Rewrite paragraph 8, changing the sentence construction to produce a different effect. You might experiment with shortening one of the long sentences or subordinating some parts of them.

JOYCE MAYNARD

JOYCE MAYNARD, *the journalist and novelist, writes about American life and particularly the lives of women and the generation of the 1970s. She writes in her book* Looking Back *(1973): "My generation's definition of The Good Life is harder to arrive at. Our plans for the future are vague, because so many of us don't believe in planning, because we don't quite believe in the future. Perhaps we make too much of growing up with tension, from as far back as the Cuban Missile Crisis, but the fact is that the tension of the sixties put us in a kind of suspension." In the following passage she writes about another aspect of growing up.*

The Pressure of The Group

The pressure of The Group is strong in any period. There 1
was a new kind of pressure affecting us during the sixties
though—not just the push toward conformity and the fear
and distrust that people have by nature (and that public
schools seem to reinforce) of anything that's different. In
the fifties, I think, groups pretty rigidly conformed, but they
were indiscriminating too. A pair of bobby sox, a V-necked
sweater, and you were *in*. The sixties were a more critical-
minded, sophisticated time, full of more negative adjectives
than lavish superlatives, a time when it was easier to do
things wrong than to do them right. Products, ourselves, of
hours spent listening to TV commercials, we had become
comparative shoppers, suspicious and demanding, minutely
analyzing one another's actions and appearances—new
haircuts with unevenly trimmed sideburns, cowlicks, un-
matched socks, Band-Aids that, we suspected, concealed
pimples, new dresses, new shoes. We knew each other's
faces and bodies and wardrobes so well that any change
was noticed at once, the fuel for endless notes. That's why I
dressed so carefully mornings—I was about to face the
scrutiny of fifteen gossip-seeking girls, ten only slightly less
observant boys ready to imitate my voice and walk, and one
stern, prune-faced teacher who would check my spelling
and my long division with the care my enemies gave to my
hems. At every moment—even at home, with no one but
family there—I'd be conscious of what the other kids, The
Group, would think if they could see me now.

They ruled over us all—and over each other—like a 2
supreme court. Their presence was frightening, their judgments quick and firm and often damning, and the tightness
of the circle when I was in it only made the times when I was
outside seem more miserable. The hierarchy was re-
established a hundred times a day—in choosing partners
for science experiments, in study halls, when the exchange

of homework problems began, and at lunch. But most of all in note passing. We rarely needed to take notes, and so we passed them. We could have whispered easily enough, of course, or remained silent. (It wasn't ever that we had important things to say.) But note passing was far more intriguing, spylike. (Those were "The Man from U.N.C.L.E." days, all of us playing Illya Kuryakin.) Most of all, note passing was exclusive. Whispers were impermanent and could be overheard. Notes could be tightly sealed and folded, their journeys followed down the rows to make sure none was intercepted along the way. Getting a note, even an angry one, was always a compliment. Whenever I received one, I was amazed and grateful that I had made some slight impression on the world, that I was worthy of someone's time and ink. There were kids, I knew, whose letters died, like anonymous fan mail, unanswered and unread.

I think it was in notes more than in conversations or 3 Girl Scout meetings or Saturday mornings together on our bikes, that friendships and hatreds were established. We committed ourselves on paper to things we never would have said out loud (this seems odd to me now) and we saved them all—round-lettered, backhand messages written on blue-lined loose-leaf paper, the corners of old workbook pages, candy wrappers, lunch bags; they circulated around the classroom from desk to desk and year to year (once, in the seventh grade, we even had a pulley between desks). These were, I think, the greatest writing practice we got in school. Sometimes the notes contained news, stretched out in soap opera-type installment doses, to last us through an uneventful day. Stories leaked slowly—"Guess what?" would travel down my row to Becky till, at last, the teacher's mind deep in another matter, my note would cross the hardest point along its course, the latitudinal gulch between our rows (not within them) and she would unwrap it, folded like an origami bird, and write her answer, "What?" and pass it back to me. We wrote about TV shows watched the night before, about how we hated math and what our weekend and after-school plans were ("Are you going to walk home or take the bus?" "Short cut or long way around?").

Great wars, or so they seemed to us, were waged in notes, based on elaborate strategies we worked out, like homework, the night before. If things were getting dull, I'd plan to pick a fight with accusations of two-facedness (talking about someone behind his back was the most common offense) or cruelty to an underdog. Realizing early that I wasn't going to be a leader among the *in*, and refusing to simply follow, I became the champion of the class failures. The boy with the harelip, the girl who lived in a trailer and smelled bad, the one who tended to drool a little on her collar, I defended (enjoying the image of myself as kind and gentle benefactress, protecting the sensitive, the poet soul) from the group I loved and envied—for their coolness—and hated for the fact that they had never quite admitted me. I lectured Margie in suffering, histrionic moralistic tones ("You, who have always been popular, cannot know what it's like not to be. Think, for a moment, what Franny feels like when you laugh at her or lead her on to make a fool of herself, because she thinks that then you'll be her friend. I *know*—I know what it's like on this side of the fence . . .") Margie, a genuinely friendly girl, would be first puzzled and defensive. And then, as her troops moved in on me, sarcastic and coldly vicious. She'd write back to deny the charges, and there would be the ghastly period I always forgot about, setting out on my battles, when I seemed to be sinking and friendless, and wished I'd never started the whole thing.

QUESTIONS

1. Maynard varies the length of the sentences of paragraph 2 for emphasis. Which sentences are the shortest? Do they convey greater emphasis than the longer ones?

2. What sentences in paragraph 1 might the author break up to gain emphasis in the same way?

3. What does Maynard gain in paragraph 3 by coordinating the two parts of the second sentence with a semicolon? What is gained through the extreme use of coordination in the fifth sentence?

4. How many sentences in paragraph 4 are moderately periodic? How many of them are loose? How close are these sentences to the sentences of ordinary speech?

5. Was "the pressure of The Group" strong in your high school?

WRITING ASSIGNMENTS

1. Rewrite one of Maynard's paragraphs, achieving different emphasis in some of the sentences by reducing or expanding their length.

2. Analyze the pressures exerted by The Group in your high school experience. In the course of this analysis, compare your experience with Maynard's.

3. Discuss the similarities and differences you observe between boys in a group and girls in a group, at a particular age. Draw a conclusion about boys and girls in the early 1980s.

DICTION

Usage

None of us speaks or writes in the same way on all occasions: the differences depend on how formal the occasion is. A letter of application for a job will be more formal than a letter to a friend; a graduation speech will sound different from a locker-room conversation.

Each of us has a formal and informal language and, whether we know it or not, standards for judging their effectiveness. These standards come from the different groups we belong to—each group with its special idioms and vocabulary. Teenagers share a common language, which sometimes they have to translate for their parents; teenagers of a particular racial or ethnic background share a special dialect or language. So do teenagers of a particular city or region of the country. Though teenagers in Los Angeles share expressions and idioms with all other teenagers in the city, they may share a special dialect with their families and with their friends. At school they may share a language with their teachers different from the dialect they speak at home. Even a family may have its own private language—special words and expressions to describe acts and feelings.

Cutting across these differences is a standardized English we hear on television and read in newspapers—a language sometimes less colorful and personal than these other languages, but serving as a medium for communication among diverse groups of people, not only in the United States but in other English-speaking countries. This standard is of long growth, and it changes less than the informal language and slang of particular groups. This standard, represented in the readings in this book, falls between

191

two extremes—one formal and abstract in its content and sentences, the other informal and concrete:

> [Formal] Of the influences that shape men's actions, none is more powerful than the images we carry in our heads. Every subject is apt to invoke in our minds a specific image, made up of concrete information, misinformation, folklore, desire and prejudice. Thus, how people see themselves as a nation determines to a large extent how they will respond to any new challenge. The roles we play in our family life, particularly with respect to our children, depend greatly on what roles we assign ourselves in the society around us.—Gerald Holton, "The False Images of Science"

> [*Informal*] Bryant's specializes in barbecued spareribs and barbecued beef—the beef sliced from briskets of steer that have been cooked over a hickory fire for thirteen hours. When I'm away from Kansas City and depressed, I try to envision someone walking up to the counterman at Bryant's and ordering a beef sandwich to go—for me. The counterman tosses a couple of pieces of bread onto the counter, grabs a half-pound of beef from the pile next to him, slaps it onto the bread, brushes on some sauce in almost the same motion, and then wraps it all up in two thicknesses of butcher paper in a futile attempt to keep the customer's hand dry as he carries off his prize.—Calvin Trillin, *American Fried*

The abstract ideas of Holton could be stated less formally. But usage is a matter of convention and occasion as well as personal choice, and if we would not be surprised to find his ideas stated informally, we probably would be surprised to find barbecue described in formal language.

As a rule, informal writing is closer to the patterns of everyday speech; formal writing seems impersonal if it departs widely from these patterns. Much standard writing today has both formal and informal features: we find colloquialisms (*grabs a half-pound of beef, slaps it onto*) in company with abstract or less familiar words (*envision*). We also find striking balance and antithesis—a feature of formal sentences—in company with looser, more familiar phrasing and expressions:

> What I would like to know is: how should I feel about the earth, these days? Where has all the old nature gone? What became of the wild, writhing, unapproachable mass of the life of the world, and what happened to our old, panicky excitement about it? Just in fifty

years, since I was a small boy in a suburban town, the world has become a structure of steel and plastic intelligible and diminished.—Lewis Thomas, "A Trip Abroad"

NEWSWEEK

In its special fiftieth anniversary issue, NEWSWEEK *magazine traced the history of five families in Springfield, Ohio—typical of the life of Americans from 1933 to 1983. The description here is of Dick Hatfield, the "guru of cool" in Springfield in the 1950s. Dick was so well known that advertisers used words he invented, paying tribute to "his gift of unintelligible gab and his authority as an arbiter of cool taste." On returning home from the Armed Forces Reserves, he worked for the railroad and as a disc jockey before taking a job with a steel company.* Newsweek *concludes: "Nothing remains now of the age of cool in Springfield except its last few survivors, baldish men in their middle and late 40s with two or three divorces behind them, still driving the old cruising routes as if in familiar motion they could catch up with the past and recover the last innocent time."*

Being Cool

Being cool, Hatfield remembers now, had to do first with 1
how you looked and what you wore. Cool guys did not wear
leather jackets or chinos and sweat socks, either. Cool guys
wore pleated gray-flannel pants, custom pegged by a
needlewoman named Ma Weiner for 75 cents a pair, with a
skinny belt buckled on the side and a shirt with the billowing
Mr. B collar popularized by the singer Billy Eckstine, who
was *very* cool. Cool guys had cool walks, too, working at
them till they had just the right hunch to the shoulders, just

the right swing to the arms. "Sometimes," Hatfield recalls, "you would just *stand* there and be cool. Some chick would come by and say, 'He's cool,' just by the way you stood."

Cool guys did not sit home watching family sitcoms or 2 the Mouseketeers. When they were home at all, cool guys watched "77 Sunset Strip" mostly for Kookie, the eighth avatar of cool, or Dick Clark's "American Bandstand"; it was the constant intention of Hatfield's crowd to go to Philly, where the Bandstand was produced, and really show them how to dance, but somehow they never saved up enough money. They did their stepping instead at El Som (for sombrero) dances at the Y on football and basketball Friday nights, or later, when they came of drinking age, at upscale clubs like the Melody Showbar—the Four Freshmen played there once—or funkier joints like the Frolics out on Lagonda Avenue. Hatfield, ultracool, preferred the Frolics for its ambience, which included a bouncer with a .357 magnum and featured a rhythm-and-blues band presided over by a large black man named H-Bomb Ferguson. You could do the dirty boogie at the Frolics, "a modified jitter-bug," as Hatfield remembered it, "with like more hips," and find out quickly which guys and chicks were truly cool.

Cool guys hung out, at Frisch's Big Boy for the burgers, 3 or under the clock at Woolworth's for the girl-watching, or at East High Billiards for the action; Hatfield was taking tickets there one March day in 1954 when the great Willie Mosconi came in and sank 526 straight balls for a world's record. But mostly cool guys cruised, customizing their cars and living an automotive life later imitated by art in the film "American Graffiti." Hatfield's wheels supported a mink-white Chevy with scallops in three colors, regatta blue, Bahama blue and Inca gray, and the what-me-worry like-ness of Alfred E. Neuman hand-done on the gas cap by a local painter. For a final touch of style, he installed a dummy telephone with a real-sounding Ma Bell ring, activated by a push button under the dashboard. Sometimes he would set it off with his knee at Frisch's just as one of the carhop girls came over to take his order. "Hold on a second, will you, honey," he would say, picking up the receiver. "I got an important call here."

The cruising route favored by cool guys was downtown 4 when it still *was* downtown, its streets alive with life; Hatfield figured he spent very nearly every evening for four years going around the core block in the heart of the city, so many times he imagined that his tire tracks must have been indelibly imprinted in the left-hand lane. You cruised for a while, checking out the happenings; then you did the joints, O'Brien's Tavern at 9, then the Savoy, and then, at 1 a.m., the Alibi or the Shady Lady Saloon.

But suddenly everything began changing, and the cool 5 life began to chill. Hatfield noticed it around the time he was called up into the Reserves in 1960, at 22. Guys were getting restless, itchy for something new; some were disappearing into the military, some into marriages. The music was changing; five white guys named the Beach Boys were bleaching out Chuck Berry's black sound, and the dirty boogie was washed under by the twist, the pony and the mashed potato. "It was like everybody knew how to do *our* dance," Hatfield recalls. "The dirty boogie was no longer new." Downtown was changing, too, emptying out and beginning to go seedy. The difference struck Hatfield one day in the early '60s when he pulled up at East High Billiards and found a parking space right across the street. There was nobody around; being cool wasn't cool anymore.

QUESTIONS

1. How do the details help to explain the meaning of the phrase "being cool" to teenagers in the late 1950s? Does *Newsweek* state the meaning directly?

2. What other slang does *Newsweek* identify? How do you discover the meaning of these words or expressions?

3. What does the language of these teenagers tell you about their world and values? Is the *Newsweek* account a sympathetic one? Or is *Newsweek* merely reporting what happened to teenagers in the 1950s?

4. How different is the voice of *Newsweek* from the voice of Hatfield and the other teenagers described? What words and sentences tell you that the voices are different?

5. How different are Hatfield's world and values from your own? What language expresses the values of teenagers today? What influence does popular music have on current teenager slang and values?

WRITING ASSIGNMENTS

1. Analyze the language of two sports columnists, noting the degree of formality or informality in each, and the extent to which each depends on sports jargon. Use your analysis to define the difference in the voice of each writer.

2. Describe a special jargon or slang that you share with friends or your family. Discuss the special meanings of these words and the values they express.

3. Every profession and trade has a special language or jargon that provides a "shorthand" or concise means of communicating. Examine a trade journal or popular magazine directed to a particular audience—*Popular Mechanics, Field and Stream, Stereo Review*—and identify particular words and phrases of this kind. Discuss the special meanings conveyed by several of these words or phrases.

4. Examine an issue of a professional journal in political science, sociology, medicine or a similar field to find out how alike the various articles are in style. Consider the level of the writing as well as the choice of words. Take note especially of any special language or jargon.

DERECK WILLIAMSON

> DERECK WILLIAMSON *was a frequent contributor of articles to the "Phoenix Nest" column of the* Saturday Review, *an important magazine devoted to politics and the arts. The column usually published humorous*

sketches on a variety of subjects. From Williamson the reader could learn how to mix cement or make a fake hi-fi system (the secret is to generate a "clutter" of wires and equipment). In the essay reprinted here, Williamson satirizes the language of rule books in an unusual way.

Tell It Like It Was

A browse through the Little League Baseball Official Rules 1
indicates that times have changed since my sandlot baseball days. I'll tell it like it is now, and then try to tell it like it was then.

> PLAYING EQUIPMENT—Each team must have at least twelve conventional baseball uniforms. The Official Little League Shoulder Patch must be affixed to the upper left sleeve of the uniform blouse. Games may not be played except in uniforms. These uniforms are the property of the League, and are to be loaned to the players for such period as the League may determine.

Playing equipment—Each guy came out to the ballfield 2
looking like a bum. Shirts were optional. Patches went on pants because they were torn up sliding. Anybody wearing a clean or neat garment was jumped on, and rubbed around in the dirt.

> Each League must provide in each dugout at least six (6) protective helmets approved by Little League Headquarters. The wearing of such approved helmets by the batter, all base runners, and coaches is mandatory. Shoes with metal spikes or cleats are prohibited. Catchers must wear masks during practice, pitcher warm-up, and regular games.

There were no dugouts—only the ditch that ran across 3
the field just behind second base. In the ditch were at least sixty (60) frogs. Headgear was optional. The most popular

were brimless caps and capless brims. There was only one helmet in the league—a leather aviator's helmet, with goggles, owned by Spike Snyder. Shoes with metal spikes or cleats could not be worn, because they all belonged to big brothers in high school and didn't fit. Catchers didn't wear masks. To avoid being hit in the head they stood eight feet behind the plate and let the ball bounce once.

> PITCHERS—Any player on the team roster may pitch. A player shall not pitch in more than six (6) innings in a calendar week. Delivery of a single pitch shall constitute having pitched in an inning.

Pitchers—Any player who owned the ball pitched. A player could not pitch on more than seven (7) days in a calendar week, or more than one hundred (100) innings a day, because it got too dark. Delivery of a pitch straight down and the pitcher falling senseless beside the ball constituted exhaustion.   4

> EQUIPMENT—The ball shall weigh not less than five ounces or more than five and one-quarter (5¼) ounces avoirdupois. It shall measure not less than nine (9) inches nor more than nine and one-quarter (9¼) inches in circumference. The bat shall be round and made of wood. It shall not be more than thirty-three (33) inches in length. Bats may be taped for a distance not exceeding sixteen (16) inches from the small end. The first baseman is the only fielder who may wear a mitt. All other fielders must use fielder's gloves.

Equipment—The ball could be of any weight, and anybody stupid enough to say "avoirdupois" out loud deserved what he got. Circumferences of the ball depended on the amount of tape wrapped around it. Sometimes the tape came loose when you hit the ball, and the circumference changed rapidly. Sometimes it was just tape by the time it reached the fielder, and the circumference was zero (0).   5

Bats were made of wood and were round unless they had been used for hitting rocks. After bats were broken   6 they were taped for their entire length and it was hard to tell which was the small end. The first baseman was lucky if he got either a mitt or a glove. The only mitt belonged to the fat right fielder, who wore it even when he was at bat.

> PROTESTS—Protests shall be considered only when based on the violation or interpretation of a playing rule or the use of an ineligible player. No protest shall be considered on a decision involving an umpire's judgment.

Protests—A protest was considered only when you 7 were awfully sure you could lick the other guy. There was no umpire, unless some kid was on crutches and couldn't play. Nobody paid any attention to his calls, because he was just another kid.

> FIELD DECORUM—The actions of players, managers, coaches, umpires, and League officials must be above reproach.

Field decorum—There were no managers, or coaches, 8 or any of those big people. Only players who swore and spat. Anyone caught being above reproach got clobbered.

QUESTIONS

1. Williamson contrasts two kinds of baseball through two attitudes toward it—attitudes expressed not only in the details of the games but in ways of talking or writing about it. What is the chief difference between the language of Little League Baseball Official Rules and that of his account of sandlot baseball?
2. Is Williamson approving of Little League baseball, critical of it, or merely amused? Or is his feeling neutral? Do you share his attitude?

WRITING ASSIGNMENTS

1. Rewrite the Little League Baseball Official Rules for the information of children playing the game. Then analyze the changes

that you made in vocabulary and sentence construction and the reasons for these changes.

2. Write a one-paragraph letter to a former high-school teacher asking for advice about a present course or a possible future career. Write a second one-paragraph letter to a friend who has taken the course or embarked on such a career, asking the same advice. In a third paragraph discuss the adjustments in usage you made and the reasons for them.

Tone

By the tone of a piece of writing, we mean the reflection of the attitude of the writer toward the subject or reader. The possibilities are many: our writing may be sarcastic, bitter, angry, mocking, whimsical, facetious, joyful, admiring—and even indifferent. And we can reveal this attitude in numerous ways. We can state it directly, as H. L. Mencken does in an essay on education:

> There should be more sympathy for school children. The idea that they are happy is of a piece with the idea that the lobster in the pot is happy.

Or we can express it indirectly: we may exaggerate to the point of absurdity for a humorous effect; or understate so there is an obvious discrepancy between what we show and what we say, producing an ironic effect; or present the facts without deliberate exaggeration or understatement, our attitude emerging in the selection of facts or details.

In short, the tone of a paragraph or essay is conveyed by the voice we choose in writing. The voice of the writer depends on the rhythms and nuances of speech, carried into the modulations and rhythms of the sentences and paragraphs. False starts in writing are often failures to discover the voice or tone we want. Too formal a sentence or choice of words may create an impression of distance or unconcern; a highly informal style may suggest over-friendliness or lack of seriousness or flippancy. We find as we write that we need to adjust the tone. For an essay need not express one dominant tone: the expression of our attitude changes as we turn to new ideas and details.

CALVIN TRILLIN

CALVIN TRILLIN *has since 1967 written about his travels in the United States for* The New Yorker, *in a series called "U.S. Journal." His articles for various magazines*

on eating habits in America are collected in his book
American Fried, *subtitled "Adventures of a Happy*
Eater." Trillin here describes the annual crawfish eating
contest at Breaux Bridge, Louisiana—the Crawfish
Capital of the World by resolution of the state legisla-
ture. At the contest, a fraternity boy jeers when a
crawfish Trillin enters in a race loses.

The Crawfish-Eating Contest

Somehow, the fraternity boy did not impress me as a threat   1
to my enjoyment, maybe because he did not treat ten o'clock
in the morning as a time to be drinking sodapop wine but as
a time to be drinking a nice old-fashioned can of Schlitz. I
was also untroubled by the displays of crawfish T-shirts,
crawfish beer mugs, and crawfish aprons. Breaux Bridge
could shine through almost any amount of commercialism
and Lauderdale-ism as, in fact, the Crawfish Capital of the
World. Breaux Bridge people are incapable of turning out
the kind of leaden junk food usually peddled to tourists even
when they try. Woody Marshall, for instance, invented
something called a crawfish dog—he is, as I have said, a
man of many accomplishments—and although that may
sound pretty awful, it happens to be delicious, except for the
hotdog bun. (The recipe in the official program says, "Make
roux with shortening and flour, cook until light brown, sauté
onions, add crawfish and fat and water and seasoning.
Cook 20 minutes and serve on an open-face hotdog bun." If
someone could figure out how to make hotdogs taste like
crawfish dogs, he could bring back baseball.) The same
booth that served beer and ordinary hotdogs sold, for fifty
cents, something called a crawfish patty, which is also
known as crawfish pie, and which if served in some
expense-account French restaurant in New York would keep
that restaurant jammed on rainy recession Tuesday eve-

nings. ("Six dollars, is of course, a lot to ask for an appetizer," the review would say, "but the exquisite *Écrevisses à la Teche* at the Cajun d'Or happen to be worth every penny of it.")

A crawfish patty is what I happened to be eating when 2 the time for the crawfish-eating contest approached. I was also drinking a glass (nonbreakable plastic) of non-sodapop wine and reclining under an oak tree and listening to some fine music played by Celbert Cormier and his Musical Kings (a violin, an accordion, two electric guitars, and a drum) and discussing the logistics involved in timing our departure the next day in a way that would put us at a restaurant called The Yellow Bowl in Jeannerette around mealtime. Peter Wolf, who was doing all of those things himself, was saying that we had waited too late to register and would be unable to participate, since only ten eaters are allowed. (Otherwise, everyone would be up there gobbling up the free crawfish.) I happened to know that only nine people had registered, but I also knew that they included such formidable eaters as the oyster-eating champion of Louisiana, who had downed fifteen and a half dozen oysters in an hour at the Oyster Festival in Galliano—a festival that was somehow kept secret from me for years. I also knew that we had been invited to dinner that evening at the home of Mrs. Harris Champagne, who, according to experts in Breaux Bridge, was the first person to serve crawfish *étouffée* in a restaurant, and I realized that sitting down to a plate of her legendary *étouffée* when already stuffed with boiled would be an act of irresponsibility. It had also occurred to me that if I did become full before approaching Mrs. Champagne's table, I would prefer to become full of patties. Boiled, after all, is not my sport. I told Peter it was a shame we hadn't registered in time.

The oyster-eating champion, a specialist away from his 3 specialty, was the first contestant to drop out. "I'm not full. I could have a hotdog," he said, when I asked him what happened. "But these things don't taste right." The first female contestant in the history of the contest, a trim secretary, dropped out some time later. ("I'm not as hungry as I thought I was," she said.) The winner, Chester McGear, looked like one of the fraternity boys everyone had been so worried about, although he had actually graduated a couple of years before. He wore a sweatshirt emblematic of having consumed ten pitchers of beer in some tavern in Chicago, and he had a small rooting section that chanted "Go, Chester, Go!" or *"Allons, Chester, Allons!"* or "Come on, Chester, Eat That Meat!" He was on his twenty-second pound of crawfish when his final opponent dropped out. I was pleased to see that McGear acted the part of a traditional eating champion. They never admit to being full. My father always used to tell me about a boy who won a pie-eating contest in St. Joe by eating thirty-three pies and then said, "I wooda ate more but my ma was calling me for supper." When the reporters went up on the stand to interview McGear, he remained at his place, and as he answered the questions he absently reached toward the platter in front of him and peeled crawfish and popped them into his mouth, like a man working on the peanut bowl during a cocktail party.

QUESTIONS

1. What is Trillin's attitude toward Breaux Bridge and toward the crawfish-eating contest? How do you discover it—through what Trillin says or implies or shows?

2. What is his attitude toward the various contestants—in particular, Chester McGear?

3. Do you find one dominant tone in Trillin's narrative, or does the tone change?

4. Mark Twain finds humor in the manner of telling a story. What kind of humor do you find in the manner or way Trillin tells his?

5. How informal is the writing? How close to the spoken idiom are Trillin's sentences?

WRITING ASSIGNMENTS

1. Describe one of the following, establishing a dominant tone through the details you select. Let the reader discover your attitude through these details: don't state it directly.
   a. a meeting of a school organization
   b. a meeting of a social or sports club
   c. an exhibition or fair
   d. a contest
2. Describe the same event from a different point of view. Establish a different tone through a different selection of detail.

LIANE ELLISON NORMAN

> LIANE ELLISON NORMAN, *who teaches English at the University of Pittsburgh, has written on a range of subjects including education and the life of women in the United States. As her essay on college students shows, Norman uses the personal essay to write about important issues—with humor and insight. The unusual analogy that develops the essay is particularly worth study.*

Pedestrian Students and High-Flying Squirrels

The squirrel is curious. He darts and edges, profile first, one bright black eye on me, the other alert for enemies on the other side. Like a fencer, he faces both ways, for every impulse toward me, an impulse away. His tail is airy. He flicks and flourishes it, taking readings of some subtle kind.

I am enjoying a reprieve of warm sun in a season of rain and impending frost. Around me today is the wine of the garden's final ripening. On the zucchini, planted late, the flagrant blossoms flare and decline in a day's time.

I am sitting on the front porch thinking about my stu- 3 dents. Many of them earnestly and ardently want me to teach them to be hacks. Give us ten tricks, they plead, ten nifty fail-safe ways to write a news story. Don't make us think our way through these problems, they storm (and when I am insistent that thinking *is* the trick, "You never listen to us," they complain.) Who cares about the First Amendment? they sneer. What are John Peter Zenger and Hugo Black to us? Teach us how to earn a living. They will be content, they explain, with know-how and jobs, satisfied to do no more than cover the tedium of school board and weather.

Under the rebellion, there is a plaintive panic. What if, 4 on the job—assuming there is a job to be on—they fear-lessly defend the free press against government, grand jury, and media monopoly, but don't know how to write an obitu-ary. Shouldn't obituaries come first?

I hope not, but even obituaries need good information 5 and firm prose, and both, I say, require clear thought.

The squirrel does not share my meditation. He grows 6 tired of inquiring into me. His dismissive tail floats out behind as he takes a running leap into the tree. Up the bark he goes and onto a branch, where he crashes through the leaves. He soars from slender perch to slender perch, shak-ing up the tree as if he were the west wind. What a madcap he is, to go racing from one twig that dips under him to another at those heights!

His acrobatic clamor loosens buckeyes in their prickly 7 armor. They drop, break open, and he is down the tree in a twinkling, picking, choosing. He finds what he wants and carries it, an outsize nut which is burnished like a fine cello, across the lawn, up a pole, and across the tightrope tele-phone line to the other side, where he disappears in maple foliage.

Some inner clock or calendar tells him to stock his 8 larder against the deep snows and hard times that are coming. I have heard that squirrels are fuzzy-minded, that they collect their winter groceries and store them, and then forget where they are cached. But this squirrel is purposeful; he appears to know he'd better look ahead. Faced with necessity, he is prudent, but not fearful. He prances and flies as he goes about his task of preparation, and he never fails to look into whatever startles his attention.

Though he is not an ordinary pedestrian, crossing the 9 street far above, I sometimes see the mangled fur of a squirrel on the street, with no flirtation left. Even a high-flying squirrel may zap himself on an aerial live wire. His days are dangerous and his winters are lean, but still he lays in provisions the way a trapeze artist goes about his work, with daring and dash.

For the squirrel, there is no work but living. He gathers 10 food, reproduces, tends the children for a while, and stays out of danger. Doing these things with style is what distinguishes him. But for my students, unemployment looms as large as the horizon itself. Their anxiety has cause. And yet, what good is it? Ten tricks or no ten tricks, there are not enough jobs. The well-trained, well-educated stand in line for unemployment checks with the unfortunates and the drifters. Neither skill nor virtue holds certain promise. This being so, I wonder, why should these students not demand, for the well-being of their souls, the liberation of their minds?

It grieves me that they want to be pedestrians, earth- 11 bound and always careful. You ask too much, they say. What you want is painful and unfair. There are a multitude of pressures that instruct them to train, not free, themselves.

Many of them are the first generation to go to college; 12 family aspirations are in their trust. Advisers and models tell them to be doctors, lawyers, engineers, cops, and public-relations people; no one ever tells them they can be poets, philosophers, farmers, inventors, or wizards. Their elders are anxious too; they reject the eccentric and the novel. And, realism notwithstanding, they cling to talismanic determination; play it safe and do things right and I, each one thinks, will get a job even though others won't.

I tell them fondly of my college days, which were a dizzy 13 time (as I think the squirrel's time must be), as I let loose and pitched from fairly firm stands into the space of intellect and imagination, never quite sure what solid branch I would light on. That was the most useful thing I learned, the practical advantage (not to mention the exhilaration) of launching out to find where my propellant mind could take me.

A luxury? one student ponders, a little wistfully.   14

Yes, luxury, and yet necessity, and it aroused that flight, 15 a fierce unappeasable appetite to know and to essay. The luxury I speak of is not like other privileges of wealth and power that must be hoarded to be had. If jobs are scarce, the heady regions of treetop adventure are not. Flight and gaiety cost nothing, though of course they may cost everything.

The squirrel, my frisky analogue, is not perfectly free. 16 He must go on all fours, however nimbly he does it. Dogs are always after him, and when he barely escapes, they rant up the tree as he dodges among the branches that give under his small weight. He feeds on summer's plenty and pays the price of strontium in his bones. He is no freer of industrial ordure than I am. He lives, mates, and dies (no obituary, first or last, for him), but still he plunges and balances, risking his neck because it is his nature.

I like the little squirrel for his simplicity and bravery. He 17 will never get ahead in life, never find a good job, never settle down, never be safe. There are no sure-fire tricks to make it as a squirrel.

QUESTIONS

1. What is the difference in Norman's attitude toward the squirrel and toward the students she teaches? Do you hear a different tone of voice in the paragraphs dealing with each?

2. Does the essay end in the same tone in which it begins?

3. In what ways does the writer resemble the squirrel? How does she establish these points of resemblance?

4. Do you agree with Norman's characterization of college students today? Are the students you know different from the journalism students she is describing?

5. What point is the writer making in her final sentence, "There are no sure-fire tricks to make it as a squirrel"? Could this sentence be taken as the central idea or thesis of the essay?

WRITING ASSIGNMENT

Discuss your own goals in life, what you hope to gain from a college education, and what experiences and circumstances have shaped you as a student. In the course of your essay, discuss the extent to which you fit the characterization of college students in the essay.

JAMES BALDWIN

JAMES BALDWIN *is known throughout the world for his stories, novels, and plays, and particularly for his essays on black life in America. Baldwin, in an essay first published in 1948 and reprinted in his famous book,* Notes of a Native Son, *says that the Harlem he has known from boyhood wears a face that "... is, indeed, somewhat excessively casual and may not be as open or as careless as it seems." In a later essay on Harlem of the 1950s, in his book* Nobody Knows My Name, *Baldwin describes that face from a different point of view.*

Fifth Avenue, Uptown

There is a housing project standing now where the house in which we grew up once stood, and one of those stunted city trees is snarling where our doorway used to be. This is on the rehabilitated side of the avenue. The other side of the avenue—for progress takes time—has not been rehabilitated yet and it looks exactly as it looked in the days when we sat with our noses pressed against the windowpane, longing to be allowed to go "across the street." The grocery store which gave us credit is still there, and there can be no doubt that it is still giving credit. The people in the project certainly need it—far more, indeed, than they ever needed the project. The last time I passed by, the Jewish proprietor was still standing among his shelves, looking sadder and heavier but scarcely any older. Farther down the block stands the shoe-repair store in which our shoes were repaired until reparation became impossible and in which, then, we bought all our "new" ones. The Negro proprietor is still in the window, head down, working at the leather.

These two, I imagine, could tell a long tale if they would 2 (perhaps they would be glad to if they could), having watched so many, for so long, struggling in the fishhooks, the barbed wire, of this avenue.

The avenue is elsewhere the renowned and elegant 3 Fifth. The area I am describing, which, in today's gang parlance, would be called "the turf," is bounded by Lenox Avenue on the west, the Harlem River on the east, 135th Street on the north, and 130th Street on the south. We never lived beyond these boundaries; this is where we grew up. Walking along 145th Street—for example—familiar as it is, and similar, does not have the same impact because I do not know any of the people on the block. But when I turn east on 131st Street and Lenox Avenue, there is first a soda-pop joint, then a shoeshine "parlor," then a grocery story, then a dry cleaners', then the houses. All along the street there are people who watched me grow up, people who grew up with me, people I watched grow up along with my brothers and sisters; and, sometimes in my arms, sometimes underfoot, sometimes at my shoulder—or on it—their children, a riot, a forest of children, who include my nieces and nephews.

When we reach the end of this long block, we find 4 ourselves on wide, filthy, hostile Fifth Avenue, facing that project which hangs over the avenue like a monument to the folly, and the cowardice, of good intentions. All along the block, for anyone who knows it, are immense human gaps, like craters. These gaps are not created merely by those who have moved away, inevitably into some other ghetto; or by those who have risen, almost always into a greater capacity for self-loathing and self-delusion; or yet by those who, by whatever means—War II, the Korean war, a policeman's gun or billy, a gang war, a brawl, madness, an overdose of heroin, or, simply, unnatural exhaustion—are dead. I am talking about those who are left, and I am talking principally about the young. What are they doing? Well, some, a minority, are fanatical churchgoers, members of the more extreme of the Holy Roller sects. Many, many more are "moslems," by affiliation or sympathy, that is to say that they are united by nothing more—and nothing less—than a hatred of the white world and all its works. They are present, for example, at every Buy Black street-corner meeting—meetings in which the speaker urges his hearers to cease trading with white men and establish a separate economy. Neither the speaker nor his hearers can possibly do this, of course, since Negroes do not own General Motors or RCA or the A & P, nor, indeed, do they own more than a wholly insufficient fraction of anything else in Harlem (those who *do* own anything are more interested in their profits than in their fellows). But these meetings nevertheless keep alive in the participators a certain pride of bitterness without which, however futile this bitterness may be, they could scarcely remain alive at all. Many have given up. They stay home and watch the TV screen, living on the earnings of their parents, cousins, brothers, or uncles, and only leave the house to go to the movies or to the nearest bar. "How're you making it?" one may ask, running into them along the block, or in the bar. "Oh, I'm TV-ing it"; with the saddest, sweetest, most shamefaced of smiles, and from a great distance. This distance one is compelled to respect; anyone who has traveled so far will not easily be dragged again into the world. There are further retreats, of course, than the TV screen or the bar. There are those who are simply sitting on their stoops, "stoned," animated for a moment only, and hideously, by the approach of someone who may lend them the money for a "fix." Or by the approach of someone from whom they can purchase it, one of the shrewd ones, on the way to prison or just coming out.

And the others, who have avoided all of these deaths, 5 get up in the morning and go downtown to meet "the man." They work in the white man's world all day and come home in the evening to this fetid block. They struggle to instill in their children some private sense of honor or dignity which will help the child to survive. This means, of course, that they must struggle, stolidly, incessantly, to keep this sense alive in themselves, in spite of the insults, the indifference, and the cruelty they are certain to encounter in their working day. They patiently browbeat the landlord into fixing the heat, the plaster, the plumbing; this demands prodigious patience; nor is patience usually enough. In trying to make their hovels habitable, they are perpetually throwing good money after bad. Such frustration, so long endured, is driving many strong, admirable men and women whose only crime is color to the very gates of paranoia.

One remembers them from another time—playing 6 handball in the playground, going to church, wondering if they were going to be promoted at school. One remembers them going off to war—gladly, to escape this block. One remembers their return. Perhaps one remembers their wedding day. And one sees where the girl is now—vainly looking for salvation from some other embittered, trussed, and struggling boy—and sees the all-but-abandoned children in the streets.

QUESTIONS

1. What is Baldwin's general attitude toward upper Fifth Avenue and Harlem? Is his attitude toward the inhabitants of the street markedly different from his attitude toward the street itself? Does he state his attitude directly or instead imply it in his details?

2. Does Baldwin maintain an overall tone in these paragraphs, or does his tone shift at some point?

3. Is he writing to persuade the reader to take action on the social evils suffered by the people on the street, or is he merely describing a street he knows well?

4. What impression do you get of Baldwin? What seem to be his most prominent qualities as an observer and writer?

WRITING ASSIGNMENTS

1. Analyze three paragraphs from different articles in an issue of a newspaper or newsmagazine to show how usage varies according to subject, attitude, and the approach of individual writers. You might compare the diction of two reports of the same event—in two newsmagazines or newspapers—to illustrate the possible variations.

2. Describe a street you remember well from your high-school days. Establish a dominant tone as you write. If you shift your tone, do so without being abrupt.

Concreteness

Writing is *concrete* when it makes an observation or impression perceptible to the senses. Eric Sevareid makes concrete the changes that occurred in his hometown in North Dakota:

> Sounds have changed; I heard not once the clopping of a horse's hoof, nor the mourn of a coyote. I heard instead the shriek of brakes, the heavy throbbing of the once-a-day Braniff airliner into Minot, the shattering sirens born of war, the honk of a diesel locomotive which surely cannot call to faraway places the heart of a wakeful boy like the old steam whistle in the night.—"Velva, North Dakota"

Complex ideas can be made concrete with vivid examples; indeed, examples are essential to our understanding:

> I have described the hand when it uses a tool as an instrument of discovery. . . . We see this every time a child learns to couple hand and tool together—to lace its shoes, to thread a needle, to fly a kite or to play a penny whistle. With the practical action there goes another, namely finding pleasure in the action for its own sake—in the skill that one perfects, and perfects by being pleased with it. This at bottom is responsible for every work of art, and science too: our poetic delight in what human beings do because they can do it.—J. Bronowski, *The Ascent of Man*

As we will see, imagery and figurative language can increase the vividness of specific details.

Whatever the purpose of the writer, excessive detail will blur the focus and perhaps make the writing incoherent. Voltaire said, "The secret of being a bore is to tell everything." A boring movie may show everything in what seems like an endless stream of detail; a boring paragraph or essay does the same thing. To develop an idea or impression effectively, detail must be *selected*. Good writing is economical.

214

CLAUDE BROWN

CLAUDE BROWN *describes his youth in New York and the life of a black man in America in his autobiography,* Manchild in the Promised Land. *He was a member of a Harlem youth gang, served time in reformatories, and later finished his education, graduating from Howard University in 1965. Brown has done much work with young black people and writes about the present life of young black men* The Children of Ham, *which the following description of a Harlem tenement introduces.*

A Building in Upper Harlem

[1]There is a building in upper Harlem on a shabby side street with several other buildings that resemble it in both appearance and condition. [2]"This building" is in an advanced state of deterioration; only cold water runs through the water pipes, the rats here are as large as cats. [3]The saving grace of this building might very well be the erratic patterns of the varied and brilliant colors of the graffiti which adorn it internally and externally from basement to roof. [4]This building has no electricity in the apartments, but the electricity in the hallway lamp fixtures is still on. [5]Some of the apartments have garbage piled up in them five feet high and that makes opening the door a very difficult task for those whose nasal passages are sufficiently insensitive to permit entry. [6]In some of the apartments and on the rooftop, the garbage and assorted debris are piled only one or two feet high, and the trash has been there so long that plant life has generated. [7]The most rapid tour possible through this building will necessitate boiling oneself in a hot tub of strong disinfectant for a couple of hours, and even then this astonishingly formidable breed of lice will continue to make its presence felt throughout a long itchy night. [8]This

building is adjacent to a fully occupied tenement whose inhabitants are families, some of which include several children. ⁹This building has a few steps missing from the staircase above the second floor and there are no lightbulbs in the hallway; it's a very unsafe place for trespassers, even during the day. ¹⁰This building's last family of tenants was emancipated several weeks ago; they hit the numbers and moved to the Bronx, shouting, "Free at last, free at last; thank God for the number man." ¹¹Prior to their liberation, the "last family" had lived a most unusual existence. ¹²Somebody had to be at home at all times to protect the family's second-hand-hot television from becoming a third-hand-hot television; there were too many junkies in and out who used the vacant apartments to stash their loot until they could "down" it and who also used some of the apartments for sleeping and as "shooting galleries." ¹³For protection, the last family had a large, vicious German shepherd. ¹⁴This dog was needed for the rats as well as the junkies. ¹⁵A cat would be no help at all. ¹⁶The sight of the rats in this building would give any cat smaller than a mountain lion instant heart failure. ¹⁷The last family considered itself fortunate, despite the many unpleasant, unhealthy and unsafe aspects of its residence. ¹⁸"We ain't paid no rent in two years. ¹⁹I guess the city just forgot that we was here or they was just too embarrassed to ask for it," said the head of the last family. ²⁰This building has holes in the walls large enough for a man to walk through two adjacent apartments. ²¹This building has holes in the ceilings on the fourth and fifth floors, and when it rains, the rain settles on the floor of a fourth-story apartment. ²²This building is not unique, there are many others like it in the ghettos of New York City; and like many others . . . this building is owned by the City of New York.

QUESTIONS

1. Brown's description of a Harlem slum building depends on an accretion of detail. From what physical angle of vision is the

building described in sentences 1–9? Are we given an overall view from a single point of observation?

2. What is gained by reserving the information about the adjacent building for the middle of the paragraph—following the description of the deserted building? What is gained in the whole paragraph by saving the information about the owner of the building for the end? What is the principle of order in the whole paragraph?

3. The final sentence indicates that the author is making the building representative or symbolic of an *attitude*, reflected in a particular environment. What is that attitude and how does the selection of detail help us to understand it?

4. Did Brown succeed in shocking you about the Harlem building? How else might he have done so?

WRITING ASSIGNMENT

Discuss the implications of the details of the paragraph: what the building reveals about the city that owns it and what it suggests about the lives of its inhabitants.

JOHN UPDIKE

JOHN UPDIKE'S *essay on Central Park in New York shows how details selected from a particular point of view can tell us much about a world without the need of direct commentary. From his casual and humorous description of the park, we get an impression of Updike himself. Notice the sharp contrasts in the details and their arrangement in the essay.*

Central Park

On the afternoon of the first day of spring, when the gutters 1 were still heaped high with Monday's snow but the sky itself was swept clean, we put on our galoshes and walked up the sunny side of Fifth Avenue to Central Park. There we saw:

Great black rocks emerging from the melting drifts, 2 their craggy skins glistening like the backs of resurrected brontosaurs.

A pigeon on the half-frozen pond strutting to the edge 3 of the ice and looking a duck in the face.

A policeman getting his shoe wet testing the ice. 4

Three elderly relatives trying to coax a little boy to 5 accompany his father on a sled ride down a short but steep slope. After much balking, the boy did, and, sure enough, the sled tipped over and the father got his collar full of snow. Everybody laughed except the boy, who sniffled.

Four boys in black leather jackets throwing snowballs 6 at each other. (The snow was ideally soggy, and packed hard with one squeeze.)

Seven men without hats. 7

Twelve snowmen, none of them intact. 8

Two men listening to the radio in a car parked outside 9 the Zoo; Mel Allen was broadcasting the Yanks-Cardinals game from St. Petersburg.

A tahr (*Hemitragus jemlaicus*) pleasantly squinting in 10 the sunlight.

An aoudad absently pawing the mud and chewing. 11

A yak with its back turned. 12

Empty cages labeled "Coati," "Orang-outang," 13 "Ocelot."

A father saying to his little boy, who was annoyed 14 almost to tears by the inactivity of the seals, "Father [Father Seal, we assumed] is very tired; he worked hard all day."

Most of the cafeteria's out-of-doors tables occupied. 15

A pretty girl in black pants falling on them at the 16 Wollman Memorial Rink.

"BILL & DORIS" carved on a tree. "REX & RITA" written in 17 the snow.

Two old men playing, and six supervising, a checkers 18 game.

The Michael Friedsam Foundation Merry-Go-Round, 19

nearly empty of children but overflowing with calliope music.

A man on a bench near the carrousel reading, through 20 sunglasses, a book on economics.

Crews of shinglers repairing the roof of the Tavern-on- 21 the-Green.

A woman dropping a camera she was trying to load, 22 the film unrolling in the slush and exposing itself.

A little colored boy in aviator goggles rubbing his ears 23 and saying, "He really hurt me." "No, he didn't," his nurse-maid told him.

The green head of Giuseppe Mazzini staring across the 24 white softball field, unblinking, though the sun was in its eyes.

Water murmuring down walks and rocks and steps. A 25 grown man trying to block one rivulet with snow.

Things like brown sticks nosing through a plot of 26 cleared soil.

A tire track in a piece of mud far removed from where 27 any automobiles could be.

Footprints around a KEEP OFF sign.   28

Two pigeons feeding each other.   29

Two showgirls, whose faces had not yet thawed the 30 frost of their makeup, treading indignantly through the slush.

A plump old man saying "Chick, chick" and feeding 31 peanuts to squirrels.

Many solitary men throwing snowballs at tree trunks.   32

Many birds calling to each other about how little the 33 Ramble has changed.

One red mitten lying lost under a poplar tree.   34

An airplane, very bright and distant, slowly moving 35 through the branches of a sycamore.

QUESTIONS

1. How do Updike's details create a dominant impression, or is he trying to avoid creating a dominant impression?

2. What does he gain by presenting these impressions in phrases—actually shortened sentences?

3. What impression do you get of Updike from the essay—particularly from what he notices and chooses to describe?

WRITING ASSIGNMENT

Describe an afternoon in a park or athletic field, as Updike does. Make your details as vivid as you can, without developing each impression.

RENATA ADLER

> RENATA ADLER *has written film criticism, fiction, and numerous essays on American life and social issues for various periodicals, including* The New York Times *and* The New Yorker *magazine. Her description of a radio station in the early 1950s, taken from a collection of essays published in 1969, gives us a different picture of a world also described by James Baldwin and* Newsweek. *Adler tells us something about the same youth culture of the period through a careful mounting of vivid details.*

WABC

Let's assume that a former radio addict who kicked the habit in 1954 now switches to WABC, 770 on the AM dial. If he is under thirty and has tuned in during news time, he may think for a moment that nothing has changed: Fred Foy, one of the newscasters, used to be the announcer for "The Lone Ranger," and another, George Ansboro, used to be the announcer for "Young Widder Brown." In a few minutes, however, he will hear one of the disc jockeys— 1

Herb Oscar Anderson, Bob Dayton, Dan Ingram, Bruce Morrow, Charlie Greer, or Bob Lewis—and then, the chances are, his mood and Weltanschauung will change entirely. To begin with, he is likely to be addressed at once, familiarly, as "cousin," for it is customary, on jukebox-music stations, to enlist disc jockeys and fans in some sort of group or family. At WABC, listeners are "cousins" and disc jockeys are "All Americans"; at WMCA, listeners are simply listeners, but disc jockeys are "Good Guys"; and at WINS, where disc jockeys are simply disc jockeys and listeners are simply listeners, the disc jockeys show their solidarity by playing basketball as a team and challenging all comers.

However that may be, in any given quarter hour, our 2
hypothetical WABC listener will be joining a chronologically mixed but aesthetically unified new generation of about a quarter of a million child cousins, teenage cousins, and perennially young adult cousins who are listening to the new music—the New Sound—over what has become, according to The Pulse Inc., a rating service, the most popular radio station in New York. (WOR, its nearest competitor, is a relatively non-generational "talk" station.) Our listener can hear WABC in most of New England and at least as far south as the United States Naval Base at Guantanamo. (Later at night, according to Station KOB, which is bringing suit, he can also hear it as far west as Albuquerque, New Mexico, where it allegedly interferes with local stations.)

Our listener will probably begin by turning the volume 3
down, for, depending on the hour, he may be greeted by astral screams of *"Swing,* Charlie, *swing!"* "All the *way* with HOA!" *"More* music and *much* more *excitement, here* at *Day*ton *Place!"* "Boba*loo*, the big fat *Da*ddy *Poo!"* or "Cousin *Bru*cie!" *Cou*sin Brucie! Cousin Bru*cie! Cou*sin *Bru*cie! *Cousin Brucie!"* There may also be voices— apparently submerged in several feet of water—gurgling "Your music authority, seventy-seven, WA-BeatleC!" and conversation thereafter always proceeds at fever pitch. The listener may be urgently invited to vote in the "Principal of the Year Contest" (sixteen million handwritten votes were

received last year), to send in for a "Kissin' Cousin Card" or a "Kemosabe Card" (a hundred and fifty thousand requests have been filled in a single week), to participate in a "Beatle Drawing Contest" (seveny-five thousand entries have been received, the winning entries to be exhibited in Huntington Hartford's Gallery of Modern Art), or to send in a box top—any old box top—"just as a whim!" (A few days later, he may be asked whether he knows anyone who can use a warehouseful of box tops.)

If he has tuned in during the early morning, our listener 4 will hear Herb Oscar Anderson crooning his theme song. "Hello Again," and reading notices about dogs and persons who have disappeared during the night. ("Dear Nancy, eighteen years old. We're sorry you left. Please come back and we'll forget all about it. Love, Mom and Dad." Nancy usually hears it and comes back; the lost dogs are usually found and returned, also.) In the late morning, he will hear Bob Dayton welcoming his listeners to "Dayton Place" and wishing a happy birthday to many of them. In the early afternoon, there is Dan Ingram, on "Your Ingram Singram" or "Your Ingram Flingram," announcing that he is there "laughing and biting, and scratching." Now and then, Dan will shout "Charge!" or announce a weather report as having come to him from "Peter the Meter Reader and our weather girl Fat Pontoon and her Soggy Stockings." In the evening, there is Bruce Morrow announcing, with terrific intensity, that it is or will soon be "Date Night," and giving all his girl listeners a big kiss (pronounced "mmmwa") as he asks all fans in cars to blow their horns at once. (If our listener has his window open, he will doubtless hear horns blowing all up and down the street.) Bruce Morrow may recount some recent escapade, like a breaking down of his car that forced him to buy a horse from the owner of an applecart and to ride it at full gallop through the Lincoln Tunnell on his way to a record hop in Palisades Park.

Then it is time for Bob Lewis, "the big fat Daddy Poo," 5 making weird choking noises to introduce a commercial for an exam cram book ("Kids, have exams got you by the throat?") and announcing record hops as far away as Galesburg, Michigan ("I don't think many of you will be able to attend this one, but . . ."). Finally, there is Charlie Greer, on "Your All Night Office Party," who repeatedly warns the listener, "Don't be a dial twister or I'll give you a Charlie Greer blister," until it is morning and time for Herb Oscar Anderson to sing "Hello Again" again. All the disc jockeys will keep up this continuous stream of chatter, singing with or answering back to records, relaying personal messages to fans, reading traffic reports phoned in by regular "cousins" (like Eddie Schmeltz, a construction worker in Passaic, and Joe Firmata, a hearse driver in Brooklyn), coughing, sneezing, groaning, chortling, or laughing wildly, until our listener is more than likely to be stunned into becoming a non-generational cousin himself.

QUESTIONS

1. What qualities of the radio station is Adler trying to convey? What aspects of the broadcast does she focus on?

2. How different are the disc jockeys in personality and style? What point is Adler making in noting these differences?

3. What point is she making about the audience of the station?

4. What is the dominant tone of the description? Does the tone shift from paragraph to paragraph?

5. In what order does she present the details?

6. How different are disc jockeys today from those described?

WRITING ASSIGNMENTS

1. Describe a radio station you listen to. Do not comment directly on the qualities of the station. Let your details reveal these qualities, and your attitude toward the station.

2. Write one or two paragrahs that develop one of the following ideas in specific detail. Draw your details from several areas of experience if you can—home, school, place of recreation, place of work:

a. "I have known people to stop and buy an apple on the corner and then walk away as if they had solved the unemployment problem."—Heywood Broun

b. "Heroes are created by popular demand, sometimes out of the scantiest materials."—Gerald Johnson

c. "Everything is funny as long as it is happening to somebody else."—Will Rogers

Imagery

Images convey sensory impressions: impressions of sight, hearing, smell, taste, or touch. The following passage from a story by James Joyce illustrates most of these:

> The cold air stung us and we played till our bodies glowed. Our shouts echoed in the silent street. The career of our play brought us through the dark muddy lanes behind the houses where we ran the gauntlet of the rough tribes from the cottages, to the back doors of the dark dripping gardens where odors arose from the ashpits, to the dark odorous stables where a coachman smoothed and combed the horse or shook music from the buckled harness. —"Araby"

We think in images constantly. Joyce could not have expressed his sense of a particular street on a particular night in abstract language. The more evocative our imagery, when the situation calls for vivid impressions, the more directly will our words express experience. A passage will seem overwritten if a vivid representation of experience is not needed; so-called fine writing tries to be too evocative of sense experience. In the passage quoted above, Joyce selects only those details that will give the reader an impression of the physical sensations experienced in the darkness. The imagery suggests the vitality of imagination, a theme of the story; Joyce probably could not have conveyed that vitality without it.

RACHEL CARSON

The American naturalist and conservationist RACHEL CARSON *(1907–1964) worked as a marine biologist for the U.S. Fish and Wildlife Service and, returning to the Fisheries later, edited the magazine* Fish *and* Wildlife. *She retired from government service in 1952. Carson wrote several books about the natural life of the Atlantic coast and waters including* The Edge of the Sea, *from which the following descriptive passage is taken;*

Under the Sea-Wind; *and* The Sea Around Us, *which
received the National Book Award in 1951. In 1962 she
published her most influential book,* Silent Spring,
*which warned of the increasing pollution of the envi-
ronment by insecticides and chemicals.*

Walking to the Seacoast

One of my own favorite approaches to a rocky seacoast is by   1
a rough path through an evergreen forest that has its own
peculiar enchantment. It is usually an early morning tide
that takes me along that forest path, so that the light is still
pale and fog drifts in from the sea beyond. It is almost a
ghost forest, for among the living spruce and balsam are
many dead trees—some still erect, some sagging earthward,
some lying on the floor of the forest. All the trees, the living
and the dead, are clothed with green and silver crusts of
lichens. Tufts of the bearded lichen or old man's beard hang
from the branches like bits of sea mist tangled there. Green
woodland mosses and a yielding carpet of reindeer moss
cover the ground. In the quiet of that place even the voice of
the surf is reduced to a whispered echo and the sounds of
the forest are but the ghosts of sound—the faint sighing of
evergreen needles in the moving air; the creaks and heavier
groans of half-fallen trees resting against their neighbors
and rubbing bark against bark; the light rattling fall of a
dead branch broken under the feet of a squirrel and sent
bounding and ricocheting earthward.

But finally the path emerges from the dimness of the   2
deeper forest and comes to a place where the sound of surf
rises above the forest sounds—the hollow boom of the sea,
rhythmic and insistent, striking against the rocks, falling
away, rising again.

Up and down the coast the line of the forest is drawn   3
sharp and clean on the edge of a seascape of surf and sky

and rocks. The softness of the sea fog blurs the contours of the rocks; gray water and gray mists merge offshore in a dim and vaporous world that might be a world of creation, stirring with new life.

QUESTIONS

1. Carson appeals to our senses of sight and sound in describing her walk to the seacoast. At what point do sounds become important? How many sounds does she describe? What contrasts does she develop, and why are these important to her dominant impression.

2. How does sight reinforce sound in the passage? Does Carson appeal to other senses for reinforcement?

WRITING ASSIGNMENT

Describe a walk you have taken, selecting details to create a dominant impression, and appealing to two or more of the senses as Carson does.

LARRY WOIWODE

LARRY WOIWODE, *born and raised in North Dakota, has written much about the Middle West in his fiction and essays. His writing about outdoor life is particularly extraordinary, as his description of the killing of a deer, from an essay on guns in America published in* Esquire *magazine shows. The point of view is sharply different from Peter Matthiessen's description of the killing of a whale and Ernest Hemingway's of the shooting of a water buffalo—both guided by a different purpose.*

Killing a Deer

Once in the middle of a Wisconsin winter I shot a deer, my 1
only one, while my wife and daughter watched. It had been
hit by a delivery truck along a country road a few miles from
where we lived and one of its rear legs was torn off at the
hock; a shattered shin and hoof lay steaming in the red-
beaded snow. The driver of the truck and I stood and
watched as it tried to leap a fence, kicked a while at the top
wire it was entangled in, flailing the area with fresh ropes of
blood, and then went hobbling across a pasture toward a
wooded hill. Placid cows followed it with a curious awe. "Do
you have a rifle with you?" the driver asked. "No, not with
me. At home." He looked once more at the deer, then got in
his truck and drove off.

I went back to our Jeep where my wife and daughter 2
were waiting, pale and withdrawn, and told them what I
was about to do, and suggested that they'd better stay at
home. No, they wanted to be with me, they said; they
wanted to watch. My daughter was three and a half at the
time. I got my rifle, a .22, a foolishly puny weapon to use on
a deer but the only one I had, and we came back and saw
that the deer was lying in some low brush near the base of
the hill; no need to trail its blatant spoor. When I got about a
hundred yards off, marveling at how it could have made it
so far in its condition through snow that came over my boot
tops, the deer tried to push itself up with its front legs, then
collapsed. I aimed at the center of its skull, thinking, *This
will be the quickest*, and heard the bullet ricochet off and go
singing through the woods.

The deer was on its feet, shaking its head as though 3
stung, and I fired again at the same spot, quickly, and
apparently missed. It was now moving at its fastest hobble
up the hill, broadside to me, and I took my time to sight a
heart shot. Before the report even registered in my mind,
the deer went down in an explosion of snow and lay struggling there, spouting blood from its stump and a chest wound.

I was shaking by now. Deer are color-blind as far as science can say, and as I went toward its quieting body to deliver the coup de grace, I realized I was being seen in black and white, and then the deer's eye seemed to home in on me, and I was struck with the understanding that I was its vision of approaching death. And then I seemed to enter its realm through its eye and saw the countryside and myself in shades of white and grey. *But I see the deer in color,* I thought.

A few yards away, I aimed at its head once more, and there was the crack of a shot, the next-to-last round left in the magazine. The deer's head came up, and I could see its eye clearly now, dark, placid, filled with an appeal, it seemed, and then felt the surge of black and white surround and subsume me again. The second shot, or one of them, had pierced its neck; a grey-blue tongue hung out over its jaw; urine was trickling from below its tail; a doe. I held the rifle barrel inches from its forehead, conscious of my wife's and daughter's eyes on me from behind, and as I fired off the final and fatal shot, felt myself drawn by them back into my multicolored, many-faceted world again.

QUESTIONS

1. To what senses does Woiwode appeal in describing the killing of the doe?

2. What emotions does he convey through the specific details he gives us?

3. The killing of the doe is a necessary one, a fact Woiwode emphasizes through details of the suffering of the wounded animal. What are his other details meant to show?

4. Why does he stress the difference between his view of the doe and what he imagines is the doe's view of him?

WRITING ASSIGNMENTS

1. Rewrite the description from the viewpoint of the wounded doe—beginning with the circumstances of the wounding, and

ending with her death. Let your details make the point of the essay.

2. Narrate an experience in which you learned something unexpected about the world of nature. Let your reader see that world and undergo the experience as you did. Choose images that appeal to several of the senses, not just to one.

THOMAS WOLFE

In his stories and novels, THOMAS WOLFE *(1900–1938) wrote about his native Asheville, North Carolina— most memorably in* Look Homeward, Angel—*and about his life in New York City where he taught English at New York University from 1924 to 1930. Wolfe wrote about ten thousand words a day, leaving at his early death an immense amount of fiction. His account of a boyhood experience in Asheville, in his book* From Death to Morning, *shows Wolfe's ability to evoke a world through its sights, sounds and smells.*

Circus at Dawn

There were times in early autumn—in September—when 1 the greater circuses would come to town—the Ringling Brothers, Robinson's, and Barnum and Bailey shows, and when I was a route-boy on the morning paper, on those mornings when the circus would be coming in I would rush madly through my route in the cool and thrilling darkness that comes just before break of day, and then I would go back home and get my brother out of bed.

Talking in low excited voices we would walk rapidly 2 back toward town under the rustle of September leaves, in cool streets just grayed now with that still, that unearthly

and magical first light of day which seems suddenly to
re-discover the great earth out of darkness, so that the earth
emerges with an awful, a glorious sculptural stillness, and
one looks out with a feeling of joy and disbelief, as the first
men on this earth must have done, for to see this happen is
one of the things that men will remember out of life forever
and think of as they die.

At the sculptural still square where at one corner, just   3
emerging into light, my father's shabby little marble shop
stood with a ghostly strangeness and familiarity, my brother
and I would "catch" the first street car of the day bound for
the "depot" where the circus was—or sometimes we would
meet some one we knew, who would give us a lift in his
automobile.

Then, having reached the dingy, grimy, and rickety   4
depot section, we would get out, and walk rapidly across the
tracks of the station yard, where we could see great flares
and steamings from the engines, and hear the crash and
bump of shifting freight cars, the swift sporadic thunders of
a shifting engine, the tolling of bells, the sounds of great
trains on the rails.

And to all these familiar sounds, filled with their exul-   5
tant prophecies of flight, the voyage, morning, and the shining cities—to all the sharp and thrilling odors of the
trains—the smell of cinders, acrid smoke, of musty, rusty
freight cars, the clean pine-board of crated produce, and the
smells of fresh stored food—oranges, coffee, tangerines
and bacon, ham and flour and beef—there would be added
now, with an unforgettable magic and familiarity, all the
strange sounds and smells of the coming circus.

The gay yellow sumptuous-looking cars in which the   6
star performers lived and slept, still dark and silent, heavily
and powerfully still, would be drawn up in long strings upon
the tracks. And all around them the sounds of the unloading
circus would go on furiously in the darkness. The receding
gulf of lilac and departing night would be filled with the
savage roar of the lions, the murderously sudden snarling of
great jungle cats, the trumpeting of the elephants, the stamp

of the horses, and with the musty, pungent, unfamiliar odor
of the jungle animals: the tawny camel smells, and the smells
of panthers, zebras, tigers, elephants, and bears.

Then, along the tracks, beside the circus trains, there 7
would be the sharp cries and oaths of the circus men, the
magical swinging dance of lanterns in the darkness, the
sudden heavy rumble of the loaded vans and wagons as
they were pulled along the flats and gondolas, and down the
runways to the ground. And everywhere, in the thrilling
mystery of darkness and awakening light, there would be
the tremendous conflict of a confused, hurried, and yet
orderly movement.

The great iron-gray horses, four and six to a team, 8
would be plodding along the road of thick white dust to a
rattling of chains and traces and the harsh cries of their
drivers. The men would drive the animals to the river which
flowed by beyond the tracks, and water them; and as first
light came one could see the elephants wallowing in the
familiar river and the big horses going slowly and carefully
down to drink.

QUESTIONS

1. Wolfe builds his description through a contrast between the
   town, seen in the first light of dawn, and the circus, unloading
   at the train depot. What images does he give us of the town? In
   particular, what image does the word "sculptural" convey in
   paragraphs 2 and 3?

2. What visual images of the circus unloading contrast with the
   earlier images of the town? What feelings is Wolfe contrasting
   through these images?

3. To images of sight Wolfe adds images of smell in paragraph 5.
   Odors, like taste, are difficult to describe. But the writer can
   remind us of objects we associate with strong odors, and this
   reminder makes the odors alive to us. How does Wolfe give us
   this reminder?

4. Wolfe draws the world of the town and the world of the circus
   together in paragraphs 7 and 8. What may he be trying to
   show, or what feelings is he conveying in doing so?

WRITING ASSIGNMENTS

1. Wolfe is contrasting two kinds of mystery, represented by the different worlds of the town and the circus. Discuss what the imagery tells you about the mystery of each and what Wolfe may be saying to us through this contrast.

2. Describe a comparable experience in your life involving two worlds, as different as those of the town and the circus. Use your description to develop an idea suggested by the experience.

Figurative Language

A simile is an explicit comparison (using *like* or *as*) that usually develops or implies one or more simple points of resemblance:

> Will Brangwen ducked his head and looked at his uncle with swift, mistrustful eyes, like a caged hawk.—D. H. Lawrence

A metaphor is an implicit comparison in which an object is presented as if it were something else:

> Some people are molded by their admirations, others by their hostilities.—Elizabeth Bowen

Personification is the attribution of human qualities to abstract ideas or objects. Simile, metaphor, and personification unite in the following passage:

> Then Sunday light raced over the farm as fast as the chickens were flying. Immediately the first straight shaft of heat, solid as a hickory stick, was laid on the ridge.—Eudora Welty

One purpose of figures of speech is to evoke the qualities of experience and give shape or substance to an emotion or awareness that up to the moment of its expression may be indefinite. In exposition a writer will depend on metaphor because of its property of expressing an attitude as well as representing an idea:

> England is not the jewelled isle of Shakespeare's much-quoted passage, nor is it the inferno depicted by Dr. Goebbels. More than either it resembles a family, a rather stuffy Victorian family, with not many black sheep in it but with all its cupboards bursting with skeletons. It has rich relations who have to be kowtowed to and poor relations who are horribly sat upon, and there is a deep conspiracy of silence about the source of the family income. It is a family in which the young are generally thwarted and most of the power is in the hands of irresponsible uncles and bedridden aunts.—George Orwell, "England, Your England"

JOHN McPHEE

JOHN MCPHEE *has been a contributing editor and columnist for* Time *magazine and since 1965 has been a staff writer for* The New Yorker *magazine. His articles, collected in a number of books including* Pieces of the Frame, Giving Good Weight, *and* The Curve of Binding Energy, *deal with a range of subjects from sports to nuclear terrorism. He is particularly well known for his writing about the outdoors. The passage reprinted here is from his book* Encounters with the Archdruid, *published in 1971.*

Running the Rapids

¹There is something quite deceptive in the sense of acceleration that comes just before a rapid. ²The word "rapid" itself is, in a way, a misnomer. ³It refers only to the speed of the white river relative to the speed of the smooth water that leads into and away from the rapid. ⁴The white water is faster, but it is hardly "rapid." ⁵The Colorado, smooth, flows about seven miles per hour, and, white, it goes perhaps fifteen or, at its whitest and wildest, twenty miles per hour—not very rapid by the standards of the twentieth century. ⁶Force of suggestion creates a false expectation. ⁷The mere appearance of the river going over those boulders—the smoky spray, the scissoring waves—is enough to imply a rush to fatality, and this endorses the word used to describe it. ⁸You feel as if you were about to be sucked into some sort of invisible pneumatic tube and shot like a bullet into the dim beyond. ⁹But the white water, though faster than the rest of the river, is categorically slow. ¹⁰Running the rapids in the Colorado is a series of brief experiences, because the rapids themselves are short. ¹¹In them, with the raft folding and bending—sudden hills of water filling the immediate skyline—things happen in slow motion. ¹²The projector of your own existence slows way

down, and you dive as in a dream, and gradually rise, and fall again. ¹³The raft shudders across the ridgelines of water cordilleras to crash softly into the valleys beyond. ¹⁴Space and time in there are something other than they are out here. ¹⁵Tents of water form overhead, to break apart in rags. ¹⁶Elapsed stopwatch time has no meaning at all.

QUESTIONS

1. Why does McPhee explain that the word *rapid* is a misnomer? Would the experience he describes seem different if he had not given this information?

2. What images do the metaphors *smoky* and *scissoring* create in sentence 7? How many similes do you find in sentence 8, and what do they add to the sentence?

3. What metaphors convey the "slow motion" of the experience described in sentences 12–16?

4. Are the words *folding* and *bending* used literally or metaphorically in sentence 11?

5. What use of personification do you find in sentence 13?

WRITING ASSIGNMENTS

1. Rewrite McPhee's paragraph, eliminating the metaphors, similes, and personification. Then write a second version, supplying metaphors and similes of your own.

2. Describe an experience similar to McPhee's—trying to keep your balance on an icy street, descending a steep hill—and use metaphors, similes, and personification to heighten the vividness of your details.

ANNIE DILLARD

A poet and nature writer, ANNIE DILLARD *lived for ten years in the Roanoke valley in Virginia. She wrote about her experiences with nature there in her book* Pilgrim at Tinker Creek, *awarded the Pulitzer Prize in 1974. Keeping "a meteorological journal of the mind," Dillard sought at Tinker Creek what Henry David Thoreau sought at Walden Pond. She tells us toward the beginning of the book, "But if I can bear the nights, the days are a pleasure. I walk out; I see something, some event that would otherwise have been utterly missed and lost; or something sees me, some enormous power brushes me with its clean wing, and I resound like a beaten bell." Dillard develops this idea later in the book in the following passage.*

Looking at the World

Once I visited a great university and wandered, a stranger, 1 into the subterranean halls of its famous biology department. I saw a sign on a door: ichthyology department. The door was open a crack, and as I walked past I glanced in. I saw just a flash. There were two white-coated men seated opposite each other on high lab stools at a hard-surfaced table. They bent over identical white enamel trays. On one side, one man, with a lancet, was just cutting into an enormous preserved fish he'd taken from a jar. On the other side, the other man, with a silver spoon, was eating a grapefruit. I laughed all the way back to Virginia.

Michael Goldman wrote in a poem, "When the Muse 2 comes She doesn't tell you to write;/ She says get up for a minute, I've something to show you, stand here." What made me look up at that roadside tree?

The road to Grundy, Virginia, is, as you might expect, a 3 narrow scrawl scribbled all over the most improbably peaked and hunched mountains you ever saw. The few people who live along the road also seem peaked and hunched. But what on earth—? It was hot, sunny summer. The road was just bending off sharply to the right. I hadn't seen a house in miles, and none was in sight. At the apogee of the road's curve grew an enormous oak, a massive bur oak two hundred years old, one hundred and fifty feet high, an oak whose lowest limb was beyond the span of the highest ladder. I looked up: there were clothes spread all over the tree. Red shirts, blue trousers, black pants, little baby smocks—they weren't hung from branches. They were outside, carefully spread, splayed as if to dry, on the outer leaves of the great oak's crown. Were there pillowcases, blankets? I can't remember. There was a gay assortment of cotton underwear, yellow dresses, children's green sweaters, plaid skirts. . . . You know roads. A bend comes and you take it, thoughtlessly, moving on. I looked behind me for another split second, astonished; both sides of the tree's canopy, clear to the top, bore clothes. Trompe!

But there is more to the present than a series of snap-   4
shots. We are not merely sensitized film; we have feelings, a memory for information and an eidetic memory for the imagery of our own pasts.

Our layered consciousness is a tiered track for an un-   5
matched assortment of concentrically wound reels. Each one plays out for all of life its dazzle and blur of translucent shadow-pictures; each one hums at every moment its own secret melody in its own unique key. We tune in and out. But moments are not lost. Time out of mind is time nevertheless, cumulative, informing the present. From even the deepest slumber you wake with a jolt—older, closer to death, and wiser, grateful for breath. You quit your seat in a darkened movie theatre, walk past the empty lobby, out the double glass doors, and step like Orpheus into the street. And the cumulative force of the present you've forgotten sets you reeling, staggering, as if you'd been struck broadside by a plank. It all floods back to you. Yes, you say, as if you'd been asleep a hundred years, this is it, this is the real weather, the lavender light fading, the full moisture in your lungs, the heat from the pavement on your lips and palms—not the dry orange dust from horses' hooves, the salt sea, the sour Coke—but this solid air, the blood pumping up your thighs again, your fingers alive. And on the way home you drive exhilarated, energized, under scented, silhouetted trees.

QUESTIONS

1. What does Dillard want to show us in the "snapshots" of the two white-coated men and of the oak spread with clothes? Does she explain why these scenes caught her eye?

2. Dillard tells us in paragraph 4 that "we are not merely sensitized film." What makes this statement metaphorical? What are the two meanings of "sensitized"? What is "eidetic memory," and is the word "eidetic" metaphorical?

3. Why is "sensitized film" an incomplete description—or metaphor—for the human being in the act of observing something?

4. Dillard introduces in paragraph 5 a new and more appropriate metaphor to describe our minds. What is that metaphor, and how does she develop it through the words "plays out," "hums," and "tune in and out"? Why is this metaphor more appropriate?

5. How does Dillard illustrate the "cumulative" quality of "time out of mind" through the experience of leaving a movie theater?

6. In the Greek myth Orpheus enters the world of the dead in search of his wife, Eurydice, and returns to earth after finding her. What is the point of the simile, "step like Orpheus into the street," in paragraph 5? What other similes does Dillard use in this paragraph and to what effect?

7. What is the central idea of the passage, and where does Dillard first introduce it and later restate it?

WRITING ASSIGNMENTS

1. Write a series of "snapshots" of your own, selecting ones that generate different feelings. Try through your detail and the use of figurative language to convey these feelings to your reader. Build your series to a comment about them as Dillard does.

2. Develop the following statement with an experience of your own, using figurative language to make the experience vivid: "We tune in and out. But moments are not lost. Time out of mind is time nevertheless, cumulative, informing the present."

Faulty Diction

We hear much today about the abuse of language—particularly about euphemism and equivocation like that cited by George Orwell in his classic essay on language and politics included in this section:

> Defenseless villages are bombarded from the air, the inhabitants driven out into the countryside, the cattle machine-gunned, the huts set on fire with incendiary bullets: this is called pacification. Millions of peasants are robbed of their farms and sent trudging along the roads with no more than they can carry: this is called transfer of population or rectification of frontiers.

Writing in 1946, Orwell bluntly tells his readers that "In our time, political speech and writing are largely the defense of the indefensible," and he adds that this language "has to consist largely of euphemism, question-begging, and sheer cloudy vagueness." We can guess what Orwell would have said about political language in our own time—about such phrases as "credibility gap" and "positive reference input" to describe the good and bad reputations of office holders and candidates, and in nonpolitical discourse, "learning resource centers" and "interfaces between student and teacher" to describe libraries and conferences. Such vague and pretentious language can be comical, as Russell Baker shows in his retelling of "Little Red Riding Hood," but as Orwell explains, the abuses of language have consequences: ". . . if thought corrupts language, language can also corrupt thought."

The three essays in this section offer an opportunity to consider many of these abuses and their possible causes. So do other essayists in this book—William Zinsser in his discussion of "clutter" and *Time* in its discussion of euphemism.

GEORGE ORWELL

GEORGE ORWELL *(1903–1950) was the pseudonym of the English novelist and essayist Eric Hugh Blair. Orwell*

*was born in India where his father was a customs offi-
cial for the British colonial government. At the age of 8
he was sent to a school in England, and he later attended Eton School on a scholarship. Instead of attend-
ing Cambridge University for which he had prepared,
Orwell took a job with the Indian Imperial Police and
from 1922 to 1927 served in Burma—an experience he
writes about in "Shooting an Elephant" later in this
book. When he left the service, he returned to Europe
where he began his career as journalist and novelist.
The rise of totalitarianism in Europe led Orwell to write
increasingly about its causes in essays like the classic
study of political language reprinted here and in his
most famous novels,* Animal Farm *(1945) and* Nineteen
Eighty-Four *(1949).*

Politics and the English
Language

Most people who bother with the matter at all would admit 1
that the English language is in a bad way, but it is generally
assumed that we cannot by conscious action do anything
about it. Our civilization is decadent and our language—so
the argument runs—must inevitably share in the general
collapse. It follows that any struggle against the abuse of
language is a sentimental archaism, like preferring candles
to electric light or hansom cabs to aeroplanes. Underneath
this lies the half-conscious belief that language is a natural
growth and not an instrument which we shape for our own
purposes.

Now, it is clear that the decline of a language must 2
ultimately have political and economic causes: it is not due
simply to the bad influence of this or that individual writer.
But an effect can become a cause, reinforcing the original
cause and producing the same effect in an intensified form,
and so on indefinitely. A man may take to drink because he
feels himself to be a failure, and then fail all the more

completely because he drinks. It is rather the same thing that is happening to the English language. It becomes ugly and inaccurate because our thoughts are foolish, but the slovenliness of our language makes it easier for us to have foolish thoughts. The point is that the process is reversible. Modern English, especially written English, is full of bad habits which spread by imitation and which can be avoided if one is willing to take the necessary trouble. If one gets rid of these habits one can think more clearly, and to think clearly is a necessary first step toward political regeneration: so that the fight against bad English is not frivolous and is not the exclusive concern of professional writers. I will come back to this presently, and I hope that by that time the meaning of what I have said here will have become clearer. Meanwhile, here are five specimens of the English language as it is now habitually written.

These five passages have not been picked out because 3 they are especially bad—I could have quoted far worse if I had chosen—but because they illustrate various of the mental vices from which we now suffer. They are a little below the average, but are fairly representative samples. I number them so that I can refer back to them when necessary:

(1) I am not, indeed, sure whether it is not true to say that the Milton who once seemed not unlike a seventeenth-century Shelley had not become, out of an experience ever more bitter in each year, more alien [*sic*] to the founder of that Jesuit sect which nothing could induce him to tolerate.
Professor Harold Laski (Essay in *Freedom of Expression*)

(2) Above all, we cannot play ducks and drakes with a native battery of idioms which prescribes such egregious collocations of vocables as the Basic *put up with* for *tolerate* or *put at a loss* for *bewilder.*
Professor Lancelot Hogben (*Interglossa*)

(3) On the one side we have the free personality: by definition it is not neurotic, for it has neither conflict nor dream. Its desires, such as they are, are transparent, for they are just

what institutional approval keeps in the forefront of consciousness; another institutional pattern would alter their
number and intensity; there is little in them that is natural,
irreducible, or culturally dangerous. But *on the other side,*
the social bond itself is nothing but the mutual reflection of
these self-secure integrities. Recall the definition of love.
Is not this the very picture of a small academic? Where is
there a place in this hall of mirrors for either personality or
fraternity?

Essay on psychology in *Politics* (New York)

(4) All the "best people" from the gentlemen's clubs, and all
the frantic fascist captains, united in common hatred of
Socialism and bestial horror of the rising tide of the mass
revolutionary movement, have turned to acts of provocation,
to foul incendiarism, to medieval legends of poisoned wells,
to legalize their own destruction of proletarian organizations, and rouse the agitated petty-bourgeoisie to chauvinistic
fervor on behalf of the fight against the revolutionary way
out of the crisis.

Communist pamphlet

(5) If a new spirit *is* to be infused into this old country, there
is one thorny and contentious reform which must be tackled,
and that is the humanization and galvanization of the B.B.C.
Timidity here will bespeak canker and atrophy of the soul.
The heart of Britain may be sound and of strong beat, for
instance, but the British lion's roar at present is like that of
Bottom in Shakespeare's *Midsummer Night's Dream*—as
gentle as any sucking dove. A virile new Britain cannot
continue indefinitely to be traduced in the eyes or rather
ears, of the world by the effete languors of Langham Place,
brazenly masquerading as "standard English." When the
Voice of Britain is heard at nine o'clock, better far and
infinitely less ludicrous to hear aitches honestly dropped
than the present priggish, inflated, inhibited, school-
ma'amish arch braying of blameless bashful mewing
maidens!

Letter in *Tribune*

Each of these passages has faults of its own, but, quite
apart from avoidable ugliness, two qualities are common to

all of them. The first is staleness of imagery; the other is lack of precision. The writer either has a meaning and cannot express it, or he inadvertently says something else, or he is almost indifferent as to whether his words mean anything or not. This mixture of vagueness and sheer incompetence is the most marked characteristic of modern English prose, and especially of any kind of political writing. As soon as certain topics are raised, the concrete melts into the abstract and no one seems able to think of turns of speech that are not hackneyed: prose consists less and less of *words* chosen for the sake of their meaning, and more and more of *phrases* tacked together like the sections of a prefabricated henhouse. I list below, with notes and examples, various of the tricks by means of which the work of prose-construction is habitually dodged:

Dying metaphors. A newly invented metaphor assists   5
thought by evoking a visual image, while on the other hand a metaphor which is technically "dead" (e.g. *iron resolution*) has in effect reverted to being an ordinary word and can generally be used without loss of vividness. But in between these two classes there is a huge dump of worn-out metaphors which have lost all evocative power and are merely used because they save people the trouble of inventing phrases for themselves. Examples are: *Ring the changes on, take up the cudgels for, toe the line, ride roughshod over, stand shoulder to shoulder with, play into the hands of, no axe to grind, grist to the mill, fishing in troubled waters, on the order of the day, Achilles' heel, swan song, hotbed.* Many of these are used without knowledge of their meaning (what is a "rift," for instance?), and incompatible metaphors are frequently mixed, a sure sign that the writer is not interested in what he is saying. Some metaphors now current have been twisted out of their original meaning without those who use them even being aware of the fact. For example, *toe the line* is sometimes written *tow the line*. Another example is *the hammer and the anvil*, now always used with the implication that the anvil gets the worst of it. In real life it is always the anvil that breaks the hammer, never the

other way about: a writer who stopped to think what he was saying would be aware of this, and would avoid perverting the original phrase.

Operators or *verbal false limbs.* These save the trouble 6 of picking out appropriate verbs and nouns, and at the same time pad each sentence with extra syllables which give it an appearance of symmetry. Characteristic phrases are *render inoperative, militate against, make contact with, be subjected to, give rise to, give grounds for, have the effect of, play a leading part (role) in, make itself felt, take effect, exhibit a tendency to, serve the purpose of, etc., etc.* The keynote is the elimination of simple verbs. Instead of being a single word, such as *break, stop, spoil, mend, kill,* a verb becomes a *phrase*, made up of a noun or adjective tacked on to some general-purpose verb such as *prove, serve, form, play, render.* In addition, the passive voice is wherever possible used in preference to the active, and noun constructions are used instead of gerunds (*by examination of* instead of *by examining*). The range of verbs is further cut down by means of the *-ize* and *de-* formations, and the banal statements are given an appearance of profundity by means of the *not un-* formation. Simple conjunctions and prepositions are replaced by such phrases as *with respect to, having regard to, the fact that, by dint of, in view of, in the interests of, on the hypothesis that;* and the ends of sentences are saved from anticlimax by such resounding commonplaces as *greatly to be desired, cannot be left out of account, a development to be expected in the near future, deserving of serious consideration, brought to a satisfying conclusion,* and so on and so forth.

Pretentious diction. Words like *phenomenon, element,* 7 *individual* (as noun), *objective, categorical, effective, virtual, basic, primary, promote, constitute, exhibit, exploit, utilize, eliminate, liquidate,* are used to dress up simple statements and give an air of scientific impartiality to biased judgments. Adjectives like *epoch-making, epic, historic, unforgettable, triumphant, age-old, inevitable, inexorable, veritable,* are used to dignify the sordid processes of international politics, while writing that aims at glorifying war usually takes on an archaic color, its characteristic words being: *realm, throne, chariot, mailed fist, trident, sword, shield, buckler, banner, jackboot, clarion.* Foreign words and expressions such as *cul de sac, ancien régime, deus ex machina, mutatis mutandis, status quo, gleichschaltung, weltanschauung,* are used to give an air of culture and elegance. Except for the useful abbreviations *i.e., e.g.,* and *etc.,* there is no real need for any of the hundreds of foreign phrases now current in English. Bad writers, and especially scientific, political, and sociological writers, are nearly always haunted by the notion that Latin or Greek words are grander than Saxon ones, and unnecessary words like *expedite, ameliorate, predict, extraneous, deracinated, clandestine, subaqueous,* and hundreds of others constantly gain ground from their Anglo-Saxon opposite numbers.* The jargon peculiar to Marxist writing (*hyena, hangman, cannibal, petty bourgeois, these gentry, lackey, flunkey, mad dog, White Guard,* etc.) consists largely of words and phrases translated from Russian, German, or French; but the normal way of coining a new word is to use a Latin or Greek root with the appropriate affix and, where necessary, the size formation. It is often easier to make up words of this kind (*deregionalize, impermissible, extramarital, nonfragmentary* and so forth) than to think up the English words that will cover one's meaning. The result, in general, is an increase in slovenliness and vagueness.

   Meaningless words. In certain kinds of writing, particu-   8
larly in art criticism and literary criticism, it is normal to come across long passages which are almost completely lacking in meaning.† Words like *romantic, plastic, values,*

---

*An interesting illustration of this is the way in which the English flower names which were in use till very recently are being ousted by Greek ones, *snapdragon* becoming *antirrhinum, forget-me-not* becoming *myosotis,* etc. It is hard to see any practical reason for this change of fashion: it is probably due to an instinctive turning away from the more homely word and a vague feeling that the Greek word is scientific.

†Example: "Comfort's catholicity of perception and image, strangely Whitmanesque in range, almost the exact opposite in aesthetic compulsion, continues to

human, dead, sentimental, natural, vitality, as used in art criticism, are strictly meaningless, in the sense that they not only do not point to any discoverable object, but are hardly ever expected to do so by the reader. When one critic writes, "The outstanding feature of Mr. X's work is its living quality," while another writes, "The immediately striking thing about Mr. X's work is its peculiar deadness," the reader accepts this as a simple difference of opinion. If words like *black* and *white* were involved, instead of the jargon words *dead* and *living,* he would see at once that language was being used in an improper way. Many political words are similarly abused. The word *Fascism* has now no meaning except in so far as it signifies "something not desirable." The words *democracy, socialism, freedom, patriotic, realistic, justice,* have each of them several different meanings which cannot be reconciled with one another. In the case of a word like *democracy,* not only is there no agreed definition, but the attempt to make one is resisted from all sides. It is almost universally felt that when we call a country democratic we are praising it: consequently the defenders of every kind of régime claim that it is a democracy, and fear that they might have to stop using the word if it were tied down to any one meaning. Words of this kind are often used in a consciously dishonest way. That is, the person who uses them has his own private definition, but allows his hearer to think he means something quite different. Statements like *Marshal Pétain was a true patriot, The Soviet press is the freest in the world, The Catholic Church is opposed to persecution,* are almost always made with intent to deceive. Other words used in variable meanings, in most cases more or less dishonestly, are: *class, totalitarian, science, progressive, reactionary, bourgeois, equality.*

Now that I have made this catalogue of swindles and perversions, let me give another example of the kind of 9

---

evoke that trembling atmospheric accumulative hinting at a cruel, an inexorably serene timelessness. ... Wrey Gardiner scores by aiming at simple bull's-eyes with precision. Only they are not so simple, and through this contented sadness runs more than the surface bittersweet of resignation." *(Poetry Quarterly.)*

writing that they lead to. This time it must of its nature be an imaginary one. I am going to translate a passage of good English into modern English of the worst sort. Here is a well-known verse from *Ecclesiastes:*

> I returned and saw under the sun, that the race is not to the swift, nor the battle to the strong, neither yet bread to the wise, nor yet riches to men of understanding, nor yet favour to men of skill; but time and chance happeneth to them all.

Here it is in modern English:

> Objective consideration of contemporary phenomena compels the conclusion that success or failure in competitive activities exhibits no tendency to be commensurate with innate capacity, but that a considerable element of the unpredictable must invariably be taken into account.

This is a parody, but not a very gross one. Exhibit (3), 10 above, for instance, contains several patches of the same kind of English. It will be seen that I have not made a full translation. The beginning and ending of the sentence follow the original meaning fairly closely, but in the middle the concrete illustrations—race, battle, bread—dissolve into the vague phrase "success or failure in competitive activities." This had to be so, because no modern writer of the kind I am discussing—no one capable of using phrases like "objective consideration of contemporary phenomena"—would ever tabulate his thoughts in that precise and detailed way. The whole tendency of modern prose is away from concreteness. Now analyze these two sentences a little more closely. The first contains forty-nine words but only sixty syllables, and all its words are those of everyday life. The second contains thirty-eight words of ninety syllables: eighteen of its words are from Latin roots, and one from Greek. The first sentence contains six vivid images, and only one phrase ("time and chance") that could be called vague. The second contains not a single fresh, arresting phrase, and in spite of its ninety syllables it gives only a shortened version of the meaning contained in the first. Yet without a doubt it is the second kind of sentence that is gaining ground in modern English. I do not want to exaggerate. This kind of writing is not yet universal, and outcrops of simplicity will occur here and there in the worst-written page. Still, if you or I were told to write a few lines on the uncertainty of human fortunes, we should probably come much nearer to my imaginary sentence than to the one from *Ecclesiastes.*

As I have tried to show, modern writing at its worst 11 does not consist in picking out words for the sake of their meaning and inventing images in order to make the meaning clearer. It consists in gumming together long strips of words which have already been set in order by someone else, and making the results presentable by sheer humbug. The attraction of this way of writing is that it is easy. It is easier—even quicker, once you have the habit—to say *In my opinion it is not an unjustifiable assumption that* than to say *I think.* If you use ready-made phrases, you not only don't have to hunt about for words; you also don't have to bother with the rhythms of your sentences, since these phrases are generally so arranged as to be more or less euphonious. When you are composing in a hurry—when you are dictating to a stenographer, for instance, or making a public speech—it is natural to fall into a pretentious, Latinized style. Tags like *a consideration which we should do well to bear in mind* or *a conclusion to which all of us would readily assent* will save many a sentence from coming down with a bump. By using stale metaphors, similes, and idioms, you save much mental effort, at the cost of leaving your meaning vague, not only for your reader but for yourself. This is the significance of mixed metaphors. The sole aim of a metaphor is to call up a visual image. When these images clash—as in *The Fascist octopus has sung its swan song, the jackboot is thrown into the melting pot*—it can be taken as certain that the writer is not seeing a mental image of the objects he is naming; in other words he is not really thinking. Look again at the examples I gave at the beginning of this essay. Professor Laski (1) uses five negatives in fifty-three words. One of these is superfluous, making nonsense of the whole passage, and in addition there is the slip—*alien* for akin—making further nonsense, and several avoidable pieces of clumsiness which increase the general vaguenes. Professor Hogben (2) plays ducks and drakes with a battery which is able to write prescriptions, and, while disapproving of the everyday phrase *put up with,* is unwilling to look *egregious* up in the dictionary and see what it means; (3) if one takes an uncharitable attitude towards it, is simply meaningless: probably one could work out its intended meaning by reading the whole of the article in which it occurs. In (4), the writer knows more or less what he wants to say, but an accumulation of stale phrases chokes him like tea leaves blocking a sink. In (5), words and meaning have almost parted company. People who write in this manner usually have a general emotional meaning—they dislike one thing and want to express solidarity with another—but they are not interested in the detail of what they are saying. A scrupulous writer, in every sentence that he writes, will ask himself at least four questions, thus: What am I trying to say? What words will express it? What image or idiom will make it clearer? Is this image fresh enough to have an effect? And he will probably ask himself two more: Could I put it more shortly? Have I said anything that is avoidably ugly? But you are not obliged to go to all this trouble. You can shirk it by simply throwing your mind open and letting the ready-made phrases come crowding in. They will construct your sentences for you—even think your thoughts for you, to a certain extent—and at need they will perform the important service of partially concealing your meaning even from yourself. It is at this point that the special connection between politics and the debasement of language becomes clear.

In our time it is broadly true that political writing is bad 12 writing. Where it is not true, it will generally be found that the writer is some kind of rebel, expressing his private opinions and not a "party line." Orthodoxy, of whatever color, seems to demand a lifeless, imitative style. The political dialects to be found in pamphlets, leading articles, manifestoes, White Papers and the speeches of undersecretaries do, of course, vary from party to party, but they are all alike in that one almost never finds in them a fresh, vivid, homemade turn of speech. When one watches some tired hack on the platform mechanically repeating the familiar phrases—*bestial atrocities, iron heel, bloodstained tyranny, free peoples of the world, stand shoulder to shoulder*—one often has a curious feeling that one is not watching a live human being but some kind of dummy: a feeling which suddenly becomes stronger at moments when the light catches the speaker's spectacles and turns them into blank discs which seem to have no eyes behind them. And this is not altogether fanciful. A speaker who uses that kind of phraseology has gone some distance toward turning himself into a machine. The appropriate noises are coming out of his larynx, but his brain is not involved as it would be if he were choosing his words for himself. If the speech he is making is one that he is accustomed to make over and over again, he may be almost unconscious of what he is saying, as one is when one utters the responses in church. And this reduced state of consciousness, if not indispensable, is at any rate favorable to political conformity.

In our time, political speech and writing are largely the 13 defense of the indefensible. Things like the continuance of British rule in India, the Russian purges and deportations, the dropping of the atom bombs on Japan, can indeed be defended, but only by arguments which are too brutal for most people to face, and which do not square with the professed aims of political parties. This political language has to consist largely of euphemism, question-begging and sheer cloudy vagueness. Defenseless villages are bombarded from the air, the inhabitants driven out into the countryside, the cattle machine-gunned, the huts set on fire with incendiary bullets: this is called *pacification*. Millions of peasants are robbed of their farms and sent trudging along the roads with no more than they can carry: this is called *transfer of population* or *rectification of frontiers*.

People are imprisoned for years without trial, or shot in the back of the neck or sent to die of scurvy in Arctic lumber camps: this is called *elimination of unreliable elements*. Such phraseology is needed if one wants to name things without calling up mental pictures of them. Consider for instance some comfortable English professor defending Russian totalitarianism. He cannot say outright, "I believe in killing off your opponents when you can get good results by doing so." Probably, therefore, he will say something like this:

"While freely conceding that the Soviet régime exhibits certain features which the humanitarian may be inclined to deplore, we must, I think, agree that a certain curtailment of the right to political opposition is an unavoidable concomitant of transitional periods, and that the rigors which the Russian people have been called upon to undergo have been amply justified in the sphere of concrete achievement."

The inflated style is itself a kind of euphemism. A mass 14 of Latin words falls upon the facts like soft snow, blurring the outlines and covering up all the details. The great enemy of clear language is insincerity. When there is a gap between one's real and one's declared aims, one turns as it were instinctively to long words and exhausted idioms, like a cuttlefish squirting out ink. In our age there is no such thing as "keeping out of politics." All issues are political issues, and politics itself is a mass of lies, evasions, folly, hatred, and schizophrenia. When the general atmosphere is bad, language must suffer. I should expect to find—this is a guess which I have not sufficient knowledge to verify—that the German, Russian and Italian languages have all deteriorated in the last ten or fifteen years, as a result of dictatorship.

But if thought corrupts language, language can also 15 corrupt thought. A bad usage can spread by tradition and imitation, even among people who should and do know better. The debased language that I have been discussing is in some ways very convenient. Phrases like *a not unjustifi-*

*able assumption, leaves much to be desired, would serve no
good purpose, a consideration which we should do well to
bear in mind,* are a continuous temptation, a packet of
aspirins always at one's elbow. Look back through this essay, and for certain you will find that I have again and again
committed the very faults I am protesting against. By this
morning's post I have received a pamphlet dealing with
conditions in Germany. The author tells me that he "felt
impelled" to write it. I open it at random, and here is almost
the first sentence that I see: "[The Allies] have an opportunity not only of achieving a radical transformation of Germany's social and political structure in such a way as to
avoid a nationalistic reaction in Germany itself, but at the
same time of laying the foundations of a co-operative and
unified Europe." You see, he "feels impelled" to write—
feels, presumably, that he has something new to say—and
yet his words, like cavalry horses answering the bugle,
group themselves automatically into the familiar dreary pattern. This invasion of one's mind by ready-made phrases
(*lay the foundations, achieve a radical transformation*) can
only be prevented if one is constantly on guard against
them, and every such phrase anaesthetizes a portion of
one's brain.

I said earlier that the decadence of our language is 16
probably curable. Those who deny this would argue, if they
produced an argument at all, that language merely reflects
existing social conditions, and that we cannot influence its
development by any direct tinkering with words and constructions. So far as the general tone or spirit of a language
goes, this may be true, but it is not true in detail. Silly words
and expressions have often disappeared, not through any
evolutionary process but owing to the conscious action of a
minority. Two recent examples were *explore every avenue*
and *leave no stone unturned,* which were killed by the jeers
of a few journalists. There is a long list of flyblown
metaphors which could similarly be got rid of if enough
people would interest themselves in the job; and it should

also be possible to laugh the *not un-* formation out of existence,* to reduce the amount of Latin and Greek in the average sentence, to drive out foreign phrases and strayed scientific words, and, in general, to make pretentiousness unfashionable. But all these are minor points. The defense of the English language implies more than this, and perhaps it is best to start by saying what it does *not* imply.

To begin with it has nothing to do with archaism, with 17 the salvaging of obsolete words and turns of speech, or with the setting up of a "standard English" which must never be departed from. On the contrary, it is especially concerned with the scrapping of every word or idiom which has outworn its usefulness. It has nothing to do with correct grammar and syntax, which are of no importance so long as one makes one's meaning clear, or with the avoidance of Americanisms, or with having what is called a "good prose style." On the other hand it is not concerned with fake simplicity and the attempt to make written English colloquial. Nor does it even imply in every case preferring the Saxon word to the Latin one, though it does imply using the fewest and shortest words that will cover one's meaning. What is above all needed is to let the meaning choose the word, and not the other way about. In prose, the worst thing one can do with words is to surrender to them. When you think of a concrete object, you think wordlessly, and then, if you want to describe the thing you have been visualizing you probably hunt about till you find the exact words that seem to fit it. When you think of something abstract you are more inclined to use words from the start, and unless you make a conscious effort to prevent it, the existing dialect will come rushing in and do the job for you, at the expense of blurring or even changing your meaning. Probably it is better to put off using words as long as possible and get one's meaning as clear as one can through pictures or sensations. Afterward one can choose—not simply *accept*—the phrases that

---

*One can cure oneself of the *not un-* formation by memorizing this sentence: *A not unblack dog was chasing a not unsmall rabbit across a not ungreen field.*

will best cover the meaning, and then switch round and decide what impression one's words are likely to make on another person. This last effort of the mind cuts out all stale or mixed images, all prefabricated phrases, needless repetitions, and humbug and vagueness generally. But one can often be in doubt about the effect of a word or a phrase, and one needs rules that one can rely on when instinct fails. I think the following rules will cover most cases:

(i) Never use a metaphor, simile, or other figure of speech which you are used to seeing in print.

(ii) Never use a long word where a short one will do.

(iii) If it is possible to cut a word out, always cut it out.

(iv) Never use the passive where you can use the active.

(v) Never use a foreign phrase, a scientific word, or a jargon word if you can think of an everyday English equivalent.

(vi) Break any of these rules sooner than say anything outright barbarous.

These rules sound elementary, and so they are, but they demand a deep change of attitude in anyone who has grown used to writing in the style now fashionable. One could keep all of them and still write bad English, but one could not write the kind of stuff that I quoted in those five specimens at the beginning of this article.

I have not here been considering the literary use of 18 language, but merely language as an instrument for expressing and not for concealing or preventing thought. Stuart Chase and others have come near to claiming that all abstract words are meaningless, and have used this as a pretext for advocating a kind of political quietism. Since you don't know what Fascism is, how can you struggle against Fascism? One need not swallow such absurdities as this, but one ought to recognize that the present political chaos is connected with the decay of language, and that one can probably bring about some improvement by starting at the verbal end. If you simplify your English, you are freed from the worst follies of orthodoxy. You cannot speak any of the necessary dialects, and when you make a stupid remark its stupidity will be obvious, even to yourself. Political language—and with variations this is true of all political parties, from Conservatives to Anarchists—is designed to make lies sound truthful and murder respectable, and to give an appearance of solidity to pure wind. One cannot change this all in a moment, but one can at least change one's own habits, and from time to time one can even, if one jeers loudly enough, send some worn-out and useless phrase—some *jackboot, Achilles' heel, hotbed, melting pot, acid test, veritable inferno,* or other lump of verbal refuse—into the dustbin where it belongs.

QUESTIONS

1. How does the third example in Orwell's paragraph 3 help to explain the statement in paragraph 4 that "the concrete melts into the abstract"?

2. What visual image did *iron resolution* in paragraph 5 originally convey? What other dead metaphors can you cite, and what was the original significance?

3. Among the characteristic phrases cited in paragraph 6, Orwell might have included *in terms of.* Compare the following:

   > He explained his failure in terms of his attitude toward school.

   > Einstein was a creative thinker in physics because he thought in terms of mathematics instead of mystical concepts.

   In which sentence is the phrase used less awkwardly,, and why?

4. Why is the passage cited in the footnote to paragraph 8 "almost completely lacking in meaning"? Given Orwell's criticisms in paragraph 8, what would be the proper use of language in art criticism?

5. Compare the passage from Ecclesiastes quoted in paragraph 9 (King James Version) with modern renderings of it. Do you think these modern renderings are superior to Orwell's parody or to the King James version? Why?

6. "If you or I were to write a few lines on the uncertainty of human fortunes," why would the writing come nearer to Orwell's parody than to the sentence from Ecclesiastes?

7. Given the assumptions Orwell makes in the whole essay, why are all issues "political issues"?

8. Orwell says in paragraph 17 that his concern has not been to promote a "standard English" or "to make written English colloquial." Explain what he means here. Has he not recommended the use of plain English words? What exceptions would he allow?

WRITING ASSIGNMENTS

1. Analyze a paragraph from the catalog of your college or university to discover its tone and judge the writing according to the criteria Orwell proposes.

2. Analyze a letter to the editor of a newspaper or magazine and indicate the self-impression the writer wishes to create, the qualities of the prose, and the virtues or defects of the letter.

3. Analyze three paragraphs from a current textbook in one of your courses to determine how much needless jargon is employed and how well the writing meets the standard of good writing Orwell proposes.

4. Analyze a published speech of a major political figure (see *The New York Times, Vital Speeches,* or *Congressional Record*). How honest is the use of language? Compare this speech with another by the same person. How consistent is he or she in use of language?

More on Faulty Diction

The following suggestions supplement those of Orwell in his essay, and will help you identify the faults in diction that Russell Baker is satirizing in the following essay:

1. Using the same word more than once in a sentence can be confusing if the senses are different:

   We were present for the presentation of the award.

   However, we need not avoid repeating a word if the senses are the same. Indeed, substituting can also be confusing:

   The person who entered was not the individual I was expecting.

   Though *individual* is a popular synonym for *person,* it has other meanings. The substitution may confuse the reader.

2. Needless repetition can make sentences hard to understand:

   There are necessary skills that writers need to make their ideas easy to understand and comprehensible.

3. Words that overlap in meaning can have the same effect:

   The result of the survey should produce a change in policy.

   The words *result* and *produce* mean the same thing in the sentence.

4. Euphemism—providing a mild or pleasant substitute for a blunt term—can be a source of ambiguity. The euphemism "delinquent" to describe a juvenile criminal or the words "slow" and "retarded" to describe children who have trouble learning or are crippled mentally help us avoid giving pain. What words should we use in speaking about children who have trouble learning or have broken the law? No easy answers exist: we know the price of speaking bluntly, but also the price of hiding facts.

5. Equivocal terms are also a source of ambiguity because they have double meanings. The word *exceptional* is widely used to

describe bright children as well as crippled ones or children who have broken the law. We need to know what children we are talking about.

6. A cliché is a phrase or saying that has become trite through overuse: *sweet as sugar, conspicuous by his absence, more sinned against than sinning.* A bromide is a comforting platitude: *it's the effort that counts, not the winning.* Both rob prose of conviction and vigor.

7. Mixed metaphors cause confusion and can be unintentionally funny:

   Blows to one's pride stick in the craw.

8. Technical words or jargon can also have the same effect. The words *interface* (to describe the boundary between two independent machines) and *software* (to describe accessory equipment) are useful words in computer language. They become jargon in a different sense of the word—to quote H. W. Fowler, "talk that is considered both ugly-sounding and hard to understand"—when borrowed to describe other things. A conference is not an "interface," and referring to a book as "software" suggests something mechanical or perhaps dispensable.

9. Circumlocution means taking the long way around—in other words, saying something in inflated language: saying "he has difficulty distinguishing the real from the imagined" when we mean "he lies." Euphemisms often depend on inflation of this kind.

RUSSELL BAKER

RUSSELL BAKER *grew up in Loudon County, Virginia. After studying at John Hopkins University, he began his career in journalism as a reporter for the* Baltimore Sun, *and in 1954 began his long association with* The New York Times. *His column for the* Times *began in 1962.*

Baker is a keen observer of life in America and, as the essay reprinted here shows, a satirist of the pretentious language we often speak and write. His essays are collected in a number of books including All Things Considered *and* So This is Depravity, *and he has written about his boyhood in his recent autobiography,* Growing Up. *In 1979 he was awarded the Pulitzer Prize for Journalism.*

Little Red Riding Hood Revisited

In an effort to make the classics accessible to contemporary readers, I am translating them into the modern American language. Here is the translation of "Little Red Riding Hood":

Once upon a point in time, a small person named Little Red Riding Hood initiated plans for the preparation, delivery and transportation of foodstuffs to her grandmother, a senior citizen residing at a place of residence in a forest of indeterminate dimension.

In the process of implementing this program, her incursion into the forest was in mid-transportation process when it attained interface with an alleged perpetrator. This individual, a wolf, made inquiry as to the whereabouts of Little Red Riding Hood's goal as well as inferring that he was desirous of ascertaining the contents of Little Red Riding Hood's foodstuffs basket, and all that.

"It would be inappropriate to lie to me," the wolf said, displaying his huge jaw capability. Sensing that he was a mass of repressed hostility intertwined with acute alienation, she indicated.

"I see you indicating," the wolf said, "but what I don't see is whatever it is you're indicating at, you dig?"

Little Red Riding Hood indicated more fully, making one thing perfectly clear—to wit, that it was to her grandmother's residence and with a consignment of foodstuffs that her mission consisted of taking her to and with.

At this point in time the wolf moderated his rhetoric and proceeded to grandmother's residence. The elderly person was then subjected to the disadvantages of total consumption and transferred to residence in the perpetrator's stomach. 7

"That will raise the old woman's consciousness," the wolf said to himself. He was not a bad wolf, but only a victim of an oppressive society, a society that not only denied wolves' rights, but actually boasted of its capacity for keeping the wolf from the door. An interior malaise made itself manifest inside the wolf. 8

"Is that the national malaise I sense within my digestive tract?" wondered the wolf. "Or is it the old person seeking to retaliate for her consumption by telling wolf jokes to my duodenum?" It was time to make a judgment. The time was now, the hour had struck, the body lupine cried out for decision. The wolf was up to the challenge. He took two stomach powders right away and got into bed. 9

The wolf had adopted the abdominal-distress recovery posture when Little Red Riding Hood achieved his presence. 10

"Grandmother," she said, "your ocular implements are of an extraordinary order of magnitude." 11

"The purpose of this enlarged viewing capability," said the wolf "is to enable your image to register a more precise impression upon my sight systems." 12

"In reference to your ears," said Little Red Riding Hood, "it is noted with the deepest respect that far from being underprivileged, their elongation and enlargement appear to qualify you for unparalleled distinction." 13

"I hear you loud and clear, kid," said the wolf, "but what about these new choppers?" 14

"If it is not inappropriate," said Little Red Riding Hood, "it might be observed that with your new miracle masticating products you may even be able to chew taffy again." 15

This observation was followed by the adoption of an aggressive posture on the part of the wolf and the assertion 16 that it was also possible for him, due to the high efficiency ratio of his jaw, to consume little persons, plus, as he stated, his firm determination to do so at once without delay and with all due process and propriety, notwithstanding the fact that the ingestion of one entire grandmother had already provided twice his daily recommended cholesterol intake.

There ensued flight by Little Red Riding Hood accompanied by pursuit in respect to the wolf and a subsequent intervention on the part of a third party, heretofore unnoted in the record. 17

Due to the firmness of the intervention, the wolf's stomach underwent ax-assisted aperture with the result that Red Riding Hood's grandmother was enabled to be removed with only minor discomfort. 18

The wolf's indigestion was immediately alleviated with such effectiveness that he signed a contract with the intervening third party to perform with grandmother in a television commercial demonstrating the swiftness of this dramatic relief for stomach discontent. 19

"I'm going to be on television," cried grandmother. 20

And they all joined her happily in crying, "What a phenomena!" 21

QUESTIONS

1. The faddish language Baker parodies reflects faddish ideas. Here is one example: "An interior malaise made itself manifest inside the wolf." What current attitude toward human predators is Baker satirizing? How does the language help him to satirize the idea?

2. Red Riding Hood prefers the farfetched to the simple, as in the expression "ocular implements." What other examples can you cite of euphemism, circumlocution, and other faults of diction?

3. What examples of repetitious phrasing and sentence padding do you find?

4. What kind of advertising language is Baker satirizing toward the end of his version?

5. What is the difference between the wolf's language and Red Riding Hood's? What does the wolf's language tell you about his personality and view of the world?

6. What other ideas is Baker satirizing in the course of his telling of the story?

WRITING ASSIGNMENT

Rewrite another fairy tale in the modish language of advertising or other contemporary jargons and styles. Let your choice of jargon and style make a point—or several points—as Baker's telling of "Little Red Riding Hood" does.

SYDNEY J. HARRIS

SYDNEY J. HARRIS, *born in England and educated in the United States, began his distinguished career in journalism as a columnist for the* Chicago Daily News *in 1941. His essays are collected in numerous books, which include* Majority of One, On the Contrary, *and* For the Time Being. *Harris is unusual for the range of philosophical and social issues he deals with in the brief journalistic essay. His ability to write with depth, yet plainly and concisely, puts him in the company of other great essayists of this kind. The essay reprinted here reveals his interest in language that we use to flatter or deceive ourselves.*

The Man in the Middle

I am the man in the middle; for where I stand determines 1
where the middle is.

I am compassionate; those less compassionate than I 2

are "cold," and those more compassionate than I are "sentimental."

I am steadfast; those less steadfast than I are "fickle," 3 and those more steadfast than I are "stubborn."

I am friendly; those less friendly than I are "stand- 4 offish," and those more friendly than I are "pushy."

I am decent; those less decent than I are "disreputa- 5 ble," and those more decent than I are "priggish."

I am civil; those less civil than I are "rude," and those 6 more civil than I are "obsequious."

I am dutiful; those less dutiful than I are "irresponsi- 7 ble," and those more dutiful than I are "subservient."

I am an individualist; those less individualistic than I 8 are "conformists," and those more individualistic than I are "kooks."

I am brave; those less brave than I are "lily-livered," 9 and those more brave than I are "hotheads."

I am a moderate; those less moderate than I are "ex- 10 tremists," and those more moderate than I are "fence-sitters."

I am firm; those less firm than I are "soft-hearted," and 11 those more firm than I are "hard-nosed."

I am competitive; those more competitive than I are 12 "wolves," and those less competitive than I are "worms."

I am normally sexed; those less so are "repressed," and 13 those more so are "promiscuous."

I am prudent; those less prudent are "spendthrifts," 14 and those more prudent are "skinflints."

I am patriotic; those less patriotic are "un-American," 15 and those more patriotic are "jingoists."

I am reasonable; those less reasonable are "too emo- 16 tional," and those more reasonable are "too logical."

I am a fond parent; those less fond than I are "au- 17 thoritarian," and those more fond than I are "permissive."

I am a careful driver; those less careful than I are 18 "reckless," and those more careful than I are "slowpokes."

I am the man in the middle, for where I stand deter- 19 mines where the middle is.

QUESTIONS

1. How do the examples explain what Harris means by the phrase, "the man in the middle"?
2. Is Harris illustrating differences in connotation or denotation—or both—in each of his examples?
3. Is Harris pointing to real differences between himself and others in his series of comparisons?
4. What examples can you provide of similar comparisons you make or that you hear made?

WRITING ASSIGNMENTS

1. Analyze a letter to the editor of a newspaper to illustrate the point Harris is making. Analyze the way particular words in the letter are used to put the writer in the "middle."
2. Show how the following statements illustrate the same use of language Harris satirizes in his essay:

> There must be no majority decisions, but only responsible persons . . . Surely every man will have advisers by his side, but the decision will be made by one man. . . . only he may possess the authority and the right to command . . . It will not be possible to dispense with Parliament. But their councilors will then actually give counsel . . . In no chamber does a vote ever take place. They are working institutions and not voting machines. This principle—absolute responsibility unconditionally combined with absolute authority—will gradually breed an elite of leaders such as today, in this era of irresponsible parliamentarianism, is utterly inconceivable.—Adolf Hitler, describing his opponents in *Mein Kampf*; quoted by William L. Shirer, *The Rise and Fall of the Third Reich.*

PART TWO

THE
WHOLE ESSAY

EXPOSITION

Thesis

The thesis of an essay is its central or controlling idea, the proposition or chief argument—the point of the essay. The topic sentence of a paragraph may be either a full or a partial statement of the controlling idea: the thesis is always a full statement of it.

Where the thesis appears depends largely on the audience. If we believe that the audience requires no introduction to the thesis—no background or explanation of the issue or important terms—we may state it in the first sentence. Many newspaper editorials begin with a statement of the thesis—a practice consistent with that of putting the important information in the opening sentences of a news story. Most essayists, by contrast, prefer to build to the thesis—stating it partially or fully in the introductory paragraphs, in company with an explanation of important terms and the issues to be discussed. George Orwell gives such an explanation in the opening paragraph of "Politics and the English Language":

> Most people who bother with the matter at all would admit that the English language is in a bad way, but it is generally assumed that we cannot by conscious action do anything about it. Our civilization is decadent and our language—so the argument runs—must inevitably share in the general collapse. It follows that any struggle against the abuse of language is a sentimental archaism, like preferring candles to electric light or hansom cabs to airplanes. Underneath this lies the half-conscious belief that language is a natural growth and not an instrument which we shape for our own purposes.

Orwell has built to a partial statement of his thesis in his concluding sentence: Language, he will show, is an instrument that we shape to our purposes. And in the opening sentence of his second paragraph he expands this statement to cover the specific concern of the essay—the political uses of language:

> Now, it is clear that the decline of a language must ultimately have political and economic causes. . . .

And in later paragraphs he restates his thesis as he presents various evidence in support of it:

> In our time it is broadly true that political writing is bad writing.
>
> In our time, political speech and writing are largely the defense of the indefensible.
>
> But if thought corrupts language, language can also corrupt thought.

Orwell introduces his thesis early in his essay and restates it throughout. If the thesis needs extensive background and discussion to be understood or perhaps is so controversial that we will win our audience by building to it slowly, we may put it at the end of the essay. In some essays we may not wish to state the thesis at all, but rather let the reader draw conclusions from the details or facts we provide. In this case the thesis is said to be implied.

PEGGY AND PIERRE STREIT

PIERRE STREIT *(1923–1975) and his wife,* PEGGY, *collaborated on numerous newspaper and magazine articles, many of them published in* The New York Times Magazine. *He was also a producer of documentaries for television and business corporations. The Streits wrote much about life in the Middle East and Asia—as in their remarkable portrait of a low caste Indian woman and her world. The caste to which Shanti belongs was commonly referred to as "untouchable," but largely through the influence of the great political leader, Mahatma Gandhi, is now called Harijan—meaning*

*"Child of God." In 1949 the Indian government made
discrimination against Harijans unlawful, but as the
Streits show traditional attitudes remain powerful.*

A Well in India

The hot dry season in India. . . . A corrosive wind drives 1
rivulets of sand across the land; torpid animals stand at the
edge of dried-up water holes. The earth is cracked and in
the rivers the sluggish, falling waters have exposed the
sludge of the mud flats. Throughout the land the thoughts of
men turn to water. And in the village of Rampura these
thoughts are focused on the village well.

It is a simple concrete affair, built upon the hard earth 2
worn by the feet of five hundred villagers. It is surmounted
by a wooden structure over which ropes, tied to buckets, are
lowered to the black, placid depths twenty feet below. Fan-
ning out from the well are the huts of the villagers—their
walls white from sun, their thatched roofs thick with dust
blown in from the fields.

At the edge of the well is a semi-circle of earthen pots 3
and, crouched at some distance behind them, a woman. She
is an untouchable—a sweeper in Indian parlance—a
scavenger of the village. She cleans latrines, disposes of
dead animals and washes drains. She also delivers village
babies, for this—like all her work—is considered unclean
by most of village India.

Her work—indeed, her very presence—is considered 4
polluting, and since there is no well for untouchables
in Rampura, her water jars must be filled by upper-caste
villagers.

There are dark shadows under her eyes and the flesh 5
has fallen away from her neck, for she, like her fellow
outcastes, is at the end of a bitter struggle. And if, in her
narrow world, shackled by tradition and hemmed in by

poverty, she had been unaware of the power of the water of the well at whose edge she waits—she knows it now.

Shanti, 30 years old, has been deserted by her husband, 6 and supports her three children. Like her ancestors almost as far back as history records, she has cleaned the refuse from village huts and lanes. Hers is a life of inherited duties as well as inherited rights. She serves, and her work calls for payment of one chapatty—a thin wafer of unleavened bread—a day from each of the thirty families she cares for.

But this is the hiatus between harvests; the oppressive 7 lull before the burst of monsoon rains; the season of flies and dust, heat and disease, querulous voices and frayed tempers—and the season of want. There is little food in Rampura for anyone, and though Shanti's chores have continued as before, she has received only six chapatties a day for her family—starvation wages.

Ten days ago she revolted. Driven by desperation, she 8 defied an elemental law of village India. She refused to make her sweeper's rounds—refused to do the work tradition and religion had assigned her. Shocked at her audacity, but united in desperation, the village's six other sweeper families joined in her protest.

Word of her action spread quickly across the invisible 9 line that separates the untouchables' huts from the rest of the village. As the day wore on and the men returned from the fields, they gathered at the well—the heart of the village—and their voices rose, shrill with outrage: a *sweeper* defying them all! Shanti, a sweeper *and* a woman challenging a system that had prevailed unquestioned for centuries! Their indignation spilled over. It was true, perhaps, that the sweepers had not had their due. But that was no fault of the upper caste. No fault of theirs that sun and earth and water had failed to produce the food by which they could fulfill their obligations. So, to bring the insurgents to heel, they employed their ultimate weapon; the earthen water jars of the village untouchables would remain empty until they returned to work. For the sweepers of Rampura the well had run dry.

No water: thirst, in the heat, went unslaked. The em- 10
bers of the hearth were dead, for there was no water for
cooking. The crumbling walls of outcaste huts went un-
tended, for there was no water for repairs. There was no
fuel, for the fires of the village were fed with dung mixed
with water and dried. The dust and the sweat and the filth
of their lives congealed on their skins and there it stayed,
while life in the rest of the village—within sight of the
sweepers—flowed on.

The day began and ended at the well. The men, their 11
dhotis wrapped about their loins, congregated at the water's
edge in the hushed post-dawn, their small brass water jugs
in hand, their voices mingling in quiet conversation as they
rinsed their bodies and brushed their teeth. The buffaloes
were watered, their soft muzzles lingering in the buckets
before they were driven off to the fields. Then came the
women, their brass pots atop their heads, to begin the ritual
of water drawing: the careful lowering of the bucket in the
well, lest it come loose from the rope; the gratifying splash
as it touched the water; the maneuvering to make it sink; the
squeal of rope against wooden pulley as it ascended. The
sun rose higher. Clothes were beaten clean on the rocks
surrounding the well as the women gossiped. A traveler
from a near-by road quenched his thirst from a villager's
urn. Two little boys, hot and bored, dropped pebbles into
the water and waited for their hollow splash, far below.

As the afternoon wore on and the sun turned orange 12
through the dust, the men came back from the fields. They
doused the parched, cracked hides of their water buffaloes
and murmured contentedly, themselves, as the water
coursed over their own shoulders and arms. And finally, as
twilight closed in, came the evening procession of women,
stately, graceful, their bare feet moving smoothly over the
earth, their full skirts swinging about their ankles, the heavy
brass pots once again balanced on their heads.

The day was ended and life was as it always was— 13
almost. Only the fetid odor of accumulated refuse and the
assertive buzz of flies attested to strife in the village. For,

while tradition and religion decreed that sweepers must clean, it also ordained that the socially blessed must not. Refuse lay where it fell and rotted.

The strain of the water boycott was beginning to tell on 14 the untouchables. For days they had held their own. But on the third their thin reserve of flesh had fallen away. Movements were slower; voices softer; minds dull. More and more the desultory conversation turned to the ordinary: the delicious memory of sliding from the back of a wallowing buffalo into a pond; the feel of bare feet in wet mud; the touch of fresh water on parched lips; the anticipation of monsoon rains.

One by one the few tools they owned were sold for 15 food. A week passed, and on the ninth day two sweeper children were down with fever. On the tenth day Shanti crossed the path that separated outcaste from upper caste and walked through familiar, winding alleyways to one of the huts she served.

"Your time is near," she told the young, expectant 16 mother. "Tell your man to leave his sickle home when he goes to the fields. I've had to sell mine." (It is the field sickle that cuts the cord of newborn babies in much of village India.) Shanti, the instigator of the insurrection, had resumed her ancestral duties; the strike was broken. Next morning, as ever, she waited at the well. Silently, the procession of upper-caste women approached. They filled their jars to the brim and without a word they filled hers.

She lifted the urns to her head, steadied them, and 17 started back to her quarters—back to a life ruled by the powers that still rule most of the world: not the power of atoms or electricity, nor the power of alliances or power blocs, but the elemental powers of hunger, of disease, of tradition—and of water.

QUESTIONS

1. The Streits build to a statement of their thesis at the end of paragraph 5. Why is it necessary to portray the world of the untouchable before stating the thesis?

2. Where in the essay is the thesis restated? Is the restatement more informative or detailed than the original statement of it?

3. What is the attitude of the authors toward the world they portray and the fate of Shanti? Do they seem to be taking sides?

4. Is it important to the thesis that Shanti is a woman? Are the authors concerned with her as a woman, in addition to their concern for her as an untouchable?

5. Is the concern of the essay equality with the power of water and the power of tradition? Or are these considerations subordinate to the portrayal of the untouchable and the courage shown?

6. Are we given a motive directly for what Shanti does—or is the motive implied?

7. How are transitions made through the seventeen short paragraphs?

WRITING ASSIGNMENTS

1. Develop an idea relating to the power of tradition and illustrate it from personal experience and observation. Provide enough background so that your reader understands why the tradition is important to the people who observe it.

2. Describe a conflict between you and your parents or school officials or between a person and a group of some sort. Explain how the conflict arises from a basic difference in attitude, ideas, or feelings—a difference that reveals something important about you and the other people involved.

GEORGE ORWELL

In his great essay based on his experience as a colonial policeman in Burma in the 1920s, GEORGE ORWELL *tells us much not only about himself but about colonial powers and their agents. He combines his description of the small town and its people with a narrative of what happens when he is summoned to deal with a temporarily crazed elephant that has trampled a townsman. In telling this incident, Orwell is arguing a thesis in a special way—through an example that he wishes to persuade us is typical of the situation faced by the colonial power. Great Britain no longer governs India or Burma, yet the ideas Orwell develops still have pertinence to the world today. More than this, Orwell has something important to say about human nature in general.*

Shooting an Elephant

In Moulmein, in lower Burma, I was hated by large numbers of people—the only time in my life that I have been important enough for this to happen to me. I was subdivisional police officer of the town, and in an aimless, petty kind of way anti-European feeling was very bitter. No one had the guts to raise a riot, but if a European woman went through the bazaars alone somebody would probably spit betel juice over her dress. As a police officer I was an obvious target and was baited whenever it seemed safe to do so. When a nimble Burman tripped me up on the football field and the referee (another Burman) looked the other way, the crowd yelled with hideous laughter. This happened more than once. In the end the sneering yellow faces of young men that met me everywhere, the insults hooted after me when I was at a safe distance, got badly on my nerves. The young Buddhist priests were the worst of all. There were several thousands of them in the town and none of them seemed to have anything to do except stand on street corners and jeer at Europeans. 1

All this was perplexing and upsetting. For at that time I had already made up my mind that imperialism was an evil thing and the sooner I chucked up my job and got out of it the better. Theoretically—and secretly, of course—I was all 2 for the Burmese and all against their oppressors, the British. As for the job I was doing, I hated it more bitterly than I can perhaps make clear. In a job like that you see the dirty work of Empire at close quarters. The wretched prisoners huddling in the stinking cages of the lock-ups, the gray, cowed faces of the long-term convicts, the scarred buttocks of the men who had been flogged with bamboos—all these oppressed me with an intolerable sense of guilt. But I could get nothing into perspective. I was young and ill educated and I had had to think out my problems in the utter silence that is imposed on every Englishman in the East. I did not even know that the British Empire is dying, still less did I know that it is a great deal better than the younger empires that are going to supplant it. All I knew was that I was stuck between my hatred of the empire I served and my rage against the evil-spirited little beasts who tried to make my job impossible. With one part of my mind I thought of the British Raj as an unbreakable tyranny, as something clamped down, in *saecula saeculorum*, upon the will of prostrate peoples; with another part I thought that the greatest joy in the world would be to drive a bayonet into a Buddhist priest's guts. Feelings like these are the normal by-products of imperialism; ask any Anglo-Indian official, if you can catch him off duty.

One day something happened which in a roundabout 3 way was enlightening. It was a tiny incident in itself, but it gave me a better glimpse than I had had before of the real nature of imperialism—the real motives for which despotic governments act. Early one morning the sub-inspector at a police station the other end of the town rang me up on the 'phone and said that an elephant was ravaging the bazaar. Would I please come and do something about it? I did not know what I could do, but I wanted to see what was happening and I got on to a pony and started out. I took my rifle, an old .44 Winchester and much too small to kill an elephant, but I thought the noise might be useful *in terrorem*. Various Burmans stopped me on the way and told me about the elephant's doings. It was not, of course, a wild elephant, but a tame one which had gone "must." It had been chained up, as tame elephants always are when their attack of "must" is due, but on the previous night it had broken its chain and escaped. Its mahout, the only person who could manage it when it was in that state, had set out in pursuit, but had taken the wrong direction and was now twelve hours' journey away, and in the morning the elephant had suddenly reappeared in the town. The Burmese population had no weapons and were quite helpless against it. It had already destroyed somebody's bamboo hut, killed a cow and raided some fruit-stalls and devoured the stock; also it had met the municipal rubbish van and, when the driver jumped out and took to his heels, had turned the van over and inflicted violences upon it.

The Burmese sub-inspector and some Indian consta- 4 bles were waiting for me in the quarter where the elephant had been seen. It was a very poor quarter, a labyrinth of squalid bamboo huts, thatched with palm-leaf, winding all over a steep hillside. I remember that it was a cloudy, stuffy morning at the beginning of the rains. We began questioning the people as to where the elephant had gone and, as usual, failed to get any definite information. That is invariably the case in the East; a story always sounds clear enough at a distance, but the nearer you get to the scene of events the vaguer it becomes. Some of the people said that the elephant had gone in one direction, some said that he had gone in another, some professed not even to have heard of any elephant. I had almost made up my mind that the whole story was a pack of lies, when we heard yells a little distance away. There was a loud, scandalized cry of "Go away, child! Go away this instant!" and an old woman with a switch in her hand came round the corner of a hut, violently shooing away a crowd of naked children. Some more women followed, clicking their tongues and exclaiming; evidently there was something that the children ought not to have seen. I rounded the hut and saw a man's dead body sprawling in the mud. He was an Indian, a black Dravidian coolie, almost naked, and he could not have been dead many minutes. The people said that the elephant had come suddenly upon him round the corner of the hut, caught him with its trunk, put its foot on his back and ground him into the earth. This was the rainy season and the ground was soft, and his face had scored a trench a foot deep and a couple of yards long. He was lying on his belly with arms crucified and head sharply twisted to one side. His face was coated with mud, the eyes wide open, the teeth bared and grinning with an expression of unendurable agony. (Never tell me, by the way, that the dead look peaceful. Most of the corpses I have seen looked devilish.) The friction of the great beast's foot had stripped the skin from his back as neatly as one skins a rabbit. As soon as I saw the dead man I sent an orderly to a friend's house nearby to borrow an elephant rifle. I had already sent back the pony, not wanting it to go mad with fright and throw me if it smelt the elephant.

The orderly came back in a few minutes with a rifle and 5 five cartridges, and meanwhile some Burmans had arrived and told us that the elephant was in the paddy fields below, only a few hundred yards away. As I started forward practically the whole population of the quarter flocked out of the houses and followed me. They had seen the rifle and were all shouting excitedly that I was going to shoot the elephant. They had not shown much interest in the elephant when he was merely ravaging their homes, but it was different now that he was going to be shot. It was a bit of fun to them, as it would be to an English crowd; besides they wanted the meat. It made me vaguely uneasy. I had no intention of shooting the elephant—I had merely sent for the rifle to defend myself if necessary—and it is always unnerving to have a crowd following you. I marched down the hill, looking and feeling a fool, with the rifle over my shoulder and an ever-growing army of people jostling at my heels. At the bottom, when you got away from the huts, there was a metalled road and beyond that a miry waste of paddy fields a thousand yards across, not yet ploughed but soggy from the first rains and dotted with coarse grass. The elephant was standing eight yards from the road, his left side toward us. He took not the slightest notice of the crowd's approach. He was tearing up bunches of grass, beating them against his knees to clean them, and stuffing them into his mouth.

I had halted on the road. As soon as I saw the elephant 6 I knew with perfect certainty that I ought not to shoot him. It is a serious matter to shoot a working elephant—it is comparable to destroying a huge and costly piece of machinery—and obviously one ought not to do it if it can possibly be avoided. And at that distance, peacefully eating, the elephant looked no more dangerous than a cow. I thought then and I think now that his attack of "must" was already passing off; in which case he would merely wander harmlessly about until the mahout came back and caught him. Moreover, I did not in the least want to shoot him. I decided that I would watch him for a little while to make sure that he did not turn savage again, and then go home.

But at that moment I glanced round at the crowd that 7 had followed me. It was an immense crowd, two thousand at the least and growing every minute. It blocked the road for a long distance on either side. I looked at the sea of yellow faces above the garish clothes—faces all happy and excited over this bit of fun, all certain that the elephant was going to be shot. They were watching me as they would watch a conjurer about to perform a trick. They did not like me, but with the magical rifle in my hands I was momentarily worth watching. And suddenly I realized that I should have to shoot the elephant after all. The people expected it of me and I had got to do it; I could feel their two thousand wills pressing me forward, irresistibly. And it was at this moment, as I stood there with the rifle in my hands, that I first grasped the hollowness, the futility of the white man's dominion in the East. Here was I, the white man with his gun, standing in front of the unarmed native crowd—seemingly the leading actor of the piece; but in reality I was only an absurd puppet pushed to and fro by the will of those yellow faces behind. I perceived in this moment that when the white man turns tyrant it is his own freedom that he destroys. He becomes a sort of hollow, posing dummy, the conventionalized figure of a sahib. For it is the condition of his rule that he shall spend his life in trying to impress the "natives," and so in every crisis he has got to do what the "natives" expect of him. He wears a mask, and his face grows to fit it. I had got to shoot the elephant. I had committed myself to doing it when I sent for the rifle. A sahib has got to act like a sahib; he has got to appear resolute, to know his own mind and do definite things. To come all that way, rifle in hand, with two thousand people marching at my heels, and then to trail feebly away, having done nothing—no, that was impossible. The crowd would laugh at me. And my whole life, every white man's life in the East, was one long struggle not to be laughed at.

But I did not want to shoot the elephant. I watched him 8 beating his bunch of grass against his knees with that preoccupied grandmotherly air that elephants have. It seemed to me that it would be murder to shoot him. At that age I was not squeamish about killing animals, but I had never shot an elephant and never wanted to. (Somehow it always seems worse to kill a *large* animal.) Besides, there was the beast's owner to be considered. Alive, the elephant was worth at least a hundred pounds; dead, he would only be worth the value of his tusks, five pounds, possibly. But I had got to act quickly. I turned to some experienced-looking Burmans who had been there when we arrived, and asked them how the elephant had been behaving. They all said the same thing: he took no notice of you if you left him alone, but he might charge if you went too close to him.

It was perfectly clear to me what I ought to do. I ought 9 to walk up to within, say, twenty-five yards of the elephant and test his behavior. If he charged, I could shoot; if he took no notice of me, it would be safe to leave him until the mahout came back. But also I knew that I was going to do no such thing. I was a poor shot with a rifle and the ground was soft mud into which one would sink at every step. If the elephant charged and I missed him, I should have about as much chance as a toad under a steam-roller. But even then I was not thinking particularly of my own skin, only of the watchful yellow faces behind. For at that moment, with the crowd watching me, I was not afraid in the ordinary sense, as I would have been if I had been alone. A white man mustn't be frightened in front of "natives"; and so, in general, he isn't frightened. The sole thought in my mind was that if anything went wrong those two thousand Burmans would see me pursued, caught, trampled on, and reduced to a grinning corpse like that Indian up the hill. And if that happened it was quite probable that some of them would laugh. That would never do. There was only one alternative. I shoved the cartridges into the magazine and lay down on the road to get a better aim.

The crowd grew very still, and a deep, low, happy sigh, 10 as of people who see the theater curtain go up at last, breathed from innumerable throats. They were going to have their bit of fun after all. The rifle was a beautiful German thing with crosshair sights. I did not then know that in shooting an elephant one would shoot to cut an imaginary bar running from ear-hole to ear-hole. I ought, therefore, as the elephant was sideways on, to have aimed straight at his ear-hole; actually I aimed several inches in front of this, thinking the brain would be further forward.

When I pulled the trigger I did not hear the bang or feel 11 the kick—one never does when a shot goes home—but I heard the devilish roar of glee that went up from the crowd. In that instant, in too short a time, one would have thought, even for the bullet to get there, a mysterious, terrible change had come over the elephant. He neither stirred nor fell, but every line of his body had altered. He looked suddenly stricken, shrunken, immensely old, as though the frightful impact of the bullet had paralyzed him without knocking him down. At last, after what seemed a long time—it might have been five seconds, I dare say—he sagged flabbily to his knees. His mouth slobbered. An enormous senility seemed to have settled upon him. One could have imagined him thousands of years old. I fired again into the same spot. At the second shot he did not collapse but climbed with desperate slowness to his feet and stood weakly upright, with legs sagging and head drooping. I fired a third time. That was the shot that did for him. You could see the agony of it jolt his whole body and knock the last remnant of strength from his legs. But in falling he seemed for a moment to rise, for as his hind legs collapsed beneath him he seemed to tower upward like a huge rock toppling, his trunk reaching skyward like a tree. He trumpeted, for the first and only time. And then down he came, his belly toward me, with a crash that seemed to shake the ground even where I lay.

I got up. The Burmans were already racing past me 12 across the mud. It was obvious that the elephant would never rise again, but he was not dead. He was breathing very rhythmically with long rattling gasps, his great mound of a side painfully rising and falling. His mouth was wide open—I could see far down into caverns of pale pink throat. I waited a long time for him to die, but his breathing did not weaken. Finally I fired my two remaining shots into the spot where I thought his heart must be. The thick blood welled out of him like red velvet, but still he did not die. His body did not even jerk when the shots hit him, the tortured breathing continued without a pause. He was dying, very slowly and in great agony, but in some world remote from me where not even a bullet could damage him further. I felt that I had got to put an end to that dreadful noise. It seemed dreadful to see the great beast lying there, powerless to move and yet powerless to die, and not even to be able to finish him. I sent back for my small rifle and poured shot after shot into his heart and down his throat. They seemed to make no impression. The tortured gasps continued as steadily as the ticking of a clock.

In the end I could not stand it any longer and went 13 away. I heard later that it took him half an hour to die. Burmans were bringing dahs and baskets even before I left, and I was told they had stripped his body almost to the bones by the afternoon.

Afterward, of course, there were endless discussions 14 about the shooting of the elephant. The owner was furious, but he was only an Indian and could do nothing. Besides, legally I had done the right thing, for a mad elephant has to be killed, like a mad dog, if its owner fails to control it. Among the Europeans opinion was divided. The older men said I was right, the younger men said it was a damn shame to shoot an elephant for killing a coolie, because an elephant was worth more than any damn Coringhee coolie. And afterward I was very glad that the coolie had been killed; it put me legally in the right and it gave me a sufficient pretext for shooting the elephant. I often wondered whether any of the others grasped that I had done it solely to avoid looking a fool.

QUESTIONS

1. Orwell states in paragraph 3: "One day something happened which in a roundabout way was enlightening. It was a tiny incident in itself, but it gave me a better glimpse than I had had before of the real nature of imperialism—the real motives for which despotic governments act." The incident, in its details, reveals the psychology of the imperialist ruler. What effect do the stuffy, cloudy weather and the behavior of the Burmans and their attitude toward the elephant have on this psychology? Why is the dead coolie described in detail in paragraph 4? Why is the shooting of the elephant described in detail in paragraph 11? In general, how does the incident reveal the motives Orwell mentions?

2. The incident reveals more than just the motives of the imperialist ruler: What does it reveal about mob and crisis psychology and the man in the middle?

3. Where in the essay is the thesis stated, and how do you account for its placement? Does Orwell restate it?

4. The exact diction contributes greatly to the development of the thesis, for Orwell does not merely *tell us*, he makes us see. In paragraph 11, for example, he states: ". . . I heard the devilish roar of *glee* that went up from the crowd." He might have chosen *laughter, hilarity,* or *mirth* to describe the behavior of the crowd, but *glee* is the exact word because it connotes something that the other three words do not—malice. And the

elephant "*sagged* flabbily to his knees," not *dropped* or *sank*, because *sagged* connotes weight and, in the context of the passage, age. What does Orwell mean in the same paragraph by "His mouth slobbered" and "An enormous senility seemed to have settled upon him"? In paragraph 12 why "*caverns* of pale pink throat" rather than *depths*? In paragraph 4 why is the corpse *grinning* rather than *smiling*? (Consult the synonym listings in your dictionary, or compare definitions.)

WRITING ASSIGNMENTS

1. Illustrate the last sentence of the essay from your own experience. Build the essay to the moment when you acted to avoid looking like a fool. Make your reader see and feel what you saw and felt.

2. Orwell states: "And my whole life, every white man's life in the East, was one long struggle not to be laughed at." Drawing on your experience and observation, discuss what you see as the feelings and motives of people charged with enforcing rules of some sort—perhaps hall monitors in high school, or lifeguards at a swimming pool, or supervisors at a playground, or baby-sitters. Use your discussion to draw a conclusion, as Orwell does.

ERIC SEVAREID

Born in 1912 in Velva, North Dakota, ERIC SEVAREID *graduated from the University of Minnesota in 1935 and immediately began his career as a journalist with the* Minneapolis Journal. *He later reported for the Paris edition of* The New York Herald Tribune. *In 1939 Sevareid began his long association with the Columbia Broadcasting Company as a war correspondent in Europe. From 1964 to 1977 he delivered his commentary on the CBS Evening News. His numerous books include* Small Sounds in the Night *(1956) and an au-*

tobiography, Not So Wild a Dream *(1976). Like Orwell in "Shooting an Elephant," Sevareid builds through a careful presentation of detail to increasingly broad truths about the world of his youth and human nature generally.*

Velva, North Dakota

My home town has changed in these thirty years of the American story. It is changing now, will go on changing as America changes. Its biography, I suspect, would read much the same as that of all other home towns. Depression and war and prosperity have all left their marks; modern science, modern tastes, manners, philosophies, fears and ambitions have touched my town as indelibly as they have touched New York or Panama City.

Sights have changed: there is a new precision about street and home, a clearing away of chicken yards, cow barns, pigeon-crested cupolas, weed lots and coulees, the dim and secret adult-free rendezvous of boys. An intricate metal "jungle gym" is a common backyard sight, the sack swing uncommon. There are wide expanses of clear windows, designed to let in the parlor light, fewer ornamental windows of colored glass designed to keep it out. Attic and screen porch are slowly vanishing and lovely shades of pastel are painted upon new houses, tints that once would have embarrassed farmer and merchant alike.

Sounds have changed; I heard not once the clopping of a horse's hoof, nor the mourn of a coyote. I heard instead the shriek of brakes, the heavy throbbing of the once-a-day Braniff airliner into Minot, the shattering sirens born of war, the honk of a diesel locomotive which surely cannot call to faraway places the heart of a wakeful boy like the old steam whistle in the night. You can walk down the streets of my town now and hear from open windows the intimate voices of the Washington commentators in casual converse on the great affairs of state; but you cannot hear on Sunday morning the singing in Norwegian of the Lutheran hymns; the old country seems now part of a world left long behind and the old-country accents grow fainter in the speech of my Velva neighbors.

The people have not changed, but the *kinds of* people 4 have changed: there is no longer an official, certified town drunk, no longer a "Crazy John," spitting his worst epithet, "rotten chicken legs," as you hurriedly passed him by. People so sick are now sent to places of proper care. No longer is there an official town joker, like the druggist MacKnight, who would spot a customer in the front of the store, have him called to the phone, then slip to the phone behind the prescription case, and imitate the man's wife to perfection with orders to bring home more bread and sausage and Cream of Wheat. No longer anyone like the early attorney J. L. Lee, who sent fabulous dispatches to that fabulous tabloid, the *Chicago Blade*, such as his story of the wild man captured on the prairie and chained to the wall in the drugstore basement. (This, surely, was Velva's first notoriety; inquiries came from anthropologists all over the world.)

No, the "characters" are vanishing in Velva, just as they 5 are vanishing in our cities, in business, in politics. The "well-rounded, socially integrated" personality that the progressive schoolteachers are so obsessed with is increasing rapidly, and I am not at all sure that this is good. Maybe we need more personalities with knobs and handles and rugged lumps of individuality. They may not make life more smooth; more interesting they surely make it.

They eat differently in Velva now; there are frozen 6 fruits and sea food and exotic delicacies we only read about in novels in those meat-and-potato days. They dress differently. The hard white collars of the businessmen are gone with the shiny alpaca coats. There are comfortable tweeds now, and casual blazers with a touch in their colors of California, which seems so close in time and distance.

It is distance and time that have changed the most and 7 worked the deepest changes in Velva's life. The telephone,

the car, the smooth highway, radio and television are con-
solidating the entities of our country. The county seat of
Towner now seems no closer than the state capital of Bis-
marck; the voices and concerns of Presidents, French pre-
miers and Moroccan pashas are no farther away than the
portable radio on Aunt Jessey's kitchen table. The national
news magazines are stacked each week in Harold Anderson's drugstore beside the new soda fountain, and the excellent *Minot Daily News* smells hot from the press each
afternoon.

Consolidation. The nearby hamlets of Sawyer and 8
Logan and Voltaire had their own separate banks and papers and schools in my days of dusty buggies and Model T's
and marooned in the snowdrifts. Now these hamlets are
dying. A bright yellow bus takes the Voltaire kids to Velva
each day for high school. Velva has grown—from 800 to
1,300—because the miners from the Truax coal mine can
commute to their labors each morning and the nearby
farmers can live in town if they choose. Minot has tripled in
size to 30,000. Once the "Magic City" was a distant and
splended Baghdad, visited on special occasions long prepared for. Now it is a twenty-five minute commuter's jump
away. So P. W. Miller and Jay Louis Monicken run their
businesses in Minot but live on in their old family homes in
Velva. So Ray Michelson's two girls on his farm to the west
drive up each morning to their jobs as maids in Minot
homes. Aunt Jessey said, "Why, Saturday night I counted
sixty-five cars just between here and Sawyer, all going up to
the show in Minot."

The hills are prison battlements no longer; the prairies 9
no heart-sinking barrier, but a passageway free as the swelling ocean, inviting you to sail home and away at your whim
and your leisure. (John and Helen made an easy little jaunt
of 700 miles that week-end to see their eldest daughter in
Wyoming.)

Consolidation. Art Kumm's bank serves a big region 10
now; its assets are $2,000,000 to $3,000,000 instead of the

$200,000 or $300,000 in my father's day. Eighteen farms near Velva are under three ownerships now. They calculate in sections; "acres" is an almost forgotten term. Aunt Jessey owns a couple of farms, and she knows they are much better run. "It's no longer all take out and no put in," she said. "Folks strip farm now; they know all about fertilizers. They care for it and they'll hand on the land in good shape." The farmers gripe about their cash income, and not without reason at the moment, but they will admit that life is good compared with those days of drought and foreclosure, manure banked against the house for warmth, the hand pump frozen at 30 below and the fitful kerosene lamp on the kitchen table. Electrification has done much of this, eased back-breaking chores that made their wives old as parchment at forty, brought life and music and the sound of human voices into their parlors at night.

And light upon the prairie. "From the hilltop," said 11 Aunt Jessey, the farms look like stars at night."

Many politicians deplore the passing of the old family- 12 size farm, but I am not so sure. I saw around Velva a release from what was like slavery to the tyrannical soil, release from the ignorance that darkens the soul and from the loneliness that corrodes it. In this generation my Velva friends have rejoined the general American society that their pioneering fathers left behind when they first made the barren trek in the days of the wheat rush. As I sit here in Washington writing this, I can feel their nearness. I never felt it before save in my dreams.

But now I must ask myself: Are they nearer to one 13 another? And the answer is no; yet I am certain that this is good. The shrinking of time and distance has made contrast and relief available to their daily lives. They do not know one another quite so well because they are not so much obliged to. I know that democracy rests upon social discipline, which in turn rests upon personal discipline; passions checked, hard words withheld, civic tasks accepted, work well done, accountings honestly rendered. The old-fashioned small town was this discipline in its starkest, most primitive form; without this discipline the small town would have blown itself apart.

For personal and social neuroses festered under this 14 hard scab of conformity. There was no place to go, no place to let off steam; few dared to voice unorthodox ideas, read strange books, admire esoteric art or publicly write or speak of their dreams and their soul's longings. The world was not "too much with us," the world was too little with us and we were too much with one another.

The door to the world stands open now, inviting them 15 to leave anytime they wish. It is the simple fact of the open door that makes all the difference; with its opening the stale air rushed out. So, of course, the people themselves do not have to leave, because, as the stale air went out, the fresh air came in.

Human nature is everywhere the same. He who is not 16 forced to help his neighbor for his own existence will not only give him help, but his true good will as well. Minot and its hospital are now close at hand, but the people of Velva put their purses together, built their own clinic and homes for the two young doctors they persuaded to come and live among them. Velva has no organized charity, but when a farmer falls ill, his neighbors get in his crop; if a townsman has a financial catastrophe his personal friends raise a fund to help him out. When Bill's wife, Ethel, lay dying so long in the Minot hospital and nurses were not available, Helen and others took their turns driving up there just to sit with her so she would know in her gathering dark that friends were at hand.

It is personal freedom that makes us better persons, 17 and they are freer in Velva now. There is no real freedom without privacy, and a resident of my home town can be a private person much more than he could before. People are able to draw at least a little apart from one another. In drawing apart, they gave their best human instincts room for expansion.

QUESTIONS

1. Where does Severeid indicate his attitude toward his home town? What is his thesis?

2. How does the selection of detail in the whole essay support the dominating impression Sevareíd creates of the town in his opening paragraph? Is any of this detail unrelated to this impression?

3. What is the tone of the comment on the story of the wild man, and how is the comment related to the thesis?

4. How does Sevareid emphasize the causes of the change in life in Velva? Does he indicate a main cause?

5. What does Sevareid mean by the statement in paragraph 13, "without this discipline the small town would have blown itself apart"?

6. Sevareid points up a series of paradoxes toward the end. What are these, and what do they contribute to the tone of the conclusion?

WRITING ASSIGNMENTS

1. Analyze how Eric Sevareid introduces his thesis and keeps it before the reader. Then discuss another way he might have organized the essay.

2. Describe the changes that have occurred in the neighborhood in which you grew up and discuss the reasons for these changes.

ART BUCHWALD

Born in Mount Vernon, New York, ART BUCHWALD *attended the University of Southern California and during the Second World War served in the Marine Corps. Most of his columns for* The Washington Post *and other newspapers are devoted to Washington politics, which*

*Buchwald satirizes with abundant humor and wit. Oc-
casionally, as in this dialogue illustrating the "generation gap," he turns his gaze on other aspects of American life.*

Clean Your Room

You don't really feel the generation gap in this country
until a son or daughter comes home from college for
Christmas. Then it strikes you how out of it you really are.

This dialogue probably took place all over America last
Christmas week:

"Nancy, you've been home from school for three days
now. Why don't you clean up your room?"

"We don't have to clean up our rooms at college,
Mother."

"That's very nice, Nancy, and I'm happy you're going to
such a freewheeling institution. But while you're in the
house, your father and I would like you to clean up your
room."

"What difference does it make? It's *my* room."

"I know, dear, and it really doesn't mean that much to
me. But your father has a great fear of the plague. He said
this morning if it is going to start anywhere in this country,
it's going to start in your room."

"Mother, you people aren't interested in anything that's
relevant. Do you realize how the major corporations are
polluting our environment?"

"Your father and I are very worried about it. But right
now we're more concerned with the pollution in your bedroom. You haven't made your bed since you came home."

"I never make it up at the dorm."

"Of course you don't, and I'm sure the time you save
goes toward your education. But we still have those old-
fashioned ideas about making beds in the morning, and we
can't shake them. Since you're home for such a short time,
why don't you do it to humor us?"

"For heaven's sake, Mother, I'm grown up now. Why do you have to treat me like a child?"

"We're not treating you like a child. But it's very hard for us to realize you're an adult when you throw all your clothes on the floor."

"I haven't thrown all my clothes on the floor. Those are just the clothes I wore yesterday."

"Forgive me. I exaggerated. Well, how about the dirty dishes and empty soft-drink cans on your desk? Are you collecting them for a science project?"

"Mother, you don't understand us. You people were brought up to have clean rooms. But our generation doesn't care about things like that. It's what you have in your head that counts."

"No one respects education more than your father and I do, particularly at the prices they're charging. But we can't see how living in squalor can improve your mind."

"That's because of your priorities. You would rather have me make up my bed and pick up my clothes than become a free spirit who thinks for myself."

"We're not trying to stifle your free spirit. It's just that our Blue Cross has run out, and we have no protection in case anybody in the family catches typhoid."

"All right, I'll clean up my room if it means that much to you. But I want you to know you've ruined my vacation."

"It was a calculated risk I had to take. Oh, by the way, I know this is a terrible thing to ask of you, but would you mind helping me wash the dinner dishes?"

"Wash dishes? Nobody washes dishes at school."

"Your father and I were afraid of that."

QUESTIONS

1. Do you think Buchwald is making some real point, or is his purpose merely to amuse the reader? Is he successful in what he tries to do?

2. Is he poking fun at both Nancy and her parents—or at one of them only?

3. What is gained by presenting the parents and daughter through dialogue rather than through a summary of what happened?

WRITING ASSIGNMENTS

1. Write a dialogue or an essay on a humorous situation involving teenagers and parents that reveals something about both of them—perhaps an attitude typical of these groups. Let the reader discover this truth through your details; don't state the truth directly.

2. Discuss how much Buchwald's observations of parents and teenagers correspond to your own observations or personal experience.

MARTIN GANSBERG

A native of Brooklyn, New York, MARTIN GANSBERG *studied at St. John's University and later taught at Fairleigh Dickinson University. In 1942 he joined the staff of* The New York Times; *his famous account of the murder of Kitty Genovese appeared in* The Times *on March 17, 1964. In his article Gansberg presents a situation that sociologists and psychologists were to examine in later years: the unwillingness of witnesses of a crime to report it or help the victim. Later in this book, two social psychologists, John M. Darley and Bibb Latané, offer an explanation for the behavior of those who witnessed the killing of Kitty Genovese and did nothing.*

38 Who Saw Murder

For more than half an hour 38 respectable, law-abiding 1 citizens in Queens watched a killer stalk and stab a woman in three separate attacks in Kew Gardens.

Twice their chatter and the sudden glow of their bed- 2
room lights interrupted him and frightened him off. Each
time he returned, sought her out, and stabbed her again.
Not one person telephoned the police during the assault;
one witness called after the woman was dead.

That was two weeks ago today. 3

Still shocked is Assistant Chief Inspector Frederick M. 4
Lussen, in charge of the borough's detectives and a veteran
of 25 years of homicide investigations. He can give a
matter-of-fact recitation on many murders. But the Kew
Gardens slaying baffles him—not because it is a murder,
but because the "good people" failed to call the police.

"As we have reconstructed the crime," he said, "the 5
assailant had three chances to kill this woman during a
35-minute period. He returned twice to complete the job. If
we had been called when he first attacked, the woman might
not be dead now."

This is what the police say happened beginning at 3:20 6
A.M. in the staid, middle-class, tree-lined Austin Street area:

Twenty-eight-year-old Catherine Genovese, who was 7
called Kitty by almost everyone in the neighborhood, was
returning home from her job as manager of a bar in Hollis.
She parked her red Fiat in a lot adjacent to the Kew Gardens Long Island Rail Road Station, facing Mowbray Place.
Like many residents of the neighborhood, she had parked
there day after day since her arrival from Connecticut a year
ago, although the railroad frowns on the practice.

She turned off the lights of her car, locked the door, and 8
started to walk the 100 feet to the entrance of her apartment
at 82–70 Austin Street, which is in a Tudor building, with
stores in the first floor and apartments on the second.

The entrance to the apartment is in the rear of the 9
building because the front is rented to retail stores. At night
the quiet neighborhood is shrouded in the slumbering
darkness that marks most residential areas.

Miss Genovese noticed a man at the far end of the lot, 10
near a seven-story apartment house at 82–40 Austin Street.
She halted. Then, nervously, she headed up Austin Street

toward Lefferts Boulevard, where there is a call box to the 102nd Police Precinct in nearby Richmond Hill.

She got as far as a street light in front of a bookstore 11 before the man grabbed her. She screamed. Lights went on in the 10-story apartment house at 82–67 Austin Street, which faces the bookstore. Windows slid open and voices punctuated the early-morning stillness.

Miss Genovese screamed: "Oh, my God, he stabbed 12 me! Please help me! Please help me!"

From one of the upper windows in the apartment 13 house, a man called down: "Let that girl alone!"

The assailant looked up at him, shrugged and walked 14 down Austin Street toward a white sedan parked a short distance away. Miss Genovese struggled to her feet.

Lights went out. The killer returned to Miss Genovese, 15 now trying to make her way around the side of the building by the parking lot to get to her apartment. The assailant stabbed her again.

"I'm dying!" she shrieked. "I'm dying!" 16

Windows were opened again, and lights went on in 17 many apartments. The assailant got into his car and drove away. Miss Genovese staggered to her feet. A city bus, O–10, the Lefferts Boulevard line to Kennedy International Airport, passed. It was 3:35 A.M.

The assailant returned. By then, Miss Genovese had 18 crawled to the back of the building, where the freshly painted brown doors to the apartment house held out hope for safety. The killer tried the first door; she wasn't there. At the second door, 82–62 Austin Street, he saw her slumped on the floor at the foot of the stairs. He stabbed her a third time—fatally.

It was 3:50 by the time the police received their first call, 19 from a man who was a neighbor of Miss Genovese. In two minutes they were at the scene. The neighbor, a 70-year-old woman, and another woman were the only persons on the street. Nobody else came forward.

The man explained that he had called the police after 20 much deliberation. He had phoned a friend in Nassau

County for advice and then he had crossed the roof of the building to the apartment of the elderly woman to get her to make the call.

"I didn't want to get involved," he sheepishly told the 21 police.

Six days later, the police arrested Winston Moseley, a 22 29-year-old business-machine operator, and charged him with homicide. Moseley had no previous record. He is married, has two children and owns a home at 133–19 Sutter Avenue, South Ozone Park, Queens. On Wednesday, a court committed him to Kings County Hospital for psychiatric observation.

When questioned by the police, Moseley also said that 23 he had slain Mrs. Annie May Johnson, 24, of 146–12 133d Avenue, Jamaica, on Feb. 29 and Barbara Kralik, 15, of 174–17 140th Avenue, Springfield Gardens, last July. In the Kralik case, the police are holding Alvin L. Mitchell, who is said to have confessed that slaying.

The police stressed how simple it would have been to 24 have gotten in touch with them. "A phone call," said one of the detectives, "would have done it." The police may be reached by dialing "O" for operator or SPring 7-3100.

Today witnesses from the neighborhood, which is made 25 up of one-family homes in the $35,000 to $60,000 range with the exception of the two apartment houses near the railroad station, find it difficult to explain why they didn't call the police.

A housewife, knowingly if quite casually, said, "We 26 thought it was a lover's quarrel." A husband and wife both said, "Frankly, we were afraid." They seemed aware of the fact that events might have been different. A distraught woman, wiping her hands in her apron, said, "I didn't want my husband to get involved."

One couple, now willing to talk about that night, said 27 they heard the first screams. The husband looked thoughtfully at the bookstore where the killer first grabbed Miss Genovese.

"We went to the window to see what was happening," 28

he said, "but the light from our bedroom made it difficult to see the street." The wife, still apprehensive, added: "I put out the light and we were able to see better."

Asked why they hadn't called the police, she shrugged 29 and replied: "I don't know."

A man peeked out from a slight opening in the doorway 30 to his apartment and rattled off an account of the killer's second attack. Why hadn't he called the police at the time? "I was tired," he said without emotion. "I went back to bed."

It was 4:25 A.M. when the ambulance arrived to take the 31 body of Miss Genovese. It drove off. "Then," a solemn police detective said, "the people came out."

QUESTIONS

1. What point or thesis is Gansberg developing through the details of what happened to Kitty Genovese? Does he state the point directly—through a statement of his own or through one of the participants?

2. What aspects of the incident does he emphasize? What details best reveal this emphasis?

3. What is the tone of the narrative? Does Gansberg dramatize what happened through heightened characterization of the participants and through a heightened setting? Need the episode be dramatized to make the point it does?

4. What do you think is Gansberg's purpose in writing—to inform the reader of the facts, to awaken the reader's conscience, to promote confidence in the police, or what?

5. How effective is the essay in achieving its purpose?

WRITING ASSIGNMENTS

1. Give an account of an event you witnessed—a traffic accident, for example—and describe the behavior of the participants, including that of observers and others not directly involved. Let your details make your point, and emphasize those that develop it most.

2. Write an interpretation of the episode, discussing what the details reveal to you about the world Gansberg describes—its attitudes and values in particular. Defend your interpretation, explaining why you interpret the details as you do.

3. Compare Kew Gardens with your own neighborhood in its attitudes and values. Be concrete in discussing these attitudes and values: don't merely name them, or characterize the people of your neighborhood in general terms. Build your comparison to an idea that it supports.

Main and Subordinate Ideas

The thesis is the most important idea in an essay. When an essay builds to its thesis through a series of subordinate ideas and details, we may sense a rising importance of ideas in it, even perhaps a sense of climax. As in the paragraph, it is important that we sense at least the relative importance of these ideas and details. An essay in which all of these seemed to have the same importance would be extremely hard to read.

We can sense this relative importance of ideas even in the topic sentences, as in these sentences that open the first seven paragraphs of Sevareid's essay on Velva, North Dakota. The different indentations show the relative weight of each idea:

> My home town has changed in these thirty years. . . .
>> Sights have changed. . . .
>> Sounds have changed. . . .
>> The people have not changed, but the kinds of people have changed.
>>> No, the "characters" are vanishing in Velva. . . .
>> They eat differently in Velva now. . . .
> It is distance and time that have changed the most and worked the deepest changes in Velva's life.

Sevareid builds to his thesis through a series of increasingly broad generalizations. Here are the opening sentences of the last five paragraphs:

>> Many politicians deplore the passing of the old family-size farm, but I am not so sure.
>> But now I must ask myself: Are they nearer to one another?
>> For personal and social neuroses festered under this hard scab of conformity.
>> The door to the world stands open now. . . .
> Human nature is everywhere the same.
> It is personal freedom that makes us better persons, and they are freer in Velva now [THESIS].

Sevareid's sentences show that we do not always need formal transitions to tell us which ideas are main and subordinate. The clear logical relationship of Sevareid's shows their relative importance. But as in the paragraph, formal transitions are sometimes needed. Having a sense of the relative importance of our ideas and details is important as we write.

IRWIN EDMAN

The American philosopher and essayist IRWIN EDMAN, *born in 1896, received his education at Columbia University, where he taught until his death in 1954. Edman did much to generate popular interest in philosophy through his many essays and books, including* Philosopher's Holiday *and* Under Whatever Sky—*from which the essay reprinted here is taken. He was a master of the formal essay, writing in a plain style that frequently conveys a quiet humor and friendliness.*

Sincerity as a Fine Art

I remember often during my early adolescence listening to older people making conversation. I vowed I would never willingly be a conspirator at such transparent hypocrisies. When *I* went out to dinner, I found myself saying, I should speak only when I felt like it, and I should say only what was on my mind. I used to listen while my elders pretended to have a fascinated interest in visitors with whom I knew they had only the most remote concern, and hear them discuss with affected animation matters that I knew bored them to pain. I remember having had it explained to me that this was the least that good manners demanded. It was at this moment that I came to the conclusion that good manners and dubious morals had much in common.

In these matters, I have become subdued to the general   2
color of civilized society. It has long ago been brought home
to me that a guest has obligations in addition to that of
eating the food provided by his host. It is fair enough that
one should, if not sing, at least converse for one's supper. I
have even come to believe that my elders of long ago were
more interested in their visitors than I had supposed. I have
lighted upon the fact that questions asked out of politeness
may elicit answers that are fascinating on their own. An
enchanting story may be the unearned increment of a con-
ventional inquiry.

And yet I have not ceased to be troubled at the momen-   3
tum with which on a social occasion one is embarked on a
brief career of insincerity. I have found myself expressing
opinions on Russia or on psychiatry that I had not known I
possessed. I have sometimes, out of sheer inability to get out
of it, maintained a position on old age-security, or on old age
itself, that, save for some impulsive remark I had let fall, I
should not have considered it a point of honor to defend as
my considered philosophy on the subject. On shamefully
numerous occasions, I have repeated an anecdote by which I
was myself bored to death. I have talked with dowagers
about literature, art, and education, at moments when all
three of these lofty themes seemed to me insufferably tedious and stuffy.

I have come to admire those sturdy individualists who   4
say—as I once planned to say—only whatever comes into
their minds, and speak only when they are spoken to, and
perhaps not even then. But I must admit I find them difficult
socially, these high-minded boors who can be pricked into
only the most minimal of replies, these dedicated rough-
necks who find a savage pleasure in telling you without
compromise what they think of everything, including your
loyalties and your enthusiasms—and possibly yourself.

There must be some way of acting both agreeably and   5
sincerely. It is a fine art, practiced, one is told, by a few witty
eighteenth-century courtiers. But wits today are rather cele-
brated for their malignity. It is a difficult alternative, that

between truth and charm, and I confess that I am tempted to seek the easier and more genial path. If one plumped for sincerity, one would get to be known simply as a bear, a bear who would soon be walking alone, a boorish bear who at any rate would seldom be invited out to dinner. As Santayana remarks somewhere, "For a man of sluggish mind and bad manners, there is decidedly no place like home."

QUESTIONS

1. The main idea of paragraph 1 may be stated as follows: In my youth I was disturbed by the hypocrisy of adults. What subordinate ideas develop it in the paragraph?

2. The main idea of paragraph 2 may be stated as follows: As an adult I see the matter somewhat differently. What subordinate ideas develop it in the paragraph?

3. What are the main ideas of paragraphs 3–5?

4. Which of these ideas would you select as the thesis, and why?

5. To what extent does Edman depend on transitions to distinguish the main and subordinate ideas?

6. Does Edman offer a solution to the problem discussed in paragraphs 1–4? Is he suggesting, for example, that he found a middle course between two extremes? Can you offer a better solution?

WRITING ASSIGNMENTS

1. Edman's essay is organized in a traditional form: statement of a problem (paragraphs 1–4), discussion of a solution (paragraph 5). Write an essay in which you explore a similar problem and, like Edman, explore a solution, examining the difficulties of finding one.

2. Write an essay on one of the following topics. Give your thesis emphasis by putting it in a prominent place in the essay— perhaps at the end of your opening paragraph, or in the final paragraph. If you begin the essay with your thesis, you may want to give it emphasis by repeating or restating it at key points:

a. the art of keeping friends
b. on not giving advice
c. the art of persuading children
d. on getting along with neighbors or roommates
e. on living away from home

MARGARET MEAD AND RHODA METRAUX

MARGARET MEAD (1901–1978) was for more than forty years an ethnologist at the Museum of Natural History in New York City. She taught at numerous universities, mostly at Columbia, and wrote some of the most influential books in the field of social anthropology—including Male and Female *and* Growing Up in New Guinea. *RHODA METRAUX, an anthropologist also associated with the Museum of Natural History, collaborated with Mead on the writing of several books and a series of magazine essays, later collected in the book* A Way of Seeing. *Mead and Metraux look at the same subject Art Buchwald does—from the point of view of the anthropologist. Their ideas on how children can be encouraged to develop an independent judgment might be compared with those of John Holt later in this book.*

The Gift of Autonomy

Every gift we give carries with it our idea of what a present 1
is. Perhaps it expresses our personality; perhaps, on the
contrary, it is what we believe the recipient really wants, a
choice based on careful listening for the slightest hint of
what he longs for or needs or should have, even though he
may not realize it.

Gifts from parents to children always carry the most 2

meaningful messages. The way parents think about presents goes one step beyond the objects themselves—the ties, dolls, sleds, record players, kerchiefs, bicycles and model airplanes that wait by the Christmas tree. The gifts are, in effect, one way of telling boys and girls, "We love you even though you have been a bad boy all month" or, "We love having a daughter" or, "We treat all our children alike" or, "It is all right for girls to have some toys made for boys" or, "This alarm clock will help you get started in the morning all by yourself." Throughout all the centuries since the invention of a Santa Claus figure who represented a special recognition of children's behavior, good and bad, presents have given parents a way of telling children about their love and hopes and expectations for them.

When I was a child, my parents used to give me a pair 3 of books each Christmas. One was "light," easy reading; the other was "heavy," a book I had to think about if I was to enjoy it. This combination carried with it the message that there are different kinds of pleasure to be gained through reading and that I should discover each kind for myself.

If we think about all the presents we have given our 4 children over the years, we will see how they fit into the hopes we have for each child. I do not mean this in the simple sense that we delight in a little girl's femininity, and so give her dolls, or that we implement a boy's masculinity by giving him model planes and boxing gloves. We do, of course, speak to our children in this simplest form of symbolism. And we do, of course, personalize what we say when we give our outdoors son a fishing rod and his experiment-minded brother a microscope.

However, our giving also carries more subtle and com- 5 plex messages. For example, we can ask ourselves: "What am I saying to my children about growing up to be independent, autonomous people?" An abstract question of this kind can be posed in relation to a whole range of presents for children of both sexes and of different ages. Where the choice to be made is between a simple toy engine that the child himself can wind up and a more complicated one that I shall have to wind up for him, which one do I give him? Choosing a doll for a little girl, do I buy her a perishable costume doll with one beautiful dress, a washable doll with a wardrobe or a doll for which she will make dresses out of the materials I also give her? The costume doll can perhaps be dressed and undressed, but that is all. A bath would be ruinous. A sturdy doll with a ready-made wardrobe places choice in the child's own hands. She herself can dress and undress it, bathe it safely and decide whether her "little girl" will wear pink or blue, plaid or plain. Giving my child materials out of which to fashion doll dresses is a lovely idea, and may perhaps encourage her to learn how to sew. But choice and autonomy both are reduced because now I must help her at every step.

We can ask questions of this kind also about the pres- 6 ents of money that are given our children by grandparents and godparents, aunts and uncles and family friends. What do we tell our children about the bright silver dollar tucked into the toe of a Christmas stocking or the grown-up looking check that is made out in the child's own name? Is the money meant to be used now for some specific purpose— for the charm bracelet a little girl has admired or the radio a boy wants for his own room? Or is it an inducement, perhaps, to begin saving for the car a teen-ager must wait five years to own? Is the child told, directly or indirectly: "This is your money to do with as you like"? Or is the child asked: "Would you rather spend it or put it in the bank?"

By defining the alternatives so sharply, we are, in effect, 7 robbing the child of choice. In fact, when you tell him that the money is his and then give directions, hint at alternatives or reproach him for spending it in one way instead of another, the gift carries a very definite message: "I don't really trust your choices. I don't really want you to choose." If, on the other hand, the message is simple and direct ("This is your money, yours, to dispose of as you like"), then the child may even solicit your advice. But there is no real turning back once you have said, "This is your money."

Over the years, there are always new ways of reinforc- 8

ing or detracting from our children's growing sense of independence. For example, if you give a boy a box of stationery imprinted with his name and a supply of postage stamps, you are showing him that you expect him to write, address and mail his own letters. This means, of course, that you may never see the letters he writes, or you may become a consultant on appropriate terms of address or the correct abbreviations of names of states. At this point you can give him an almanac in which he himself can look up the answers to his questions—or you can keep the almanac on your own desk and become the mediator between his questions and the information he needs.

Giving a girl a diary with a key is a way in which a mother can tell her daughter (boys, on the whole, do not keep diaries) that she respects her child's growing sense of identity and independence. Giving a boy a desk is one way of fostering his sense of personal privacy; but if we continually tidy it up or complain about its untidiness, as we see it, the original message miscarries. 9

In many families the climax, and in some the crisis, of their individual pattern of giving comes as the children approach college, when their parents prepare to give them the most expensive "gift" of all—a college education. Of course, parents are not, as a rule, literally "giving" their children an education. What they are giving them is the opportunity to become educated. 10

Many parents today meet the responsibility of supporting their children through the college years, wholly or in part, by taking out insurance policies for this special purpose. Usually such policies, whatever their specific form, are payable to the parents. Then the choice of a college and the course of study remains firmly in the parents' hands. Americans believe very strongly that he who pays the pipe calls the tune. 11

This is the *customary* way of doing things. It carries with it the message that our children, although approaching adulthood, are still children in our eyes. But this need not be. The money instead can be set up as a fund available to 12 the boy or girl. Its purpose can be specified: This is not money for just anything. It is money for higher education, intended to give you freedom and choice within this area of your life.

For children who have grown up with an ever-enlarging 13 sense of their own autonomy and independence, intelligent handling of the opportunity for further education will come naturally and easily. They are free, if they like, to postpone going to college for a year. Or they can drop out for a semester or a year without fearing that the tuition money will have vanished when they want to go back. A girl can marry before she goes to college, or while she is still a student, knowing that the choice of when and where she will continue her education remains open to her. Next year or ten years from now the money will be there, waiting, ready for her when she wants and needs it.

Like the small presents of early childhood that carry the 14 message "You need my help," the educational insurance policy in the parents' names places responsibility in the parents' hands. In many cases parents are not even required to spend the money on the education of the child in whose interest the policy was acquired. But when money is placed in the child's own name, a trust for a special purpose, the parents are saying: "This is what I hope to give you— the right of choice. I respect your right to choose. My gift is intended to underwrite your freedom to be a person. Long ago I gave you stamps so you could mail your own letters. I gave you an allowance so you could move more freely in your own world. Now, as then, I want you to be an autonomous, self-starting person, someone who enjoys interdependence with other people because instead of fighting for your independence, you have grown into it."

All our giving carries with it messages about ourselves, 15 our feelings about those to whom we give, how we see them as people and how we phrase the ties of relationship. Christmas giving, in which love and hope and trust play such an intrinsic part, can be an annual way of telling our children that we think of each of them as a person, as we also hope they will come to think of us.

QUESTIONS

1. If the statement in paragraph 11—"Americans believe very strongly that he who pays the piper calls the tune"—were the thesis of the essay, how might the essay have been organized to develop it? What parts of the present essay would you omit?

2. Where does the thesis of the essay first appear, and how is it restated later?

3. In what order are the various problems of giving presents discussed in paragraphs 4–10?

4. Why do the authors devote a considerable part of the essay to the educational insurance policy?

5. Is the purpose of the essay to analyze the practice of gift giving, or to give advice to parents and others on this matter? Do the authors address their readers as colleagues, or clients seeking advice, or merely as general readers?

WRITING ASSIGNMENTS

1. Analyze the gifts you gave members of your family last Christmas or Chanukah, and discuss the reasons for your choices. Give particular attention to your expectations in choosing the gift for each person.

2. Discuss the ways high school teachers can encourage or discourage students from doing their best work. Distinguish the problems that arise in two different subjects like English and mathematics.

WILLIAM ZINSSER

WILLIAM ZINSSER, *whose definition of cluttered language appears earlier in this book, shows that behind the popular term "dropout" are attitudes toward success and failure that we need to examine closely. Like Eric Sevareid and George Orwell earlier in this part of the book, he uses a specific situation to develop some general truths. The subject Zinsser writes about is one that*

invites a special jargon—terms like "dropout" that ig-
nore individual differences and concerns. Like Orwell,
Sevareid and other writers of the journalistic essay, he
shows that complex ideas can be discussed in an easy
and clear style without sacrifice of depth.

The Right to Fail

I like "dropout" as an addition to the American language   1
because it's brief and it's clear. What I don't like is that we
use it almost entirely as a dirty word.

We only apply it to people under twenty-one. Yet an   2
adult who spends his days and nights watching mindless TV
programs is more of a dropout than an eighteen-year-old
who quits college, with its frequently mindless courses, to
become, say, a VISTA volunteer. For the young, dropping
out is often a way of dropping in.

To hold this opinion, however, is little short of treason   3
in America. A boy or girl who leaves college is branded a
failure—and the right to fail is one of the few freedoms that
this country does not grant its citizens. The American dream
is a dream of "getting ahead," painted in strokes of gold
wherever we look. Our advertisements and TV commercials
are a hymn to material success, our magazine articles a toast
to people who made it to the top. Smoke the right cigarette
or drive the right car—so the ads imply—and girls will be
swooning into your deodorized arms or caressing your expensive lapels. Happiness goes to the man who has the
sweet smell of achievement. He is our national idol, and
everybody else is our national fink.

I want to put in a word for the fink, especially the   4
teen-age fink, because if we give him time to get through his
finkdom—if we release him from the pressure of attaining
certain goals by a certain age—he has a good chance of
becoming our national idol, a Jefferson or a Thoreau, a
Buckminster Fuller or an Adlai Stevenson, a man with a

mind of his own. We need mavericks and dissenters and dreamers far more than we need junior vice-presidents, but we paralyze them by insisting that every step be a step up to the next rung of the ladder. Yet in the fluid years of youth, the only way for boys and girls to find their proper road is often to take a hundred side trips, poking out in different directions, faltering, drawing back, and starting again.

"But what if we fail?" they ask, whispering the dreadful 5 word across the Generation Gap to their parents, who are back home at the Establishment, nursing their "middle-class values" and cultivating their "goal-oriented society." The parents whisper back: "Don't!"

What they should say is "Don't be afraid to fail!" Fail- 6 ure isn't fatal. Countless people have had a bout with it and come out stronger as a result. Many have even come out famous. History is strewn with eminent dropouts, "loners" who followed their own trail, not worrying about its odd twists and turns because they had faith in their own sense of direction. To read their biographies is always exhilarating, not only because they beat the system, but because their system was better than the one that they beat.

Luckily, such rebels still turn up often enough to prove 7 that individualism, though badly threatened, is not extinct. Much has been written, for instance, about the fitful scho-lastic career of Thomas P. F. Hoving, New York's former Parks Commissioner and now director of the Metropolitan Museum of Art. Hoving was a dropout's dropout, entering and leaving schools as if they were motels, often at the request of the management. Still, he must have learned something during those unorthodox years, for he dropped in again at the top of his profession.

His case reminds me of another boyhood—that of Hol- 8 den Caulfield in J. D. Salinger's *The Catcher in the Rye*, the most popular literary hero of the postwar period. There is nothing accidental about the grip that this dropout con-tinues to hold on the affections of an entire American gen-eration. Nobody else, real or invented, has made such an engaging shambles of our "goal-oriented society," so gratified our secret belief that the "phonies" are in power and the good guys up the creek. Whether Holden has also reached the top of his chosen field today is one of those speculations that delight fanciers of good fiction. I speculate that he has. Holden Caulfield, incidentally, is now thirty-six.

I'm not urging everyone to go out and fail just for the 9 sheer therapy of it, or to quit college just to coddle some vague discontent. Obviously it's better to succeed than to flop, and in general a long education is more helpful than a short one. (Thanks to my own education, for example, I can tell George Eliot from T. S. Eliot, I can handle the pluperfect tense in French, and I know that Caesar beat the Helvetii because he had enough frumentum.) I only mean that failure isn't bad in itself, or success automatically good.

Fred Zinnemann, who has directed some of Hol- 10 lywood's most honored movies, was asked by a reporter, when *A Man for All Seasons* won every prize, about his previous film *Behold a Pale Horse*, which was a box-office disaster. "I don't feel any obligation to be successful," Zinnemann replied. "Success can be dangerous—you feel you know it all. I've learned a great deal from my failures." A similar point was made by Richard Brooks about his ambitious money loser, *Lord Jim*. Recalling the three years of his life that went into it, talking almost with elation about the troubles that befell his unit in Cambodia, Brooks told me that he learned more about his craft from this considerable failure than from his many earlier hits.

It's a point, of course, that applies throughout the arts. 11 Writers, playwrights, painters and composers work in the expectation of periodic defeat, but they wouldn't keep going back into the arena if they thought it was the end of the world. It isn't the end of the world. For an artist—and perhaps for anybody—it is the only way to grow.

Today's younger generation seems to know that this is 12 true, seems willing to take the risks in life that artists take in art. "Society," needless to say, still has the upper hand—it sets the goals and condemns as a failure everybody who won't play. But the dropouts and the hippies are not as afraid of failure as their parents and grandparents. This could mean, as their elders might say, that they are just plumb lazy, secure in the comforts of an affluent state. It could also mean, however, that they just don't buy the old standards of success and are rapidly writing new ones.

Recently it was announced, for instance, that more than 13 two hundred thousand Americans have inquired about service in VISTA (the domestic Peace Corps) and that, according to a Gallup survey, "more than three million American college students would serve VISTA in some capacity if given the opportunity." This is hardly the road to riches or to an executive suite. Yet I have met many of these young volunteers, and they are not pining for traditional success. On the contrary, they appear more fulfilled than the average vice-president with a swimming pool.

Who is to say, then, if there is any right path to the top, 14 or even to say what the top consists of? Obviously the colleges don't have more than a partial answer—otherwise the young would not be so disaffected with an education that they consider vapid. Obviously business does not have the answer—otherwise the young would not be so scornful of its call to be an organization man.

The fact is, nobody has the answer, and the dawning 15 awareness of this fact seems to me one of the best things happening in America today. Success and failure are again becoming individual visions, as they were when the country was younger, not rigid categories. Maybe we are learning again to cherish this right of every person to succeed on his own terms and to fail as often as necessary along the way.

QUESTIONS

1. Zinsser develops his thesis in paragraphs 1–4. What is his thesis, and what sentence states it most fully?

2. Paragraphs 5–8 provide support for the thesis by *defending* the right to fail. What form does this defense take? What does Zinsser gain by citing the hero of *Catcher in the Rye*?

3. Paragraphs 9–12 *qualify* what has been said earlier: Zinsser tells us what he does not mean by "the right to fail." What does he not mean, and how does he qualify his idea of failure through discussion of success and failure in the arts, the film art specifically?

4. Paragraphs 13–15 provide additional supporting evidence that the maverick has a role to play in American society (Zinsser's point in paragraphs 6 and 7) and restate the thesis to conclude the essay. What is that evidence, and how is the thesis restated?

5. Do you agree with Zinsser that parents and society provide teenagers with rigid standards of success? Do you agree with his belief that failure is a means to growth?

WRITING ASSIGNMENTS

1. Discuss your agreement or disagreement with Zinsser about the demands made on teenagers today, drawing on your own experiences and ideas of success and failure. Do not try to speak for all teenagers. Limit yourself to your experience and personal goals.

2. Discuss the value of two or three different courses you took in high school, with attention to the effect of these courses on your choice of a college or a college major, or the development of long-term goals (or all of these).

3. Write an essay on one of the following topics. Develop it as Zinsser develops his essay: state a thesis and explain it, defend it with supporting evidence, qualify it (explaining what you do not mean and limiting your generalizations), provide additional evidence for one or more of your supporting ideas, and restate your thesis in conclusion:
   a. unintended lessons taught in high school classes
   b. lessons that cannot be taught in school
   c. discovering the nature of prejudice
   d. "rules" that work at home or at school

Beginning and Ending

If we want to make our ideas convincing, we will want to capture the attention of our readers and hold it. We will lose this attention if we describe in too much detail how we intend to proceed. We need usually to indicate a point of view and perhaps also the ways we will develop the subject. There may be excellent reasons for beginning an essay with the thesis, but in most instances the thesis needs an introduction: We can build to it by showing why the subject is worth discussing and why the thesis is worth the reader's attention. The following opening paragraphs effectively accomplish this purpose:

> The administration of criminal justice and the extent of individual moral responsibility are among the crucial problems of a civilized society. They are indissolubly linked, and together they involve our deepest personal emotions. We often find it hard to forgive ourselves for our own moral failures. All of us, at some time or other, have faced the painful dilemma of when to punish and when to forgive those we love—our children, our friends. How much harder it is, then, to deal with the stranger who transgresses.—David L. Bazelon, "The Awesome Decision"

> The aim of this book is to delineate two types of clever schoolboy: the converger and the diverger. The earlier chapters offer a fairly detailed description of the intellectual abilities, attitudes and personalities of a few hundred such boys. In the later chapters, this description is then used as the basis for a more speculative discussion—of the nature of intelligence and originality and of the ways in which intellectual and personal qualities interact. Although the first half of the book rests heavily on the results of psychological tests, and the last two chapters involve psychoanalytic theory, I have done my best to be intelligible, and, wherever possible, interesting to everyone interested in clever schoolboys: parents, schoolteachers, dons, psychologists, administrators, clever schoolboys—Liam Hudson, *Contrary Imaginations*

In the first of these paragraphs, the author eases readers into the subject: personal consideration—their attitude toward themselves, their children, their friends—arouses their interest. The author assumes that this interest needs to be aroused. The second opening paragraph challenges interest: no easing into the subject here, for the opening sentence announces both the subject of the book and a key distinction. The bonus is the wit of the author— and the promise of more.

An effective ending will not let the discussion drop; the reader should not have a sense of loose ends, of lines of thought left uncompleted. In the formal essay, the ending may be used for a restatement of the thesis or perhaps a full statement of it—if we have chosen to build to it. One of the most effective conclusions is the reference back to ideas that opened the essay.

THE NEW YORKER

The following essay appeared in THE NEW YORKER *magazine—in "The Talk of the Town," a collection of short essays, sketches, and occasional political comments that open each issue. They are written by the staff of the magazine. As the title of the column suggests, their purpose is to converse with the reader about the world and New York City in particular as observed that week. This sketch of an upper Manhatten street lets the details make their point without discussion. It is particularly effective in developing a thesis by example, though "thesis" is perhaps misleading as a term for the impression* The New Yorker *gives us of Columbus Avenue.*

Street Writing

One recent evening, we spent an interesting couple of hours   1
observing the fate of a strip of wet concrete that lay unprotected in front of the Food City on Columbus Avenue at Seventieth Street. Wet concrete, we noted, provides a simple and efficient test of human character, separating those with

a streak of devilishness from those temperate souls who
have never had the urge to write on a wall or carve their
names on a tree. We found that it is impossible to predict
how a man or a woman will behave on being confronted by
an unguarded stretch of newly poured concrete; nothing in
a person's dress, sex, age, haircut, or apparent relationship
to the world indicates whether or not he is the type to make
a sudden change from a normal to an unusual street position (standing to squatting), grab an implement, and start
engraving his initials. In the time we spent in front of Food
City—which was closed for the night, its dimmed lights
giving a lunar glow to a line of honeydew melons in the
window—we saw in the behavior of passersby a sort of
small drama of conscience. We saw Columbia Avenue stroll-
ers succumb to the temptation to write in the concrete; we
saw temptation pondered and successfully resisted; and we
saw manifestations of outrage at those who had succumbed.
As the evening fleets of taxis raced down the avenue toward
midtown, we watched a well-groomed man of perhaps sixty,
wearing a pin-striped summer-weight suit and carrying a
briefcase with gold initials on the side, pause, stare at the
concrete, and then, without a hint of self-consciousness,
bend down in a dignified swooping motion and scratch two
initials with the end of a pen that he produced from his
jacket pocket. (We couldn't see if the letters were the same as
those on his briefcase.) He studied his handiwork for a
second and then walked briskly away. A young man with
thinning curly hair who was wearing a Pac-Man T-shirt
stepped in a gingerly fashion into the center of the concrete
with his eight- or nine-year-old daughter, who had blond
braids and was wearing starched overalls and a battery-
powered light-up visor. They began writing their names.
"Put a heart around mine, Daddy, please?" said the little
girl, hopping up and down.

    A deeply suntanned man, barechested under an unbut- 2
toned shirt, came strolling by with a tall woman in bloomers
and started berating the father and daughter for writing in
the concrete. "It's disgraceful," he said. "How would you

like someone to come and write his name on the walkway to your apartment? How about in your living room?" The bare-chested man seemed to have just finished dinner at one of the restaurants on Columbus Avenue, and to be in a bumptious mood; he spoke loudly and at length to the father, the daughter, and the rest of a little group that had quickly gathered around the strip of wet concrete, and he moved on, finally, with the self-satisfied gait of one who feels himself to be entirely in the right.

"What a loudmouth!" said the curly-haired father to his ₃ daughter, who had been standing with her lips contracted as if she were about to burst out laughing. "Don't listen to *anyone* who goes around with his belly button showing."

The number of people around the stretch of concrete ₄ was growing, and enough of them were crouching to give it the look of a minor archeological site. Two young women, both wearing pedal pushers and sneakers, excused themselves as they elbowed their way past us. One of them wrote a name and surrounded it with a sketch of a canine creature.

"Is that a dog or a coyote?" we asked.   ₅

"A coyote," she said, walking away rapidly.   ₆

A bearded man in his sixties or seventies who was ₇ wearing hiking boots and a pair of very short shorts in an Army camouflage pattern paused to study the scene with a disdainful expression on his face. "It's absolutely the same thing as writing graffiti in the subways," he remarked to a woman dressed entirely in yellow, who had been watching for a while. "Most of these people complain about subway graffiti, but look at them now. And it's so egotistical. Everyone is just writing names and initials."

"It's not egotistical, it's romantic," said the woman in ₈ yellow. "Look at this." She pointed to an inscription that read "Peg is a Goddess."

"They look like adults making mud pies," said the ₉ bearded man, with another disdainful glance at the writers.

A group of black teen-agers on bicycles paused to watch ₁₀ the scene for a minute and then rode whooping toward the Park. An Oriental woman in a red T-shirt came up to a young man who had just finished scratching two sets of initials within a heart. "I think it's terrible that you people walk through our neighborhood and deface the sidewalks," she said. "You wouldn't like it if this happened on your street."

"But this *is* my street," replied the young man, who had 11 an angular jaw and was wearing the kind of thick rubber sandals that Californians call beachwalkers. "I live in that apartment bulding over there, and I always thought that this was one of the most boring sidewalks I ever saw. Anything is an improvement."

Like most impromptu public events in New York, the 12 sidewalk-writing session soon attracted the police. When a patrol car pulled up in front of Food City, members of the small crowd around the concrete began a swift mass sidling movement toward the street corner, their faces as guiltily blank as those of a pack of schoolchildren caught scribbling in the halls. "Hey, you!" a policeman shouted at the dispersing crowd, and one conscience-stricken man in jogging clothes turned his head. "Come here, you!" the policeman thundered, and the jogger, who was wearing a Walkman with the earphones like a collar around his neck, came slowly back to stand in front of the officer.

"Did you know," the policeman said in a sarcastic voice, 13 "that there's a law against defacing public property? Didn't you think that what you were doing just might be against the law?"

"Everybody else was doing it," said the jogger. 14

"And if everybody went and jumped off the Empire 15 State Building, I suppose you'd do *that*, too!" the policeman said, looking slightly sheepish as he uttered this age-old retort of nannies.

The officer dismissed the jogger (who settled his ear- 16 phones defiantly on his head as he walked away) and told the remaining loiterers to move along.

For the next few hours, patrol cars hovered around the 17 concrete strip, and any late-night saunterer on Columbus Avenue who felt a surge of temptation as he looked at the concrete had to keep it to himself. Walking in front of Food City next morning, we found that the orgy of lawlessness of the night before had resulted in a tangle of names, initials, and hearts, including one verse (unreadable) and several drawings (including the coyote). As we strolled down the avenue a few nights later, we saw that the letters in the concrete had already been worn faint by the passage of feet and by the friction of grocery boxes delivered to the market. By now, like the results of most minor sins, the concrete writing is a scarcely visible part of the daily landscape.

QUESTIONS

1. What kind of introduction to the essay do we receive in paragraph 1?

2. What is the thesis of the essay? Does the essay build to a statement of the thesis, perhaps in the closing paragraph, or instead introduce it early?

3. We are told in paragraph 1 that "nothing in a person's dress, sex, age, haircut, or apparent relationship to the world" will predict behavior in the situation described. What details in the description of the man with the briefcase, the man in the T-shirt, and the suntanned man make this point? Are the descriptions of other participants also significant?

4. What impression do you have of the writer, and how is this impression created? Do you notice a special point of view—a way of seeing people and city life? Does the writer seek to be objective in reporting the episode? In general, what does the point of view contribute to the essay?

WRITING ASSIGNMENTS

1. Describe a similar episode which taught you something important about the people of your neighborhood or school. Use your opening paragraph to give enough information about the setting to permit your reader to see what you did. If you introduce your thesis early in the essay, restate it in your conclusion— drawing together the various observations you have made.

2. Develop the idea that "nothing in a person's dress, sex, age, haircut, or apparent relationship to the world" can predict what this person will do in a situation similar to that in the essay. Present several examples to make this point.

BOB GREENE

> BOB GREENE, *a columnist for the* Chicago Tribune, *also writes a column for* Esquire Magazine—*where the essay reprinted here first appeared in 1982. Like George Plimpton, who practiced with the Detroit Lions to experience professional football firsthand, Greene once joined a rock band to discover firsthand the life of a rock musician. In this essay he writes about the world he knows best—that of the newspaperman. From an account of his personal experiences with newspapers he builds to a general consideration of the media today.*

Paper Boy

When I was twelve, maybe thirteen, I would ride the bus 1 downtown with my best friend, Jack Roth, and we would kill the day just walking around the stores.

When darkness came we would wait for the bus to take 2 us home. Standing on Broad Street just east of High, we would look over at the big building across the street from the statehouse. It was the building that was the home of *The Columbus Dispatch*. Atop the building was a red neon sign that spelled the paper's name out in Old English script, and beneath the logo was the slogan: OHIO'S GREATEST HOME NEWSPAPER.

We would stand there, Saturday dusk after Saturday 3 dusk, and we would stare up at that sign, blazing red in the

sky, and it would seem that there was nothing more powerful in all this world than *The Columbus Dispatch.*

I've been thinking about that lately because, with the 4
seemingly endless stories of great newspapers wheezing
and dying, I figure it is unlikely that young boys and girls
stand on corners in awe of newspaper buildings anymore.

Which is probably not all that unhealthy; there was a 5
time when newspapers were thought of as so all-potent that
nothing on earth could stand in their way. They were burly
and arrogant and at times despotic; they ruled their cities,
and to cross the publisher or editor of the town's leading
newspaper was akin to political suicide. Newspapers were in
fact what governments were supposed to be in theory: the
rulers of their constituents, the monarchs of their municipalities.

So it is probably good, in a way, that such a thing is 6
disappearing. But I find it mostly melancholy; I am a newspaperman, I have been a newspaperman since I was sixteen
years old, and I sense the passing of an era. Newspapers
will surely survive, in one form or another. But many newspapers will die—many already have—and even the ones
that live are unlikely to cause young boys to stand on the
street corner in reverie.

When *The Washington Star* was going down, Mary 7
McGrory, the paper's superlative columnist, complained
that people often stopped her as she went about her rounds
and said, "And how is the *Star* doing?" It made her feel
awful; the question was asked as one might ask about a
relative with a terrible and incurable disease. More than
anything else, that question made her understand how
things were changing. In a past that seems shockingly recent, such a question might have sounded absurd. Newspapers occasionally died before, yes; but never did they seem
so generically weak, so fragile; never did they seem worthy
of the public's worried concern.

Newspapers have been hated, and they have survived 8
that; newspapers have been idealized, and they have survived that. But never before have newspapers been pa-

tronized, and even pitied. It is happening now, in each town where a great newspaper faces death. Speeches are made on city-council floors, and statements are read by concerned mayors, and eulogies are delivered by television anchormen to audiences the newspapers would love to have. It used to be the newspapers that told the councilmen and the mayors and the television reporters what the agenda was. Everything seems to be turning around.

There is a temptation to go overboard in telling what it feels like to walk into a newspaper's city room. The fact of the matter is, there is no way to go overboard. When I first entered a city room it was the most intoxicating feeling I had ever experienced, and that feeling stays with me to this day. 9

Much of the sensory onslaught has changed in this electronic age; but twenty years ago, to hear the clatter of a floor full of typewriters, and smell the musk from the paste-pots, and hear the reporters yelling "Boy!" as they summoned the copykids to pick up their stories—to wander into that atmosphere for the first time was to know, instantly, what you wanted to do for the rest of your life. 10

Forget literature; immortality lay in a front-page by-line about a four-car fatal on I-70. In the city room, suddenly nothing seemed small-town anymore; if you went out and saw something, and then came back and wrote it up, everyone you knew—all of your neighbors, all of your family, all of your friends—would know about it in the morning, too. If you hadn't seen it, no one would know it had happened; because you were there, everyone would know. 11

There was no feeling in the world like finishing your last paragraph on deadline and seeing the sheet of yellow paper move from city editor to copy editor to slot man to pneumatic tube—and then, forty-five minutes later, while the rest of the city slept, to see the first papers come up with that story on Page One, and your name riding atop it. 12

It was a guarantee of eternal adolescence; the world was reinvented each day, each morning you were going to see something you had never seen before . . . and then you were going to get paid to tell people about it. And the people 13 were out there; that was a given, they needed you, they had always needed their newspaper, they were waiting for that paper boy to show up with their daily news. You sat in the city room and you could almost sense those people waiting for that thump on the front stoop, the sound that announced that you and your newspaper had arrived again.

There was no real hint that the audience was not always 14 going to be there. Television was a presence, true, but it seemed not to threaten the local morning and afternoon papers. In the city room, you sensed that over at the TV stations they were waiting for that thump at their front door, too, to learn what the news really was. All through the decade of the 1960s, that was the case; television was everywhere, but it was taking its cues from the papers.

It was during the 1970s that this changed. Working in 15 the city room, you did not notice it right away. You were too busy fashioning the day's facts into newspaper stories; that consumed so much of your time that it did not occur to you that, just maybe, people weren't reading the front page the same way they used to. They didn't particularly like to read, and now they didn't have to. Television had become the front page, and if you were candid with yourself, you had to admit that television was pretty good at it. This skill you were so proud of—this boiling of accidents and local disasters into swallowable stories—was easily transferable to the television screen. And those people who were waiting for that thump at the front door . . . now they were waiting for the anchormen whose names they knew instantly. A byline suddenly seemed like something out of the Gay Nineties.

If you were lucky, your publishers and editors were 16 anticipating what was going on, and were changing your newspaper into something it had never been before. They were conceding the front page to television, and concentrating on special sections and features and columns. If you were unlucky, your publishers and editors were pretending that nothing had changed, and the product you were putting out every day was being delivered to an audience that, maybe without even knowing it, felt that it was somehow quaint in the 1980s. The delivery process itself—the printing of thousands of papers, each to be hand delivered or peddled individually—seemed ominous in an age of electronic efficiency and economic peril. In any event, the newspaper you dreamed of as a kid—the newspaper that was your town's major way of finding out what happened yesterday—was gone forever. You could pretend it was still the same, but there were days when you noticed that even you didn't read most of the front-page stories past the first two paragraphs. And you were a newspaperman.

When newspaper reporters gather these days, it is this 17 kind of thing they talk about. They have all had the experience: They have run around on a story all day, hurried back to the office, gone over their notes, crafted the information into a smooth and concise report. And they have gone to bed knowing that, by the time the readers reach out the front door for their papers in the morning, all of the information will seem very old. The readers will have heard all about it on the late-night TV news before going to sleep. As often as not, the newspaper reporters will have watched the same broadcasts.

The common response among most of us is to try to do 18 what we do better or in a different way than the television reporters. Give the story a different twist, or a literary flair that can't be carried off on TV. Sometimes this works; many newspapers prosper. But they aren't what they were before. They aren't their communities' principal source for news— and that is what made us go into newspaper work in the first place. If someone had told us that we were going to be working for a sort of daily magazine published on newsprint, we probably would have said no thanks.

I have hedged my bets. I work for this magazine, and I 19 also work for *ABC News Nightline*, a television program whose technological reach astounds me each time I come in touch with it.

But I am different from the other people who work for 20 *Esquire*, and I am different from the other people who work for ABC. I am different because I am a newspaperman; not a former newspaperman, but a newspaperman who walks into a city room every morning of his life. My home base is the *Chicago Tribune*, and I am a little embarrassed to admit that the feeling I get in that city room is the same I got so many years ago, when I was first allowed to feel whatever it is in the air of a newspaper office.

In many ways I am afraid to leave it; all the signs tell all of us that newspaper work is like manufacturing buggies in the days when automobiles first took to the streets, but when you are in love with something, you cannot walk away. My magazine colleagues deal with proofs for glossy pages as part of their daily routine; my television colleagues watch the news being fed to New York from satellite points around the world. I wait for the first edition to come up, just as I did when I was sixteen years old   21

Some people dream of writing great works of literature; some people dream of stirring people's imaginations with the beauty and flow of their prose.   22

For some of us, though, for some reason, the goal was considerably less grand. All we wanted to do was go out every day and see something new, and then write what we saw into stories that people would read in their newspapers the next morning. Everything else was extra.   23

And the funny thing is, the dream goes on. In today's mail I received a letter from a young man with whose work I am familiar. He has a job in a fairly secure part of the publishing industry. In his letter, though, he told me that he wanted desperately to be a newspaperman. He named the paper to which he is applying; it is a newspaper that—if I know anything about this business—will be dead within two years.   24

But I wrote him the letter of recommendation; I said that he is a fine young talent, and that he will do good work if only he is given a chance. He is not an obtuse person; he must realize that there is no certain future in what he is pursuing. But something inside him makes him want to do it, and I did not feel like talking him out of it. I just wrote the letter and mailed it off, and I hope he gets the job.   25

So it is not the best feeling when we see what is happen- 26 ing in the newspaper community. We are supposed to be fairly glib when it comes to any other subject—newspapermen, it is said, can write about cats or kings—but we stumble around when we try to explain what all of this is doing to us.

For me it's fairly simple. I have my limitations, but I 27 have the ability to do something that I doubt Saul Bellow or John Updike can do. Sitting on the rewrite bank, I can give you fifteen inches about a four-alarm fire on a twenty-minute deadline. It may not count for anything, but I can do it.

QUESTIONS

1. How do the opening four paragraphs establish a mood and state the subject of the essay?

2. Is Greene saying that newspapers are less efficient in conveying news than television is, or that they are more efficient? Or is he not concerned with the relative efficiency of these media? If he is not primarily concerned with this difference, what is his chief concern? What is his thesis?

3. What are the pleasures of writing for a newspaper, according to Greene? And what does he imply is the difference between writing for a newspaper and writing "literature"?

4. Does Greene use his concluding paragraph to state or to restate his thesis or to provide additional details or to add a final reflection?

5. At what level of usage does Green write—Formal, General, or Informal—and how do you know? Is the style suited to the subject matter and point of view of the essay?

6. What sense of Greene's personality do you get from the essay? What conveys his personality most?

WRITING ASSIGNMENTS

1. Discuss the extent to which you depend on the newspaper and television (and other sources of news) for information from day

to day. Then discuss the extent to which your experience gives support to Greene's view of newspapers.

2. Greene states: "Newspapers have been hated, and they have survived that; newspapers have been idealized, and they have survived that." Discuss your attitude toward the newspaper you read regularly—how useful or indispensable you find it, how much you respect or idealize it as a source of information or as an authority.

Order of Ideas

What we are writing about often governs the way we order ideas in the paragraph; we saw that the account of a process is usually chronological. Often, however, we organize on the basis of what we think will most interest our audience or will best make our point clear. The same is true of the order of ideas in an essay. Thus, we may introduce our thesis at the beginning if we believe our audience will understand it without explanation. But if they need explanation, we may decide to build to it through explanatory details. In general, the considerations that we make in organizing essays are those we make in organizing paragraphs.

The nature of the essay influences these choices. The essay of personal experience may be as carefully organized as the essay of ideas, but we may allow the essay to follow a freer course—perhaps presenting experiences and observations as we have come to associate them in reflecting on our experience. Annie Dillard presents her experiences in this way, as moments of the past "tune in and out" of her consciousness. A formal discussion of the same ideas probably would organize them in some way.

As Dillard shows, the ordering of ideas may reveal a characteristic way of thinking—one that we find in other essays of the same writer. We sometimes use the word *style* to describe this feature. In the larger sense of the word, style is the sum of choices we make—in diction and sentence construction as well as organization. But it is perhaps truer to say that much of what we describe as style is not chosen at all. One writer may favor long, heavily coordinated sentences, as in the speech of a nonstop talker. Another, used to speaking in clipped sentences, may write in very short sentences—or very short paragraphs. Nevertheless, we do make choices within these limits, as we occasionally make them in speaking. But we are governed here also by habits that develop as we grow up. The more writing we do, the more we become aware of what we do habitually. And in becoming aware, we have the opportunity to experiment with new ways of writing—as college gives us the opportunity to try new ways of thinking.

BEN MARSH

At the time BEN MARSH *wrote his essay on country music for* Harper's *magazine, he was a graduate student in geography at Pennsylvania State University. His interest in geography is apparent in it. Marsh at the beginning focuses on the country lyric, but as he develops his analysis he broadens this focus to the geography of the music, showing that this perspective is essential to understanding its popularity. Through country music, Marsh gives us insight not just into one important part of American culture but also into American life generally. His essay is another example of how writers can develop important ideas out of personal experience and observation—presented in concrete detail.*

A Rose-Colored Map

Country music presents two images of life—life as it should 1
be, and life as it should not be. The conflict between these
two themes is the force that drives country music; it is this
dialectic of right and wrong that makes country music exciting to the millions who listen to it. Perhaps the melodies are
formulaic, but it is the lyrics that sell the songs, the descriptions of everyday people facing problems and making right
or wrong decisions about them. The right decision is the one
that lets people be honest, faithful, moral, and therefore
happy.

Right and wrong in country music are not distributed 2
randomly across the American landscape. Goodness is concentrated in the South and in the countryside, while badness
is far more common in cities and in the North. If the lyrics of
country songs were all someone knew about America, he
would think that everything of value was in the rural South.
Country music contains a clear, if incidental, regional geography of the South, describing its terrain, its climate, its

agriculture, and its natural resources. Everybody in country songs grew up on a farm in the South, where their parents still live. The normal city in country music is Nashville, the normal river is the Mississippi, the normal beer is Lone Star, the normal crop is cotton, the normal dog is a hound, and the normal food is black-eyed peas. And if the directions given in various songs are treated like a road map, that map says it is "up" to Chicago and Cincinnati, "down" to New Orleans and Georgia, "over" or "across" to the Carolinas, and "out" to Texas or California, while it is "back" to Tennessee or Kentucky, "back" to the mountains, and "back" to the farm. The center of country music's map of America is clearly the rural South, especially the mountain states.

The South, as it is presented in country music, is the best 3 possible place to live, the standard for comparing all other places, especially the Northern city. The North, in general, is a cold, gray, hazy area at the periphery of country music's map, as far from home as one can get. Listen to one song or a hundred, the pattern is the same. If a song is about someone being unfaithful, drunken, jobless, or lonely, it will be in a city, probably in the North. If a song is about family, security, childhood, love, or other pleasant things, it will be in the South, probably on a farm. Texas usually appears as a land of heroic men and romantic women. Canada and Alaska show up as our new frontiers, important places for individualists. And California is an ambiguous place with both Southern and Northern characteristics, perhaps a reflection of the conflict between the agricultural and urban parts of that state.

There are obvious advantages for the writers of allegor- 4 ical tales like country music's to have a conventionalized geography to reinforce the message. But why does country music use *this* image of America? Why is country music so pleased with the South and so upset with the North? The answer to this question lies not in the actual geography of the United States, but in how country music's audience perceives the geography of the United States. It is not a question of what America is, but of what America means to these people. As a result, the question has to do with far more than just a style of singing, it has to do with the attitudes of the millions of Americans who listen to country music—attitudes about regional differences in American society, about the role of the media as part of the American power structure, and about the value of progress in general.

One attractive explanation of the geography *in* country music is that it is a reflection of the geography *of* country music. This argument holds that country music views the world from the South because most of the performers, or most of the audience, live in the South. However, this is untrue. Country music is not exclusively Southern in any sense but its history and its perspective. True, most of the older performers came from the South, but many were from Northern states like Illinois and Pennsylvania, or even from Canada. And modern country music stars are from all over the English-speaking world.

Country music's audience is even less Southern than its performers. The music is indisputably popular in the South, but the evidence—from the distribution of country music radio stations, from performers' itineraries, and from the regional circulation of fan magazines—indicates that country music has more listeners outside the South than in it. Some suggest that this is because a large part of country music's audience is homesick expatriate Southerners living in Northern cities, but the data does not support this. For example, country music is not, as one would expect, especially popular in industrial cities such as Detroit, which traditionally has been a pole of South-North migration.

Country music's Southern perspective on the world must be treated as symbolism, not reporting. Perhaps country music once glorified the South because it was parochial music about local places, but it is now popular nearly everywhere. In the United States country music is the typical music on stage at small-town high schools and county fairs all across America, and on the radio in machine shops and beauty parlors, on truckers' tape decks, and on jukeboxes in ten thousand little bars.

To understand how the vision of America in country 8
music is appropriate to this audience, it is necessary to look
carefully at how country music functions in American culture. Country music comes to its audience through the media
and must be viewed in that context. Country music's morality plays appear on records, in movies, in magazines, on
syndicated television shows, and especially over the radio.
The history of early country music is inseparable from the
history of early radio, and there are now over 1,700 radio
stations in the U.S. that play country music every day. Country music is a radio ministry, and the gospel it preaches—
that we should all be moral, righteous, and Southern—
makes sense when it is seen in this context.

Country music's view of America must be compared 9
with another view, as distinctive as country music's but offering a different perspective—the image projected by network television, the wire services, and mass-circulation
magazines. In these media virtually all the decisions about
content are made in New York, Washington, Chicago, and
Los Angeles. Accordingly, the brightest, most exciting, most
memorable spots on these, our most frequently reinforced
pictures of our land, are the big cities. Compared to them,
the South and the rest of the country seem almost feature-
less, perhaps a little sinister, or maybe just boring.

Country music's image of America contradicts that of 10
the "mainstream" American media—and that is its appeal.
The South is presented as a virtuous place to country music
fans all over America not for what it is, but for what it is not.
Unlike the North, the seat of the media, the South is not
responsible for the shape we are in. According to the
media's own reporting, the South has had nothing to do
with inflation, taxes, shortages, abuses of federal power,
Supreme Court rulings, and so forth. The same innocence of
the sins of power that let Jimmy Carter go from ex-governor
of Georgia to President in twenty-two months lets country
music paint the South as a haven from the sins of the nation.

The South has escaped bad press mostly because it is 11
under-reported, and this is why country music has been free
to impose whatever meaning it chooses on the South. When

the South has appeared in the national media, it has been portrayed as backward, ignorant, and reactionary. But country music can transform these attributes into virtues: backward easily becomes rustic, ignorant becomes simple and uncomplicated, and reactionary becomes old-fashioned.

The ability to see a region which is nearly ignored in the 12 media as the best part of America, and to see the centers of media power as the worst part, reflects deep displeasure by millions of Americans with the content of those media. Country music's gloomy image of the North is a reflection of what the audience feels about what is happening to America in general. The South, in contrast, is a picture of how the nation would be if it had not gone astray.

What country music's audience seeks to escape by vi- 13 carious life in the rural South is, in a word, progress. Country music's South is above all old-fashioned. Life in the South means old-fashioned family, old-fashioned religion, old-fashioned values. Life in the South is life in the past, a laundered past without smallpox and without lynchings. This is what country music's rural Southern perspective is all about—the South has none of the problems of the North, and the country has none of the problems of the city, because the past has none of the problems of the present. Country music's South provides escape from modern America.

It seems extreme to suggest that millions of Americans 14 feel the need to escape from the land they live in, yet that is the clear message of country music's picture of the world. Escape is certainly a common enough theme in the rest of country music. Drinking, divorce, traveling, prison, and death can all be considered kinds of escape, and all are quite common in country music. To Freud the countryside itself symbolized escape. The rural South is just another kind of escape; it is a place where one avoids the problems of the modern world and lives the simple, friendly, old-fashioned country life.

Who are the people who feel they need country music's 15

exit and haven from the world we all live in? It is possible to construct a picture of an average country music listener from various kinds of television, radio, and magazine marketing data. The picture of this average person is entirely consonant with his expressed desire to avoid the wrongs of modern American life. Quite simply, the person who needs to escape into the mythically old-fashioned South is the one who is losing something as America progresses. It is not the rural-urban migrant, it is not the second- or third-generation European-American, it is not the Black. All these peoples have gained as America industrializes, urbanizes, progresses. None of them fear the future and cherish the past. None of them could be as nostalgic as the country music fan for a South that never was.

Country music is for the small-town American. Country 16 music and its image of America pleases those millions of quiet people in traditional, socially conservative communities, who daily face erosion of the values that make their lives meaningful. America is moving from the nineteenth century into mass society not in a smooth glide, but in a series of painful little shocks, and the person most likely to appreciate country music is the person for whom those shocks hurt most. Country music's function is to replenish the system of values that we seem to be losing.

The image of America in country music may seem ex- 17 treme and one-sided, but it is in answer to what its audience perceives as an extreme and one-sided world. It is important to these threatened Americans everywhere to know that there is still a region in this land where life is lived as they know it should be, and where there is relief from the changes they fear. The fiction of the rural South in country music is that place.

By glorifying the South, country music departs radically 18 from nearly every other popular geography of the United States. But country music's message that America is taking drastically wrong directions is radical, too. Country music seems to have almost Marxian overtones in its treatment of the injuries of class. Poverty is ennobling, for example, while wealth imprisons its owners. And some recent songs have been surprisingly militant in their calls for greater social justice through rejection of illegitimate authority and through greater economic equity. Johnny Cash has produced several successful songs in the past few years about men's attempts to get more control on their jobs. In one an auto worker steals a Cadillac "one piece at a time" in his lunchbox; in another a hungry farmworker steals a strawberry cake from a fancy hotel, after spending weeks picking strawberries; and in a third song a machinist plots that on the day he retires he will punch out his boss as he leaves. The songs are meant to be ironic, yet they are portrayals of what would be acts of revolution if they occurred en masse. In content and even in style, these songs are reminiscent of Woody Guthrie's songs during the Depression.

Partly because of this radicalness, an odd convergence 19 has taken place between country music and the music descended from the folk/protest tradition of the Sixties, sometimes called "folk-rock." Both are displeased with modern urban America and each uses instrumentation and arrangements derived from their common Appalachian folk origins. The result is that the themes and the performances in the two genres are similar enough that performers like Kris Kristofferson or Commander Cody, who are virtually antithetical in politics, religion, and life-style to the average country fan, can compete in the same market with some performers so puritanical that they will not appear in clubs where liquor is served.

Country music shares its radically positive image of the 20 South with two other recent national movements. Neither the election of Jimmy Carter to the Presidency, nor those southward migrations of population, industry, and political power to the so-called Sun Belt, would have been possible in the face of strong anti-Southern sentiment. There are obvious differences between the motivations that determine how people vote, where they move to, and what kind of music they listen to, but perhaps all these events are best thought of as manifestations of a single change in attitude. In years to come we can only expect to see more reaction to the old alignment of power in America, power expressed through the government and the major media.

America was settled by immigrants, and we have never 21 stopped moving. From Plymouth Rock to the Cumberland Gap to the Oregon Trail, if a man did not like life where he was, he could move down the road and it would be different. But we have run out of frontiers. Today, if a new place is needed, an old place must be redefined. Country music is showing us this process in action, as a major American region acquires a new image. However, allegiance to this new South takes place at the expense of allegiance to the country as a whole. The irony of country music's audience considering itself to be an especially patriotic group is that it is loyal to a mythical earlier America as symbolized by the sunny, old-fashioned South of country music, not to America as it now exists.

QUESTIONS

1. Marsh moves from the background and definition of country music to an explanation of its characteristics. What characteristics does he emphasize, and how are these related to his thesis, stated in his opening sentence?

2. As part of his explanation, Marsh rejects a common view of country music (paragraphs 5–6). What is that view, and how does he show it to be wrong?

3. What is the purpose of the comparison with the view of the media (paragraphs 9–10), and the history of early radio (paragraph 8)?

4. What attitudes explain the popularity of country music? Why does March consider these attitudes after his discussion of the view of the media?

5. Why does Marsh conclude with a discussion of the radicalness of country music? Could he have discussed this radicalness before explaining the attitudes that make country music popular?

6. How does he restate his thesis in the concluding paragraph? How does he keep his thesis before the reader in the course of his discussion?

WRITING ASSIGNMENTS

1. Illustrate the attitudes Marsh discusses in country music you are familiar with. Discuss other attitudes that you find, and state whether these support Marsh's analysis.
2. Analyze the attitudes implied in rock lyrics or those of musical comedy written in a certain period—for example, the Rodgers and Hammerstein musicals of the 1940s.

JOAN DIDION

> JOAN DIDION *established her reputation as a magazine columnist and editor and later as a short story and screen writer and novelist. She was an associate editor of* Vogue *after graduating from the University of California, Berkeley, in 1956. and she was later a columnist for* The Saturday Evening Post *magazine and contributing editor to the* National Review *magazine. In her novels* Play It As It Lays *and* The Book of Common Prayer *and in her many essays Didion depicts personal and social values often imperceptible to the people who live by them. She explores such values in her ironic essay on the marriage business in Las Vegas.*

Marrying Absurd

To be married in Las Vegas, Clark County, Nevada, a bride   1
must swear that she is eighteen or has parental permission and a bridegroom that he is twenty-one or has parental permission. Someone must put up five dollars for the license. (On Sundays and holidays, fifteen dollars. The Clark

County Courthouse issues marriage licenses at any time of the day or night except between noon and one in the afternoon, between eight and nine in the evening, and between four and five in the morning.) Nothing else is required. The State of Nevada, alone among these United States, demands neither a premarital blood test nor a waiting period before or after the issuance of a marriage license. Driving in across the Mojave from Los Angeles, one sees the signs way out on the desert, looming up from the moonscape of rattlesnakes and mesquite, even before the Las Vegas lights appear like a mirage on the horizon: "GETTING MARRIED? Free License Information First Strip Exit." Perhaps the Las Vegas wedding industry achieved its peak operational efficiency between 9:00 p.m. and midnight of August 26, 1965, an otherwise unremarkable Thursday which happened to be, by Presidential order, the last day on which anyone could improve his draft status merely by getting married. One hundred and seventy-one couples were pronounced man and wife in the name of Clark County and the State of Nevada that night, sixty-seven of them by a single justice of the peace, Mr. James A. Brennan. Mr. Brennan did one wedding at the Dunes and the other sixty-six in his office, and charged each couple eight dollars. One bride lent her veil to six others. "I got it down from five to three minutes," Mr. Brennan said later of his feat. "I could've married them *en masse*, but they're people, not cattle. People expect more when they get married."

What people who get married in Las Vegas actually do 2 expect—what, in the largest sense, their "expectations" are—strikes one as a curious and self-contradictory business. Las Vegas is the most extreme and allegorical of American settlements, bizarre and beautiful in its venality and in its devotion to immediate gratification, a place the tone of which is set by mobsters and call girls and ladies' room attendants with amyl nitrite poppers in their uniform pockets. Almost everyone notes that there is no "time" in Las Vegas, no night and no day and no past and no future (no Las Vegas casino, however, has taken the obliteration of the ordinary time sense quite so far as Harold's Club in

Reno, which for a while issued, at odd intervals in the day
and night, mimeographed "bulletins" carrying news from
the world outside); neither is there any logical sense of
where one is. One is standing on a highway in the middle of
a vast hostile desert looking at an eighty-foot sign which
blinks "STARDUST" or "CAESAR'S PALACE." Yes, but what does
that explain? This geographical implausibility reinforces the
sense that what happens there has no connection with
"real" life; Nevada cities like Reno and Carson are ranch
towns, Western towns, places behind which there is some
historical imperative. But Las Vegas seems to exist only in
the eye of the beholder. All of which makes it an extraordi-
narily stimulating and interesting place, but an odd one in
which to want to wear a candlelight satin Priscilla of Boston
wedding dress with Chantilly lace insets, tapered sleeves
and a detachable modified train.

And yet the Las Vegas wedding business seems to ap- 3
peal to precisely that impulse. "Sincere and Dignified Since
1954," one wedding chapel advertises. There are nineteen
such wedding chapels in Las Vegas, intensely competitive,
each offering better, faster, and, by implication, more sincere services than the next: Our Photos Best Anywhere,
Your Wedding on A Phonograph Record, Candlelight with
Your Ceremony, Honeymoon Accommodations, Free
Transportation from Your Motel to Courthouse to Chapel
and Return to Motel, Religious or Civil Ceremonies, Dressing Rooms, Flowers, Rings, Announcements, Witnesses
Available, and Ample Parking. All of these services, like
most others in Las Vegas (sauna baths, payroll-check cash-
ing, chinchilla coats for sale or rent) are offered twenty-four
hours a day, seven days a week, presumably on the premise
that marriage, like craps, is a game to be played when the
table seems hot.

But what strikes one most about the Strip chapels, with 4
their wishing wells and stained-glass paper windows and
their artificial bouvardia, is that so much of their business is
by no means a matter of simple convenience, of late-night
liaisons between show girls and baby Crosbys. Of course
there is some of that. (One night about eleven o'clock in Las

Vegas I watched a bride in an orange minidress and masses of flame-colored hair stumble from a Strip chapel on the arm of her bridegroom, who looked the part of the expendable nephew in movies like *Miami Syndicate.* "I gotta get the kids," the bride whimpered. "I gotta pick up the sitter, I gotta get to the midnight show." "What you gotta get," the bridegroom said, opening the door of a Cadillac Coupe de Ville and watching her crumple on the seat, "is sober.") But Las Vegas seems to offer something other than "convenience"; it is merchandising "niceness," the facsimile of proper ritual, to children who do not know how else to find it, how to make the arrangements, how to do it "right." All day and evening long on the Strip, one sees actual wedding parties, waiting under the harsh lights at a crosswalk, standing uneasily in the parking lot of the Frontier while the photographer hired by The Little Church of the West ("Wedding Place of the Stars") certifies the occasion, takes the picture: the bride in a veil and white satin pumps, the bridegroom usually in a white dinner jacket, and even an attendant or two, a sister or a best friend in hot-pink *peau de soie*, a flirtation veil, a carnation nosegay. "When I Fall in Love It Will Be Forever," the organist plays, and then a few bars of Lohengrin. The mother cries; the stepfather, awkward in his role, invites the chapel hostess to join them for a drink at the Sands. The hostess declines with a professional smile; she has already transferred her interest to the group waiting outside. One bride out, another in, and again the sign goes up on the chapel door: "One moment please— Wedding."

I sat next to one such wedding party in a Strip restaurant the last time I was in Las Vegas. The marriage had just taken place; the bride still wore her dress, the mother her corsage. A bored waiter poured out a few swallows of pink champagne ("on the house") for everyone but the bride, who was too young to be served. "You'll need something with more kick than that," the bride's father said with heavy jocularity to his new son-in-law; the ritual jokes about the wedding night had a certain Panglossian character, since the bride was clearly several months pregnant. Another round of pink champagne, this time not on the house, and the bride began to cry. "It was just as nice," she sobbed, "as I hoped and dreamed it would be."

QUESTIONS

1. One principle of order in the Didion is spatial: we see Las Vegas as a visitor would see it from the highway. How does this spatial view change as the essay progresses?

2. The essay at the same time moves to increasingly bizarre episodes, culminating in the wedding party of the final paragraph. What is bizarre about this episode? How do the transitional sentences that open some of the paragraphs indicate this principle of order?

3. Is Didion concerned mainly with characterizing Las Vegas through the weddings performed there, or is the city a backdrop for a comment she wishes to make about wedding customs or about American values in the late 1960s?

4. In Voltaire's *Candide* the philosopher Pangloss says, "All is for the best in this best of all possible worlds." How does the wedding described in the final paragraph reflect this attitude?

5. What is the dominant tone of the essay, and how is it established?

6. Where is the thesis stated? How do the details of the essay develop it? What ideas or attitudes does Didion imply rather than state?

WRITING ASSIGNMENTS

1. Discuss the extent to which the details of the essay support the view of the American wedding developed by Marcia Seligson (see page 62).

2. Characterize a city you have visited through an activity associated with it that typifies its way of life and values. Let your details reveal this way of life and these values.

Analysis

We can analyze ideas in essays exactly as we do in paragraphs—through definition, classification, division, comparison and contrast, analogy, and the like. These methods of analysis are basic to exposition—and also to argument, as we shall see in the next section. We can, as in paragraphs, use these methods of analysis singly or in combination: the more complex the subject matter of the essay, the more of these we probably will use. And the more that we do use, the more careful we must be with our organization and transitions. The reader should understand at every point in the essay why a particular method of analysis is being used, and how it develops the thesis. Often transitions are needed to make these uses and the relationship of methods and ideas clear. We need to keep in mind as we write that we probably know more about the subject than do our readers: we are illustrating and analyzing ideas to make these clear to them. Obviously the kind and number of examples we choose depend on how much help we think our readers need. No matter how logically developed our ideas may be, if we do not explain or illustrate them clearly, we will fail to communicate them and will convince no one but ourselves.

JAMES THURBER

JAMES THURBER *(1894–1961) stands in the company of our greatest writers and humorists. An artist, playwright, and essayist, he was associated with* The New Yorker *magazine as writer and editor during his entire career. His many books include* My Life and Hard Times, *an account of his youth in Columbus, Ohio;* The Owl in the Attic; *and (with E. B. White)* Is Sex Necessary? *Thurber was particularly interested in American popular culture and the ways we think and talk about ourselves. In the satirical essay reprinted here he gives us an inventory of "a certain kind of Broad Generalization, or Sweeping Statement," abundantly illustrated.*

What a Lovely Generalization!

I have collected, in my time, derringers, snowstorm paper- 1
weights, and china and porcelain dogs, and perhaps I should explain what happened to these old collections before I go on to my newest hobby, which is the true subject of this monograph. My derringer collection may be regarded as having been discontinued, since I collected only two, the second and last item as long ago as 1935. There were originally seventeen snowstorm paperweights, but only four or five are left. This kind of collection is known to the expert as a "diminished collection," and it is not considered cricket to list it in your *Who's Who* biography. The snowstorm paperweight suffers from its easy appeal to the eye and the hand. House guests like to play with paperweights and to slip them into their luggage while packing up to leave. As for my china and porcelain dogs, I disposed of that collection some two years ago. I had decided that the collection of actual objects, of any kind, was too much of a strain, and I determined to devote myself, instead, to the impalpable and the intangible.

Nothing in my new collection can be broken or stolen or 2
juggled or thrown at cats. What I collect now is a certain kind of Broad Generalization, or Sweeping Statement. You will see what I mean when I bring out some of my rare and cherished pieces. All you need to start a collection of generalizations like mine is an attentive ear. Listen in particular to women, whose average generalization is from three to five times as broad as a man's. Generalizations, male or female, may be true ("Women don't sleep very well"), untrue ("There are no pianos in Japan"), half true ("People would rather drink than go to the theater"), debatable ("Architects have the wrong idea"), libelous ("Doctors don't

know what they're doing"), ridiculous ("You never see foreigners fishing"), fascinating but undemonstrable ("People who break into houses don't drink wine"), or idiosyncratic ("Peach ice cream is never as good as you think it's going to be").

"There are no pianos in Japan" was the first item in my 3 collection. I picked it up at a reception while discussing an old movie called "The Battle," or "Thunder in the East," which starred Charles Boyer, Merle Oberon, and John Loder, some twenty years ago. In one scene, Boyer, as a Japanese naval captain, comes upon Miss Oberon, as his wife, Matsuko, playing an Old Japanese air on the piano for the entertainment of Loder, a British naval officer with a dimple, who has forgotten more about fire control, range finding, marksmanship, and lovemaking than the Japanese commander is ever going to know. "Matsuko," says the latter, "why do you play that silly little song? It may be tedious for our fran." Their fran, John Loder, says, "No, it is, as a matter of—" But I don't know why I have to go into the whole plot. The lady with whom I was discussing the movie, at the reception, said that the detail about Matsuko and the piano was absurd, since "there are no pianos in Japan." It seems that this lady was an authority on the musical setup in Japan because her great-uncle had married a singsong girl in Tokyo in 1912.

Now, I might have accepted the declarations that there 4 are no saxophones in Bessarabia, no banjo-mandolins in Mozambique, no double basses in Zanzibar, no jews's-harps in Rhodesia, no zithers in Madagascar, and no dulcimers in Milwaukee, but I could not believe that Japan, made out in the movie as a great imitator of Western culture, would not have any pianos. Some months after the reception, I picked up an old copy of the *Saturday Evening Post* and, in an article on Japan, read that there were, before the war, some fifteen thousand pianos in Japan. It just happened to say that, right there in the article.

You may wonder where I heard some of the other 5 Sweeping Statements I have mentioned above. Well, the one about peach ice cream was contributed to my collection by a fifteen-year-old girl. I am a chocolate man myself, but the few times I have eaten peach ice cream it tasted exactly the way I figured it was going to taste, which is why I classify this statement as idiosyncratic; that is, peculiar to one individual. The item about foreigners never fishing, or, at any rate, never fishing where you can see them, was given to me last summer by a lady who had just returned from a motor trip through New England. The charming generalization about people who break into houses popped out of a conversation I overheard between two women, one of whom said it was not safe to leave rye, Scotch or bourbon in your summer house when you closed it for the winter, but it was perfectly all right to leave your wine, since intruders are notoriously men of insensitive palate, who cannot tell the difference between Nuits-St.-Georges and saddle polish. I would not repose too much confidence in this theory if I were you, however. It is one of those Comfortable Conclusions that can cost you a whole case of Château Lafite.

I haven't got space here to go through my entire collection, but there is room to examine a few more items. I'm not sure where I got hold of "Gamblers hate women"—possibly at Bleeck's—but, like "Sopranos drive men crazy," it has an authentic ring. This is not true, I'm afraid, of "You can't trust an electrician" or "Cops off duty always shoot somebody." There may be something in "Dogs know when you're despondent" and "Sick people hear everything," but I sharply question the validity of "Nobody taps his fingers if he's all right" and "People who like birds are queer." 6

Some twenty years ago, a Pittsburgh city editor came out with the generalization that "Rewrite men go crazy when the moon is full," but this is perhaps a little too special for the layman, who probably doesn't know what a rewrite man is. Besides, it is the abusive type of Sweeping Statement and should not be dignified by analysis or classification. 7

In conclusion, let us briefly explore "Generals are afraid of their daughters," vouchsafed by a lady after I had told her my General Wavell anecdote. It happens, for the sake of our present record, that the late General Wavell, of 8

His Britannic Majesty's forces, discussed his three daughters during an interview a few years ago. He said that whereas he had millions of men under his command who leaped at his every order, he couldn't get his daughters down to breakfast on time when he was home on leave, in spite of stern directives issued the night before. As I have imagined it, his ordeal went something like this. It would get to be 7 A.M., and then 7:05, and General Wavell would shout up the stairs demanding to know where everybody was, and why the girls were not at table. Presently, one of them would call back sharply, as a girl has to when her father gets out of hand, "For heaven's sake, Daddy, will you be quiet! Do you want to wake the neighbors?" The General, his flanks rashly exposed, so to speak, would fall back in orderly retreat and eat his kippers by himself. Now, I submit that there is nothing in this to prove that the General was afraid of his daughters. The story merely establishes the fact that his daughters were not afraid of him.

If you are going to start collecting Sweeping Statements 9 on your own, I must warn you that certain drawbacks are involved. You will be inclined to miss the meaning of conversations while lying in wait for generalizations. Your mouth will hang open slightly, your posture will grow rigid, and your eyes will take on the rapt expression of a person listening for the faint sound of distant sleigh bells. People will avoid your company and whisper that you are probably an old rewrite man yourself or, at best, a finger tapper who is a long way from being all right. But your collection will be a source of comfort in your declining years, when you can sit in the chimney corner cackling the evening away over some such gems, let us say, as my own two latest acquisitions: "Jewelers never go anywhere" and "Intellectual women dress funny."

Good hunting. 10

QUESTIONS

1. Is Thurber's statement that a woman's "average generalization is from three to five times as broad as a man's" any better

founded than other generalizations he cites? How do you think he wants the reader to take this statement?

2. How does each of the examples in paragraph 2 illustrate the labels Thurber gives them? Why is the statement that "People would rather drink than go to the theater" half true?

3. What is the overall tone of the essay, and how is it established? How is this tone related to Thurber's purpose in writing the essay?

WRITING ASSIGNMENTS

1. Collect examples of generalizations like those in paragraph 2, classifying them, and build your examples to a conclusion about the purpose such generalizations serve.

2. Write a characterization of Thurber from the way he talks about himself and talks to the reader of the essay. Consider his qualities as a humorist, keeping in mind Mark Twain's definition in "How To Tell a Story."

JOHN CIARDI

Born in Boston in 1916, and educated at Bates College and Tufts, the American poet and essayist JOHN CIARDI *taught at Harvard and Rutgers before giving his full time to writing. He was for many years the poetry editor of* Saturday Review *magazine, writing a column for that magazine under the title "Manner of Speaking." Ciardi is distinguished both as a poet and as a translator of Dante, and through his columns, radio commentary (most recently on PBS), and many books he has made people aware of the values of literature and the richness of our language. In the essay reprinted here, we see Ciardi's concern with American values generally.*

Is Everybody Happy?

The right to pursue happiness is issued to Americans with 1
their birth certificates, but no one seems quite sure which
way it ran. It may be we are issued a hunting license but
offered no game. Jonathan Swift seemed to think so when
he attacked the idea of happiness as "the possession of
being well-deceived," the felicity of being "a fool among
knaves." For Swift saw society as Vanity Fair, the land of
false goals.

It is, of course, un-American to think in terms of fools 2
and knaves. We do, however, seem to be dedicated to the
idea of buying our way to happiness. We shall all have made
it to Heaven when we possess enough.

And at the same time the forces of American commer- 3
cialism are hugely dedicated to making us deliberately unhappy. Advertising is one of our major industries, and advertising exists not to satisfy desires but to create them—
and to create them faster than any man's budget can satisfy
them. For that matter, our whole economy is based on a
dedicated insatiability. We are taught that to possess is to be
happy, and then we are made to want. We are even told it is
our duty to want. It was only a few years ago, to cite a single
example, that car dealers across the country were flying
banners that read "You Auto Buy Now." They were calling
upon Americans, as an act approaching patriotism, to buy
at once with money they did not have, automobiles they did
not really need, and which they would be required to grow
tired of by the time the next year's models were released.

Or look at any of the women's magazines. There, as 4
Bernard DeVoto once pointed out, advertising begins as
poetry in the front pages and ends as pharmacopoeia and
therapy in the back pages. The poetry of the front matter is
the dream of perfect beauty. This is the baby skin that must
be hers. These, the flawless teeth. This, the perfumed breath
she must exhale. This, the sixteen-year-old figure she must
display at forty, at fifty, at sixty, and forever.

Once past the vaguely uplifting fiction and feature arti- 5
cles, the reader finds the other face of the dream in the back
matter. This is the harness into which Mother must strap
herself in order to display that perfect figure. These, the
chin straps she must sleep in. This is the salve that restores
all, this is her laxative, these are the tablets that melt away
fat, these are the hormones of perpetual youth, these are the
stockings that hide varicose veins.

Obviously no half-sane person can be completely per- 6
suaded either by such poetry or by such pharmacopoeia and
orthopedics. Yet someone is obviously trying to buy the
dream as offered and spending billions every year in the
attempt. Clearly the happiness market is not running out of
customers, but what are we trying to buy?

The idea "happiness," to be sure, will not sit still for 7
easy definition: the best one can do is to try to set some
extremes to the idea and then work in toward the middle. To
think of happiness as acquisitive and competitive will do to
set the materialistic extreme. To think of it as the idea one
senses in, say, a holy man of India will do to set the spiritual
extreme. That holy man's ideal of happiness is in needing
nothing from outside himself. In wanting nothing, he lacks
nothing. He sits immobile, rapt in contemplation, free even
of his own body. Or nearly free of it. If devout admirers
bring him food he eats it; if not, he starves indifferently.
Why be concerned? What is physical is an illusion to him.
Contemplation is his joy and he achieves it through a fantas-
tically demanding discipline, the accomplishment of which
is itself a joy within him.

Is he a happy man? Perhaps his happiness is only 8
another sort of illusion. But who can take it from him? And
who will dare say it is more illusory than happiness on the
installment plan?

But, perhaps because I am Western, I doubt such 9
catatonic happiness, as I doubt the dreams of the happiness
market. What is certain is that his way of happiness would
be torture to almost any Western man. Yet these extremes
will still serve to frame the area within which all of us must
find some sort of balance. Thoreau—a creature of both

Eastern and Western thought—had his own firm sense of that balance. His aim was to save on the low levels in order to spend on the high.

Possession for its own sake or in competition with the 10 rest of the neighborhood would have been Thoreau's idea of the low levels. The active discipline of heightening one's perception of what is enduring in nature would have been his idea of the high. What he saved from the low was time and effort he could spend on the high. Thoreau certainly disapproved of starvation, but he would put into feeding himself only as much effort as would keep him functioning for more important efforts.

Effort is the gist of it. There is no happiness except as 11 we take on life-engaging difficulties. Short of the impossible, as Yeats put it, the satisfactions we get from a lifetime depend on how high we choose our difficulties. Robert Frost was thinking in something like the same terms when he spoke of "the pleasure of taking pains." The mortal flaw in the advertised version of happiness is in the fact that it purports to be effortless.

We demand difficulty even in our games. We demand it 12 because without difficulty there can be no game. A game is a way of making something hard for the fun of it. The rules of the game are an arbitrary imposition of difficulty. When the spoilsport ruins the fun, he always does so by refusing to play by the rules. It is easier to win at chess if you are free, at your pleasure, to change the wholly arbitrary rules, but the fun is in winning within the rules. No difficulty, no fun.

The buyers and sellers at the happiness market seem 13 too often to have lost their sense of the pleasure of difficulty. Heaven knows what they are playing, but it seems a dull game. The Indian holy man seems dull to us, I suppose, because he seems to be refusing to play anything at all. The Western weakness may be in the illustration that happiness can be bought. Perhaps the Eastern weakness is in the idea that there is such a thing as perfect (and therefore static) happiness.

Happiness is never more than partial. There are no 14 pure states of mankind. Whatever else happiness may be, it is neither in having nor in being, but in becoming. What the Founding Fathers declared for us as an inherent right, we should do well to remember, was not happiness but the *pursuit* of happiness. What they might have underlined, could they have foreseen the happiness market, is the cardinal fact that happiness is in the pursuit itself, in the meaningful pursuit of what is life-engaging and life-revealing, which is to say, in the idea of *becoming*. A nation is not measured by what it possesses or wants to possess, but by what it wants to become.

By all means let the happiness market sell us minor 15 satisfactions and even minor follies so long as we keep them in scale and buy them out of spiritual change. I am no customer for either puritanism or asceticism. But drop any real spiritual capital at those bazaars, and what you come home to will be your own poorhouse.

QUESTIONS

1. Ciardi organizes his discussion of happiness as an extended definition. What kind of definition of happiness does he employ—denotative, connotative, stipulative, or theoretical?

2. Ciardi builds to his full definition of happiness through a consideration of advertising and the Eastern holy man. Given his opening comments on Swift and the American way of thinking, why does he delay his definition until late in the essay? How do his comments on advertising and the Eastern holy man help to establish his definition?

3. Where, finally, does Ciardi state his definition?

4. "The pursuit of happiness" is so familiar a phrase that we are likely not to examine its full implications. Is Ciardi defining this phrase according to what he believes the founding fathers meant by it, or is he proposing his own definition?

WRITING ASSIGNMENTS

1. Ciardi deals with an abstract idea through everyday experiences. Select another phrase in common use and define it as Ciardi does. Examine its implications fully.

2. Discuss the statement "We demand difficulty even in our games" through two different games that you enjoy playing. Indicate the extent of your agreement with Ciardi.

3. Develop the following statement through your personal observations: "Whatever else happiness may be, it is neither in having nor in being, but in becoming."

4. Ciardi analyzes women's magazines in light of the idea of happiness they purvey. Analyze a man's magazine in the same way, giving attention to the articles and the advertisements.

ANDY ROONEY

For many years ANDY ROONEY *wrote for such people as Arthur Godfrey, Gary Moore, and Victor Borge on television. His face and commentary are familiar to viewers of Sixty Minutes on CBS, and his collections of these television essays in* A Few Minutes with Andy Rooney *and its sequel have won him a wide reading audience. Rooney says this about writing for television: "To be spoken aloud, the sentences have to be shorter and the writing simpler. You can't turn a clever phrase because if the audience doesn't catch it the first time, they can't go back and read it over again. At the same time, a viewer or listener expects more from something that's been written to be said than he'd expect to hear from a friend he meets on the street, so the writing has to be a little concentrated."*

Types

There are only two types of people in the world, Type A and   1
Type Z. It isn't hard to tell which type you are. How long before the plane leaves do you arrive at the airport?

Early plane catchers, Type A, pack their bags at least a   2
day in advance, and they pack neatly. If they're booked on a

flight that leaves at four in the afternoon, they get up at five-thirty that morning. If they haven't left the house by noon, they're worried about missing the plane.

Late plane catchers, Type Z, pack hastily at the last 3 minute and arrive at the airport too late to buy a newspaper.

What do you do with a new book? Type A reads more 4 carefully and finishes every book, even though it isn't any good.

Type Z skims through a lot of books and is more apt to 5 write in the margins with a pencil.

Type A eats a good breakfast; Type Z grabs a cup of 6 coffee.

Type A's turn off the lights when leaving a room and 7 lock the doors when leaving a house. They go back to make sure they've locked it, and they worry later about whether they left the iron on or not. They didn't.

Type Z's leave the lights burning and, if they lock the 8 door at all when they leave the house, they're apt to have forgotten their keys.

Type A sees the dentist twice a year, has an annual 9 physical checkup and thinks he may have something.

Type Z has been meaning to see a doctor. 10

Type A squeezes a tube of toothpaste from the bottom 11 and rolls it very carefully as he uses it, puts the top back on every time.

Type Z squeezes the tube from the middle, and he's lost 12 the cap under the radiator.

Type Z's are more apt to have some Type A charac- 13 teristics than Type A's are apt to have any Type Z characteristics.

Type A's always marry Type Z's. 14

Type Z's always marry Type A's. 15

QUESTIONS

1. What is the basis of the humorous division Rooney is making?
2. Is he saying that the division is an absolute one—in other

words, that people fall into one type or the other without exception?

3. Why do Type A's always marry Type Z's?

4. What in the essay illustrates Mark Twain's point that humor is found in the manner of telling a story (or writing a humorous essay)?

WRITING ASSIGNMENTS

1. On the basis of what you have noticed about your English teacher, discuss whether she or he is Type A or Type Z.

2. Discuss the type of person you are, developing the discussion through a series of examples as Rooney does.

3. Divide people on the basis of a different characteristic. Develop your discussion through a series of examples as Rooney does.

EDWARD T. HALL

EDWARD T. HALL, *professor of anthropology at North-western University, has studied the Pueblo Indians of the Southwest and the cultures of other parts of the world. In his book* The Hidden Dimension *he states the theme of his many writings on culture and the nonverbal forms of language: "Contrary to common belief, the many diverse groups that make up our country have proved to be surprisingly persistent in maintaining their separate identities. Superficially, these groups may all look alike and sound somewhat alike but beneath the surface there lie manifold unstated, unformulated differences in the structuring of time, space, materials, and relationships. It is these very things that, though they gave significance to our lives, so often result in the distortion of meaning regardless of good intentions*

*when peoples of different cultures interact." In this sec-
tion Hall discusses how people who speak the same
language perceive space in different ways.*

The English and the Americans

It has been said that the English and the Americans are two   1
great people separated by one language. The differences for
which language gets blamed may not be due so much to
words as to communications on other levels beginning with
English intonation (which sounds affected to many Americans) and continuing to ego-linked ways of handling time,
space, and materials. If there ever were two cultures in
which differences of the proxemic details are marked it is in
the educated (public school) English and the middle-class
Americans. One of the basic reasons for this wide disparity
is that in the United States we use space as a way of classifying people and activities, whereas in England it is the social
system that determines who you are. In the United States,
your address is an important cue to status (this applies not
only to one's home but to the business address as well). The
Joneses from Brooklyn and Miami are not as "in" as the
Joneses from Newport and Palm Beach. Greenwich and
Cape Cod are worlds apart from Newark and Miami. Businesses located on Madison and Park avenues have more
tone than those on Seventh and Eighth avenues. A corner
office is more prestigious than one next to the elevator or at
the end of a long hall. The Englishman, however, is born
and brought up in a social system. He is still Lord—no
matter where you find him, even if it is behind the counter in
a fishmonger's stall. In addition to class distinctions, there
are differences between the English and ourselves in how
space is allotted.

The middle-class American growing up in the United   2
States feels he has a right to have his own room, or at least
part of a room. My American subjects, when asked to draw

an ideal room or office, invariably drew it for themselves and no one else. When asked to draw their present room or office, they drew only their own part of a shared room and then drew a line down the middle. Both male and female subjects identified the kitchen and the master bedroom as belonging to the mother or the wife, whereas Father's territory was a study or a den, if one was available; otherwise, it was "the shop," "the basement," or sometimes only a workbench or the garage. American women who want to be alone can go to the bedroom and close the door. The closed door is the sign meaning "Do not disturb" or "I'm angry." An American is available if his door is open at home or at his office. He is expected not to shut himself off but to maintain himself in a state of constant readiness to answer the demands of others. Closed doors are for conferences, private conversations, and business, work that requires concentration, study, resting, sleeping, dressing, and sex.

The middle- and upper-class Englishman, on the other 3 hand, is brought up in a nursery shared with brothers and sisters. The oldest occupies a room by himself which he vacates when he leaves for boarding school, possibly even at the age of nine or ten. The difference between a room of one's own and early conditioning to shared space, while seeming inconsequential, has an important effect on the Englishman's attitude toward his own space. He may never have a permanent "room of his own" and seldom expects one or feels he is entitled to one. Even Members of Parliament have no offices and often conduct their business on the terrace overlooking the Thames. As a consequence, the English are puzzled by the American need for a secure place in which to work, an office. Americans working in England may become annoyed if they are not provided with what they consider appropriate enclosed work space. In regard to the need for walls as a screen for the ego, this places the Americans somewhere between the Germans and the English.

The contrasting English and American patterns have 4 some remarkable implications, particularly if we assume that man, like other animals, has a built-in need to shut himself off from others from time to time. An English student in one of my seminars typified what happens when hidden patterns clash. He was quite obviously experiencing strain in his relationships with Americans. Nothing seemed to go right and it was quite clear from his remarks that we did not know how to behave. An analysis of his complaints showed that a major source of irritation was that no American seemed to be able to pick up the subtle clues that there were times when he didn't want his thoughts intruded on. As he stated it, "I'm walking around the apartment and it seems that whenever I want to be alone my roommate starts talking to me. Pretty soon he's asking 'What's the matter?' and wants to know if I'm angry. By then I am angry and say something."

It took some time but finally we were able to identify   5
most of the contrasting features of the American and British problems that were in conflict in this case. When the American wants to be alone he goes into a room and shuts the door—he depends on architectural features for screening. For an American to refuse to talk to someone else present in the same room, to give them the "silent treatment," is the ultimate form of rejection and a sure sign of great displeasure. The English, on the other hand, lacking rooms of their own since childhood, never developed the practice of using space as a refuge from others. They have in effect internalized a set of barriers, which they erect and which others are supposed to recognize. Therefore, the more the Englishman shuts himself off when he is with an American the more likely the American is to break in to assure himself that all is well. Tension lasts until the two get to know each other. The important point is that the spatial and architectural needs of each are not the same at all.

QUESTIONS

1. What is Hall's thesis, and where does he first state it? Where does he restate it later in the essay?

2. How does he organize the contrast between the English and the Americans? Does he contrast the English and American patterns point by point or instead deal with one set of patterns first, another set afterwards? Or does he mix these methods of organization?

3. How does he illustrate these patterns? Does he illustrate all of them?

4. Hall traces cause-and-effect relations through contrast of living patterns. What are the chief relations he traces?

5. How do the examples explain the phrase *internalized a set of barriers*, in the concluding paragraph? What does Hall mean by *screening*?

6. What use does he make of classification in the whole essay? On what basis does he divide the English and the Americans?

WRITING ASSIGNMENTS

1. Discuss the extent to which your study habits fit the English or the American pattern. Use your analysis to comment on the accuracy of Hall's thesis.

2. Contrast two of your friends or relatives on the basis of their attitude toward space and architecture or toward privacy. State the similarities before commenting on the differences. Notice that the differences may be slight ones, and even slight differences may be revealing of people.

JOSHUA E. MILLS

JOSHUA E. MILLS *teaches journalism and mass communication at New York University. His essay on the special problems of the journalism student appeared in* Quill *in 1981. Writing from the special viewpoint of the teacher, Mills defines an ethical issue important to the working journalist. Mills defines the issue chiefly through the contrast between the professional journalist and the nonprofessional student.*

The Journalism Student and the Free Lance

On local television news one Saturday evening last year, 1
Edward I. Koch, the outspoken mayor of New York City,
acknowledged that he had smoked marijuana.

Although the report was the lead story on WNEW-TV's 2
news, it had been reported and recorded not by professional journalists, but by several student reporters from
New York University.

With a minicam and video recorder, the students had 3
covered the several thousand demonstrators marching
down Fifth Avenue in Manhattan, headed for Washington
Square Park, in a protest supporting more liberal laws on
the use of marijuana.

To the students' delight, they found Koch nearby—not 4
participating in the parade, but out for a walk. They asked
him for an interview and Koch agreed. He was asked what
he thought of the demonstration and gave a response that
was not particularly newsworthy.

Then one of the students asked, "Have you ever smoked 5
marijuana?" Koch said, "Yes. I tried it. It didn't get me high.
I wouldn't recommend it to someone else."

Not earth-shaking news, perhaps, but it was the first- 6
time the mayor had acknowledged publicly that he had
smoked marijuana, the students thought. What's more, few
public officials ever conceded such experimentation. But the
students had no ready outlet for their "scoop." NYU does
not have a television station; its FM station is a part-timer
that gets lost among the more than 70 stations in New York.

The students decided to try to sell the tape to a commercial television news show.

They went first to the local television stations owned by the three major networks. WABC, WCBS and WNBC. They were turned down and told, they said, that the stations were not permitted to buy videotape from non-union personnel. At their fourth stop, WNEW-TV, they made a sale. The money ($50) wasn't important; they were elated that their story would be aired. It ran that night.

No complaint was filed by the mayor and no eyebrows were raised by other news operations, but it seemed to me then—and it still does—that the incident raised an ethical question about student journalism that is rarely examined. How did the student reporters identify themselves to the mayor? If they identified themselves as journalism students, did they communicate implicitly that what followed was a classroom exercise, not intended for public distribution?

In this case, the reporters' identification was odd, and perhaps unethical in a different way. The student holding the microphone was an Italian citizen and a stringer for Italian television; he told the mayor he was a journalist for Italian television. He did not identify the other students at all.

With thousands of journalism students reporting public affairs these days, often working side-by-side with professional reporters, it's worth taking a look at the ambiguous position of the student journalist.

Are they members of the press? Or merely journalists in training? Are they subject to a press code of ethics? Or do different standards apply? How are these journalism students perceived by their sources? And how are they taught to identify themselves?

When professional journalists ask for an interview or other material, the clear implication is that they intend to report their findings. No cautionary word is needed to the source. But when a student tells an interviewee, "Hi, I'm a journalism student and I'd like to ask you a few questions," no such implication is clear. Sources might infer that the students' work is a class exercise, and that their comments are off-the-record.

What of students who seek to sell an article or a tape 13 that was a class assignment? Don't they have an obligation to notify the people to whom they talked and to ask their permission? That would eliminate the ethical dilemma of misrepresentation, but it carries with it an invitation to censor.

There is an alternative. Students could identify them- 14 selves as students *and* free-lance writers or journalists: "Excuse me, I'm a journalist and a student at NYU. Would you mind talking to me for a few minutes?"

This approach would make it harder for students to do 15 reporting. Fewer people would be willing to talk.

Well, so what? No one promises students that reporting 16 will be an easy career; professionals have to deal with these problems every day. But should every class reporting exercise be hampered by the obstacles facing professional reporters?

If every time students go out on the street they are 17 trying to convince people to talk to them, they'll learn a lot about how hard it is to be a reporter—but perhaps not enough of the skills instructors are trying to teach them: how to ask questions, take notes and keep the conversation going at the same time.

In courses that are likely to produce work that is pub- 18 lishable or suitable for broadcast, students must be taught to identify themselves both as journalists and as students. They are ethically obligated *not* to imply—even through silence—that their work is for classroom use only. In basic courses, when the instructor is clear that there is no likelihood of work being published, it should be adequate for students to identify themselves simply as journalism students. And students should be taught both the differences in the identifications, and the reasons for them.

The result, we hope, is that students will emerge with 19 not only the skills of the professional journalist, but with an understanding of a reporters' ethical responsibility to sources.

QUESTIONS

1. The ethical issue Mills analyzes depends on stated and implied differences between the professional journalist and the journalism student. What are these differences?

2. Mills analyzes the issue through an example. How does the example help clarify it? Would the issue have been clear to you without the example?

3. If Mills had not depended on the example, in what other way might he have analyzed the issue?

4. Do you see an alternative to the solution Mills proposes? Do you agree with him that journalism students have an obligation to state what use they will make of information given them in interviews?

WRITING ASSIGNMENT

Mills organizes his essay in a familiar and highly useful way: he states a problem, then explores a solution. Write an essay on the ethical issue raised by one of the following questions, or on an issue of your own choosing—organizing the essay in this way:

a. Should the reviewer of a student production apply the same standard of judgment as would be applied to a professional one?

b. Should boxers be required to wear protective headgear?

c. Should motorcyclists be required to wear helmets if automobile drivers are not required to wear seatbelts?

d. Should fines for driving offenses be lower for juveniles because of their immaturity?

e. Should the buyers of second-hand cars be given information about previous owners?

f. Should grades be curved in different sections of the same course?

NANCY K. HILL

NANCY K. HILL, *a native of Minnesota, taught at Yale and now teaches the humanities at the University of Colorado in Boulder. Her essay on teaching, like that of Liane Ellison Norman earlier, depends on comparison—but with the difference that Hill explores a number of popular analogies as a way of establishing her idea that teaching is best compared to mountaineering. Hill in this way combines exposition—her explanation of what makes a good teacher—with argumentative analogy, to be considered in a later section of this book.*

Teaching as Mountaineering

Just recently a committee meeting at the University of Colorado was interrupted by the spectacle of a young man scaling the wall of the library just outside the window. Discussion of new interdisciplinary courses halted as we silently hoped he had discipline enough to return safely to the earth. Hope was all we could offer from our vantage point in Ketchum Hall, the impulse to rush out and catch him being checked by the realization of futility.

The incident reinforced my sense that mountaineering serves as an apt analogy for the art of teaching. The excitement, the risk, the need for rigorous discipline all correspond, though the image I have in mind is not that of the solitary adventurer rappelling off a wall, but that of a Swiss guide leading an expedition.

I remember a mountaineer named Fritz who once led a group up the Jungfrau at the same time a party was climbing the north face of the Eiger. My own mountaineering skill was slender, and my enthusiasm would have faltered had I not felt Fritz was capable of hauling not only me but all the rest of us off that mountain. Strong, self-assured, calm, he radiated that solid authority that encouraged me to tie on to his rope. But I soon realized that my presence on his line constituted a risk for Fritz. Had I been so foolhardy as to try to retrieve my glove which went tumbling off a precipice, or had I slipped into one of those inexplicably opening crevasses, I might well have pulled the noble Fritz down with me. It was a sobering realization. I, the novice, and he, the expert, were connected by the same lifeline in an experience of mutual interdependence. To give me that top of the world exaltation he, too, was taking a risk.

The analogy to teaching seems to me apt, and not just 4 for professors who happen to live in Colorado, for the analogy implies an active acceptance of responsibility for one's own fate, whereas most other analogies to teaching suggest passivity. What is needed to restore teachers' confidence that the profession is significant is a new analogy, a new metaphor (I shy away from the PR word, "image") that conveys more of the essence of teaching than the worn-out analogies we have known. Most previous analogies are seriously inadequate, for while they may describe a part of the teaching activity, they also suggest patterns that are not fully applicable to teaching. It is not a simple matter, for those faulty analogies create misunderstandings about the professor's role, not only in the lay public, but in the professoriate itself. These wrong analogies have contributed to growing demoralization within the profession, and have confused the difficult issue of proper evaluation.

The most common analogies to the teacher are the 5 preacher, the shepherd, the curator, the actor, the researcher, and, most insidiously, the salesman. None captures the special relationship between teacher and students, a relationship better described by Socrates as a coming together of friends. Rather than emphasizing the mutuality of the endeavor, each of these common analogies turns on a separation between the professional and his clients. Each leads to a certain kind of evaluation.

The preacher exhorts, cajoles, pleads with a congrega- 6 tion often so benighted as to exist in a state of somnolence.

He measures his success by the number of souls so stirred as either to commit themselves to his cause, or vehemently to reject it. Somewhat like the preacher is the shepherd who gathers and watches over a flock clearly inferior to himself. The analogy may be apt for the Lord and his subangelic followers, but it will not do for teacher and students, or, especially, for Socrates and his friends. The Shepherd is likely to be evaluated by the gulf separating his wisdom from that of his flock.

If the poor country curate has often furnished an anal- 7 ogy to the bleating professor, so has the curator of a museum. Lips pursed so as to distill a purer essence of hauteur, the curator as connoisseur points out the rarities of classical cultures to the uninitiated who can scarcely be expected to appreciate these finer things. Since they cannot understand him anyway, the curator has no compunction about sprinkling his presentation with Latin and Greek and with English so esoteric as to sound foreign. Chances are high that the professor as connoisseur will succeed in convincing most of the class that the subject is really the province of a secret society with its own arcane practices and language, best left behind its own inaccessible walls. Indeed, colleagues of the connoisseur measure his success by the paucity of devotees allowed in to the society through this winnowing process.

The teacher as actor also plays to a passive audience, 8 but he measures success by larger numbers. A certain aura of the magician clings to him as he lures spectators into witnessing his academic sleight-of-hand without their ever really getting in on the trick. A certain tinge of the stand-up comedian colors the performance as the actor plays to the audience to register laughs big enough to drown out the lecturer droning on next door.

A bastardized version of the actor is that figure now 9 thought so apt an analogy in our consumer-conscious society: the salesman. His predecessors include the snake-oil man and the door-to-door purveyor of anything from brushes to Britannicas. He or she takes the product to the people, wherever they are, and tailors the pitch to their pockets. While all of these analogies create a certain level of despair in the professoriate either struggling to pattern themselves in a particular mode or hopelessly realizing they can never achieve it, the salesman analogy has the most deleterious effects. No longer adhering even to a prepared script, the salesman shamelessly alters his or her presentation so it will draw the largest number of contented consumers.

The researcher as teacher differs from the previous 10 analogies, and that very distinction is often thought to make him or her a good teacher. Taciturn, solitary, he disdains the performing arts and is content merely to mutter out an assortment of scattered facts to the young only dimly perceived beyond his clouded trifocals. His measure of success is his students' capacity to regurgitate factual data.

None of these analogies comes close enough to the 11 essential magic and majesty of a real learning experience. None even dimly anticipates that self-eradicating feature that is built in to the teaching process, for those who have truly mastered what their teacher has presented no longer need him or her. None accepts as a necessary ingredient in the learning process, activity, the sense of an intellectual excitement so compelling that one's whole being is caught up in it. None acknowledges the peril, and the joy, of encountering those mental deeps Hopkins described.

> . . . the mind, mind has mountains; cliffs of fall
> Frightful, sheer, no-man-fathomed. Hold them cheap
> May who ne'er hung there.

Mountaineering furnishes the needed analogy. The 12 Swiss mountain guide, like the true teacher, has a quiet authority about his very person. He or she engenders trust and confidence so that one is willing to join the endeavor. The mountaineer accepts his leadership role, yet recognizes

Exposition

that the success of the journey (measured by the scaling of the heights) depends upon close cooperation and active participation by each member of the group. He has crossed the terrain before and is familiar with the landmarks, but each trip is new, and generates its own anxiety and excitement. Essential skills must be mastered if the trip is to be successful; lacking them, disaster looms as an ominous possibility. The very precariousness of the situation necessitates keen focus and rapt attention; slackness, misjudgment, or laziness can bring doom.

The teacher as mountaineer learns, as E. M. Forster 13 urged, to connect. The guide rope links mountaineers together so that they may assist each other in the ascent. The effective teacher does something similar by using the oral and written contributions of the students as instructional materials. The teacher also makes other connections, locating the text in its historical setting, forging inter and intra-disciplinary links where plausible, joining the material of the course with the lives of the students, where possible, and with the wider national life beyond the classroom where pertinent.

Teaching as mountaineering does not encourage the 14 yellowed lecture note syndrome. Indeed, the analogy does not really encourage lecturing at all. If the student as mountaineer is to be challenged, the student must come to each class session ready and prepared to assist in scaling the next peak, ready to test his or her own abilities against those of the master teacher. Only by arduous and sustained effort does the student approach the mastery of the teacher, and only then is the student ready to assume the role of guide—well-trained in the art of mountaineering, able to take controlled risks, ready to lead others to a mountain-top experience. Not a huckster, not a performer, not a pleader, but a confident, exuberant guide on expeditions of shared responsibility.

To encourage and further such mountain-top experi- 15 ences the society must recognize teaching for the sublime art it is—not merely an offshoot of research, not merely a performance before a passive audience, but a guided expedition into the most exciting and least understood terrain on earth—the mind itself.

QUESTIONS

1. What are the similarities between the teacher and the preacher, the shepherd, the curator, the actor, the researcher and the salesman? And what differences weaken each analogy for Hill?

2. What are the similarities between the teacher and the mountaineer? What is the mind parallel to in the analogy? What are the differences, and why do they not weaken the analogy for Hill?

3. In what way is the teaching process "self-eradicating"? Why is this feature basic to the true teacher?

4. Does Hill begin the essay with a statement of her thesis, or does she build to it? What do you think she has assumed about her audience in organizing the essay?

WRITING ASSIGNMENTS

1. Discuss the extent to which you hold one or more of the conceptions of the teacher that Hill believes are mistaken, and give your reasons for holding them. Use this discussion to defend your conception of the ideal teacher.

2. Compare your conception of the ideal teacher with that of Hill. Defend your conception through an example, as she does.

3. Compare two effective teachers in your life. Describe their similarities and differences—in attitude toward students and teaching methods, for example. In a concluding paragraph, discuss how closely these teachers meet the definition of teacher as mountaineer.

4. Discuss how close Hill is in her conception of the teacher to that of John Holt in his essay on discipline in education.

ARGUMENT AND PERSUASION

Inductive Reasoning

Our discussion so far has been about expository writing—writing that explains or gives reasons or analyzes. We discussed the importance in exposition of illustrating and supporting our ideas with personal experience and observation and, where appropriate, factual evidence gathered from reputable sources. The process by which we draw conclusions or generalize from evidence of this kind is called induction. An example is the statement which is drawn from my personal experience that parents and teenagers I know do not like the same kind of music.

This generalization is sometimes called a perfect induction because it is limited to those people I actually surveyed or observed. But most inductive generalizations deal with groups or classes containing a very large number of members—a number much too great to survey. An example is the statement that parents and teenagers do not like the same kind of music. Notice how difficult it would be to establish the truth of this statement. It would be quite impossible to find out whether the statement is true of teenagers and parents in the past, and it would be very hard to find out whether the statement is true of teenagers and parents today. It would be hard but not impossible—if we could prove that the people we had observed were typical of all present teenagers and their parents. That is one major problem in induction: to choose particular instances that we can say are truly representative of the group or class about which we are generalizing.

When we generalize in this way, it is obvious that we need to qualify the generalization—that is, to explain that it is probable only. Inductive generalizations (except for the perfect ones) can be probable only—never certain—because of the difficulty of guaranteeing that the limited number of people sampled are typical or representative. A "hasty generalization" is a judgment that we make on the basis of insufficient evidence or on the basis of special cases. Our example above would be a hasty generalization if there were special circumstances that led the particular teenagers and parents under discussion to dislike the same music: There might, for example, be misunderstandings and conflicts in these families that have led to disagreements about music.

Let us consider another example—the argument that people over seventy should be denied driving licenses because an extraordinary number of them were involved in traffic accidents over a period of time. This argument might be worth considering if the behavior of these people could be shown to be typical. But other relevant evidence must be considered: an extraordinary number of drivers might have been involved in accidents during the same period—during a harsh winter, perhaps. Many beliefs we hold arise from such hasty observations: Small towns are safer than large cities; Irishmen have short tempers; New Yorkers are rude. But the New Yorkers who prompted the statement, to deal with just the last of these, may have been observed on a crowded, stalled bus on the hottest day of the year.

We will consider some special forms of inductive reasoning in the discussions that follow.

ALVIN TOFFLER

For many years the Washington correspondent and an editor of Fortune Magazine, ALVIN TOFFLER *has taught at the New School for Social Research in New York City and at other institutions. The author of numerous articles on social change, he is perhaps best known for his book* Future Shock. *In his most recent book* The Third Wave, *Toffler explores the changes that new technologies are bringing about in our lives. Previously, he argues, people's dual roles as producers and consumers*

*split their personalities. As producers they were taught
to develop restraint and defer pleasure; as consumers
they were taught to seek immediate gratification and
abandon restraint. But modern technology is increasingly bringing the consumer into manufacture —
producing a new class of what Toffler calls "prosumers,"
that is, people who produce what they consume, like the
"do-it-yourselfers" described in the section of the book
reprinted here. Though he does not predict the exact
changes to come, Toffler asks whether it is possible for a
society "to attain a high material standard of living
without obsessively focusing all its energies on production for exchange."*

The Do-It-Yourselfers

In 1956 the American Telephone & Telegraph Company, 1
creaking under the burden of exploding communications
demand, began introducing new electronic technology that
made it possible for callers to direct-dial their long-distance
calls. Today it is even possible to direct-dial many over-
seas calls. By punching in the appropriate numbers, the
consumer took on a task previously done for him by the
operator.

In 1973–74 the oil squeeze triggered by the Arab em- 2
bargo sent gasoline prices soaring. Giant oil companies
reaped bonanza profits, but local filling-station operators
had to fight a desperate battle for economic survival. To cut
costs many introduced self-service fuel pumps. At first these
were an oddity. Newspapers wrote funny feature stories
about the motorist who tried to put the fuel hose into the car
radiator. Soon, however, the sight of consumers pumping
their own gas became a commonplace.

Only 8 percent of U.S. gas stations were on a self- 3
service basis in 1974. By 1977 the number reached nearly 50
percent. In West Germany, of 33,500 service stations some

15 percent had shifted to self-service by 1976, and this 15 percent accounted for 35 percent of all the gasoline sold. Industry experts say that it will soon be 70 percent of the total. Once more the consumer is replacing a producer and becoming a prosumer.

The same period saw the introduction of electronic 4 banking, which not only began to break down the pattern of "banker's hours" but also increasingly eliminated the teller, leaving the customer to perform operations previously done by the bank staff.

Getting the customer to do part of the job—known to 5 economists as "externalizing labor cost"—is scarcely new. That's what self-service supermarkets are all about. The smiling clerk who knew the stock and went and got it for you was replaced by the push-it-yourself shopping cart. While some customers lamented the good old days of personal service, many liked the new system. They could do their own searching and they wound up paying a few cents less. In effect, they were paying themselves to do the work the clerk had previously done.

Today this same form of externalization is occurring in 6 many other fields. The rise of discount stores, for example, represents a partial step in the same direction. Clerks are far and few between; the customer pays a bit less but works a bit harder. Even shoe stores, in which a supposedly skilled clerk was long regarded as a necessity, are moving to self-service, shifting work to the consumer.

The same principle can be found elsewhere, too. As 7 Caroline Bird has written in her perceptive book, *The Crowding Syndrome*, "More things come knocked down for supposedly easy assembly at home ... and during the Christmas season shoppers in some of the proudest New York stores have to make out sales slips for clerks unable or unwilling to write."

In January 1978 a thirty-year-old government worker in 8 Washington, D.C., heard strange noises emanating from his refrigerator. The customery thing to do in the past was to call in a mechanic and pay him to fix it. Given the high cost and the difficulty of getting a repairman at a convenient hour, Barry Nussbaum read the instructions that came with his refrigerator. On it he discovered an 800 telephone number that he could use to call the manufacturer—Whirlpool Corporation of Benton Harbor, Michigan—free of charge.

This was the "Cool-Line" set up by Whirlpool to help 9 customers with service problems. Nussbaum called. The man at the other end then "talked him through" a repair, explaining to Nussbaum exactly which bolts to remove, which sounds to listen for and—later—what part would be needed. "That guy," says Nussbaum, "was super-helpful. He not only knew what I needed to do, he was a great confidence builder." The refrigerator was fixed in no time.

Whirlpool has a bank of nine full-time and several 10 part-time advisers, some of them former service field men, who wear headsets and take such calls. A screen in front of them instantly displays for them a diagram of whatever product is involved (Whirlpool makes freezers, dishwashers, air-conditioners, and other appliances in addition to refrigerators) and permits them to guide the customer. In 1978 alone Whirlpool handled 150,000 such calls.

The Cool-Line is a rudimentary model for a future sys- 11 tem of maintenance that permits the homeowner to do much of what a paid outside mechanic or specialist once did. Made possible by advances that have driven down the cost of long-distance telephoning, it suggests future systems that might actually display step-by-step fix-it-yourself instructions on the home television screen as the adviser speaks. The spread of such systems would reserve the repair mechanic only for major tasks, or turn the mechanic (like the doctor or social worker) into a teacher, guide, and guru for prosumers.

What we see is a pattern that cuts across many 12 industries—increasing externalization, increasing involvement of the consumer in tasks once done for her or him by others—and once again, therefore, a transfer of activity from Sector B of the economy to Sector A, from the exchange sector to the prosumption sector.

QUESTIONS

1. Toffler builds through a series of examples to a generalization supported by them. We call this order of ideas or method of organizing an essay—moving from the specific to the general, from particulars of experience to conclusions based on them—inductive. Would the generalization be unclear or difficult to understand if Toffler had begun with it?

2. How various are the examples Toffler presents? Has he chosen examples from a single area or from several?

3. How do Toffler's examples suggest the meaning of the terms *prosumer* and *prosumption*?

4. Does Toffler say or imply that the changes he describes are an improvement in any way, or is he merely presenting the facts?

5. What other conclusions about American society or the American economy do you think are supported by these facts, and how are they supported?

WRITING ASSIGNMENTS

1. Present a series of observations of your own about how people today behave as consumers. Build these observations to one or more conclusions they support. Be careful not to generalize more broadly than the evidence you have presented allows.

2. Discuss the extent to which your own experience and observation support the conclusion Toffler reaches. If you believe his conclusion needs qualification, explain why it does.

Analogy

We discussed earlier the use of analogy, or a point by point comparison of two things, for the purpose of illustration. Analogy can also be used to argue that similar objects or situations imply other similarities. For example, if identical twins are law students, wear the same clothes, like the same movies and music, play the same sports, and have the same hobbies, it may be argued that their respective friends will be similar in their tastes and interests. Arguments from analogy are a form of inductive argument because of their dependence on such particulars of experience as these. Indeed, it may be argued that all inductions depend upon the relation of similarity. As a rule, the greater number of points of similarity, the stronger the probability of the conclusion. But notice that these points of similarity must be relevant to the conclusion and give strength to it. The particulars cited do not, for example, establish that the twins have the same friends or always will.

More than this, the dissimilarities between the things being compared must not weaken the conclusion. If in seeking a job as a shoe salesman I argue that my experience as a Marine drill sergeant fits me for the job, I will have to show that both jobs require roughly the same skills and that the differences or dissimilarities are insignificant. It is significant, notice, that customers can walk out of the store whereas recruits cannot voluntarily walk off the parade ground. Dissimilarities may increase the strength of an argument, too. If I argue further that a number of former drill sergeants are now successful shoe salesmen, my argument will be strengthened if these sergeants are different in age, background, and experience in selling.

In general, a limited conclusion may be drawn from a limited analogy if the points of similarity are clearly specified (or at least agreed upon), if these points are relevant to the conclusion, and if inferences are drawn from these points only. If these limits are not observed, the analogy may be judged false or poor. The salesman who thinks of himself as a "tiger" and his customers as the prey may discover the falsity of this analogy: deceived customers (unlike the tiger's dinner) are permitted to learn from their mistakes.

BROOKS ATKINSON

BROOKS ATKINSON *was associated through his career as a journalist with the* New York Times, *as war correspondent, drama critic, and essayist. In 1947 he won the*

Pulitzer Prize for Foreign Correspondence. In later years he became increasingly concerned with the environment. The essay reprinted here, one of his finest on this subject, is particularly effective in its use of analogy.

The Warfare in the Forest Is Not Wanton

After thirty-five years the forest in Spruce Notch is tall and sturdy. It began during the Depression when work gangs planted thousands of tiny seedlings in abandoned pastures on Richmond Peak in the northern Catskills. Nothing spectacular has happened there since; the forest has been left undisturbed.

But now we have a large spread of Norway spruces a foot thick at the butt and 40 or 50 feet high. Their crowns look like thousands of dark crosses reaching into the sky.

The forest is a good place in which to prowl in search of wildlife. But also in search of ideas. For the inescapable fact is that the world of civilized America does not have such a clean record. Since the seedlings were planted the nation has fought three catastrophic wars, in one of which the killing of combatants and the innocent continues. During the lifetime of the forest 350,000 Americans have died on foreign battlefields.

Inside America civilized life is no finer. A President, a Senator, a man of God have been assassinated. Citizens are murdered in the streets. Riots, armed assaults, looting, burning, outbursts of hatred have increased to the point where they have become commonplace.

Life in civilized America is out of control. Nothing is out of control in the forest. Everything complies with the instinct for survival—which is the law and order of the woods.

Although the forest looks peaceful it supports incessant warfare, most of which is hidden and silent. For thirty-five years the strong have been subduing the weak. The blueberries that once flourished on the mountain have been destroyed. All the trees are individuals, as all human beings are individuals; and every tree poses a threat to every other tree. The competition is so fierce that you can hardly penetrate some of the thickets where the lower branches of neighboring trees are interlocked in a blind competition for survival.

Nor is the wildlife benign. A red-tailed hawk lived there 7 last summer—slowly circling in the sky and occasionally drawing attention to himself by screaming. He survived on mice, squirrels, chipmunks and small birds. A barred owl lives somewhere in the depth of the woods. He hoots in midmorning as well as at sunrise to register his authority. He also is a killer. Killing is a fundamental part of the process. The nuthatches kill insects in the bark. The woodpeckers dig insects out. The thrushes eat beetles and caterpillars.

But in the forest, killing is not wanton or malicious. It is 8 for survival. Among birds of equal size most of the warfare consists of sham battles in which they go through the motions of warfare until one withdraws. Usually neither bird gets hurt.

Nor is the warfare between trees vindictive. Although 9 the spruces predominate they do not practice segregation. On both sides of Lost Lane, which used to be a dirt road, maples, beeches, ashes, aspens and a few red oaks live, and green curtains of wild grapes cover the wild cherry trees. In the depths of the forest there are a few glades where the spruces stand aside and birches stretch and grow. The forest is a web of intangible tensions. But they are never out of control. Although they are wild they are not savage as they are in civilized life.

For the tensions are absorbed in the process of growth, 10 and the clusters of large cones on the Norway spruces are certificates to a good future. The forest gives an external impression of discipline and pleasure. Occasionally the pleasure is rapturously stated. Soon after sunrise one morning last summer when the period of bird song was nearly over, a solitary rose-breasted grosbeak sat on the top of a tall spruce and sang with great resonance and beauty. He flew a few rods to another tree and continued singing: then to another tree where he poured out his matin again, and so on for a half hour. There was no practical motive that I was aware of.

After thirty-five uneventful years the spruces have 11 created an environment in which a grosbeak is content, and this one said so gloriously. It was a better sound than the explosion of bombs, the scream of the wounded, the crash of broken glass, the crackle of burning buildings, the shriek of the police siren.

The forest conducts its affairs with less rancor and 12 malevolence than civilized America.

QUESTIONS

1. One sometimes hears the argument that violence is natural to human beings, since we are a part of a warring natural world. How does Atkinson implicitly reject this analogy? More specifically, what are the points of dissimilarity between the world of the forest and the world of humans?

2. How might the world of the forest be used to argue that competition in the world of humans need not be destructive of some of those competing—as the argument that only the "fit" survive in the world of business implies?

3. How does Atkinson increase the probability of his argument through the details he marshals in support of it?

WRITING ASSIGNMENT

Each of the following statements suggests an analogy. Write on one of them, discussing points of similarity and dissimilarity and using this discussion to argue a thesis.
a. The family is a small nation.
b. The nation is a large family.
c. College examinations are sporting events.
d. Choosing a college is like buying a car.

Cause and Effect

Earlier we discussed some ways cause and effect can be analyzed in paragraphs. These include tracing an effect to its recent or immediate cause (dropping in grade point average because of failing a course) and to its more distant or remote cause (failing to study). We also discussed the analysis of an object according to the material out of which it is made (material cause), the shape given it (formal cause), its maker (efficient cause), and use (final cause). In writing about an event or object, we may not use these formal terms, but we do imply these ideas about cause in our informal discussion.

We also use the words necessary and sufficient, as when we say that getting an "A" on the first examination is necessary for an "A" in the course but not sufficient: an "A" on every examination is sufficient if the course depends only on examinations. Notice what these words imply about cause when we use them: we are talking about the conditions of getting an "A" only—circumstances in which this event might occur. Reasoning about necessary and sufficient conditions is one of the ways scientists today reason about cause. Thus, when scientists say that a necessary condition of getting a cold is exposure to a virus, they are saying only that a virus of some kind must be present. They are not saying that we must get the cold if it is. Other conditions obviously need to be present, but they do not claim to know what these are—or if they do know, they may talk about one necessary condition, perhaps to show how to prevent colds, or about a sufficient condition of our getting a cold, if they know of one.

Notice that, in using the words *necessary* and *sufficient*, we implicitly recognize that events, like the reasons for our actions, are complex—never simple. Yet this is not what some of our statements show—statements that generalize about "the" cause of a cold or some other physical or social or political ill, as if a single cause could be identified and dealt with. Many weak generalizations are of this sort. Another kind arises from the idea that one event must be the cause of another because it precedes it: I caught the cold "because" I was soaked in a rainstorm. The sequence of events does not necessarily make one event the cause of the next. Clearly we might have caught the cold even if we had not been soaked, and we cannot know whether getting soaked will always give one a cold—even if it has always in the past. This kind of reasoning (discussed by George F. Will, "The Not-So-Mighty Tube") is given a Latin name—the *post hoc* fallacy, from the expression *post hoc, ergo propter hoc* (after this, therefore because of this).

NORMAN COUSINS

NORMAN COUSINS *is inseparably linked with the* Saturday Review, *which he edited from 1940 to 1977. He won numerous awards for his journalism and his work on behalf of world peace, including the Peace Medal of the United Nations in 1971. His columns were collected in a number of books that provide a continuous political commentary on postwar America and the world. His essay on Benny Paret, whose fatal knockout in the ring Normal Mailer describes earlier in this book, raises important questions about boxing and spectator sports generally—and also about the responsibility of the public for the violence encouraged in them.*

Who Killed Benny Paret?

Sometime about 1935 or 1936 I had an interview with Mike   1
Jacobs, the prize-fight promoter. I was a fledgling newspaper reporter at that time; my beat was education, but during the vacation season I found myself on varied assignments, all the way from ship news to sports reporting. In this way I found myself sitting opposite the most powerful figure in the boxing world.

There was nothing spectacular in Mr. Jacob's manner   2
or appearance; but when he spoke about prize fights, he was no longer a bland little man but a colossus who sounded the way Napoleon must have sounded when he reviewed a battle. You knew you were listening to Number One. His saying something made it true.

We discussed what to him was the only important ele- 3
ment in successful promoting—how to please the crowd. So
far as he was concerned, there was no mystery to it. You put
killers in the ring and the people filled your arena. You hire
boxing artists—men who are adroit at feinting, parrying,
weaving, jabbing, and dancing, but who don't pack dyna-
mite in their fists—and you wind up counting your empty
seats. So you searched for the killers and sluggers and
maulers—fellows who could hit with the force of a baseball bat.

I asked Mr. Jacobs if he was speaking literally when he 4
said people came out to see the killer.

"They don't come out to see a tea party," he said evenly. 5
"They come out to see the knockout. They come out to see a
man hurt. If they think anything else, they're kidding themselves."

Recently a young man by the name of Benny Paret was 6
killed in the ring. The killing was seen by millions; it was on
television. In the twelfth round he was hit hard in the head
several times, went down, was counted out, and never came
out of the coma.

The Paret fight produced a flurry of investigations. 7
Governor Rockefeller was shocked by what happened and
appointed a committee to assess the responsibility. The New
York State Boxing Commission decided to find out what was
wrong. The District Attorney's office expressed its concern.
One question that was solemnly studied in all three probes
concerned the action of the referee. Did he act in time to
stop the fight? Another question had to do with the role of
the examining doctors who certified the physical fitness of
the fighters before the bout. Still another question involved
Mr. Paret's manager; did he rush his boy into the fight
without adequate time to recuperate from the previous one?

In short, the investigators looked into every possible 8
cause except the real one. Benny Paret was killed because
the human fist delivers enough impact, when directed
against the head, to produce a massive hemorrhage in the
brain. The human brain is the most delicate and complex

mechanism in all creation. It has a lacework of millions of highly fragile nerve connections. Nature attempts to protect this exquisitely intricate machinery by encasing it in a hard shell. Fortunately, the shell is thick enough to withstand a great deal of pounding. Nature, however, can protect man against everything except man himself. Not every blow to the head will kill a man—but there is always the risk of concussion and damage to the brain. A prize fighter may be able to survive even repeated brain concussions and go on fighting, but the damage to his brain may be permanent.

In any event, it is futile to investigate the referee's role 9 and seek to determine whether he should have intervened to stop the fight earlier. This is not where the primary responsibility lies. The primary responsibility lies with the people who pay to see a man hurt. The referee who stops a fight too soon from the crowd's viewpoint can expect to be booed. The crowd wants the knockout; it wants to see a man stretched out on the canvas. This is the supreme moment in boxing. It is nonsense to talk about prize fighting as a test of boxing skills. No crowd was ever brought to its feet screaming and cheering at the sight of two men beautifully dodging and weaving out of each other's jabs. The time the crowd comes alive is when a man is hit hard over the heart or the head, when his mouthpiece flies out, when blood squirts out of his nose or eyes, when he wobbles under the attack and his pursuer continues to smash at him with poleax impact.

Don't blame it on the referee. Don't even blame it on 10 the fight managers. Put the blame where it belongs—on the prevailing mores that regard prize fighting as a perfectly proper enterprise and vehicle of entertainment. No one doubts that many people enjoy prize fighting and will miss it if it should be thrown out. And that is precisely the point.

QUESTIONS

1. Cousins distinguishes between the immediate and the remote causes of Paret's death. What does he show to be the immediate cause, and why can this cause be stated with near certainty?

2. Cousins is concerned chiefly with the remote cause of Paret's death. How is this concern basic to his purpose in writing the essay? What are the chief indications of that purpose?

3. How would a different purpose have required Cousins to focus instead on the immediate cause?

4. How does Cousins establish the remote cause? Is his evidence statistical—based on a sample of statements of boxing fans? Is it theoretical—based on a discussion of "human nature"? Is he concerned with the psychology of the crowd or the sociology of boxing? Is his analysis of the event intended to offer a complete explanation?

WRITING ASSIGNMENTS

1. Analyze a mass sport like pro football or hockey to determine the extent of its appeal to violent emotions.

2. Contrast Cousins' view of the causes of Paret's death with Mailer's view in "The Death of Benny Paret."

HERBERT HENDIN

HERBERT HENDIN *has practiced psychiatry in New York City since 1952. His association with the Columbia Psychoanalytic Clinic began in 1963. He is particularly noted for his studies of psychosocial problems in such books as* Black Suicide *(1969) and* The Age of Sensation *(1975), from which this section on students and drugs is taken. Hendin identifies conditions present in the lives of particular users, without trying to suggest that these are necessary—that is, are always present. In the preface he states the basic assumptions of his study: "Social facts are empty numbers unless translated into psychosocial facts that reflect the dynamism of life, the emotion behind the fact, the cause for the statistic. Culture is a two-way street, a flow between individuals and institutions, single minds and collective forces."*

Students and Drugs

No more dramatic expression of the dissatisfaction students   1
feel with themselves can be found than students abusing
drugs. Students often become drug abusers, that is, heavy
and habitual users, in an attempt to alter their emotional
lives, to transform themselves into the people they wish they
could be, but feel they never could be without drugs. What
they crave is to restructure their own emotions, not to be
themselves, but to live as some "other." What this "other" is
like and how it can be achieved cut to the center of the
changing American psyche.

The turmoil over performance, achievement, and suc-   2
cess, the increasing terror of becoming "too" involved with
anyone; the attempt to find in fragmentation the means of
effecting a pervasive change in one's total relation to life—
all these are everywhere prevalent on campus. Students
abusing drugs are often attempting to cure themselves of
the malaise they see everywhere around them and in themselves.

Why do some students take LSD or heroin while others   3
take marijuana or amphetamines? Why do still others take
anything and everything? Students who are intrigued by
drugs can learn through trial and error and from other
students to find and favor the drugs which most satisfy their
particular emotional needs. They rapidly become expert
psychopharmacologists, able to locate the specific drug cure
for what disturbs them. One student who by seventeen had
tried just about everything and had become a daily, in-
travenous heroin user, had rejected LSD early in his drug
career, explaining, "I can't see what anyone gets out of it. It
just sort of makes you schizy—quiet one minute and freaked
out the next."

Some students were initially drawn to the "cops-and-   4
robbers" quality of drug abuse. While they were clearly out
to defy their parents and the whole structure of authority,
they were often unaware that their abuse had anything to

do with their families, so profoundly had they pushed their rage at them out of their consciousness. Such students were invariably unable to deal with their parents directly and were bound in a need to defy them and a simultaneous need to punish themselves for their rebellion.

Drugs provided these students with both crime and 5 punishment, while removing their defiance out of the direct presence of their parents. One student would "let his mind float away" and concentrate on music he liked whenever his father berated him. Afterward he went out and took whatever drugs he could buy. While he never connected his drug abuse with his anger toward his father, he often dreamed of it as a crime for which he would be punished. He had a dream in which a riot was going on in another part of town while he was shooting heroin. He was afraid that somehow he would be arrested along with the rioters. Drugs were clearly his way of rioting, of diverting the crime of rebellion to the crime of drug abuse and focusing his destructive potential on himself. The expectation this student had that he would be arrested was typical, and revelatory of the appeal of drugs for him. Jail signified to such students a concrete way of locking up their rage. Drugs permitted them to both contain their rage and to express it in a way that gave them a sense of defiance, however self-damaging that defiance may be. Often, students who are most in trouble with the police over drugs are those for whom the need for crime and punishment was more significant than the need for drugs.

For most of the students who abused them, drugs also 6 provided the illusion of pleasurable connection to other people while serving to detach them from the emotions real involvement would arouse. Drugs were, for these students, the best available means of social relations. Heroin abusers found in the junkie underworld a sense of security, belonging, and acceptance derived from the acknowledgment and the shared need for heroin. LSD abusers felt their most intimate experiences involved tripping with another person. Marijuana abusers felt that drugs "took the edge off their personality" enough to permit them to be gentle and to empathize with other people. Amphetamine abusers were pushed into the social round on amphetamine energy, often being enabled to go through sexual experience they would otherwise have found unendurable.

For many students drug abuse is the means to a life 7 without drugs. Such students take drugs to support the adaptation they are struggling to make. Once it is established, they are often able to maintain it without drugs. The period of heavy drug abuse often marks the crisis in their lives when they are trying to establish a tolerable relation to the world and themselves. Appealing, tumultuous, sometimes frighteningly empty, the lives of students who turn to drugs are an intense, dramatic revelation of the way students feel today, what they are forced to grapple with not only in the culture, but in themselves.

QUESTIONS

1. Does Hendin single out a sufficient cause of drug use among students, or instead identify a number of realted (or unrelated) necessary causes?

2. Does he distinguish psychological from social causes, or does he assume these are one and the same?

3. Is Hendin generalizing about all students today—even those who do not use drugs—or is he commenting merely on student drug users?

4. How does drug use foster "fragmentation" in the drug user? How can "fragmentation" provide a solution to the problems Hendin identifies in paragraph 2?

5. What does Hendin mean by the statement, "For many students drug abuse is the means to a life without drugs"?

WRITING ASSIGNMENT

Describe the tensions you have observed in yourself or in fellow students, and discuss the extent to which these tensions resemble those that Hendin identifies. Suggest some of the causes for those you have experienced or observed.

GEORGE F. WILL

GEORGE F. WILL *taught political science at Michigan State Univresity and the University of Toronto, before turning to political commentary. After serving as an aide to Senator Gordon Allott of Colorado, Will served as Washington editor of the* National Review *magazine from 1972 to 1976, and began his political column for* Newsweek *magazine in 1975. His columns also appear in* The Washington Post *and other newspapers. In 1977 Will received the Pulitzer Prize for distinguished commentary. In the following essay Will discusses an unusually interesting example of "post hoc" reasoning about the effects of television.*

The Not-So-Mighty Tube

In simpler days it was said that the hand that rocked the cradle ruled the world. Today, says Professor Michael J. Robinson of Catholic University (in *The Public Interest*), the rule of television rocks the world: "In the 1950s television was a *reflection* of our social and political opinions, but by the 1960s it was an important *cause* of them." He insists that television journalism did "engender" fundamental changes, "moving us" toward conservatism, and entertainment programing is a "fomenter" of social liberalism, "fostering" and "pushing us toward" change.

"Mary Tyler Moore and 'Mary Tyler Mooreism' seem to have been unusually effective in 'consciousness raising.' Between 1958 and 1969, the percentage of women accepting the idea that a woman could serve effectively as President actually *declined* by 3 percent. But between 1969 and 1972, the proportion of women who came to accept the idea of a female President *increased* by 19 percent. . . . During those first two seasons in which Mary Richards and Rhoda Morgenstern came to television, the level of public support among women for a female President increased more than

among any other two-year—or ten year—period since the
1930s."

The *post hoc, ergo propter hoc* fallacy involves mistak-   3
ing mere antecedents for causes: the cock crows and then
the sun rises, so the crowing caused the sunrise. Did prim
Mary cause consciousness to rise? Does the water wheel
move the river? Television conforms entertainment to market research, struggling to paddle as fast as the current.
Robinson finds it ironic that entertainment programing, the
servant of commerce, is supportive of "social liberalism,"
which he identifies with "hedonism and libertarianism"
(and "Maude"). But commerce, which profits from the
sovereignty of appetites, has never been a conservative
force.

Television is not always benign or even innocuous.   4
When vacuous or violent it is enervating and desensitizing;
and it has influenced, often unfortunately, the way Americans campaign for office and for change. But it is more
mirror than lever.

Robinson believes the "audio-visual orgy of the 1960s"   5
shifted "power" upward toward the President and down-
ward toward "have-nots" such as the civil-rights movement,
and other "groups wretched or angry or clever enough to do
what was needed to become photogenic." But Kennedy,
constantly on television and consistently stymied by Congress, learned that conspicuousness is not power. Jimmy
Carter, who uses television even more assiduously than
Kennedy did, is learning that television does not make governing easier. Americans have developed fine filters for
what they consider static, commercial and political, so Carter's media blitz about the energy crisis was like water
thrown on sand: it left little trace. Thanks in part to broadcasting, political rhetoric has become like advertising, audi-
ble wallpaper, always there but rarely noticed.

Robinson notes that the 1963 "March on Washington"   6
("the greatest public-relations gambit ever staged") capped
five months of intense civil-rights coverage, during which
the percentage of Americans regarding civil rights as "the

most important problem facing America" soared from 4 to 52. But it is unhistorical to say that this means the networks had begun "to define our political agenda."

Television did not give civil-rights leaders the idea of a   7
March on Washington or make the idea effective. In 1941 the mere threat (by A. Philip Randolph) of a march frightened FDR into important policy changes. The civil-rights movement did not start with television, but with the moral and social changes wrought by the Second World War. The movement's first great victory was the Supreme Court's 1954 desegregation decision, when television was in its infancy. (During the two television decades the least "photogenic" branch of government, the judiciary, has grown in importance relative to the other branches.) The movement had on its side great leaders, centuries of grievances, the Constitution, and justice. It benefited from television, but did not depend upon it. Television hastened change a bit, but probably did not determine the direction or extent of change. What television did on its own (for example, manufacturing Stokely Carmichael as a "black leader") was as evanescent as most shoddy fiction.

When Robinson says "Nixon would have lost in 1968   8
had it not been for network news coverage of politics between 1964 and his election," he must mean either that LBJ would have been re-elected but for disintegration at home and defeat abroad; or that without television Americans would not have minded disintegration and defeat; or that without television there would not have been disintegration and defeat. The first idea is true but trivial; the last two are false.

The United States has never had national newspapers,   9
so the focus of news was local. But network news is "national news." So, Robinson says, television has shifted frustrations toward the national government. But the centralization of power in Washington began well before television and would have "nationalized" news, and frustrations, with no help from television. Robinson believes that television journalism, although accused of liberal bias, has recently

stimulated political conservatism. But the limitations of government would have become apparent, and the conservative impulse would have had its day, even if television had developed only as an entertainment industry.

To represent situation-comedy shows as shapers of the 10 nation's consciousness is to portray the public as more passive and plastic than it is. To represent television journalism as a fundamentally transforming force is to make the nation's politics seem less purposeful, more mindless, more a matter of random causes than is the case. The contours of history are not determined by communications technology, however much it pleases people to think that history is what, and only what, can be seen at home. To see the rise of blacks, or the fall of LBJ, as primarily a consequence of television is to hollow out history. It discounts the noble and ignoble ideas and passions, heroes and villains and common people who make history.

In the silly movie *Network*, millions of Americans are 11 prompted by a deranged anchor man to sprint to their windows to shout, "We're mad as hell and we won't take it any more." Modern man, proudly sovereign beneath a blank heaven, is prone to believe that "they" (evil persons, irresistible impulses, impersonal forces) control the world. Astrology, vulgar Marxism and Freudianism, and other doctrines nourish this need. So does the exaggeration of media influence. Journalists and perhaps even serious scholars, such as Robinson, who study television, are prone to believe that it turns the world. But the world is not that easy to turn.

QUESTIONS

1. What in the reasoning that Will disputes illustrates the *post hoc* fallacy?
2. What evidence does Will present to show that television may not have created the civil rights movement and other social movements or influenced national politics to the extent that some people believe?

3. What alternative influences does he propose?

4. Does Will say or imply that television exerts no influence on our social and political life and thinking or that the media in general exert greater influence than they should?

5. Where does Will first state his thesis, and where does he restate it?

6. Do you agree with Will that media blitzes, like the one discussed in paragraph 5, exert less influence than some believe? On what evidence do you base your opinion?

WRITING ASSIGNMENTS

1. Trace an idea you hold about energy conservation or the ERA or nuclear power or a similar social or political issue today to its sources—family, friends, school, church, the media, or your own thinking on the issue. State which of these influences was the greatest, and present evidence for your reasons.

2. Discuss the extent to which television influences your attitude toward or thinking about a current social or political issue—the power of the presidency or the Supreme Court, for example. Build your discussion to a general assessment of the influence of television on your thinking on social and political issues.

ALAN WERTHEIMER

ALAN WERTHEIMER, *who teaches political science at the University of Vermont, writes often on issues of public policy. His essay, published in the* New York Times *in 1980, explores the dilemma that he believes underlies much discussion today about government spending— the choice between "helping identifiable lives and saving statistical lives." Knowing that a large segment of his audience supports what he refers to as "welfare-state humanitarianism," Wertheimer uses the dilemma to force these people to recognize that the issue is complex, does not present a simple choice between right and wrong, and demands an examination of basic assumptions.*

[*Statistical*] *Lives*

Suppose the following were true: 1

At least some money spent on open-heart surgery could   2
be used to prevent heart disease. True, patients in need of
such surgery might die, but many more lives would be saved.

Some money spent treating tooth decay among low-   3
income children might be used on fluoridation and dental
hygiene. True, some decay would go untreated, but fewer
children would ever need such treatment.

We could prohibit ransom payments to kidnappers.   4
True, kidnapped children might die, but by lowering the
incentive to kidnap, fewer children would be taken.

We could drastically reduce unemployment compensa-   5
tion. True, the unemployed would suffer, but by converting
the money saved to private investment and by lowering the
incentive to stay jobless, there would be substantially less
unemployment.

These cases exhibit a similar structure. All involve   6
choosing between a policy designed to help specific persons
and one that seeks to prevent the need for such help. These
choices are especially difficult because we know who needs
help. The patient requiring open-heart surgery, the kidnapped child, the unemployed auto worker—they have
names and faces; they are "identifiable" lives. On the other
hand, we do not know whose lives will be saved or who will
benefit from the prevention of heart disease, tooth decay,
kidnappings, or creation of new jobs. Some people will, and
we may be able to estimate their numbers with precision.
These are real lives, but they are only "statistical" lives.

We might say we do not have to choose between helping   7
those in need and preventing future needs. After all, we
could do both. But resources are scarce, and even when

resources are not at issue (as in the kidnapping case), we often must choose between competing persons or goals. We cannot do everything we might like to the extent we might like. We must often choose between helping identifiable lives and saving statistical lives.

I wish to make three points about these dilemmas. First, 8 we do seem to favor the interests of identifiable lives (saving the kidnapped child) and it may not be irrational to do so. Second, we nevertheless do see the need to attend to the interests of statistical lives, even if this injures identifiable lives. Thus it is now common to hear people advocating directing more medical resources to primary prevention of disease and fewer to treatment. Israel's policy of refusing to negotiate with terrorists may risk the lives of some hostages, but we do see the point. Third, welfare-state policies focus on identifiable lives, whereas conservative economists prefer to focus on statistical lives.

Monetary theory and other technical issues aside, the 9 new Adam Smiths tell us that however well-intentioned, welfare-state policies have not (always) worked—on the policies' own terms. Minimum-wage laws, unemployment compensation, consumer protection, occupational safety, Medicaid, Social Security—by interfering with market efficiency, by discouraging individual initiative, by impeding private-capital formation, by incurring large-scale expenditures on governmental bureaucracies—all these policies (and others) have been self-defeating. They argue that liberal economics, filled with concern for the genuine needs of identifiable lives, has swelled the future ranks of statistical lives in need. Welfare-state humanitarianism is short-sighted, they say, and is thus less humanitarian than we may believe.

We need not dwell on the accuracy of this account. 10 Conservative economists may be wrong about the facts. We certainly need not assume that market choices and private-capital formation always serve the interests of all social groups, that regulation always does more harm than good. But suppose conservative economists are (sometimes) right about the facts. Suppose that attempts to serve the needs of identifiable lives do end up harming future statistical lives.

Should we turn our back on the needs that we see in order to prevent those that we cannot see? Regrettably, the answer may sometimes be yes.

QUESTIONS

1. Wertheimer's argument is in part inductive: he shows that well-established facts and expert testimony make the dilemma real, not fictitious. What are these facts and testimony? What in the wording of paragraphs 9–10 shows that Wertheimer considers this evidence highly probable and not certain?

2. If we choose to save specific persons, what would be the consequences? What would they be if we choose to save "statistical" lives?

3. One way of refuting a dilemma is to "grasp the horns" and show that at least one of the alternatives is false or would not lead to the alleged consequences. Another way is to "go between the horns" and show that a third alternative exists—a policy that would save specific persons and "statistical" lives both. In paragraphs 7–8, Wertheimer anticipates refutation of the dilemma and answers it. What kind of refutation might be presented, and how does he answer it?

4. Do you agree with Wertheimer's response to the dilemma in paragraph 10? On what evidence do you base your agreement or disagreement—facts, expert testimony, or assumptions that you regard as self-evident?

WRITING ASSIGNMENTS

1. Present examples of your own of the dilemma Wertheimer presents, and use them to explore their implications of your own beliefs and conclusions.

2. Present a dilemma that you believe should concern Americans today. Introduce facts or expert testimony to show that the dilemma is a real one, anticipate a refutation of your dilemma and answer it, and state your own views on what can or should be done.

Deductive Reasoning

Induction, as we saw, is sometimes reasoning from particular instances to a general conclusion or truth:

> I studied the equations but didn't do the practice problems, and I failed algebra. I studied my French but skipped the language lab and did poorly in French. I studied the formulas and performed the experiments carefully and passed Chemistry (three particular instances). Therefore, learning seems to depend on practice as well as study (probable truth).

Deduction, by contrast, is the process of inference—of reasoning from a general truth to another general truth or a particular instance:

> Since learning depends on constant study and practice (general truth), I passed algebra because I studied the equations and did the practice problems (particular instance).

In ordinary conversation we say informally, "I passed algebra because I studied and did the practice problems." This statement is a shortening of the following syllogism or formal argument:

> The act of learning is an act that depends on study and practice.
> The mastery of algebra is an act of learning.
> Therefore, the mastery of algebra is an act that depends on study and practice.

Notice that the first two statements—called the major and minor premises respectively—were left unstated in our shortened statement (called an *enthymeme*). Where the full argument is stated, the premises and conclusion may occur in a different order:

> The child needs to acquire fundamental skills in communication—to learn to read, write, and express himself flexibly and clearly—in order to function as a social creature (*major premise*). The television experience does not further his verbal development (*conclusion*) because it does not require any verbal participation on his part, merely passive intake (*minor premise*).—Marie Winn, *The Plug-In Drug*

Where inductive arguments depend on the weight of factual evidence beyond the premises, deductive arguments depend on the premises alone as evidence for the conclusion. No other evidence is required because the premises are regarded to be true—as in the *Declaration of Independence:*

> We hold these truths to be self-evident: that all men are created equal; that they are endowed by their creator with certain unalienable rights; that among these are life, liberty, and the pursuit of happiness.

From truths such as these, or long-held beliefs, or generalizations well supported by long experience, we make inferences as in our original example. Thus, if it is true that learning depends on study and practice and true also that the mastery of algebra is an act of learning, it must be true that mastering algebra depends on study and practice. Though no other evidence but the premises *need* be provided, I may decide to illustrate or defend one or both. For a true statement is not always obvious to everyone.

The argument, thus, must satisfy two requirements: the propositions that form the premises must be true, and the process of reasoning must be correct, or to use the technical term, must be valid.

Note that "valid" does not mean "true": an argument may be false in its premises, but still be valid if the process of inference from these premises is correct. Here is a valid argument, both of whose premises are false:

> All Texans are taxpayers.
> All property owners are Texans.
> Therefore, all property owners are taxpayers.

We ask of an argument that it be valid in its reasoning and true in its premises. A valid argument whose premises are true is called sound. The argument just cited would be sound if, in fact, all Texans do pay taxes, and all property owners (everywhere) are Texans. Logicians have complex techniques for testing the validity of the many kinds of syllogism; we cannot review them here. But we need to keep in mind a few characteristics that invalidate deductive arguments:

Someone says to us: "My neighbors must all be property owners because they all pay taxes." Something strikes us as wrong here, but what is it? We can construct the whole argument as follows:

> All property owners are taxpayers.
> My neighbors are taxpayers.
> Therefore, my neighbors are property owners.

The trouble is with the middle term, taxpayers. The major term of a syllogism is the predicate term of its conclusion; the subject of the conclusion is the minor term. The term that appears in the premises but not in the conclusion is called the middle term:

All	A	is	B
	middle		MAJOR
All	C	is	A
	MINOR		middle
All	C	is	B
	MINOR		MAJOR

(The argument may not have more than these three terms.) For the argument to be valid, this middle term must be "distributed" in at least one of the premises; that is, it must refer to—that is, be distributed among—all members of the class named. In the argument above, the middle term, taxpayers, is undistributed in both premises—referring in each to some members of the class taxpayers, but not to all:

> All property owners are taxpayers.
> My neighbors are taxpayers.

Though all property owners are taxpayers, not all taxpayers may own property. And though all my neighbors are taxpayers, not all taxpayers may be my neighbors. But that is exactly what the conclusion asserts. The argument is thus invalid because the conclusion says more than the premises do.

Other invalid arguments can be analyzed more easily. The middle term must not be ambiguous, as in the following argument:

> Whoever helps himself is helped by God.
> A thief helps himself.
> Therefore, a thief is helped by God.

And both premises must be affirmative if the conclusion is so: if one of the premises is negative, so must be the conclusion. And, if both premises are negative, no conclusion follows. The following argument is invalid for this reason:

> No dogs are welcome visitors.
> Children are not dogs.
> Therefore, children are welcome visitors.

In developing arguments of our own, it is important to remember that an argument may seem "logical" because the process of reasoning is correct, and yet be unsound because the premises are questionable or false. In reading arguments, we need to consider both the premises that form it and the way the writer reasons from them.

H. L. MENCKEN

HENRY LOUIS MENCKEN *(1880–1956) wrote for Baltimore newspapers and other periodicals most of his life, and was one of the founders and editors of the* American Mercury *magazine. His satirical essays on American life and politics were collected in six volumes under the title* Prejudices. *His three volumes of autobiography describe his youth in Baltimore and his later career in journalism. Mencken's interests were wide, and he wrote extensively about American democracy and the American language, whose characteristics he describes in a classic book on the subject. His ironic, and often sarcastic, style is well illustrated by these reflections, published after his death in* Minority Report.

Reflections on War

The thing constantly overlooked by those hopefuls who talk 1
of abolishing war is that it is by no means an evidence of
decay but rather a proof of health and vigor. To fight seems
to be as natural to man as to eat. Civilization limits and wars
upon the impulse but it can never quite eliminate it. Whenever the effort seems to be most successful—that is, whenever man seems to be submitting most willingly to discipline,
the spark is nearest to the powder barrel. Here repression
achieves its inevitable work. The most warlike people under
civilization are precisely those who submit most docilely to
the rigid inhibitions of peace. Once they break through the
bounds of their repressed but steadily accumulating pugnac-
ity, their destructiveness runs to great lengths. Throwing off
the chains of order, they leap into the air and kick their legs.
Of all the nations engaged in the two World Wars the Germans, who were the most rigidly girded by conceptions of
renunciation and duty, showed the most gusto for war for its
own sake.

The powerful emotional stimulus of war, its evocation 2
of motives and ideals which, whatever their error, are at
least more stimulating than those which impel a man to get
and keep a safe job—this is too obvious to need laboring.
The effect on the individual soldier of its very horror, filling
him with a sense of the heroic, increases enormously his
self-respect. This increase in self-respect reacts upon the
nation, and tends to save it from the deteriorating effects of
industrial discipline. In the main, soldiers are men of humble position and talents—laborers, petty mechanics, young
fellows without definite occupation. Yet no one can deny that
the veteran shows a certain superiority in dignity to the
average man of his age and experience. He has played his
part in significant events; he has been a citizen in a far more
profound sense than any mere workman can ever be. The
effects of all this are plainly seen in his bearing and his
whole attitude of mind. War may make a fool of man, but it

by no means degrades him; on the contrary, it tends to exalt him, and its net effects are much like those of motherhood on women.

That war is a natural revolt against the necessary but extremely irksome discipline of civilization is shown by the difficulty with which men on returning from it re-adapt themselves to a round of petty duties and responsibilities. This was notably apparent after the Civil War. It took three or four years for the young men engaged in that conflict to steel themselves to the depressing routine of everyday endeavor. Many of them, in fact, found it quite impossible. They could not go back to shovelling coal or tending a machine without intolerable pain. Such men flocked to the West, where adventure still awaited them and discipline was still slack. In the same way, after the Franco-Prussian War, thousands of young German veterans came to the United States, which seemed to them one vast Wild West. True enough, they soon found that discipline was necessary here as well as at home, but it was a slacker discipline and they themselves exaggerated its slackness in their imagination. At all events, it had the charm of the unaccustomed.

We commonly look upon the discipline of war as vastly more rigid than any discipline necessary in time of peace, but this is an error. The strictest military discipline imaginable is still looser than that prevailing in the average assembly-line. The soldier, at worst, is still able to exercise the highest conceivable functions of freedom—that is, he is permitted to steal and to kill. No discipline prevailing in peace gives him anything even remotely resembling this. He is, in war, in the position of a free adult; in peace he is almost always in the position of a child. In war all things are excused by success, even violations of discipline. In peace, speaking generally, success is inconceivable except as a function of discipline.

The hope of abolishing war is largely based upon the fact that men have long since abandoned the appeal to arms in their private disputes and submitted themselves to the jurisdiction of courts. Starting from this fact, it is contended that disputes between nations should be settled in the same manner, and that the adoption of the reform would greatly promote the happiness of the world.

Unluckily, there are three flaws in the argument. The 6 first, which is obvious, lies in the circumstances that a system of legal remedies is of no value if it is not backed by sufficient force to impose its decisions upon even the most powerful litigants—a sheer impossibility in international affairs, for even if one powerful litigant might be coerced, it would be plainly impossible to coerce a combination, and it is precisely a combination of the powerful that is most to be feared. The second lies in the fact that any legal system, to be worthy of credit, must be administered by judges who have no personal interest in the litigation before them— another impossibility, for all the judges in the international court, in the case of disputes between first-class powers, would either be appointees of those powers, or appointees of inferior powers that were under their direct influence, or obliged to consider the effects of their enmity. The third objection lies in the fact, frequently forgotten, that the courts of justice which now exist do not actually dispense justice, but only law, and that this law is frequently in direct conflict, not only with what one litigant honestly believes to be his rights, but also with what he believes to be his honor. Practically every litigation, in truth, ends with either one litigant or the other nursing what appears to him as an outrage upon him. For both litigants to go away satisfied that justice has been done is almost unheard of.

In disputes between man and man this dissatisfaction is 7 not of serious consequence. The aggrieved party has no feasible remedy; if he doesn't like it, he must lump it. In particular, he has no feasible remedy against a judge or a juryman who, in his view, has treated him ill; if he essayed vengeance, the whole strength of the unbiased masses of men would be exerted to destroy him, and that strength is so enormous, compared to his own puny might, that it would swiftly and certainly overwhelm him. But in the case of first-class nations there would be no such overwhelming force in restraint. In a few cases the general opinion of the world might be so largely against them that it would force them to acquiesce in the judgment rendered, but in perhaps a majority of important cases there would be sharply divided sympathies, and it would constantly encourage resistance. Against that resistance there would be nothing save the counter-resistance of the opposition—*i.e.,* the judge against the aggrieved litigant, the twelve jurymen against the aggrieved litigant's friends, with no vast and impersonal force of neutral public opinion behind the former.

QUESTIONS

1. In paragraphs 1–4, Mencken argues that war will not be easily abolished, and he states his major premise explicitly: "To fight seems to be as natural to man as to eat." How do the wording of this statement and the wording of others in these paragraphs show that Mencken regards these premises as certain and decisive evidence for his conclusions? What conclusions does he reach based on these premises?

2. Though he regards his premises as certain, Mencken explains and illustrates them. What examples does he present? Does he discuss one civilization or instead generalize about "warlike people" on the basis of observations made over a period of time?

3. Paragraph 1 of the Mencken contains the makings of several syllogisms; in the first of these, the major premise may be stated in these words: "The expression of a natural instinct is evidence of health and vigor." What are the minor premise and conclusion?

4. In paragraph 1 Mencken argues that repression of a natural instinct leads to increased destructiveness. What are the minor premise and conclusion?

5. L. A. White, in *Science of Culture*, argues that the need for military conscription refutes the assumption that people are naturally warlike. Given his assumptions and evidence, how might Mencken answer this objection? What do paragraphs 5–7 suggest?

6. In paragraphs 5–7 Mencken challenges "the hope of abolishing war," a hope based on the assumption that people have long since "submitted themselves to the jurisdiction of courts." What flaws does Mencken find in the argument, and what kind of evidence does he present in refutation? Does he deal with particular instances or instead generalize from observations made over a period of time?

7. Decide whether the following arguments are valid or invalid. It may be necessary to reword the premises:
   a. Since all voters are citizens and I am a voter, I am a citizen.
   b. Since all voters are citizens and I am a citizen, I am a voter.
   c. Since the Irish are vegetarians and Bernard Shaw was Irish, Shaw was a vegetarian.
   d. Those who made 93 or better on the exam will receive an A in the course. Seven of us received an A in the course and therefore must have made 93 or better on the exam.
   e. Since beneficent acts are virtuous and losing at poker benefits others, losing at poker is virtuous.

8. An *enthymeme* is a condensed syllogism, one of whose premises is implied: Because I did not study the equations, I failed algebra. In the following enthymemes, reconstruct the original syllogism by supplying the missing premise, and evaluate the argument. The premises and conclusion may need rewording:
   a. John F. Kennedy was a good President because he supported the space program and other kinds of scientific research.
   b. Capital punishment protects society from depraved individuals.
   c. I am a successful businessman because I once had a paper route.
   d. I am an independent voter, just as my father and grandfather were.

WRITING ASSIGNMENT

Write an argument for or against one of the following. In an additional paragraph identify one or more assumptions that underlie your argument, and explain why you hold these assumptions:

a. building more nuclear power plants
b. a ban on smoking in public transportation
c. the 55-mile-per-hour speed limit
c. periodic examination of licensed drivers
e. required attendance in college classes
f. compulsory gun registration

KENNETH B.CLARK

KENNETH B. CLARK *taught psychology at City College of New York from 1942 to 1975, and has taught at other universities including Columbia and Harvard. His writings on black life in America have exerted wide influence on social legislation and judicial thinking on civil rights. Among his influential books are* Dark Ghetto *(1965) and* Pathos of Power *(1974), from which this discussion of the idea of "relevance" in education is taken. Clark raises issues that Holt and Cousins also explore from different points of view and assumptions.*

The Limits of Relevance

As one who began himself to use the term "relevant" and to   1
insist on its primacy years ago, I feel an obligation to protest
the limits of relevance or to propose a redefinition of it to
embrace wider terms.

Definitions of education that depend on immediate rel-   2
evance ignore a small but critical percentage of human beings, the individuals who for some perverse reason are in
search of an education that is not dominated by the important, socially and economically required pragmatic needs of
a capitalist or a communist or a socialist society. Such an

individual is not certain what he wants to be; he may not even be sure that he wants to be successful. He may be burdened with that perverse intelligence that finds the excitement of life in a continuous involvement with ideas.

For this student, education may be a lonely and tortuous 3 process not definable in terms of the limits of course requirements or of departmental boundaries, or the four- or six-year span of time required for the bachelor's or graduate degree. This student seems unable to seek or to define or to discuss relevance in terms of externals. He seems somehow trapped by the need to seek the dimensions of relevance in relation to an examination and re-examination of his own internal values. He may have no choice but to assume the burden of seeking to define the relevance of the human experience as a reflection of the validity of his own existence as a value-seeking, socially sensitive, and responsive human being. He is required to deny himself the protective, supporting crutch of accepting and clutching uncritically the prevailing dogmatisms, slogans, and intellectual fashions.

If such a human being is to survive the inherent and 4 probably inevitable aloneness of intellectual integrity, he must balance it by the courage to face and accept the risks of his individuality; by compassion and empathetic identification with the frailties of his fellow human beings as a reflection of his own; by an intellectual and personal discipline which prevents him from wallowing in introspective amorphousness and childlike self-indulgence. And, certainly, he must demonstrate the breadth of perspective and human sensitivity and depth of affirmation inherent in the sense of humor which does not laugh at others but laughs with man and with the God of Paradox who inflicted upon man the perpetual practical joke of the human predicament.

American colleges, with few notable exceptions, pro- 5 vide little room for this type of student, just as American society provides little room for such citizens. Perhaps it is enough to see that institutions of higher education do not destroy such potential. One could hope wistfully that our colleges and even our multiuniversities could spare space and facilities to serve and to protect those students who want to experiment without being required to be practical, pragmatic, or even relevant.

Is it possible within the complexity and cacophony of 6 our dynamic, power-related, and tentatively socially sensitive institutions for some few to have the opportunity to look within, to read, to think critically, to communicate, to make mistakes, to seek validity, and to accept and enjoy this process as valid in itself? Is there still some place where relevance can be defined in terms of the quest—where respect for self and others can be taken for granted as one admits not knowing and is therefore challenged to seek?

May one dare to hope for a definition of education 7 which makes it possible for man to accept the totality of his humanity without embarrassment? This would be valuable for its own sake, but it might also paradoxically be the most pragmatic form of education—because it is from these perverse, alone-educated persons that a practical society receives antidotes to a terrifying sense of inner emptiness and despair. They are the font of the continued quest for meaning in the face of the mocking chorus of meaninglessness. They offer the saving reaffirmation of stabilizing values in place of the acceptance of the disintegration inherent in valuelessness. They provide the basis for faith in humanity and life rather than surrender to dehumanization and destruction. From these impracticals come our poets, our artists, our novelists, our satirists, our humorists. They are our models of the positives, the potentials, the awe and wonder of man. They make the life of the thinking human being more endurable and the thought of a future tolerable.

QUESTIONS

1. How does Clark explain the meanings of the term *relevant*? Why does he briefly review these meanings?

2. What assumptions does Clark make about the educational needs of people?

3. What conclusions does he derive from his assumptions?

4. Do you agree that American colleges have little room for the kind of student described in paragraph 4? What is your answer to the questions Clark asks in paragraph 6?

5. Does Clark seek to refute those who argue the "pragmatic needs" of education? Or does he present confirming arguments only?

WRITING ASSIGNMENT

Evaluate one of the following statements on the basis of your experience and observation:

a. "American colleges, with few notable exceptions, provide little room for this type of student, just as American society provides little room for such citizens."

b. ". . . it is from these perverse, alone-educated pesons that a practical society receives antidotes to a terrifying sense of inner emptiness and despair."

JOHN HOLT

In his earlier essay on kinds of discipline in learning, we discover one of the assumptions that guides JOHN HOLT*'s thinking in this essay from his book* Escape from Childhood. *In another of his books, Holt states another of his assumptions: "Human experience, knowledge, culture is everyone's. No one ought to have to prove that he deserves it or has a right to it. It ought to have been used for a great upward leveling, to make a universal aristocracy of wisdom and learning." And he summarizes the argument that the learned use to justify their authority: "We know more than you, therefore we*

are better than you, we have a right to tell you what to
do, you have no right to question us or argue with us, in
fact, you have no right to any serious opinions at all."

The Right to Control One's
Learning

Young people should have the right to control and direct 1
their own learning, that is, to decide what they want to
learn, and when, where, how, how much, how fast, and with
what help they want to learn it. To be still more specific, I
want them to have the right to decide if, when, how much,
and by whom they want to be *taught* and the right to decide
whether they want to learn in a school and if so which one
and for how much of the time.

No human right, except the right to life itself, is more 2
fundamental than this. A person's freedom of learning is
part of his freedom of thought, even more basic than his
freedom of speech. If we take from someone his right to
decide what he will be curious about, we destroy his freedom of thought. We say, in effect, you must think not about
what interests and concerns *you*, but about what interests
and concerns *us*.

We might call this the right of curiosity, the right to ask 3
whatever questions are most important to us. As adults, we
assume that we have the right to decide what does or does
not interest us, what we will look into and what we will leave
alone. We take this right for granted, cannot imagine that it
might be taken away from us. Indeed, as far as I know, it
has never been written into any body of law. Even the
writers of our Constitution did not mention it. They thought
it was enough to guarantee citizens the freedom of speech
and the freedom to spread their ideas as widely as they
wished and could. It did not occur to them that even the
most tyrannical government would try to control people's

minds, what they thought and knew. That idea was to come later, under the benevolent guise of compulsory universal education.

This right of each of us to control our own learning is now in danger. When we put into our laws the highly authoritarian notion that someone should and could decide what all young people were to learn and, beyond that, could do whatever might seem necessary (which now includes dosing them with drugs) to compel them to learn it, we took a long step down a very steep and dangerous path. The requirement that a child go to school, for about six hours a day, 180 days a year, for about ten years, whether or not he learns anything there, whether or not he already knows it or could learn it faster or better somewhere else, is such a gross violation of civil liberties that few adults would stand for it. But the child who resists is treated as a criminal. With this requirement we created an industry, an army of people whose whole work was to tell young people what they had to learn and to try to make them learn it. Some of these people, wanting to exercise even more power over others, to be even more "helpful" or simply because the industry is not growing fast enough to hold all the people who want to get into it, are now beginning to say, "If it is good for children for us to decide what they shall learn and to make them learn it, why wouldn't it be good for everyone? If compulsory education is a good thing, how can there be too much of it? Why should we allow anyone, of any age, to decide that he has had enough of it? Why should we allow older people, any more than young, not to know what we know when their ignorance may have bad consequences for all of us? Why should we not *make* them know what they *ought* to know?"

They are beginning to talk, as one man did on a nationwide TV show, about "womb-to-tomb" schooling. If hours of homework every night are good for the young, why wouldn't they be good for us all—they would keep us away from the TV set and other frivolous pursuits. Some group of experts, somewhere, would be glad to decide what we all ought to know and then every so often check up on us to make sure we knew it—with, of course, appropriate penalties if we did not.

I am very serious in saying that I think this is coming 6
unless we prepare against it and take steps to prevent it. The right I ask for the young is a right that I want to preserve for the rest of us, the right *to decide what goes into our minds.* This is much more than the right to decide whether or when or how much to go to school or what school you want to go to. That right is important, but it is only part of a much larger and more fundamental right, which I might call the right to Learn, as opposed to being Educated, *i.e.,* made to learn what someone else thinks would be good for you. It is not just compulsory schooling but compulsory Education that I oppose and want to do away with.

That children might have the control of their own learn- 7
ing, including the right to decide if, when, how much, and where they wanted to go to school, frightens and angers many people. They ask me, "Are you saying that if the parents wanted the child to go to school, and the child didn't want to go, that he wouldn't have to go? Are you saying that if the parents wanted the child to go to one school, and the child wanted to go to another, that the child would have the right to decide?" Yes, that is what I say. Some people ask, "If school wasn't compulsory, wouldn't many parents take their children out of school to exploit their labor in one way or another?" Such questions are often both snobbish and hypocritical. The questioner assumes and implies (though rarely says) that these bad parents are people poorer and less schooled than he. Also, though he appears to be defending the right of children to go to school, what he really is defending is the right of the state to compel them to go whether they want to or not. What he wants, in short, is that children should be in school, not that they should have any choice about going.

But saying that children should have the right to choose 8
to go or not to go to school does not mean that the ideas and wishes of the parents would have no weight. Unless he is estranged from his parents and rebelling against them, a

child cares very much about what they think and want. Most of the time, he doesn't want to anger or worry or disappoint them. Right now, in families where the parents feel that they have some choice about their children's schooling, there is much bargaining about schools. Such parents, when their children are little, often ask them whether they want to go to nursery school or kindergarten. Or they may take them to school for a while to try it out. Or, if they have a choice of schools, they may take them to several to see which they think they will like the best. Later, they care whether the child likes his school. If he does not, they try to do something about it, get him out of it, find a school he will like.

I know some parents who for years had a running 9 bargain with their children, "If on a given day you just can't stand the thought of school, you don't feel well, you are afraid of something that may happen, you have something of your own that you very much want to do—well, you can stay home." Needless to say, the schools, with their supporting experts, fight it with all their might—Don't Give in to Your Child, Make Him Go to School, He's Got to Learn. Some parents, when their own plans make it possible for them to take an interesting trip, take their children with them. They don't ask the school's permission, they just go. If the child doesn't want to make the trip and would rather stay in school, they work out a way for him to do that. Some parents, when their child is frightened, unhappy, and suffering in school, as many children are, just take him out. Hal Bennett, in his excellent book *No More Public School*, talks about ways to do this.

A friend of mine told me that when her boy was in third 10 grade, he had a bad teacher, bullying, contemptuous, sarcastic, cruel. Many of the class switched to another section, but this eight-year-old, being tough, defiant, and stubborn, hung on. One day—his parents did not learn this until about two years later—having had enough of the teacher's meanness, he just got up from his desk and without saying a word, walked out of the room and went home. But for all his toughness and resiliency of spirit, the experience was hard on him. He grew more timid and quarrelsome, less outgoing and confident. He lost his ordinary good humor. Even his handwriting began to go to pieces—was much worse in the spring of the school year than in the previous fall. One spring day he sat at breakfast, eating his cereal. After a while he stopped eating and sat silently thinking about the day ahead. His eyes filled up with tears, and two big ones slowly rolled down his cheeks. His mother, who ordinarily stays out of the school life of her children, saw this and knew what it was about. "Listen," she said to him, "we don't have to go on with this. If you've had enough of that teacher, if she's making school so bad for you that you don't want to go any more, I'll be perfectly happy just to pull you right out. We can manage it. Just say the word." He was horrified and indignant. "No!" he said, "I couldn't do that." "Okay," she said, "whatever you want is fine. Just let me know." And so they left it. He had decided that he was going to tough it out, and he did. But I am sure knowing that he had the support of his mother and the chance to give it up if it got too much for him gave him the strength he needed to go on.

To say that children should have the right to control and 11 direct their own learning, to go to school or not as they chose, does not mean that the law would forbid the parents to express an opinion or wish or strong desire on the matter. It only means that if their natural authority is not strong enough the parents can't call in the cops to make the child do what they are not able to persuade him to do. And the law may say that there is a limit to the amount of pressure or coercion the parents can apply to the child to deny him a choice that he has a legal right to make.

When I urge that children should control their learning 12 there is one argument that people bring up so often that I feel I must anticipate and meet it here. It says that schools are a place where children can for a while be protected against the bad influences of the world outside, particularly from its greed, dishonesty, and commercialism. It says that in school children may have a glimpse of a higher way of life, of people acting from other and better motives than greed and fear. People say, "We know that society is bad enough as it is and that children will be exposed to it and corrupted by it soon enough. But if we let children go out into the larger world as soon as they wanted, they would be tempted and corrupted just that much sooner."

They seem to believe that schools are better, more hon- 13 orable places than the world outside—what a friend of mind at Harvard once called "museums of virtue." Or that people in school, both children and adults, act from higher and better motives than people outside. In this they are mistaken. There are, of course, some good schools. But on the whole, far from being the opposite of, or an antidote to, the world outside, with all its envy, fear, greed, and obsessive competitiveness, the schools are very much like it. If anything, they are worse, a terrible, abstract, simplified caricature of it. In the world outside the school, some work, at least, is done honestly and well, for its own sake, not just to get ahead of others; people are not everywhere and always being set in competition against each other; people are not (or not yet) in every minute of their lives subject to the arbitrary, irrevocable orders and judgment of others. But in most schools, a student is every minute doing what others tell him, subject to their judgment, in situations in which he can only win at the expense of other students.

This is a harsh judgment. Let me say again, as I have 14 before, that schools are worse than most of the people in them and that many of these people do many harmful things they would rather not do, and a great many other harmful things that they do not even see as harmful. The whole of school is much worse than the sum of its parts. There are very few people in the U.S. today (or perhaps anywhere, any time) in *any* occupation, who could be trusted with the kind of power that schools give most teachers over their students. Schools seem to me among the most anti-democratic, most authoritarian, most destructive, and most dangerous institutions of modern society. No other institution does more harm or more lasting harm to more people or destroys so much of their curiosity, independence, trust, dignity, and sense of identity and worth. Even quite kindly schools are inhibited and corrupted by the knowledge of children and teachers alike that they are *performing* for the judgment and approval of others—the children for the teachers; the teachers for the parents, supervisors, school board, or the state. No one is ever free from feeling that he is being judged all the time, or soon may be. Even after the best class experiences teachers must ask themselves, "Were we right to do that? Can we prove we were right? Will it get us in trouble?"

What corrupts the school, and makes it so much worse than most of the people in it, or than they would like it to be, is its power—just as their powerlessness corrupts the students. The school is corrupted by the endless anxious demand of the parents to know how their child is doing—meaning is he ahead of the other kids—and their demand that he be kept ahead. Schools do not protect children from the badness of the world outside. They are at least as bad as the world outside, and the harm they do to the children in their power creates much of the badness of the world outside. The sickness of the modern world is in many ways a school-induced sickness. It is in school that most people learn to expect and accept that some expert can always place them in some sort of rank or hierarchy. It is in school that we meet, become used to, and learn to believe in the totally controlled society. We do not learn much science, but we learn to worship "scientists" and to believe that anything we might conceivably need or want can only come, and someday will come, from them. The school is the closest we have yet been able to come to Huxley's *Brave New World*, with its alphas and betas, deltas and epsilons—and now it even has its soma. Everyone, including children, should have the right to say "No!" to it.

QUESTIONS

1. Holt states his major premise in paragraphs 1 and 2: young people have the right to "control and direct their own learn-

ing." In paragraph 3 he explains why the Constitution does not mention this right. What words in these opening paragraphs show that Holt holds the premise to be true without question?

2. What conclusions does he draw from the premise in paragraph 4? What conclusions does he show can be drawn from different premises in paragraphs 4–5?

3. What is the larger premise that Holt introduces in paragraph 6? Why do you think he did not begin his essay with it?

4. What further deductions does Holt draw from his premises in paragraph 7, and how does he answer objections to these ideas?

5. In paragraph 8, Holt now *qualifies* his ideas; that is, he states what his premises do *not* entail. What qualifications does he make in this and later paragraphs?

6. In paragraph 9, Holt shows that his proposal is feasible; in paragraph 10, that enforced schooling can have dire effects on children. How does he show that the proposal is feasible, and what are the dire effects?

7. Paragraphs 4–11 form Holt's main argument. What in the wording of paragraph 12 shows that Holt is turning now to refutation? What objections does Holt introduce to his argument, and how does he answer it in paragraphs 13–15?

8. Where in the concluding paragraph does he restate his major premise (actually the thesis of the essay)?

9. With what aspects of the argument do you agree or disagree? Do you agree with Holt's major premise and with his estimate of schools today, or do you disagree with one or both of these?

WRITING ASSIGNMENTS

1. Using Holt's major premise, draw conclusions from it relating to the rights of children in the family. If young people have the right to "control and direct their own learning," what rights and privileges with respect to money and the use of such property as the family automobile should be theirs? When you have finished your discussion of these rights, state whether you agree with Holt's premises, and discuss the feasibility of such rights and privileges that the premise entails.

2. Write an estimate of your school, and use it to test the soundness of Holt's charges in paragraphs 13–15. If you believe his conclusions need to be qualified, explain why and how they should be.

———❧———

Order of Ideas

Argumentative essays have a traditional organization that is easy to learn and put to use. Indeed this organization, derived from the oration of the law courts and legislatures of ancient Greece and Rome, shaped the expository essay that we have been considering—in particular the division of the essay into an introduction that states the purpose and gives pertinent background, the main discussion or body, and the conclusion. The argumentative essay today, like the oration of ancient times, contains these divisions but expands them to meet the needs of the argument:

> *introduction* or what was called the exordium or exhortation to the audience, appealing to the interest and good will of the audience, and stating the subject of the oration or essay;
> *division of proofs*, stating the thesis partly or fully and summarizing the evidence and arguments to be presented;
> *narration* or background, stating the facts of the case,
> *confirmation* or proof, arguing the thesis;
> *refutation*, answering opponents;
> conclusion, reinforcing and summarizing the main argument and reinforcing the original appeal to the audience.

These parts may be combined or arranged in a different order—the narration or background perhaps combined with the confirming arguments, or the refutation coming before the confirmation. Often the division or outline of the argument is omitted, and instead of coming early, the thesis may be delayed until the conclusion for reasons discussed earlier. The following argumentative essay by Norman Cousins varies this form by combining his confirmation and refutation.

NORMAN COUSINS

> COUSINS, *in this column from the* Saturday Review *magazine, turns to the general "shucking of responsiblity" that he finds pervasive in American life. In arguing that ". . . the school has no right to jettison standards just because of difficulties in enforcing them," he takes a position exactly opposite to that of Holt, who questions the authority of the school to establish standards by virtue of its authority. Cousins is writing about the world of the late 1970s, but the issues he raises continue to be pertinent today.*

Cop-out Realism

On all sides, one sees evidence today of cop-out realism— 1
ostensible efforts to be sensible in dealing with things as
they are but that turn out to be a shucking of responsibility.

Example: Until fairly recently, off-track betting was 2
illegal in New York State. Gambling on horses was regarded
as a disguised form of stealing, run by professional
gamblers who preyed upon people who could least afford to
lose. Also outlawed was the numbers game, in which people
could bet small amounts of money on numbers drawn from
the outcome of the day's horse races.

Attempts by government to drive out the gambling syn- 3
dicates had only indifferent results. Finally, state officials
decided that, since people were going to throw their money
away despite anything the law might do to protect them, the
state ought to take over off-track betting and the numbers
racket.

It is now possible to assess the effect of that legaliza- 4
tion. The first thing that is obvious is that New York State
itself has become a predator in a way that the Mafia could
never hope to match. What was intended as a plan to con-

trol gambling has become a high-powered device to promote it. The people who can least afford to take chances
with their money are not only not dissuaded from gambling
but are actually being cajoled into it by the state. Millions of
dollars are being spent by New York State on lavish advertising on television, on radio, in buses, and on billboards. At
least the Mafia was never able publicly to glorify and extol
gambling with taxpayer money. And the number of poor
people who were hurt by gambling under the Mafia is
miniscule compared to the number who now lose money on
horses with the urgent blessings of New York State.

A second example of cop-out realism is the way some 5
communities are dealing with cigarette-smoking by teenagers and pre-teenagers. Special rooms are now being set
aside for students who want to smoke. No age restrictions
are set; freshmen have the same lighting-up privileges as
seniors.

The thinking behind the new school policy is similar to 6
the "realism" behind New York's decision to legalize off-
track betting and the numbers game. It is felt that since the
youngsters are going to smoke anyway, the school might just
as well make it possible for them to do it in the open rather
than feel compelled to do it furtively in back corridors and
washrooms.

Parents and teachers may pride themselves on their 7
"realism" in such approaches. What they are actually doing
is finding a convenient rationalization for failing to uphold
their responsibility. The effect of their supposedly "realistic" policy is to convert a ban into a benediction. By sanc-
tioning that which they deplore, they become part of the
problem they had the obligation to meet. What they regard
as common sense turns out to be capitulation.

Pursuing the same reasoning, why not set aside a cor- 8
ner for a bar where students can buy alcoholic beverages?
After all, teenage drinking is a national problem, and it is
far better to have the youngsters drink out in the open than
to have them feel guilty about stealing drinks from the
cupboard at home or contriving to snatch their liquor out-

side the home. Moreover, surveillance can be exercised. Just as most public bars will not serve liquor to people who are hopelessly drunk, so the school bartender could withhold alcohol from students who can hardly stand on their feet.

It is not far-fetched to extend the same "reasoning" to 9 marijuana. If the youngsters are going to be able to put their hands on the stuff anyway, why shouldn't they be able to buy it legally and smoke it openly, perhaps in the same schoolroom that has been converted into a smoking den?

We are not reducing the argument to an absurdity; we 10 are asking that parents and teachers face up to the implications of what they are doing.

The school has no right to jettison standards just be- 11 cause of difficulties in enforcing them. The school's proper response is not to abdicate but to extend its efforts in other directions. It ought to require regular lung examinations for its youngsters. It ought to schedule regular sessions with parents and youngsters at which reports on these examinations can be considered. It ought to bring in cancer researchers who can run films for students showing the difference between the brackish, pulpy lungs caused by cigarette smoking and the smooth pink tissue of healthy lungs. The schools should schedule visits to hospital wards for lung cancer patients. In short, educators should take the U.S. Surgeon-General's report on cigarettes seriously.

In all the discussion and debate over cigarette smoking 12 by children, one important fact is generally overlooked. That fact is that a great many children *do not* smoke. The school cannot ignore its obligation to these youngsters just because it cannot persuade the others not to smoke. It must not give the nonsmokers the impression that their needs are secondary or that the school has placed a seal of approval on a practice that is condemning millions of human beings to a fatal disease.

Still another example of cop-out realism is the policy of 13 many colleges and universities of providing common dormitories and common washrooms for both sexes. The general idea seems to be that it is unrealistic to expect young people not to sleep together. Besides, it is probably reasoned, if people are old enough to vote they are old enough to superintend their own sex habits. So, the thinking goes, the school might just as well allow them to share the same sleeping and toilet facilities.

The trouble with such policies is that they put the school 14 in the position of lending itself to the breakdown of that which is most important in healthy relations between the sexes—a respect for privacy and dignity. No one ever need feel ashamed of the human body. But that doesn't mean that the human body is to be displayed or handled like a slab of raw meat. Sex is one of the higher manifestations of human sensitivity and response, not an impersonal sport devoid of genuine feeling. The divorce courts are filled to overflowing with cases in which casual, mechanistic attitudes toward sex have figured in marital collapses. For the school to foster that casualness is for it to become an agent of de-sensitization in a monstrous default.

The function of standards is not to serve as the basis for 15 mindless repressive measures but to give emphasis to the realities of human experience. Such experience helps to identify the causes of unnecessary pain and disintegration. Any society that ignores the lessons of that experience may be in a bad way.

QUESTIONS

1. Cousins states his major premise in paragraph 1. How does he illustrate this premise in paragraphs 2–6?

2. In paragraphs 2–6 Cousins confirms his premise by showing certain consequences of "cop-out realism." In paragraphs 7–10 he shows that if we adopt such a policy, certain consequences follow—consequences that he considers obvious absurdities. What are these absurd consequences?

3. In stating in paragraphs 11–14 what the schools should be doing, Cousins draws further conclusions from the policy of "cop-out realism." What are these conclusions? Do you agree with them?

4. In the concluding paragraphs, what basic premises or assumptions concerning human responsibility and dignity emerge? How does Cousins use these premises to summarize his basic argument?

WRITING ASSIGNMENTS

1. Cousins combines confirmation and refutation, in showing that "cop-out realism" entails absurd consequences, and joins narration to these, in presenting the background on gambling and schools in New York State. Write an argumentative essay in which you combine narration with confirmation or refutation in the same way. Your refutation need not take the same form as Cousins'. You may prefer to answer objections to your basic premise and proposals directly.

2. Discuss the extent to which, in your view, Cousins would disagree with Holt's premise and basic proposals on education. Support your discussion with comparison of their premises and reasoning.

LEONARD GROSS

> LEONARD GROSS *was a senior editor of* Look *magazine, serving for a time as a correspondent in Latin America. He has written numerous articles and books on a range of subjects including physical fitness. His essay here first appeared in the "My Turn" column in* Newsweek. *It is particularly noteworthy for its clear statement and defense of the assumptions of the argument.*

Is Less More?

The following superlative is offered after considerable 1 thought: Americans are, or will shortly be, in the process of making the most fundamental adjustment they have ever had to make. If this adjustment concerned solely their standard of living, the superlative would not be valid. What makes it so is that this is the first time Americans have ever had to change the *assumptions* about the manner in which they live.

There have been times of sacrifice before, particularly during wars, but the assumption was that times would be "good" again when the emergency ended. Today, however, economic factors are such that the prudent American must adjust to the likelihood that material life may never be the same again.

This country is in the process of discovering that it can no longer afford the big life. That is the downstream meaning of our present economic turmoil. From whatever area you approach the problem, be it resources, inflation, population or politics, the prospect remains the same. Solutions will necessarily require permanent alterations in the size and scope of our activities, possessions and dreams.

Already, the broadly shared dream of upper-middle-class affluence has passed the average dreamer by. He figured that if he ever earned $20,000 a year, he'd have it made. Today, he's got the salary, but he's also got hobbling debts. Gains in real income for the middle class have been tiny; there's almost no upward mobility any longer. Aspirations to send children to college have been tempered by the immense cost and inability of degree holders to find employment.

Call it "middle-class discontent." It's demonstrably higher now than at any time in recent history. It will not lessen in our lifetime, not, at least, as a consequence of improved conditions. The cost of land will not diminish. The cost of money may diminish somewhat, but not to the levels that enabled millions of Americans to build their own homes in the years after the second world war. The value of the dollar will not increase. The cost of goods and services will not diminish, if only because the cost of fuel, a major production factor in every economic sector, will never return to previous levels. Populations will increase here and abroad, compounding problems of employment, education and maintenance.

It all sounds pretty bleak. And yet, and yet. Inherent in 6 the problem is a stunning resolution—nothing less than a change in the values by which we measure life. Because there *is* one variable in all this picture: the individual. He can diminish his discontent by reordering his priorities.

What happens to a society when its members have less 7 purchasing power is already beginning to be apparent. There will be practical changes in the way people live: smaller, less elaborate houses, fewer single-family dwellings, more cluster zoning, more condominiums, better use of land so as to provide more recreation near the home. Because travel will be so expensive, the environment near the home will receive greater attention.

With the price of food so high, discretionary income will 8 be diverted to supplement food budgets. That means less money for entertainment and an increasing reliance on the home as the family entertainment center. Such vacations as will be possible will change their nature. Vacation clubs, little known in the United States but enormously successful in Europe, will come into vogue. The Club Méditerranée, originator of the concept and prototype for other clubs, has already developed an American market.

Railroads work in Europe because Europeans use rail- 9 roads. And because they work. Europeans can board a train in the evening and be at their skiing station early the next morning after an inexpensive and acceptable night in a couchette. When Americans can no longer afford long trips in automobiles or airplanes, they will return to the railroads, the least expensive and the least environment-punishing form of mass transportation.

A subtle strain runs through these eventualities. With- 10 out neglecting the individual, we address ourselves to the common good. Everyone isn't vying for first cabin any longer; we're content to get there more modestly—and happy in the knowledge that our arrival is assured. The new

American dream will esteem "small" more than "big." The trend to smaller cars, recently made concrete by the General Motors announcement that its new models will be an average of 700 pounds lighter, is thus not simply a response to the fuel shortage. Eventually, it becomes an expression of taste.

"Less is more" is a phrase attributed to Mies van der 11 Rohe, the German architect, a leader of the Bauhaus group and pivotal force in the field of modern design. That single statement crystallized the philosophy of contemporary architecture and design—to do away with frilly styles. Would a life-style that did away with unnecessary baggage achieve the same simplicity and purity? Every week, it seems, I hear of one more American who thinks so. All were successful. All had made it to the top and then decided that the prize hadn't been worth the trip. "Can you imagine spending your life getting to a place and then finding you didn't want to be there?" one of them asked rhetorically.

Economic necessity will do more to change styles of life 12 than any previous factor. Moral imperatives don't embody an imperative for change. But when you can no longer afford the life you're living, or the life you can buy for what you earn becomes unacceptable, *then* you're motivated to change.

Since our inception, the American Premise has stated 13 that happiness lay ahead, in the bigger job, the bigger home, the bigger life. The larger implication of our new economic reality is nothing less than a rejection of that premise, with profound consequences in terms of social objectives and how they're expressed commercially. That many Americans will continue to grab for the brass ring while others are letting go in no way invalidates the premise. Facts in apparent contradiction can be simultaneously true.

QUESTIONS

1. Gross organizes his essay in the argumentative form discussed earlier:

introduction (paragraph 1)
division of proofs: partial statement of thesis (paragraphs 2–3)
narration (paragraphs 4–6)
confirmation (paragraphs 7–11)
refutation (paragraphs 12–13)
conclusion (paragraph 13)

Where in the confirmation does Gross state his thesis fully? How does he restate his thesis in the concluding paragraph?

2. What information does he provide in the narration, and for what purpose? Is he writing to a special or a general audience, and how do you know?

3. Gross is writing a special kind of essay that refutes assumptions held by a large number of Americans. What are these assumptions, and how does Gross challenge them? What assumptions of his own does he make explicitly and implicitly?

4. Gross supports his own ideas from experience: he is thus showing that new assumptions can and do find support in the world today. What are these experiences?

WRITING ASSIGNMENTS

1. Discuss how an experience like a rise in the price of gas forced you to change your standard of living and perhaps your thinking. Use this discussion to support or challenge one of Gross's ideas.

2. Challenge an assumption held by people your age, or perhaps your teachers or parents. Do so by showing how this assumption is contradicted by your experiences and observations. Follow the pattern of the argumentative essay shown above. Vary this pattern as you find necessary.

WILLIAM RASPBERRY

Born in northeastern Mississippi, WILLIAM RASPBERRY *after college began his career as a newspaperman. His column for* The Washington Post *also appears in news-*

*papers throughout the United States. Raspberry has writ-
ten much about black education and black experience in
America, and he writes also on a range of other
subjects—including the perceptions of Americans about
their values and goals.*

Images on a Screen

Suppose someone came up with a device that would allow   1
mental images to be projected on a screen. And suppose he
asked a cross-section of Americans to project vignettes from
their Ideal America.

Could you, by looking at the screen, tell whether the   2
image was that of a conservative or a liberal? A man or a
woman? A northerner or a southerner? A black or a white?

Clearly the various subsets of Americans espouse dif-   3
ferent methods for achieving their ideals. One would give
government the power to make us behave; another would
get government off our backs. One would be more concerned with attitudes, another with actions. One would seek
peace; another would prepare for war. But the point, in
every case, would be toward an ideal. Are the ideals really
so different?

Would a southern conservative, for instance, suppose   4
that an ideal America must be segregated by race? Or is his
present-day support of segregation mere pragmatism based
on his assumption that in a less-than-perfect world it's better for everybody to keep the races apart? Don't both hawk
and dove long for a world at peace? Isn't the argument
between them over the best way to achieve peace?

Would anyone's idealized projection depict an America   5
in which some were exploiters and the others exploited? Or
wouldn't both big-government and free-trade advocates see
a system in which all transactions were freely undertaken
and mutually beneficial?

There would be some obvious differences, no doubt.   6
Men might be more likely to see an ideal America in which

husbands earned the family income while wives managed the home. Women might be more likely to see the blurring of sex lines in the workplace, with females no less prevalent than males in the managerial ranks.

If the projection showed a Sunday morning congrega- 7 tion that was essentially white with a smattering of bright-faced black families, you would probably guess that it was a white doing the projecting. If the congregation was thoroughly mixed, you might guess it to be the image of a minority. If the minister is female, you'd suspect the vision emanated from a woman. And what if the priest were a black woman?

Would anyone's idealized vision include neighborhoods 8 segregated by race? By income? Or would there be a random scattering of colors and professions, with mansions and cottages intermingled? Would there be exclusive schools based on anything other than ability? Would friendships cross lines of race and ethnicity? Would marriages?

Surely there would be no poverty in anyone's ideal 9 projection. But would there be servants? And would they be of a different color than the one doing the projecting?

Conservatives may demand, in the real world, bigger 10 and better jails, while liberals may feel more optimistic about the potential for crime prevention and non-prison rehabilitation. But since the ideal vision of both would be of a society without crime, would either include police officers and jails?

Would the neighborhood bar be racially or sexually 11 segregated, or would it be more like a scene from a TV beer commercial? Who would own it?

If the image involved people who were not racially 12 identifiable, just vaguely people, would you attribute the projection to a white or a black? If a particular scene included a fair number of Asians or Latin Americans, would you suppose that an Asian or a Hispanic was doing the projecting?

While the approaches we take to solving our various 13 social problems tend to depend on our own circumstances and ethnicity, how different are our visions of what the country would look like once the problems were solved? In other words, are the crucial differences between us based on disparate goals, or only on contradictory methods for achieving them?

I'd guess the latter. I don't doubt that some of the 14 scenes projected by our magic machine would be traceable to those doing the projecting. But I suspect a lot of us would be surprised to find the projections more alike than different.

Except, perhaps, for the American Indians.   15

QUESTIONS

1. Raspberry is making a series of statements about America today in the form of questions. The wording of paragraph 4 shows that he expects assent from the reader to them:

   > Would anyone's idealized projection depict an America in which some were exploiters and the others exploited? Or wouldn't both big-government and free-trade advocates see a system in which all transactions were freely undertaken and mutually beneficial?

   How does the wording of other questions show that he expects the reader to agree?

2. Raspberry assumes the reader will confirm his examples as well as the statements from which he makes a number of inferences or deductions, for example, about what we can assume about the person projecting the Sunday morning congregation on the screen (paragraph 7). What other projections allow us to make similar inferences?

3. From what projections would it be difficult or impossible to make inferences and why?

4. In general, what political and economic ideals does Raspberry believe Americans share? If they do share these ideals, what does he believe accounts for the differences in specific attitudes or beliefs?

5. Does Raspberry recognize that exceptions exist, or is he writing about all Americans?

WRITING ASSIGNMENTS

1. State Raspberry's thesis in your own words. Then discuss the extent to which your experience gives support to it.

2. Discuss what particular behavior, actions or attitudes could be predicted from one of the following actual statements by people living in the twentieth century:

   a. "There is only one real 'statesman' once in a blue moon in one nation, and not a hundred or more at a time."

   b. "There is no indispensable man."

   c. "War alone brings up to its highest tension all human energy and puts the stamp of nobility upon the peoples who have the courage to face it."

   d. "There is no finer investment for any community than putting milk into babies."

Interpretation of Evidence

In an exposition of our ideas or beliefs, or in a debate, we can draw on our personal experience and observation for support. But often we have no experience with the matter under discussion and must turn to other sources of information. In stating opinions, it is important that the facts that support them are sound ones. But finding accurate sources is not always easy. We must know how to verify these sources—to establish the authority of the writer, to look for special circumstances or biases that may color the evidence, to find out whether the book is still up-to-date. No evidence is as neutral or objective as many want to believe, nor does all evidence have the same weight of importance. These are but a few of the considerations a researcher must keep in view. And even when the researcher does not, these questions force themselves into view when contrary evidence appears.

In choosing evidence we need to distinguish between primary sources—first-hand accounts by participants or observers—and secondary sources—later reports and interpretations by those not present. The distinction between primary and secondary is often a matter of dispute, but an eyewitness account is clearly a different kind of evidence from the reconstruction of that shooting by a historian ten years later. Primary evidence is not, however, necessarily more reliable than secondary. It may indeed be contradictory in itself or be contradicted by other eyewitness evidence. And secondary evidence may be unreliable for the same reasons. Twenty years after the assassination of President John Kennedy in November of 1963, eyewitnesses disagree on what they saw and heard, and later writers, sifting through the massive evidence, disagree on what is to be accepted as evidence. In 1979 a special Congressional subcommittee looked at new evidence and reported new findings.

Few researchers work with only one kind of evidence. Secondary sources are often needed to determine what is factual in primary sources and even to establish their worth. Proving the reliability of primary sources is sometimes a difficult job. But secondary sources must be used with caution, for writers often select evidence and interpret it to fit their view of people or history. These biases are not always intentional. All interpretations are shaped by personal and cultural attitudes of which we may be unaware. This is why primary and secondary sources must supplement each other in the search for the truth of a subject.

JOHN M. DARLEY AND BIBB LATANÉ

JOHN M. DARLEY, *professor of psychology at Princeton University, and* BIBB LATANÉ, *professor of psychology at Ohio State University, have each published many articles in the field of social psychology. Their investigation of the Kitty Genovese killing—whose details Martin Gansberg provides in his article earlier in this book—and of similar cases was first published in* Psychology Today *in 1968. Their essay is notable for their clear identification of the evidence they reason from, and for their explanation of the reasoning they employ. Norman Cousins considers the same issue—the state of mind and actions of the witnesses of an act of violence—from a different point of view. The spectators at a boxing match know that the action will be violent and may end in death, unlike the witnesses to a killing or assault. Yet the question of responsibility is the same. Darley and Latané offer an unusual explanation for behavior in these situations and explore the circumstances in which people believe they have the responsibility to act.*

When Will People Help?

Kitty Genovese is set upon by a maniac as she returns home 1 from work at 3:00 a.m. Thirty-eight of her neighbors in Kew Gardens come to their windows when she cries out in terror; none come to her assistance even though her stalker takes over half an hour to murder her. No one even so much as calls the police. She dies.

Andrew Mormille is stabbed in the stomach as he rides 2 the A train home to Manhattan. Eleven other riders watch the 17-year-old boy as he bleeds to death; none come to his assistance even though his attackers have left the car. He dies.

An 18-year-old switchboard operator, alone in her 3 office in the Bronx, is raped and beaten. Escaping momentarily, she runs naked and bleeding to the street, screaming for help. A crowd of 40 passersby gathers and watches as, in broad daylight, the rapist tries to drag her back upstairs; no one interferes. Finally two policemen happen by and arrest her assailant.

Eleanor Bradley trips and breaks her leg while shop- 4 ping on Fifth Avenue. Dazed and in shock, she calls for help, but the hurrying stream of executives and shoppers simply parts and flows past. After 40 minutes a taxi driver helps her to a doctor.

The shocking thing about these cases is that so many 5 people failed to respond. If only one or two had ignored the victim, we might be able to understand their inaction. But when 38 people, or 11 people, or hundreds of people fail to help, we become disturbed. Actually, this fact that shocks us so much is itself the clue to understanding these cases. Although it seems obvious that the more people who watch a victim in distress, the more likely someone will help, what really happens is exactly the opposite. If each member of a group of bystanders is aware that other people are also present, he will be less likely to notice the emergency, less likely to decide that it is an emergency, and less likely to act even if he thinks there is an emergency.

This is a surprising assertion—what we are saying is 6 that the victim may actually be less likely to get help, the more people who watch his distress and are available to help. We shall discuss in detail the process through which an individual bystander must go in order to intervene, and we shall present the results of some experiments designed to show the effects of the number of onlookers on the likelihood of intervention.

Since we started research on bystander responses to 7 emergencies, we have heard many explanations for the lack of intervention. "I would assign this to the effect of the megapolis in which we live, which makes closeness very difficult and leads to the alienation of the individual from the group," contributed a psychoanalyst. "A disaster syndrome," explained a sociologist, "that shook the sense of safety and sureness of the individuals involved and caused psychological withdrawal from the event by ignoring it." "Apathy," claimed others. "Indifference." "The gratification of unconscious sadistic impulses." "Lack of concern for our fellow men." "The Cold Society." All of these analyses of the person who fails to help share one characteristic: they set the indifferent witness apart from the rest of us as a different kind of person. Certainly not one of us who reads about these incidents in horror is apathetic, alienated or depersonalized. Certainly not one of us enjoys gratifying his sadistic impulses by watching others suffer. These terrifying cases in which people fail to help others certainly have no personal implications for us. That is, we might decide not to ride subways any more, or that New York isn't even "a nice place to visit," or "there ought to be a law" against apathy, but we needn't feel guilty, or re-examine ourselves, or anything like that.

Looking more closely at published descriptions of the 8 behavior of witnesses to these incidents, the people involved begin to look a little less inhuman and a lot more like the rest of us. Although it is unquestionably true that the witnesses in the incidents above did nothing to save the victims, apathy, indifference and unconcern are not entirely accurate descriptions of their reactions. The 38 witnesses of Kitty Genovese's murder did not merely look at the scene once and then ignore it. They continued to stare out of their windows at what was going on. Caught, fascinated, dis-

tressed, unwilling to act but unable to turn away, their behavior was neither helpful nor heroic; but it was not indifferent or apathetic.

Actually, it was like crowd behavior in many other 9
emergency situations. Car accidents, drownings, fires and
attempted suicides all attract substantial numbers of people
who watch the drama in helpless fascination without getting
directly involved in the action. Are these people alienated
and indifferent? Are the rest of us? Obviously not. Why,
then, don't we act?

The bystander to an emergency has to make a series of 10
decisions about what is happening and what he will do
about it. The consequences of these decisions will determine
his actions. There are three things he must do if he is to
intervene: *notice* that something is happening, *interpret*
that event as an emergency, and decide that he has *personal
responsibility* for intervention. If he fails to notice the event,
if he decides that it is not an emergency, or if he concludes
that he is not personally responsible for acting, he will leave
the victim unhelped. This state of affairs is shown graphically as a "decision tree." Only one path through this decision tree leads to intervention; all others lead to a failure to
help. As we shall show, at each fork of the path in the
decision tree, the presence of other bystanders may lead a
person down the branch of not helping.

Suppose that an emergency is actually taking place; a 11
middle-aged man has a heart attack. He stops short,
clutches his chest, and staggers to the nearest building wall,
where he slowly slumps to the sidewalk in a sitting position.
What is the likelihood that a passerby will come to his
assistance? First, the bystander has to *notice* that something
is happening. The external event has to break into his thinking and intrude itself on his conscious mind. He must tear
himself away from his private thoughts and pay attention to
this unusual event.

But Americans consider it bad manners to look too 12
closely at other people in public. We are taught to respect the
privacy of others, and when among strangers, we do this by

closing our ears and avoiding staring at others—we are embarrassed if caught doing otherwise. In a crowd, then, each person is less likely to notice the first sign of a potential emergency than when alone.

Experimental evidence corroborates this everyday ob- 13 servation. Darley and Latané asked college students to an interview about their reactions to urban living. As the students waited to see the interviewer, either by themselves or with two other students, they filled out a preliminary questionnaire. Solitary students often glanced idly about the room while filling out their questionnaires; those in groups, to avoid seeming rudely inquisitive, kept their eyes on their own papers.

As part of the study, we staged an emergency: smoke 14 was released into the waiting room through a vent. Two-thirds of the subjects who were alone when the smoke appeared noticed it immediately, but only a quarter of the subjects waiting in groups saw it as quickly. Even after the room had completely filled with smoke one subject from a group of three finally looked up and exclaimed, "God! I must be smoking too much!" Although eventually all the subjects did become aware of the smoke, this study indicates that the more people present, the slower an individual may be to perceive that an emergency does exist and the more likely he is not to see it at all.

Once an event is noticed, an onlooker must decide 15 whether or not it is truly an emergency. Emergencies are not always clearly labeled as such; smoke pouring from a building or into a waiting room may be caused by a fire, or it may merely indicate a leak in a steam pipe. Screams in the street may signal an assault or a family quarrel. A man lying in a doorway may be having a coronary or be suffering from diabetic coma—he may simply be sleeping off a drunk. And in any unusual situation, Candid Camera may be watching.

A person trying to decide whether or not a given situa- 16 tion is an emergency often refers to the reactions of those around him; he looks at them to see how he should react himself. If everyone else is calm and indifferent, he will tend to remain calm and indifferent; if everyone else is reacting strongly, he will become aroused. This tendency is not merely slavish conformity; ordinarily we derive much valuable information about new situations from how others around us behave. It's a rare traveler who, in picking a roadside restaurant, chooses to stop at one with no other cars in the parking lot.

But occasionally the reactions of others provide false 17 information. The studied nonchalance of patients in a dentist's waiting room is a poor indication of the pain awaiting them. In general, it is considered embarrassing to look overly concerned, to seem flustered, to "lose your cool" in public. When we are not alone, most of us try to seem less fearful and anxious than we really are.

In a potentially dangerous situation, then, everyone 18 present will appear more unconcerned than they are in fact. Looking at the *apparent* impassivity and lack of reaction of the others, each person is led to believe that nothing really is wrong. Meanwhile the danger may be mounting, to the point where a single person, uninfluenced by the seeming calm of others, would react.

A crowd can thus force inaction on its members by 19 implying, through its passivity and apparent indifference, that an event is not an emergency. Any individual in such a crowd is uncomfortably aware that he'll look like a fool if he behaves as though it were—and in these circumstances, until someone acts, no one acts.

In the smoke-filled room study, the smoke trickling 20 from the wall constituted an ambiguous but potentially dangerous situation. How did the presence of other people affect a person's response to the situation? Typically, those who were in the waiting room by themselves noticed the smoke at once, gave a slight startled reaction, hesitated, got up and went over to investigate the smoke, hesitated again, and then left the room to find somebody to tell about the smoke. No one showed any signs of panic, but over three-quarters of these people were concerned enough to report the smoke.

Others went through an identical experience but in 21 groups of three strangers. Their behavior was radically different. Typically, once someone noticed the smoke, he would look at the other people, see them doing nothing, shrug his shoulders, and then go back to his questionnaire, casting covert glances first at the smoke and then at the others. From these three-person groups, only three out of 24 people reported the smoke. The inhibiting effect of the group was so strong that the other 21 were willing to sit in a room filled with smoke rather than make themselves conspicuous by reacting with alarm and concern—this despite the fact that after three or four minutes the atmosphere in the waiting room grew most unpleasant. Even though they coughed, rubbed their eyes, tried to wave the smoke away, and opened the window, they apparently were unable to bring themselves to leave.

These dramatic differences between the behavior of 22 people alone and those in a group indicate that the group imposed a definition of the situation upon its members which inhibited action.

"A leak in the air conditioning," said one person when 23 we asked him what he thought caused the smoke. "Must be chemistry labs in the building." "Steam pipes." "Truth gas to make us give true answers on the questionnaire," reported the more imaginative. There were many explanations for the smoke, but they all had one thing in common: they did not mention the word fire. In defining the situation as a nonemergency, people explained to themselves why the other observers did not leave the room; they also removed any reason for action themselves. The other members of the group acted as nonresponsive models for each person—and as an audience for any "inappropriate" action he might consider. In such a situation it is all too easy to do nothing.

The results of this study clearly and strongly support 24 the predictions. But are they general? Would the same effect show up with other emergencies, or is it limited to situations like the smoke study involving danger to the self as well as to others—or to situations in which there's no clearly defined "victim"? It may be that our college-age male subjects played "chicken" with one another to see who would lose face by first fleeing the room. It may be that groups were less likely to respond because no particular person was in danger. To see how generalizable these results are, Latané and Judith Rodin set up a second experiment, in which the emergency would cause no danger for the bystander, and in which a specific person was in trouble.

Subjects were paid $2 to participate in a survey of game 25 and puzzle preferences conducted at Columbia by the Consumer Testing Bureau (CTB). An attractive young woman, the market-research representative, met them at the door and took them to the testing room. On the way, they passed the CTB office and through its open door they could see filing cabinets and a desk and bookcases piled high with papers. They entered the adjacent testing room, which contained a table and chairs and a variety of games, where they were given a preliminary background information and game preference questionnaire to fill out. The representative told subjects that she would be working next door in her office for about 10 minutes while they completed the questionnaires, and left by opening the collapsible curtain which divided the two rooms. She made sure the subjects knew that the curtain was unlocked, easily opened and a means of entry to her office. The representative stayed in her office, shuffling papers, opening drawers, and making enough noise to remind the subjects of her presence. Four minutes after leaving the testing area, she turned on a high fidelity stereophonic tape recorder.

If the subject listened carefully, he heard the repre- 26 sentative climb up on a chair to reach for a stack of papers on the bookcase. Even if he were not listening carefully, he heard a loud crash and a scream as the chair collapsed and she fell to the floor. "Oh, my God, my foot. . . . I . . . I . . . can't move it. Oh . . . my ankle," the representative moaned. "I . . . can't get this . . . thing . . . off me." She cried and moaned for about a minute longer, but the cries gradually got more subdued and controlled. Finally she muttered something about getting outside, knocked over the chair as she pulled herself up, and thumped to the door, closing it behind her as she left. This drama lasted about two minutes.

Some people were alone in the waiting room when the 27 "accident" occurred. Seventy per cent of them offered to help the victim before she left the room. Many came through the curtain to offer their assistance, others simply called out to offer their help. Others faced the emergency in pairs. Only 20 per cent of this group—eight out of 40— offered to help the victim. The other 32 remained unresponsive to her cries of distress. Again, the presence of other bystanders inhibited action.

And again, the noninterveners seemed to have decided 28 the event was not an emergency. They were unsure what had happened but whatever it was, it was not too serious. "A mild sprain," some said. "I didn't want to embarrass her." In a "real" emergency, they assured us, they would be among the first to help the victim. Perhaps they would be, but in this situation they didn't help, because for them the event was not defined as an emergency.

Again, solitary people exposed to a potential 29 emergency reacted more frequently than those exposed in groups. We found that the action-inhibited effects of other bystanders works in two different situations, one of which involves risking danger to oneself and the other of which involves helping an injured woman. The result seems sufficiently general so that we may assume it operates to inhibit helping in real-life emergencies.

Even if a person has noticed an event and defined it as 30 an emergency, the fact that he knows that other bystanders also witnessed it may still make him less likely to intervene. Others may inhibit intervention because they make a person feel that his responsibility is diffused and diluted. Each soldier in a firing squad feels less personally responsible for killing a man than he would if he alone pulled the trigger. Likewise, any person in a crowd of onlookers may feel less responsibility for saving a life than if he alone witnesses the emergency.

If your car breaks down on a busy highway, hundreds 31
of drivers whiz by without anyone's stopping to help; if you
are stuck on a nearly deserted country road, whoever passes
you first is apt to stop. The personal responsibility that a
passerby feels makes the difference. A driver on a lonely
road knows that if he doesn't stop to help, the person will
not get help; the same individual on the crowded highway
feels he personally is no more responsible than any of a
hundred other drivers. So even though an event clearly is an
emergency, any person in a group who sees an emergency
may feel less responsible, simply because any other bystander is equally responsible for helping.

This diffusion of responsibility might have occurred in 32
the famous Kitty Genovese case, in which the observers
were walled off from each other in separate apartments.
From the silhouettes against windows, all that could be told
was that others were also watching.

To test this line of thought, Darley and Latané simu- 33
lated an emergency in a setting designed to resemble Kitty
Genovese's murder. People overheard a victim calling for
help. Some knew they were the only one to hear the victim's
cries, the rest believed other people were aware of the victim's distress. As with the Genovese witnesses, subjects
could not see each other or know what others were doing.
The kind of direct group inhibition found in the smoke and
fallen-woman studies could not operate.

For the simulation, we recruited male and female stu- 34
dents at New York University to participate in a group
discussion. Each student was put in an individual room
equipped with a set of headphones and a microphone and
told to listen for instructions over the headphones. The
instructions informed the participant that the discussion
was to consider personal problems of the normal college
student in a high-pressure urban university. It was explained that, because participants might feel embarrassed
about discussing personal problems publicly, several precautions had been taken to insure their anonymity: they
would not meet the other people face to face, and the experimenter would not listen to the initial discussion but would

only ask for their reactions later. Each person was to talk in turn. The first to talk reported that he found it difficult to adjust to New York and his studies. Then, very hesitantly and with obvious embarrassment, he mentioned that he was prone to nervous seizures, similar to but not really the same as epilepsy. These occurred particularly when he was under the stresses of studying and being graded.

Other people then discussed their own problems in 35 turn. The number of other people in the discussion varied. But whatever the perceived size of the group—two, three or six people—only the subject was actually present; the others, as well as the instructions and the speeches of the victim-to-be, were present only on a pre-recorded tape.

When it again was the first person's turn to talk, after a 36 few comments he launched into the following performance, getting increasingly louder with increasing speech difficulties:

"I can see a lot of er of er how other people's problems 37 are similar to mine because er er I mean er it's er I mean some of the er same er kinds of things that I have and an er I'm sure that every everybody has and er er I mean er they're not er e-easy to handle sometimes and er I er er be upsetting like er er and er I er um I think I I need er if if could er er somebody er er er er er give me give me a little er give me a little help here because er I er I'm er h-h-having a a a a a real problem er right now and I er if somebody could help me out it would it would er er s-s-sure be sure be good be . . . because er there er er a cause I er *uh* I've got a a one of the er seiz—er er things coming *on* and and and I c-could really er use er some h-help s-so if somebody would er give me a little h-help uh er-er-er-er-er c-could somebody er er help er uh uh uh (choking sounds) . . . I'm gonna die er er I'm . . . gonna . . . die er help er er seizure er er . . ." (chokes, then quiet).

While this was going on, the experimenter waited out- 38 side the student's door to see how soon he would emerge to cope with the emergency. Rather to our surprise, some people sat through the entire fit without helping; a disproportionately large percentage of these nonresponders were from the largest-size group. Eighty-five per cent of the people who believed themselves to be alone with the victim came out of their rooms to help, while 62 per cent of the people who believed there was one other bystander did so. Of those who believed there were four other bystanders, only 31 per cent reported the fit before the tape ended. The responsibility-diluting effect of other people was so strong that single individuals were more than twice as likely to report the emergency as those who thought other people also knew about it.

People who failed to report the emergency showed few 39 signs of apathy and indifference thought to characterize "unresponsive bystanders." When the experimenter entered the room to end the situation, the subject often asked if the victim was "all right." Many of these people showed physical signs of nervousness; they often had trembling hands and sweating palms. If anything, they seemed more emotionally aroused than did those who reported the emergency. Their emotional arousal was in sharp contrast to the behavior of the nonresponding subjects in the smoke and fallen-woman studies. Those subjects were calm and unconcerned when their experiments were over. Having interpreted the events as nonemergencies, there was no reason for them to be otherwise. It was only the subjects who did not respond in the face of the clear emergency represented by the fit, who felt the moral dilemma.

Why, then, didn't they respond? It is our impression 40 that nonintervening subjects had not decided *not* to respond. Rather, they were still in a state of indecision and conflict concerning whether to respond or not. The emotional behavior of these nonresponding subjects was a sign of their continuing conflict; a conflict that other people resolved by responding. The distinction seems an academic one for the victim, since he gets no help in either case, but it is an extremely important one for arriving at an understanding of why bystanders fail to help.

The evidence is clear, then, that the presence of other 41 bystanders and the various ways these other bystanders affect our decision processes, make a difference in how likely we are to give help in an emergency. The presence of strangers may keep us from noticing an emergency at all; group behavior may lead us to define the situation as one that does not require action; and when other people are there to share the burden of responsibility, we may feel less obligated to do something when action is required. Therefore, it will often be the case that the *more* people who witness his distress, the *less* likely it is that the victim of an emergency will get help.

Thus, the stereotype of the unconcerned depersonalized 42 *homo urbanis*, blandly watching the misfortunes of others, proves inaccurate. Instead, we find a bystander to an emergency is an anguished individual in genuine doubt, concerned to do the right thing but compelled to make complex decisions under pressure of stress and fear. His reactions are shaped by the actions of others—and all too frequently by their inaction.

And we are that bystander. Caught up by the apparent 43 indifference of others, we may pass by an emergency without helping or even realizing that help is needed. Aware of the influence of those around us, however, we can resist it. We can choose to see distress and step forward to relieve it.

QUESTIONS

1. What personal observations or experience suggested to the writers an idea (or hypothesis) about the circumstances under which Americans usually notice anything? How did the experiment described in paragraph 12 help them test this idea?

2. What personal observations suggested an idea about the circumstances under which Americans decide whether a situation is an emergency? How did they test this idea in the experiment described in paragraphs 13–23?

3. Why did the writers need to perform the additional experiment described in paragraphs 25–29? Did this experiment provide new insights into the behavior of people confronted with an emergency?

4. What kind of evidence do the writers provide in paragraph 31 to confirm the results of these experiments?

5. In paragraphs 32–41, the writers apply these conclusions to the Kitty Genovese case, described earlier in this book by Martin Gansberg in "38 Who Saw Murder." How is the experiment that tested human behavior in this situation different from the earlier ones described?

6. What conclusions do the writers draw about the Genovese case in particular and about the behavior of Americans in emergencies generally? What order of ideas do you find in their essay?

7. Notice that the writers generalize carefully from clearly identified evidence. How do they suggest to the reader the relative importance of the various kinds of evidence presented—that is the weight they are prepared to give it?

WRITING ASSIGNMENTS

1. Discuss the extent to which Gansberg presents confirming evidence for the points made by Darley and Latané. If you believe Gansberg presents any contrary evidence, explain why you think so.

2. Discuss the extent to which your personal experience confirms the findings of Darley and Latané. You probably will have stronger evidence for one or more of them. Discuss the relative weight of the evidence you are presenting.

3. Work out an experiment of your own designed to test one of the ideas discussed in the essay. Write a description and defense of this experiment—explaining why it makes a good test.

DAVID L. BAZELON

DAVID L. BAZELON *was Chief Judge of the United States Court of Appeals in Washington. Before his appointment to the court in 1949, he practiced law and served the government in legal posts in Illinois and Washing-*

ton, D.C. Judge Bazelon has also been clinical professor
of psychiatry at George Washington University since
1966 and has served as advisor on medicine and law to
the government, to various universities and councils, and
to the United Nations. He is the recipient of numerous
honors including the Distinguished Service Award in
1975. His essay on the insanity plea, originally published in The Saturday Evening Post magazine in 1960,
was written for a general audience, not the specialist in
criminal law. Yet, as our outline of the essay in the
questions that follow the essay shows, it has the organization of a legal argument.

The Awesome Decision

The administration of criminal justice and the extent of 1
individual moral responsibility are among the crucial problems of a civilized society. They are indissolubly linked,
and together they involve our deepest personal emotions.
We often find it hard to forgive ourselves for our own moral
failures. All of us, at some time or other, have faced the
painful dilemma of when to punish and when to forgive
those we love—our children, our friends. How much harder
it is, then, to deal with the stranger who transgresses.

Few of us view punishment realistically. Whether 2
applied to criminals or to our own flesh and blood, we are
profoundly confused about punishment. We waver between
feeling "he deserves it" and "it will do him good." The first
reaction is our immediate emotional response, the second
our rationalization after the fact. "It will do him good" can
be proved or disproved; it lies within an area of practicality.
"He deserves it" is unprovable, a proposition derived from
absolutist morality. The latter reflects the retributive theory
of justice, whereby appropriate penalties are necessary if
only to uphold the moral law. But many people cannot
accept this view. They argue that, though punishment may

not be defensible in all cases, it cannot be dispensed with because social balance requires the gratification of the need for vengeance. Or they assert that we must punish to deter potential criminals.

Nowhere is the social attitude toward individual moral responsibility more sharply focused and more dramatic than in a criminal court. Here, in the whole process of justice—symbolized by the trial—the full weight of society's official force, moral and physical, is arrayed against a single human being. More often than not, this defendant is one of life's failures—part of the human debris of civilization. Thus, the considerations which govern the determination of his responsibility are a measure of man's humanity to man, or lack of it.

We pride ourselves, and in many respects justly so, on our efforts to insure a fair trial, and so manifest the advanced state of our civilization. Yet in an essential aspect of criminal justice we remain backward. We remain backward in the way we deal with the question of responsibility as it relates to mental disease, personality disorganization and the nature of antisocial behavior. Our criminal courts do not generally welcome the psychiatrist with his greatly expanded knowledge of unconscious motivations and environmental conditioning. Instead they cling doggedly to an age-old rule of criminal responsibility which makes modern science irrelevant to the critical question of the defendant's psychic state. In effect, our courts still ask a nineteenth-century question and insist on a nineteenth-century answer.

I refer to the famous formulation of the insanity defense which resulted from the trial of Daniel McNaghten in 1843. This rule—the prevailing law both here and in England for more than a century—requires a jury to consider only whether the defendant knew what he was doing or knew that it was wrong. In relying exclusively on the rational capacity of the mind, this so-called right-wrong test reveals its ancient lineage. It is based on the prescientific view of the human psyche and behavior, wherein the whole story is the eternal conflict between reason and passion. As long as any capacity to know or to reason remains intact, so the theory goes, failure to use it to control the passions constitutes choice, and is therefore culpable. The accused should be punished because he chose to do wrong.

But today we know that a choice of behavior involves the whole functioning human, not just reason alone. We are all painfully familiar with examples of behavior in which the accompanying thought process is only rationalization. Psychiatrists continually come across mentally sick patients who retain substantial reasoning powers. Indeed, one of the commonest symptoms of serious mental disorder is such a dissociation between the rational top of the mind and the emotional underpinnings of the personality.

On January 20, 1843, Daniel McNaghten, a Scottish wood turner, fatally shot Edward Drummond, secretary to the prime minister, Sir Robert Peel, as Drummond was entering a government office in London. The assassin had mistaken the secretary for the premier. "The Tories in my native city have compelled me to do this," he explained later. "They follow and persecute me wherever I go and have entirely destroyed my peace of mind."

The sole issue of McNaghten's trial was insanity. His counsel, Alexander Cockburn, called nine physicians and surgeons to the stand. All testified that the accused was insane. The prosecution entering no medical testimony in opposition, the presiding Lord Chief Justice Tindal directed a verdict of "not guilty, on the ground of insanity." McNaghten spent the rest of his life in mental institutions.

The public reaction was indignant; many people ascribed the shooting to a political plot. Queen Victoria herself protested the verdict. As a result, the House of Lords put several questions to the fifteen judges of England. Their answers have governed the insanity defense ever since throughout most of the English-speaking world. Lord Chief Justice Tindal set forth the McNaghten Rules as follows:

> ... the jurors ought to be told in all cases ... that to establish a defense on the ground of insanity, it must be

clearly proved that, at the time of the committing of the act, the party accused was laboring under such a defect of reason, from disease of the mind, as not to know the nature and quality of the act he was doing; or, if he did know it, that he did not know he was doing what was wrong.

The insanity defense had a long history prior to Tin- 10 dal's formulation. As early as the thirteenth century, British law recognized that "a madman does not know what he is doing." In 1724 Judge Tracy held that insanity was exculpatory if the defendant "doth not know what he is doing, no more than . . . a wild beast." Thirty-six years later the "wild beast test" was abandoned in favor of the defendant's capacity to distinguish between "right and wrong"—the precursor of the McNaghten Rules.

The insanity defense reflects a concept that has per- 11 vaded the entire history of the criminal law. We call it the doctrine of *mens rea*, sometimes described as "guilty mind," or "evil intent." It can be traced back to Deuteronomy 19:4–6, "Whoso killeth his neighbor ignorantly, whom he hated not in time past . . . shall . . . live . . ." *Mens rea* is a capsule phrase used, in connection with most crimes, to describe a state of mind which makes the offender blameworthy and so subject to criminal sanctions. Whether this state of mind is a deliberate intent to commit the prohibited act, or some form of negligence, it usually involves ability to anticipate consequences and guard against them. The insanity defense is designed to relieve from criminal liability persons who are incapable of such a state of mind.

The concept of "insanity"—conceived by lawyers, not 12 by doctors—is rooted in this requirement. Originally the insane defendant was thought of as one so obviously bereft of reason that, on the basis of common experience alone, all men could agree that he was incapable of entertaining an evil intent. Through early legal history only total insanity was recognized as a defense, probably because no scientific knowledge existed to differentiate the shadings and gradations of mental disease.

It is ironical that at the very time when psychiatry was 13 beginning to emerge as a distinct medical discipline, antiquated, nonmedical ideas about insanity were frozen into the McNaghten Rules. The law closed the door in psychiatry's face.

It was in 1838 that the American psychiatrist, Dr. Isaac 14 Ray, published his classic *Treatise on the Medical Jurisprudence of Insanity*, attacking the concepts upon which, five years later, the rules were based. In fact, McNaghten's counsel cited Doctor Ray. Other psychiatrists soon joined Doctor Ray in the attack. In this century the chorus of protest has become deafening. Some of the world's leading psychiatrists have refused to testify in court under the distorting limitations of the McNaghten Rules. In a poll taken a few years ago, 80 per cent of 300 American psychiatrists pronounced those rules unsatisfactory, and numerous jurists have agreed. Justice Cardozo flatly stated, "Everyone concedes that the present definition of insanity has little relation to the truths of mental life."

The main criticisms of the right-wrong test are fourfold. 15 First, it misses the point entirely, because whatever "insanity" means, the term refers to abnormal conditions of mind that cannot all be gathered together under the rubrics "know" and "wrong." Second, the test is based on an outmoded theory of faculty psychology—derived from phrenology—that divided the topography of the mind into separate compartments. Modern psychology views a man as an integrated personality, and reason as only one element of that personality and not the sole determinant of conduct. Third, the test poses to the expert an ultimate question involving legal and moral as well as medical issues. Fourth, the test has so strait-jacketed psychiatric testimony that insanity is defined exclusively in terms of extreme psychosis and patent organic deterioration.

What arguments favor the right-wrong test? Chiefly 16 that it reflects traditional morality governing the conduct of normal persons, that it persists historically, that alternative tests are inadequate and, perhaps most important, that many courts ignore the test as often as they apply it. From the juridical point of view, what all this controversy adds up to practically is whether we are to have more and freer psychiatric testimony. With it stated this way, I myself have no hesitance in taking a position solidly in favor of freer and fuller expert testimony.

This is exactly what we did in the District of Columbia 17 in 1955 when the United States Court of Appeals adopted the Durham Rule. Under this new, more liberal rule, a modern and comprehensive body of law governing the administration of the insanity defense is being slowly built up on the basis of continuing experience. At the same time the community's fears that great numbers of dangerous persons would be freed to attack again are being put to rest. Nothing of this sort has happened. Defendants acquitted under the Durham Rule have been sent to mental hospitals, many of them for longer periods than they would have served in prison. And they appear to get into less trouble after release than prison convicts.

Although no other court has yet adopted the District of 18 Columbia precedent, it is not an eccentric backwash of American jurisprudence. For one thing, it is an adaptation of a broadened test that the Supreme Court of New Hampshire adopted in 1870. This test, which allowed the insanity plea if the unlawful act arose from mental disease, was fashioned largely under the influence of Dr. Isaac Ray. For another, the Durham Rule reflects a widespread movement among the legal, psychiatric and allied professions to work out alternatives to the rigid spirit of the McNaghten Rules. For example, in 1955 a new test designed to liberalize McNaghten was proposed by the American Law Institute, a leading body of distinguished lawyers, judges and scholars.

To recount the Durham case, on July 13, 1951, twenty- 19 three-year-old Monte Durham broke into a Georgetown home and was caught pilfering clothes. Since the age of sixteen, Durham had been charged with passing bad checks, embezzlement, parole violation, car theft and attempted suicide. Three times he had been committed to mental institutions. Psychiatrists had variously diagnosed him as "psychotic with psychopathic personality" and, oddly, "without mental disorder but with a psychopathic personality."

Following his indictment for housebreaking, he was [20] adjudged of unsound mind and again sent to a mental hospital. Sixteen months later the hospital's superintendent certified that "prolonged psychiatric study has established that [Durham] suffers from psychological illness, but is mentally competent to stand trial. . . ."

As in the McNaghten trial, the sole issue was the mental [21] condition of the defendant. The only medical witness was the Government psychiatrist who had originally found Durham incompetent to stand trial, and his testimony "was unequivocal that Durham was of unsound mind at the time of the crime." The trial judge, who heard the case without a jury, strictly applied the McNaghten test and rejected the psychiatric testimony because the Government doctor declined to answer categorically the ultimate question—did Durham know the difference between right and wrong?

On appeal, Judges Henry W. Edgerton, George T. [22] Washington and I held this was error and, in reversing the conviction, we announced a broader test to be applied in all subsequent cases. We stated that the new rule "is simply that an accused is not criminally responsible if his unlawful act was the product of mental disease or mental defect." Under this test the question would be "whether the accused acted because of a mental disorder, and not whether he displayed particular symptoms which medical science has long recognized do not necessarily, or even typically, accompany even the most serious mental disorder."

Our underlying purpose was to unfreeze the expanding [23] knowledge of psychiatry, as it could be applied to the law, in order to free the psychiatrist from having to make the moral and legal determinations required by the right-wrong test for which he has no special qualifications, and to allow him to address himself to the problems of mental disease and defect, for which he is qualified.

Finally, it was our purpose to restore to the jury its 24
traditional function of applying "our inherited ideas of
moral responsibility to individuals prosecuted for crime"
under the historically sanctioned precept that "our collective
conscience does not allow punishment where it cannot impose blame." But in making the awesome decision as to
criminal responsibility, the jury "will be guided by wider
horizons of knowledge concerning mental life."

According to the opponents of the new rule, it creates 25
more problems than it solves. If this statement be amended
to read "uncovers" instead of "creates," I would agree. I
think that any realistic revision of the insanity formula is
bound to reveal difficult problems which have been ignored
or suppressed under the McNaghten test. Many psychiatrists, for example, who admit their inability to answer the
right-wrong question, follow the mechanical practice of tes-
tifying that a psychotic cannot distinguish right from wrong,
while an individual suffering from a nonpsychotic mental
illness can. They so testify even though such an artificial
demarcation has neither a medical nor a legal basis. Under
Durham, or any broader test, there will not be the same
compulsion to dispose of the issue by means so deviously
mechanical—a practice that also wrongly relieves the jury of
its duty to decide the case.

I agree with one of the more widespread criticisms of 26
the Durham Rule, that the term "mental disease" cannot be
rigidly defined. But that is because it is a dynamic concept
undergoing continual redefinition in the course of clinical
experience. It is strange logic, however, to conclude from
this fact that the complexities behind the term should therefore be ignored or that lawyers should arrive at a definition
a priori. We must instead seek out the best current scientific
explanations.

Another frequent criticism of the Durham test holds 27
that any serious investigation of the nature of mental illness
and its effect on criminal conduct will lead to the conclusion
that all criminals are mentally ill. If that is so, then it is high
time we found it out. I am flabbergasted that some of the

most dogmatic defenders of McNaghten actually believe that all criminals are ill. If true, would this not require a complete reconstruction of our criminal law? At the very least, it would require us to abandon the special defense of insanity and the corollary concept of *mens rea*, thereby overturning our historic system.

A third objection to the new rule is that the resources of 28 psychiatry are not up to the task. This may or may not be valid, but we do know psychiatry has more to give than the law now receives. Until we accept what it has to offer, we cannot discover the actual limitations of psychiatry.

The fourth objection to the Durham formulation is that 29 it is difficult to determine whether a criminal act is "the product of" mental illness. This is true, but I think unavoidable. Other formulations involve the same difficulties—the American Law Institute proposal uses the phrase "as a result of." Moreover, juries solve a similarly difficult problem of causation every day when they decide in personal-injury cases whether it was the defendant's negligence that caused the plaintiff's injury.

But the overriding objection to Durham undoubtedly 30 derives from our deepest feelings about punishment. In the traditional mode of thinking we, the good citizens, feel that they, the criminals, should be punished. So, the argument proceeds, it is just as well that only "slobbering idiots" should be excused, as under the McNaghten Rules. A broader rule is bad just because more criminals would get off.

This objection, based on the felt need to punish, brings 31 us to an issue that transcends legalisms and all merely professional considerations—an issue embracing the whole of society. Here are involved the mutual demands of society and the individual upon each other. Here, within the democratic framework, lies the grand context of criminal responsibility.

Practically speaking, the legal term "insanity" can be 32 defined by the consequences of its use. When pronounced "not insane," the accused is sentenced to prison as a punishment. When held insane, he goes to a mental institution for treatment. This is the practical aspect, what all the theoretical discussion boils down to—punishment or treatment.

Prisons and mental hospitals fulfill a similar function to 33 the extent that both segregate undesirable persons from society. In this sense, both protect society. According to ideal penological theory, punishment reforms; after release the prisoner will behave acceptably, and society will be protected. But in reality the rate of recidivism is high—more than 60 per cent among Federal convicts. Now, it is majestically simple that, since punishment so often fails of its purpose, something else is needed. And this something else is treatment.

Punishment as such, remember, is supposed to fit the 34 crime, not the criminal. When the sentence has been served, the warden of the penitentiary signs a certificate to that effect, and the prisoner rejoins society—even though it may be obvious that the punishment has worked no cure and indeed may have intensified the prisoner's criminal impulses. On the other hand, an inmate of a mental hospital is released only when certified by the staff as cured, or at least not dangerous to himself or others. No psychiatrist, to be sure, is infallible. He may err in his prognosis and recommend release prematurely, with disastrous results to the community. Many state hospitals, moreover, are too overcrowded and understaffed to provide optimum care. But at least the effort is made to exercise responsible medical judgment, whereas the prison warden is called upon to enter no judgment at all except as to parole. Is it not evident that treatment rather than punitive incarceration offers society better protection? So much for the practical aspects.

But as I have pointed out, society tends to waver be- 35 tween the ideas, "he deserves it" and "it will do him good." A somewhat more sophisticated attitude is reflected by the so-called deterrence theory which attempts to merge "he deserves it" and "it will do him good" under the synthetic proposition, "it will do us all good." This theory not only underlies the usual learned arguments against broadening the insanity defense but forms the central theoretical problem of the entire criminal law.

The deterrence theory, like its less sophisticated antecedents, seeks to justify the existing amount of punishment meted out as a means of preserving public order. By imprisoning the criminal, it is contended, we deter others from committing crimes. The prisoner thus becomes a scapegoat. In a free society such use of an individual cannot be justified except by a survival of the "he deserves it" feeling as well as the sanguine belief that his incarceration both serves as a beneficial example to all and does the prisoner good. Thus the ancient views of retribution persist in the deterrence theory. 36

It seems to me that this theory begs the entire question of justice for the individual. Unlike the retributive theory, it assumes that though punishment may not be right, may be purposeless or downright destructive to the individual, yet it protects society and so is justified. Hence even the mentally ill and hopelessly psychopathic recidivist are sacrificed for the purported social benefit. Thus the individual is degraded—contrary to our democratic ethos. 37

Unarguably, the maintenance of public order must be backed up by a system of sanctions. Neither law nor morality can sustain itself from generation to generation without the threat of some penalties. Many of us do not steal, not because of a fear imposed from without, but because of an internal control system generated by our mores and traditional beliefs. For most of those who require external controls it is the threat of going to jail, not actual time spent there, that keeps them from stealing. We need sanctions to give substance to the threat. How much actual punishment is required in order to sustain the threat of punishment at an effective level? That is the real problem posed by the deterrence theory. Many of its supporters seem to answer, "Exactly as much as we now have." This strikes me as both too easy and antihistorical. After all, it was not so long ago that whippings and executions, carried out as public spectacles, were considered essential to the preservation of order. 38

In our society the essential aim of the criminal law 39
should not be to induce mass fear of punishment, but to
reaffirm the value of each individual by due process in his
conviction and purposeful treatment thereafter. Too often,
in our eagerness to protect society, we forget that society is
composed of individuals. In a democracy, society or the state
is no more than the sum of its individual components. The
state exists for the benefit of the individual, not vice versa, as
in Nazi Germany or Soviet Russia. Consequently, repressive
law can be justified only as an accommodation of the mutual
liberties of two or more individuals. The real difference is not
always apparent, and at times we may favor one group of
individuals over another in the interests of those liberties. But
the basic theory does not change. It remains transcendently
important. It is perhaps the central thread of continuity in
our law.

If we now consider the issue of criminal responsibility 40
on spiritual rather than practical or ideological grounds, we
discover an ancient philosophical conflict at the heart of the
problem—free will versus determinism. I am not equipped
to deal with this great problem as a philosopher or theolo-
gian would, but I want to venture one or two observations.

If the question is whether we make real choices, two 41
things are clear—we obviously seem to do so, and some
people seem to have a wider choice of action than others.
Intellectual, physical and emotional capacity, wealth, social
status, all extend or limit the area of choice. Yet, in the eyes
of the law, for example, the poor and the rich face the same
responsibility to resist the temptation to steal, even though
the poor may be overwhelmingly tempted and the rich not
at all.

Surprisingly, this free-will-determinism issue is seldom 42
discussed in the practical context of actual choice, but usually on the level of abstract theory. On that level the argument often revolves around the old issue of science versus
religion. Freudianism has carried the banner of scientific
determinism into the inner sanctum of theology—the
human soul. Darwin placed the human animal in nature,

and Freud attempted to explain what occurred inside this human animal. His success has been substantial. Freud's concept of the unconsciousness as a source of motivation, as part of the great revolution it is working in modern thought, has compelled us to reconsider the question of criminal responsibility.

As a result, an expanded category of disease has 43 supplemented or displaced the diminished category of "evil." Evil is not a scientific word. Madmen were once thought to be possessed by evil spirits, and the means of exorcising the devil included torture. If we are not yet prepared to view every juvenile car thief as ill, many of us do feel that his social and economic background may be out of joint and may itself be "ill." The notion of a perfectly personal evil no longer suffices to explain all the events in a human career.

Evil, of course, can only be punished or forgiven. But 44 illness is supposed to be ameliorated or cured. Thus the name we put to our failures makes a difference. We all tend to believe in free will when we entertain hopes for the future, but switch to determinism when recalling our past failures. I suggest we extend the same consideration to the failures of others.

As Hollingshead and Redlich suggested in their study, 45 *Social Class and Mental Illness*, neurosis is something of a class privilege. It is less common in the lower social strata. There the number of psychotics and psychopaths appears to be greater. According to the Hollingshead-Redlich findings, the neurotic containment of conflict requires certain amenities of life, especially the possession of social values to be preserved. The mentally ill of the poor classes, including many criminals, lack the leisure for inner neurotic torture, and have less to lose by "acting out" their conflicts. Though no conclusive scientific proof exists, the indications are strong that a good deal of criminal behavior should be viewed as a pathological function of marginal socioeconomic status. Some 90 per cent of the criminal cases which come before our United States Court of Appeals

involving the insanity plea concern indigent defendants. For
many people it takes certain minimum advantages in life to
"learn how to be good." With those who have clearly failed
to learn, it may be that part of the burden of social responsibility shifts from them to us, calling for something better
than punishment.

The law is neither a scientific instrument nor an adjunct 46
to any absolute moral doctrine. Our legal system is the way
we conduct our business of mediating conflicts, preserving
the peace and furthering orderly social development. It thus
stands between all opposing forces or conflicting ideologies.
In the criminal law and in the administration of the insanity
defense the wisdom of the past, including the free-will postulate, meets modern scientific views, including the postulate
of causal determinism. The legal process differs from religion in that, being concerned with factual decisions, it cannot utter moral imperatives. It differs from science in that it
cannot choose its experimental subject matter, it cannot
plead ignorance and it cannot select its hypotheses freely. A
court must resolve all conflicts presented to it, with or without adequate knowledge.

The chief inhabitants in the house of the law are the 47
members of the jury. This much maligned body carries the
final burden of redressing the social balance. In shouldering
the awful responsibility of assessing the degree of another
person's responsibility under the law, the jury—that sample
of all of us—needs all the help available. When considering
the insanity defense, obviously it needs the help of psychiatric and other scientific experts, given fully and freely. Only
then, on the basis of all possible relevant facts and scientific
insight, can the jury make its moral judgment, its awesome
decision.

In the Durham case we said, "The legal and moral 48
traditions of the western world require that those who, of
their own free will and with evil intent . . . commit acts which
violate the law, shall be criminally responsible for those
acts. Our traditions also require that where such acts stem

from and are the product of mental disease or defect . . . moral blame shall not attach, and hence there will not be criminal responsibility."

Thus, within our traditions, the case goes to the jury.   49

QUESTIONS

1. Here is an outline of Bazelon's argumentative essay:
   Introduction (paragraphs 1–6): general statement of the issue and discussion of attitudes toward punishment;
   narration, or background (paragraphs 7–14): history of the insanity defense and McNaghten Rule;
   division of proofs (end of paragraph 14; paragraphs 15–16): statement of these;
   confirmation (paragraphs 17–24):
     17–18: defense of Durham Rule;
     19–24: second narration: history;
   refutation (paragraphs 25–45):
     25: first objection to Durham Rule and answer;
     26–27: second objection and answer;
     28: third objection and answer;
     29: fourth objection and answer;
     30–45: fifth objection and answer;
       32–34: retribution theory of punishment;
       35–45: deterrence theory and answer;
   conclusion (paragraphs 46–49): restatement of Durham Rule, restatement of the thesis, consideration of the jury system. How do the opening sentences of paragraphs 7, 15, 17, 25, and 46 mark these divisions or introduce a new consideration?

2. How does Bazelon appeal to the interest and conscience of his audience in his introduction?

3. What evidence does he give in his narration for his argument that the McNaghten Rule is unscientific?

4. Bazelon uses his division to summarize the chief criticisms of the right-wrong test. These criticisms form his thesis—stated at the end of paragraph 14 through the words of Judge Cardozo. How does he restate these words in paragraph 15?

5. Though the confirmation and refutation are separated, they form a whole in presenting the argument in favor of the Durham Rule. In what order does Bazelon present and answer the five objections, in paragraphs 25–45, and how do you know?

6. To what extent does he depend on expert testimony to answer them? What other evidence does he present?

7. Begging the question means that I assume as true what I am trying to prove, as in asking whether "the useless custom of tipping should be abolished." Why does the deterrence theory beg the question of justice for the individual, according to Bazelon?

8. Bazelon bases his main argument in favor of the Durham Rule on a definition of justice and the role of justice and law in a democracy (paragraphs 37–40). What is this definition, and how does he defend it?

9. What additional evidence is given in paragraphs 40–44 to show that the McNaghten Rule is unscientific and untrue to what we know about human beings?

10. How does Bazelon restate his thesis in the concluding paragraphs? Why does he discuss the jury system here?

WRITING ASSIGNMENTS

1. Use Bazelon's opening discussion of prevailing ideas about punishment to state your own view of the insanity plea. Explain whether you hold this view on the basis of religious or social convictions or perhaps a combination of these.

2. The insanity plea was widely discussed in newspapers and magazines in 1982. Compare two articles on the subject to show how closely the writers agree with each other and with Bazelon. Try to identify the assumptions that underlie their arguments—their basic, and possibly unstated, beliefs.

Controversy

Inductive and deductive reasoning can work together, depending on the particular argument and what we consider the point at issue. Proponents of nuclear power plants may, for example, insist that the issue in making the decision to build the plant in a particular region is economic—the increasing power needs of industry. Opponents may argue that the issue is the danger of an accident or the difficulty of disposing of nuclear waste. Much of the debate may be given to establishing the point at issue. The arguments employed in such a debate can and possibly will be inductive: statistical information on productivity and nuclear fuel, eyewitness accounts of nuclear plant operation, scientific reports on waste disposal, and the like. And the argument will be deductive in the inferences drawn from certain assumptions, perhaps ones on which the participants in the debate agree: that a high standard of living is a desirable goal in the community; that risk must be taken into account in making a decision about nuclear power; that high productivity depends on a dependable source of electrical power. From such assumptions certain conclusions will be drawn—and used to different advantage. Sometimes both assumptions and conclusions are debated; sometimes the assumptions are accepted as "givens" and not debated. In all debate, fairness and sound argument ideally should prevail. It hardly needs to be said that they often do not. We will briefly identify a few of the important "logical fallacies" a good argument avoids:

> *Arguing in a circle* is closely related to begging the question, where we assume as true what we are trying to prove: "No person who cares about jobs would oppose the bill because it is one that those who care about jobs in Ohio can support." The speaker has not given a reason to support the bill, but has merely restated the opening assertion.
>
> *Non sequitur* ("it does not follow"): The assertion, I oppose nuclear power because my father does, contains a hidden assumption—that father knows best. Since this assumption is hidden, the second part of the statement does not follow from the first part clearly. Assumptions of this sort may be

hidden because, once stated, the assumption shows the statement to be questionable or absurd.

Irrelevant conclusion: If the point at issue is whether nuclear plants present a risk, the argument that they are needed is an irrelevant argument. It may, of course, be relevant to another issue.

Ad hominem argument ("to the person"): I may attack my opponents rather than the issue—for example, by arguing that proponents of nuclear power are selfish and greedy. Even if they were people of bad character, their proposals must be judged on their merits. In other circumstances, such as an election campaign, the character of a person may be the issue.

Ad populum argument ("to the people"): I may also appeal to popular prejudice to gain support—suggesting that Lincoln or some other revered and usually long-dead person would have favored (or opposed) nuclear power. Such appeals often depend on fear.

Either-or hypothesis: I may set up two alternatives—nuclear power or economic depression—without allowing for other solutions.

GEORGE BERNARD SHAW

These self-contained passages on the question of capital punishment and imprisonment are taken from BERNARD SHAW's Crude Criminology, *written in 1921–22. Born in Dublin, Ireland, in 1856, Shaw lived until 1950 and in his long lifetime wrote on an enormous range of subjects in his plays, prefaces, and political and social commentaries and tracts. His ideas on criminology are based on assumptions about the worth of the individual and the needs of well-governed societies. In the preface to his play The* Doctor's Dilemma *(1904) Shaw states that "the theory that every individual alive is of infinite value is legislatively impracticable. No doubt the higher*

*the life we secure to the individual by wise social orga-
nization, the greater his value is to the community and
the more pains we shall take to pull him through any
temporary danger or disablement. But the man who
costs more than he is worth is doomed by sound hygiene
as inexorably as by sound economics." And he was to
state this idea even more strongly in the preface to a late
play,* The Simpleton of the Unexpected Isles *(1934):
". . . we need a greatly increased intolerance of socially
injurious conduct and an uncompromising abandonment of punishment and its cruelties, together with a
sufficient school inculcation of social responsibility to
make every citizen conscious that if his life costs more
than it is worth to the community the community may
painlessly extinguish it."*

Capital Punishment and Imprisonment

Some of the popular objections to [capital punishment] may   1
be considered for a moment. Death, it is said, is irrevocable;
and after all, they may turn out to be innocent. But really
you cannot handle criminals on the assumption that they
may be innocent. You are not supposed to handle them at all
until you have convinced yourself by an elaborate trial that
they are guilty. Besides, imprisonment is as irrevocable as
hanging. Each is a method of taking a criminal's life; and
when he prefers hanging or suicide to imprisonment for life,
as he sometimes does, he says, in effect, that he had rather
you took his life all at once painlessly, than minute by minute
in long-drawn-out torture. You can give a prisoner a pardon; but you cannot give him back a moment of his imprisonment. He may accept a reprieve willingly in the hope of a
pardon or an escape or a revolution or an earthquake or
what not; but as you do not mean him to evade his sentence
in any way whatever, it is not for you to take such clutchings
at straws into account.

Another argument against the death penalty for any- 2
thing short of murder is the practical one of the policeman
and the householder, who plead that if you hang burglars
they will shoot to avoid capture on the ground that they may
as well be hanged for a sheep as for a lamb. But this can be
disposed of by pointing out, first, that even under existing
circumstances the burglar occasionally shoots, and, second,
that acquittals, recommendations to mercy, verdicts of man-
slaughter, successful pleas of insanity and so forth, already
make the death penalty so uncertain that even red-handed
murderers shoot no oftener than burglars—less often, in
fact. This uncertainty would be actually increased if the
death sentence were, as it should be, made applicable to
other criminals than those convicted of wilful murder, and
no longer made compulsory in any case.

Then comes the plea for the sacredness of human life. 3
The State should not set the example of killing, or of clubbing a rioter with a policeman's baton, or of dropping
bombs on a sleeping city, or of doing many things that
States nevertheless have to do. But let us take the plea on its
own ground, which is, fundamentally, that life is the most
precious of all things, and its waste the worst of crimes. We
have already seen that imprisonment does not spare the life
of the criminal: it takes it and wastes it in the most cruel
way. But there are others to be considered beside the criminal and the citizens who fear him so much that they cannot
sleep in peace unless he is locked up. There are the people
who have to lock him up, and fetch him his food, and watch
him. Why are their lives to be wasted? Warders, and especially wardresses, are almost as much tied to the prison by
their occupation, and by their pensions, which they dare not
forfeit by seeking other employment, as the criminals are. If
I had to choose between a spell under preventive detention
among hardened criminals in Camp Hill and one as warder in an ordinary prison, I think I should vote for Camp
Hill. Warders suffer in body and mind from their employment; and if it be true, as our examination seems to prove,
that they are doing no good to society, but very active harm,

their lives are wasted more completely than those of the criminals; for most criminals are discharged after a few weeks or months; but the warder never escapes until he is superannuated, by which time he is an older jailbird than any Lifer in the cells.

How then does the case stand with your incurable 4 pathological case of crime? If you treat the life of the criminal as sacred, you find yourself not only taking his life but sacrificing the lives of innocent men and women to keep him locked up. There is no sort of sense or humanity in such a course. The moment we face it frankly we are driven to the conclusion that the community has a right to put a price on the right to live in it. That price must be sufficient self-control to live without wasting and destroying the lives of others, whether by direct attack like a tiger, parasitic exploitation like a leech, or having to be held on a leash with another person at the end of it. Persons lacking such self-control have been thrust out into the sage-brush to wander there until they die of thirst, a cruel and cowardly way of killing them. The dread of clean and wilfull killing often leads to evasions of the commandment "Thou shalt not kill" which are far more cruel than its frank violation. [. . .]

Modern imprisonment: that is, imprisonment practised 5 as a punishment as well as a means of detention, is extremely cruel and mischievous, and therefore extremely wicked. The word extremely is used advisedly because the system has been pushed to a degree at which prison mortality and prison insanity forced it back to the point at which it is barely endurable, which point may therefore be regarded as the practicable extreme.

Although public vindictiveness and public dread are 6 largely responsible for this wickedness, some of the most cruel features of the prison system are not understood by the public, and have not been deliberately invented and contrived for the purpose of increasing the prisoner's torment. The worst of these are (a) unsuccessful attempts at reform, (b) successful attempts to make the working of the prison cheaper for the State and easier for the officials, and (*c*) accidents of the evolution of the old privately owned detention prison into the new punitive State prison.

The prison authorities profess three objects (*a*) Retribution (a euphemism for vengeance), (*b*) Deterrence (a euphemism for Terrorism), and (*c*) Reform of the prisoner. They achieve the first by simple atrocity. They fail in the second through lack of the necessary certainty of detection, prosecution, and conviction; partly because their methods are too cruel and mischievous to secure the co-operation of the public; partly because the prosecutor is put to serious inconvenience and loss of time; partly because most people desire to avoid an unquestionable family disgrace much more than to secure a very questionable justice; and partly because the proportion of avowedly undetected crimes is high enough to hold out reasonable hopes to the criminal that he will never be called to account. The third (Reform) is irreconcilable with the first (Retribution); for the figures of recidivism, and the discovery that the so-called Criminal Type is really a prison type, prove that the retributive process is one of uncompensated deterioration.

The cardinal vice of the system is the anti-Christian vice of vengeance, or the intentional duplication of malicious injuries partly in pure spite, partly in compliance with the expiatory superstition that two blacks make a white. The criminal accepts this, but claims that punishment absolves him if the injuries are equivalent, and still more if he has the worse of the bargain, as he almost always has. Consequently, when absolution on his release is necessarily denied him, and he is forced back into crime by the refusal to employ him, he feels that he is entitled to revenge this injustice by becoming an enemy of Society. No beneficial reform of our treatment of criminals is possible unless and until this superstition of expiation and this essentially sentimental vice of vengeance are unconditionally eradicated.

Society has a right of self-defence, extending to the destruction or restraint of lawbreakers. This right is separable from the right to revenge or punish: it need have no more to do with punishment or revenge than the caging or shooting of a man-eating tiger. It arises from the existence of (A) intolerably mischievous human beings, and (B) persons defective in the self-control needed for free life in modern society, but well behaved and at their ease under tutelage and discipline. Class A can be painlessly killed or permanently restrained. The requisite tutelage and discipline can be provided for Class B without rancor or insult. The rest can be treated not as criminals but as civil defendants, and made to pay for their depredations in the same manner. At present many persons guilty of conduct much viler than that for which poor men are sent to prison suffer nothing worse than civil actions for damages when they do not (unhappily) enjoy complete immunity.

The principle to be kept before the minds of all citizens 10 is that as civilized society is a very costly arrangement necessary to their subsistence and security they must justify their enjoyment of it by contributing their share to its cost, and giving no more than their share of trouble, subject to every possible provision by insurance against innocent disability. This is a condition precedent to freedom, and justifies us in removing cases of incurable noxious disability by simply putting an end to their existence.

An unconquerable repugnance to judicial killing having 11 led to the abolition of capital punishment in several countries, and to its reservation for specially dangerous or abhorrent crimes in all the others, it is possible that the right to kill may be renounced by all civilized States. This repugnance may be intensified as we cease to distinguish between sin and infirmity, or, in prison language, between crime and disease, because of our fear of being led to the extirpation of the incurable invalid who is excessively troublesome as well as to that of the incurable criminal.

On the other hand, the opposite temperament, which is 12 not squeamish about making short work of hard cases, and which is revolted by the daily sacrifice of the lives of prison officials, and of relatives and nurses, to incurable criminals and invalids, may be reinforced by the abandonment of ethical pretentiousness, vengeance, malice, and all uncharitableness in the matter, and may become less scrupulous than at present in advocating euthanasia for all incurables.

Whichever party may prevail, punishment as such is 13 likely to disappear, and with it the ear-marking of certain offences as calling for specially deterrent severities. But it does not follow that lethal treatment of extreme cases will be barred. On the contrary, it may be extended from murder to social incompatibility of all sorts. If it be absolutely barred, sufficient restraint must be effected, not as a punishment but as a necessity for public safety. But there will be no excuse for making it more unpleasant than it need be.

When detention and restraint are necessary, the crimi- 14 nal's right to contact with all the spiritual influences of his day should be respected, and its exercise encouraged and facilitated. Conversation, access to books and pictures and music, unfettered scientific, philosophic, and religious activity, change of scene and occupation, the free formation of friendships and acquaintances, marriage and parentage: in short, all the normal methods of creation and recreation, must be available for criminals as for other persons, partly because deprivation of these things is severely punitive, and partly because it is destructive to the victim, and produces what we call the criminal type, making a cure impossible. Any specific liberty which the criminal's specific defects lead him to abuse will, no doubt, be taken from him; but if his life is spared his right to live must be accepted in the fullest sense, and not, as at present, merely as a right to breathe and circulate his blood. In short, a criminal should be treated, not as a man who has forfeited all normal rights and liberties by the breaking of a single law, but as one who, through some specific weakness or weaknesses, is incapable of exercising some specific liberty or liberties.

The main difficulty in applying this concept of individ- 15 ual freedom to the criminal arises from the fact that the concept itself is as yet unformed. We do not apply it to children, at home or at school, nor to employees, nor to persons of any class or age who are in the power of other persons. Like Queen Victoria, we conceive Man as being either in authority or subject to authority, each person doing only what he is expressly permitted to do, or what the example of the rest of his class encourages him to consider as tacitly permitted. The concept of the evolving free man in an evolving society, making all sorts of experiments in conduct, and therefore doing everything he likes as far as he can unless there are express prohibitions to which he is politically a consenting party, is still unusual, and consequently terrifying, in spite of all the individualist pamphlets of the eighteenth and nineteenth centuries. It will be found that those who are most scandalized by the liberties I am claiming for the convict would be equally scandalized if I claimed them for their own sons, or even for themselves.

The conclusion is that imprisonment cannot be fully 16 understood by those who do not understand freedom. But it can be understood quite well enough to have it made a much less horrible, wicked, and wasteful thing than it is at present.

QUESTIONS

1. The Shaw passages are taken from his *Crude Criminology*, written in 1921–22. The second passage (paragraphs 5–16) is the concluding summary of the main argument in the whole book. In an earlier passage Shaw argues that some criminals cannot be changed and when released from prison continue to torture and murder people:

> Now you cannot get rid of these nuisances and monsters by simply cataloguing them as subthyroidics and superadrenals or the like. At present you torment them for a fixed period, at the end of which they are set free to resume their operations with a savage grudge against the community which has tormented them. That is stupid. Nothing is gained by punishing people who cannot help themselves and on whom deterrence is thrown away. Releasing them is like releasing the tigers from the Zoo to find their next meal in the nearest children's playing ground.

In the passages printed here, what other arguments does Shaw present in favor of capital punishment? What assumptions is he making about society and the individual in these arguments?

2. How does Shaw answer the objections to capital punishment he presents?

3. Why does he reject life imprisonment as an alternative to capital punishment? What does he believe the purpose of imprisonment should be?

WRITING ASSIGNMENT

Shaw distinguishes three attitudes toward imprisonment. Discuss which of these attitudes represents your own, and defend your reasons for holding one of them and rejecting another. Compare your assumptions about society and the individual with Shaw's.

AMERICA

> *The following editorial in* AMERICA, *a weekly journal of Catholic opinion, was published on December 11, 1976—about a month before the execution of the convicted murderer Gary Gilmore by the state of Utah, on January 17, 1977. Gilmore, the subject of Norman Mailer's later book* The Executioner's Song, *was the first man to be executed in the United States since 1967, and the imminent revival of capital punishment produced wide debate. As the editorial points out, Gilmore's demand that he be executed raised other complex issues. The controversy aroused by his execution has continued into the 1980s.*

The Injustice of the Death Penalty

Future annalists of our nation's Bicentennial year will probably note that it marked the revival of capital punishment in   1 the United States. As we go to press, Gary Mark Gilmore faces imminent execution by a Utah firing squad. Even if something happens at the last minute to defer his execution, there are 422 other inmates in the death rows of our prisons. Some of them are scheduled for execution before Christmas. Unless there is a radical change in public sentiment, the nation will soon see its first public execution since 1967.

Mr. Gilmore stunned the nation by proclaiming the 2 justice of his death sentence and demanding his immediate execution. But it does not really matter whether the first prisoner executed is Mr. Gilmore or someone else who does not want to die. What matters is that capital punishment is being revived when there is no justification for it.

Despite the fact that 35 state legislatures have revised 3 their death penalty laws since the Supreme Court declared the pre-1972 laws unconstitutional, the American public is still profoundly confused about the morality and utility of capital punishment. This confusion is the natural result of the conflict between the traditional lawfulness of the death penalty and the absence of any solid evidence to justify its continuation. Many Americans who favor the death penalty in the abstract for certain types of crimes are against it in the concrete for almost every type of individual.

Indeed, Mr. Gilmore touched a raw nerve in the public 4 conscience when he announced his desire to die. Suddenly the public executioner looked like an accomplice in suicide. But it is patently absurd to argue that the death penalty is moral when the prisoner does not want to die but immoral when he wishes to do so. The only possible justifications for capital punishment are that it "fits the crime" and that it serves to deter the rest of the population from committing a similar crime.

Americans have long since rejected the morality of the 5 "eye for an eye, tooth for a tooth" approach to criminal punishment. Experience has taught them that the appropriateness of a punishment depends upon the restitution it makes to the social order, its efficiency as a deterrent against similar criminal conduct and the contribution it makes to the rehabilitation of the criminal. The death penalty fails on all three counts. It does not restore the life of the murderer's victim. It does not seek to rehabilitate the murderer himself. It stands, for its justification, solely on its potential for deterrence.

Because the death penalty has long since ceased to be 6 either certain or swift in the United States, the deterrent effect argument in support of the death penalty has lost its force. The death penalty has become uncertain because Americans rightly insist on tailoring the punishment not just to the crime but to the individual criminal. And the death penalty has become slow because Americans rightly insist that the full panoply of legal appeals be available to those condemned to die. What Americans must now recognize is that their commendable passion for justice has made the death penalty irretrievably unjust.

Moreover, the careful studies that have been made of 7 the actual correlation between the death penalty and the commission of heinous crimes have resulted in a total failure of proof, positive or negative, that the death penalty has any deterrent effect. Faced with this fact, supporters of the death penalty have resorted to a "common sense" argument. But common sense is not an argument when it is based on hunches rather than facts.

Most supporters of capital punishment concede that it 8 can be justified only as a last resort. But given the lack of any empirical proof that the death penalty works as a deterrent, the religious, philosophical and practical arguments against capital punishment become overwhelming. When the state deliberately executes one of its members in cold blood and as an act of sovereign justice, the state acts with an insupportable claim of total lordship and with irreversible finality. Moreover, no one has yet devised a "humane" method of capital punishment, and the very grisliness of an execution dramatizes its inherent inhumanity.

The abolition of capital punishment would leave, of 9 course, the problem of the proper confinement of heinous criminals unresolved. Anyone familiar with our prison system knows that there are some inmates who behave little better than brute beasts. But the very fact that these prisoners exist is itself a telling argument against the efficacy of capital punishment as a deterrent. If the death penalty had been truly effective as a deterrent, such prisoners would long ago have vanished. The incorrigible criminal is precisely that, and no number of executions will rehabilitate him. And as long as we have faith in the dignity of man and convictions about the limited sovereignty of the state, it is better to suffer the incorrigibility of a few than for the nation to revert to the barbarism of capital punishment.

QUESTIONS

1. Paragraphs 1–5 provide the narration or background of the situation that prompted the *America* editorial, and lead into a statement of the point at issue in the argument about capital punishment. What background is provided? How does the editorial establish the point at issue?

2. What values and arguments relating to capital punishment does the editorial assume are evident to the readers of *America* and need not be stated or argued? What is gained by not doing so?

3. Paragraphs 6–8 present the chief argument against capital punishment. What is that argument?

4. Paragraph 9 concedes that the abolition of capital punishment creates a serious problem. What is that problem, and how does the editorial use it to reinforce the chief argument against capital punishment?

5. What form does refutation take in paragraphs 5–9?

WRITING ASSIGNMENTS

1. Shaw wrote his defense of capital punishment in 1921–22; the *America* editorial was published on December 11, 1976. Discuss the extent to which the issues of capital punishment changed in the intervening years, given the evidence of these two arguments.

2. Discuss the extent to which you agree with the views attributed to Americans today, including the attitude toward "eye for an eye, tooth for a tooth" morality and toward capital punishment in the abstract and in the concrete.

ANTHONY LEWIS

ANTHONY LEWIS *was the chief of the London Bureau of* The New York Times *from 1964 to 1972, and in 1969 he began his column for the* Times. *He was awarded the Pulitzer Prize for National Reporting in 1955 and 1963, and he has also been honored for his book* Gideon's Trumpet. *Lewis writes in his column on political and moral issues of the day. His statement on the Gilmore execution, published in the* Times *on January 27, 1977, focuses on Gilmore's alleged final words to his executioners, "Let's do it."*

Let's Do It

In the early morning of Nov. 13, 1849, Charles Dickens came 1 upon a crowd outside Horsemonger Lane Jail in London. People were waiting to see a Mr. and Mrs. Manning hanged for the murder of their lodger. Dickens watched through the hours until sunrise, as the crowd screamed and laughed and sang "Oh Mrs. Manning" to the tune of "Oh Susannah." Later that day he wrote a letter to The Times of London.

"A sight so inconceivably awful as the wickedness and 2 levity of the immense crowd collected at that execution could be imagined by no man . . ." he wrote. "I am solemnly convinced that nothing that ingenuity could devise to be done in this city, in the same compass of time, could work such ruin as one public execution."

Three days later, after some other comment, Dickens 3 wrote a second letter to the editor. He said executions attracted as spectators "the lowest, the most depraved, the most abandoned of mankind." And he said steps should be taken to limit titillation of the public by stories about a condemned person.

"I would allow no curious visitors to hold any communi- 4 cation with him," Dickens said. "I would place every obstacle in the way of his sayings and doings being served up in print on Sunday mornings for the perusal of families."

Not even Dickens, with his sense of the grotesque, could 5 have imagined the spectacle enacted last week in the United States. The last sayings and doings of a murderer were retailed by the press. His picture graced the weekly journals. And the grossest details of his execution were reproduced on television, to be savored by millions of families in their homes.

Most people I know who have been physically present 6 when the state killed a human being—prison wardens, priests, newspaper reporters—have thereafter been opposed to capital punishment. Twenty years ago, on assignment as a reporter, I watched an electrocution in the District of Columbia jail. When it was over, the room smelled of roasted flesh.

But to experience such scenes vicariously removes, for 7 many, the nausea factor. Television drama has made blood and violence as acceptable as cherry pie. It was only a small additional step to restage an actual execution. And so we had the scene of Gary Gilmore's death on the evening news programs, and sketches of his last moment in sober newspapers.

Some press agencies wanted to hire helicopters to circle 8 over the prison yard, but the Federal Aviation Agency vetoed that idea. Reporters were forced to rely on hourly bulletins from the prison authorities, which some complained were dull.

The great innovation in the Gilmore case was an execu- 9 tion literary agent. A movie producer named Lawrence

Schiller signed the condemned man and his relatives to an exclusive contract for a film to be shown on television. Schiller was allowed to interview Gilmore for many hours in prison, and then to attend the execution.

The agent gave the press the juicy details of the end. 10 When the execution order was read out by an official, Schiller said, "Gary looked at him, holding his own, not quivering." It was Schiller who said he "believed" Gilmore's last words were "Let's do it"—a phrase that the press flashed across the land.

Later, the press learned that Gilmore in his last days 11 had had an intense correspondence with an 11-year-old girl named Amber Hunt. Miss Hunt was interviewed, and a week later her voice was still being heard on the radio.

The slaughter of gladiators and Christians in the Circus 12 Maximus is generally regarded as a symptom of the decadence of Rome. What does it say about a country when punishment for crime becomes a circus, to be reenacted in every home? Can a society savor such spectacles without being coarsened?

Murderers do not usually deserve sympathy. But the 13 objection to having the state kill them in turn is not sentimental. Using the apparatus of official power to extinguish a life has corrupting consequences—the more so when capital punishment is, as it has become in this country, a spectacular occasion: an event cruel and unusual.

In the absence of convincing evidence that executions 14 deter murderers, there must be a suspicion that the practice goes on to satisfy an atavistic public desire for dramatized vengeance. Revival of the death penalty in the United States may in fact encourage murder by persons such as Gary Gilmore—a man with suicidal impulses, who could have seen a way to assure his own spectacular death.

Dickens saw that point. In 1845, in a letter to a friend, 15 he argued among other grounds for opposing capital punishment: "I believe it to have a horrible fascination for many of those persons who render themselves liable to it, impelling them onward to the acquisition of a frightful notoriety."

QUESTIONS

1. What is Lewis's purpose in writing—to show what Americans have become or to warn them about what they may become? Does he generalize about all Americans?
2. How strong is the argument of deterrence for Lewis?
3. How do you think Lewis would answer Shaw's defense of capital punishment?

WRITING ASSIGNMENT

Analyze newspaper and magazine reports of the Gary Gilmore legal proceedings in November and December, 1976, or those of his execution on January 17, 1977. Discuss the prominence given certain features of the case—for example, Gilmore's statements concerning the proceedings and his behavior and his "last words." Or analyze the reporting of a similar event.

THE NEW YORKER

THE NEW YORKER *magazine published this statement on the plight of civilian populations in the nuclear age in "The Talk of the Town" on February 25, 1980, in response to the revival of registration for selective service—in particular the debate over the registration of women. Where Ellen Goodman states that the effect of their nonregistration is the point at issue in the debate,* The New Yorker *states that the issue is a broader one—having to do with whole populations. Occasionally writers and editorialists do agree on the point at issue in a debate of this kind, but often discussion*

centers—as in Goodman and The New Yorker *statement—on what the issue is. Lawyers do the same in
courtroom debates on the evidence and statutes that
should govern judicial decisions.*

The Victim-Armies

President Carter's proposal to register women as well as   1
men for the draft, being opposed alike by many feminists,
who are against any draft, and by many supporters of the
draft, who believe that wars should be fought by men, has
clouded the policy that inspired the revival of registration in
the first place. Intending to demonstrate the country's unity
and resolve to the Soviet Union in response to its invasion of
Afghanistan, the Administration has instead become em-
broiled in a murky altercation about the influence of women
on men in trench warfare and about ratification of the
Equal Rights Amendment, all of it superimposed on a renewed protest movement against any draft and a swelling
debate, greatly amplified by an exceptionally crowded and
busy Presidential campaign, about just what the potential
draftees, whether men or women, might have to do under
the Carter policy. In the spreading confusion, a somber
declaration of national purpose to the world has degener-
ated into a highly visible domestic quarrel, with every member of the family loudly putting in his or her word.

So far, the argument about women and the draft has   2
centered on reasonable-sounding questions like whether or
not women are physically strong enough for combat, but
intense passions, undoubtedly fed by apprehensions of a
more primeval sort, are churning just beneath the surface.
War, of course, got its foothold in human affairs long before
women launched their drive, now in full swing in most parts
of the globe, for equality with men in the public realm. In
the traditional order, as feminist thinkers have often

pointed out, the assignment of men to the battlefield and that of women to the domestic household were closely related. The presence of a protected, even hidden, domestic sphere, presided over by women, in which new life was brought into the world and the community was sustained, was felt to give war an elemental justification. As the bearers of children, women were the symbols and substance of peace and life, and were to be spared the destruction and death of war—except in defeat. The exclusion of women from war held intact a part of life *for which* wars could be fought by men. In the logic of this scheme, just as the migration of women from home to office, if it were to be unaccompanied by any rush of men in the opposite direction, would leave the home deserted, and thus would undercut one of the original aims of work—namely, the support of life—so the dispatch of women to war would, in a manner of speaking, empty out the heart of the community and undercut any justification for fighting.

But even to describe these traditional arrangements for 3 domesticity and war, whether one looks on them fondly or with anger, is to reveal that they have broken down irreparably across the board. The most thorough transformation has taken place in war itself. Insofar as any nation's military forces ever had the ability to protect its people, they have lost it now. The invasion of the civilian realm by modern war began with universal male conscription and the bombing of cities, and was brought to completion with the advent of nuclear weapons, which assail life at its genetic foundations. War has now penetrated to the core of the domestic sphere—its capacity for the renewal of life. Nuclear weapons have overmatched the procreativity of nature, and it is now they that, in an appropriation of life's characteristics, monstrously "proliferate," and bring forth one "generation" after another, as though death itself had gained the power to give birth and multiply. In the new military strategy, the role of the civilian population, including its heretofore undrafted female half, is to be held hostage by the rival nuclear power. Indeed, it is now an essential element of global stability that each superpower in effect bare the breast of its people to a nuclear attack or counterattack by its adversary; otherwise, deterrence, which depends on the vulnerability of each side to a reprisal by the other, would break down. Our nation, in a proper display of reverence for life, has exerted itself as one man to secure the release of some fifty hostages in Iran, but, in the same period, when nuclear war over Middle Eastern oil has been under discussion we have somehow managed to pass lightly over the fates of the tens of millions of hostages which are at stake in such a conflict. Once, military forces were deployed to protect the civilian population, but now the civilian population is deployed to protect the military forces. Across the oceans, two vast victim-armies face one another. No one was ever registered to serve in this force, but we have all been conscripted into it anyway. Women, who are certainly strong enough to push the button—should any of them aspire to that doubtful honor—just as they are weak enough to die in a holocaust, don't have to be sent to the front lines; they are already there.

QUESTIONS

1. Written at a time when the registration of women as well as men was being considered by the Carter administration and was being debated nationally, this editorial comment in an important magazine shows how narration can be used to define broader issues that remain after a specific proposal is rejected or forgotten. What are these broader issues, according to paragraph 2?

2. The editorial also shows how the point at issue in the current national debate can be redefined and shown to be a less important or unimportant consideration. How does the editorial accomplish this redefinition?

3. Does the editorial take a stand on whether women should be drafted, or is this issue left unresolved?

WRITING ASSIGNMENT

Letters to the editor of a newspaper or newsmagazine are frequently concerned with redefining the point at issue in a national debate. Examine a series of letters on a current public issue, and identify the point at issue in each of them, giving particular attention to those that explicitly redefine the issue. Then discuss your own views on the issue, arguing what you believe the point at issue should be.

ELLEN GOODMAN

ELLEN GOODMAN, *another of the excellent writers of the journalistic essay in America today, was on the staff of* Newsweek *and the* Detroit Free Press *before joining the* Boston Globe *in 1967 as feature writer and columnist. Her commentary, for which she won the Pulitzer Prize in 1980, appears regularly in the Globe and other newspapers in the United States. Goodman's statement on drafting woman was first published in February of 1980 as part of the debate over the imminent registraiton of young men and women for selective service.*

Drafting Daughters

My daughter is eleven, and as we watch the evening 1
news, she turns to me seriously and says, "I don't like the
way the world is doing things." Neither do I.

My daughter is eleven years and eight months old, to be 2
precise, and I do not want her to grow up and be drafted.
Nor does she.

My daughter is almost twelve, and thinks about un- 3
kindness and evil, about endangered species and war. I
don't want her to grow up and be brutalized by war—as
soldier or civilian.

As I read those sentences over, they seem too mild. 4
What I want to say is that I am horrified by the very idea
that she could be sent to fight for fossil fuel or fossilized
ideas. What I want to say is that I can imagine no justification for war other than self-defense, and I am scared stiff
about who has the power to decide what is "defense."

But now, in the last days before President Carter de- 5
cides whether we will register young people and whether
half of those young people will be female. I wonder about
something else. Would I feel differently if my daughter were
my son? Would I be more accepting, less anguished, at the
notion of a son drafted, a son at war?

Would I beat the drums and pin the bars and stars on 6
his uniform with pride? Would I look forward to him being
toughened up, be proud of his heroism, and accept his risk
as a simple fact of life?

I cannot believe it. 7

So, when I am asked now about registering women for 8
the draft along with men I have to nod yes reluctantly. I
don't want anyone registered, anyone drafted, unless it is a
genuine crisis. But if there is a draft, this time it can't just
touch our sons, like some civilized plague that leaves
daughters alone to produce another generation of warriors.

We may have to register women along with men any- 9
way. Women may not have won equal rights yet, but they
have "won" equal responsibilities. A male-only draft may
be ruled unconstitutional.

But at a deeper level, we have to register women along 10
with men because our society requires it. For generations,
war has been part of the rage so many men have held
against women.

War is in the hard-hat yelling at an equal rights rally, 11
"Where were you at Iwo Jima?" War is in the man infuri-
ated at the notion of a woman challenging veterans' preference. War is in the mind of the man who challenges his
wife for having had a soft life.

War has often split couples and sexes apart, into lives 12

built on separate realities. It has been part of the grudge of self-sacrifice, the painful gap of understanding and experience between men's and women's lives. It is the stuff of which alienation and novels are written.

But more awesomely, as a male activity, a rite of pas- 13 sage, a test of manhood, war has been gruesomely acceptable. Old men who were warriors have sent younger men to war as if it were their birthright. The women's role until recently was to wave banners and sing slogans, and be in need of protection from the enemy.

We all pretended that war was civilized. War had rules 14 and battlegrounds. War did not touch the finer and nobler things, like women.

This was, of course, never true. The losers, the enemies, 15 the victims, the widows of war were as brutalized as the soldiers. Under duress and in defense, women always fought.

But, perhaps, stripped of its maleness and mystery, its 16 audience and cheerleaders, war can be finally disillusioned. Without the last trappings of chivalry, it can be seen for what it is: the last deadly resort.

So, if we must have a draft registration, I would include 17 young women as well as young men. I would include them because they can do the job. I would include them because all women must gain the status to stop as well as to start wars. I would include them because it has been too easy to send men alone.

I would include them because I simply cannot believe 18 that I would feel differently if my daughter were my son.

QUESTIONS

1. What is Goodman saying about war—that it is a necessary evil, or that it makes the people who fight wars fine and noble, or that it makes people worse in character, or what? Is she arguing for or against war in the essay?

2. What is her main argument for drafting women, and what are her subordinate arguments? How does she distinguish her main argument from these others?

3. How does she trace for us her reasoning on the issue of drafting women? Why do you think she does so?

4. If the main issue for Goodman in the essay is that of drafting women, what are the subordinate issues, and how does she state them?

5. What false images of women is she attacking, and how does she identify these images?

6. Do you agree with Goodman that women should be drafted? And do you agree with other points she makes in the essay?

WRITING ASSIGNMENTS

1. Write your own argumentative essay in favor of or opposing the registration and drafting of women. Trace your reasoning on the issue, and distinguish main from subordinate issues as Goodman does.

2. Write an argumentative essay on a current issue with which you have had personal experience. In the course of your argument, state what that experience is and how much authority it grants you in analyzing the issue and stating what should be done.

RUSHWORTH M. KIDDER

RUSHWORTH M. KIDDER, *another outstanding practitioner of the journalistic essay, joined the staff of the* Christian Science Monitor *in 1979 as London correspondent, and now is a columnist writing about the Boston area and contemporary issues of concern throughout the United States. Kidder in the essay reprinted here considers the banning of Walkmans and*

similar devices in a New Jersey township. This action
has been taken or is being considered by cities, towns,
and other governmental entities in the United States.

Banning the Walkman

Thirty miles south of New York City lies a town which   1
apparently holds three records in matters pertaining to vehicular traffic.

Woodbridge Township, N.J., boasts the first cloverleaf   2
interchange ever built in the United States. It may also lay
claim to being one of nation's most visited and least remembered towns. The New Jersey Turnpike and the Garden
State Parkway intersect at that cloverleaf. So millions of us
have been there—though we had no idea it was Woodbridge.

But the latest record will surely eclipse the others.   3
Woodbridge, following a unanimous vote by its town council
in July, is now The Town that Banned the Walkman.

The Walkman, like Woodbridge itself, is something   4
many have seen but fewer, perhaps, recognize. It is, in fact,
Sony Corporation's trade name for those increasingly popular stereo tape cassette players sold by various companies.
Battery-powered, held in the hand or fastened to a belt, they
deliver their gorgeous stereophonic sound through tiny earphones. Cocooning you in your own little music world, they
leave you free to walk, jog, run, cycle, or drive at will.

Unless, that is, you happen to want to do these things in   5
Woodbridge. The town fathers have nothing against music,
or electronics, or stereo. Their objection is to the headphones. They have laid down a law prohibiting the use of
them on the town's streets.

"I think it's a distraction," says Township Council pres-   6
ident Robert F. Gawroniak. He no doubt has visions of
motorists, doped in accoustical anaesthesia, gliding blithely

past the screech of brakes and other loud warnings. He
foresees, I suspect, a community full of the auditory counterparts of The Nearsighted Mr. Magoo.

In fact, Mr. Gawroniak's argument centers on safety.   7
He wants to prevent accidents rather than react to them.
"It's a shame that you have to have the horse run away
before you lock the door," he says, his metaphor appro-
priately reflecting Woodbridge's fascination with all sorts of
transportation. Last month, state officials essentially approved the ordinance, which should be in effect by early
October. "We think we're on the right track," he told me,
slipping into yet another vehicular metaphor. He may be
right. Woodbridge officials have seen what he calls "fantas-
tic" interest from other municipalities around the country. A
number of states, including Massachusetts, Illinois, and
Pennsylvania, already outlaw headphones on drivers.

But Woodbridge goes further, putting the arm on   8
pedestrians and cyclists as well.

Not, however, without an outcry. New Jersey has a   9
reputation for its commitment to home rule. Garden Staters
bristle at interference from any sort of government. "Who
are they to tell us whether we can wear headphones or not?"
one Woodbridge jogger asked a New York Times reporter
the other day. It's a classic individual-rights-versus-govern-
ment-authority issue.

So far, the industry is keeping a very low profile.   10
Spokesman Fred Wahlstrom at Sony (which has sold 5 million of the devices worldwide and sees no fall-off from the
Woodbridge Effect) says it will wait and see how the law
works. He predicts a court test, and questions the authority
of the Township Council. "We feel it's basically a question of
individual rights," he says.

What does it all mean?   11

Well, one hesitates to put too broad an interpretation   12
upon it. Maybe the Walkman fad isn't particularly important.
Maybe it doesn't much matter that music, until now a com-
munal thing, has suddenly become wholly private. Perhaps
no one worries that great groups of people will all be mov-

ing (quite literally) to different drummers. Maybe it's not a sign of the breakdown of intercommunication, the isolation of man from his environment, and the surrender of consciousness to outside manipulation.

Don't get me wrong: I am no rank earphonophobe. I 13 see the machine's potential. One can imagine learners of languages or lovers of great books making fine use of it. But why should the earphone craze have seized us at this time?

Surely it is not that the music is so beautiful, nor that 14 technology is so advanced, nor that tapes are so cheap. What lies underneath it?

I suppose, if I had to finger one culprit, I'd point to what 15 seems an increasing misunderstanding of the value of solitude. These devices, after all, allow you to imagine that you are not alone.

"I am not merely running down this city street or this 16 country lane," says the wired-up jogger. "I am grooving to my own favorite group. I no longer have to content myself with my own thinking. Ah, no. I am not alone. This is LIFE!"

And that, deep down, may be what rankles in Wood- 17 bridge. The city fathers may think they are merely freeing their curbs and highways from the ravages of the oblivious. But underneath, ironically, they may be defending, not attacking, individuality. Theirs may be an almost instinctual rebellion against the great mental drift. They have come to the defense of solitude. In their own quiet moments, perhaps they have grasped that solitude breeds thought, and that only from thought does individuality arise.

QUESTIONS

1. How does Kidder explain the Walkman fad? Does he express approval or disapproval of it?
2. What were the professed reasons of the town council for the ban? Does Kidder say or imply that these were not the real reasons?

3. What are the reasons of those opposing the ban? Does Kidder believe that these reasons are the real ones, or does he imply that there are unstated ones?

4. Does Kidder take a stand on the issue? If he does not, does he imply approval or disapproval of the ban?

WRITING ASSIGNMENTS

1. Discuss whether you are in favor of banning the Walkman in your community. In the course of your discussion, state your reasons for agreeing or disagreeing with the philosophy of the Woodbridge town council. Direct your argument to those in your community who might consider or would have authority to enact the ban.

2. Give the details of a current controversy in your community, giving the arguments of each side. Then state your reasons for agreeing with one or the other—or possibly with both or neither. In your conclusion suggest how the issue might be reconciled.

ROBERT M. CURVIN

ROBERT M. CURVIN *is a member of the editorial board of* The New York Times. *A graduate of Rutgers and Princeton, he has taught at Brooklyn College and Rutgers, and he writes often about social problems in America. His essay on heroin appeared in the* Times *on February 20, 1981.*

What If Heroin Were Free?

After years of more or less vigorous police action, American governments have failed to stop the importation, sale and use of heroin. As Leslie Maitland reported in last Sunday's

Times, the latest wave of drug imports—from the opium fields of Afghanistan, Iran and Pakistan—is running high. So is the damage to addicts, families, neighborhoods. And so is the cost to society, on which addicts prey heavily to support their habit. Their search for the money for an ever more costly fix may be a major cause of street crime.

Isn't it time to try a wholly new, admittedly risky approach? Why not give addicts free heroin, and at least be rid of their crimes and the corruption spread by their suppliers? 2

An addict may need as much as $200 a day to support his habit. How much of that does he steal? Researchers at Temple University discovered recently that 243 heroin users in Baltimore committed more than 500,000 crimes over 11 years—an average of 200 crimes by each of them each year. 3

The profits in the heroin trade are so great that no protective or punitive measures seem able to deter it. The dealers are experts at their work. They often provide free doses until a victim requires heroin more than food. Then comes the need to pay, and the victim often pays by agreeing to recruit other victims. 4

The Federal Drug Enforcement Administration has made numerous arrests of major drug dealers in the United States and abroad. But heroin still buys its way through. Local police forces are virtually helpless. 5

Methadone maintenance programs, which provide addicts with a free and less destructive narcotic than heroin, have allowed some of the victims to lead relatively normal lives. Yet as designed, these programs do not prevent thousands of new addicts from entering the criminal world of heroin every year. 6

In such desperate circumstances, it may be much more effective simply to supply addicts with the drug in exchange for their accepting medical and psychiatric help. A drug program run by governments or authorized private clinics should take much of the profit out of the heroin industry. The addicts thus removed from the illegal market would no longer have to support the habit, and the price to all others should decline. 7

Creating and supervising proper drug clinics would be 8

expensive. But the heroin they give away, or the methadone substitutes if feasible, would cost a tiny fraction of what addicts now pay. The net saving to society could be huge.

Taking the profit out of heroin isn't a new idea. It has 9 been tried in Britain, but in ways that cannot really instruct Americans. Besides, Britain's population is different, crime is less common and the criminal heroin system does not thrive there as it does in the United States.

The argument usually brought against giving heroin 10 away is that society would thus sanction and allegedly encourage drug use. But if the humane treatment of addicts is the goal, it is at least arguable that a program of heroin support would help many more people than it would injure. And when society's potential benefits—lower crime rates, savings on law enforcement and a less fearful climate—are added to the balance, the case for official drug programs is greatly strengthened.

I do not pretend to know how best to manage a pro- 11 gram of heroin support. What would be the minimum age for patients? What degree of addiction would qualify them for free doses? How to measure success and failure of such an experiment? And could an experiment run long in one locale without attracting addicts from all over? The difficulties are obvious. But given the nation's record with heroin, the risks of a new approach seem more tolerable every day.

QUESTIONS

1. What paragraphs constitute the introduction and division of proofs? And what paragraphs constitute the narration? What audience is Curvin addressing, and how do you know from these paragraphs?

2. What are his arguments in favor of making heroin available to addicts? And how does he answer those opposed to doing so?

3. Does he present his arguments and answer in a separate confirmation and refutation, or does he combine them?

4. How does Curvin qualify his argument in his conclusion—that is, how does he suggest the limits of his argument?

5. What underlying assumptions about people or society do you find in Curvin's argument? Do you agree or disagree with the proposal and with the reasons given? Do you also agree with Curvin's assumptions?

WRITING ASSIGNMENT

Write an argumentative essay on one of the following topics or on one of your own choosing. Follow the model organization described in the discussion, "Order of Ideas," and illustrated by Curvin:

a. requiring annual reexamination of licensed teenage drivers
b. ending compulsory high school attendance
c. making a "C" average a requirement for eligibility in high school team sports
d. keeping the speed limit at 55 miles an hour

Persuasion

How we choose to present our ideas depends on our purpose in speaking or writing. The demands of exposition and persuasive argument are not the same. In exposition, we are guided by the need to make our ideas clear; in persuasive argument, we need to be clear but, in addition, we want to present our ideas in the most convincing way. In describing how to sharpen a knife, our concern is to make the process clear to those who want to understand how to do it; our main concern is not to persuade them to do so. In both exposition and persuasion, the order of ideas may be determined by the audience. Writing to a general one, we may begin an exposition of a new medical treatment with definitions that an audience of physicians and nurses would not require. Directing an argument to a hostile audience, we may begin with ideas we know are acceptable and build to controversial ones.

Persuasive arguments present additional challenges. We must use exposition in presenting the background of the argument, but we must also construct a sound argument, arouse the interest of the audience through a legitimate appeal to their emotions, and show that we are honest and well-informed enough to deserve a serious hearing. Though some writers and speakers seek to avoid all emotional appeals in the belief that the soundness of an argument guarantees its persuasiveness, few if any arguments are entirely free of emotion. We need, then, to be aware of the kind of appeals we are capable of making. The English writer E. M. Forster said the following:

> The desire to devote oneself to another person or persons seems to be as innate as the desire for personal liberty.

If such desires are indeed innate, we should have little difficulty in arousing the sympathies of our readers for the plight of their fellow human beings. The difficulty would obviously be greater if our readers held a view like the following:

> Each of us has interests of great concern to himself, but not normally or naturally of great concern to other people. A few may sympathize if they hear that my life or my job is in jeopardy, but they will not bestir themselves very much.—J. R. Lucas, *Democracy and Participation*

The consideration in persuasive arguments is not *whether* to appeal to emotions, but rather what emotions we want to arouse and how, as we make the soundest argument we can.

THE NEW YORKER

THE NEW YORKER *magazine published the following comment in "The Talk of the Town" on December 6, 1982. The absence of direct comment on the news headlines illustrates what we described earlier in the book as an "implied thesis."* The New Yorker *has given us a picture without a caption, telling us only that the writer looked around and saw the world from a particular perspective.*

In Twenty-four Hours Last Week

In twenty-four hours last week, we looked around and saw: 1

Newspaper headlines: "GANG FIGHT KILLS MAN IN NYU 2
DORM," "COPS RAID QUEENS CREDIT CARD RING," "SLAYING BARES
HER SECRET LIFE," "NAB COUPLE IN CHILD PORN," "SAYS HOTEL
FORCES HER TO BE SEX SPY," "CALIF. QUARREL ENDS IN DEATH HERE,"
"HIT BY TRAIN AND DIES," "FIRE KILLS N.J. GIRL, 3," "BABY'S DEATH
PROBED," "SAY HE RAN DOWN FANS," "JEAN HARRIS WEEPS ON TV AS
SHE RELIVES MURDER NIGHT," "MADMAN SEARS 2 WITH ACID IN SUB-
WAY," "ARREST 3 IN MIDTOWN STICKUP," "FALLING DEBRIS K.O.S
WALKER," "FAMILY SUFFERS 2ND HIT-RUN," "FIRE FEM ROASTED BY
WIVES & MOMS," "3 ARRESTED AFTER NEW HIGH SCHOOL RIOT," "JOB
SITE PROTESTER SHOT IN CLASH WITH HARDHATS," "KINKY HUBBY'S
INTO BONDAGE," "SURRENDERS IN COP'S SLAYING," "2 TEEN-AGE CHIL-
DREN ARE HELD AS PLOTTERS OF FATHER'S MURDER," "WORKER FALLS
8 FLOORS IN CAR," "ARIZONA CHURCH BISHOP JAILED OVER SHOOT-

OUT," "SUSPECTED SMUGGLER SLAIN AT TEXAS BORDER," "PROGRESS REPORTED IN FIXING INDIAN PT. ATOM-DISASTER PLAN," "CITIZENS' GUN USE ON RISE IN HOUSTON," "CONSPIRACY TRIAL IS A TALE OF TAPES," "DETECTIVE SHOOTS OFFICER IN ARGUMENT IN QUEENS," "WIFE DEFENDS LECH ON SEX TAPE CHARGES," "POPE BLASTS MAFIA," "INDONESIA SQUEEZING GUERRILLAS IN EAST TIMOR," "NIGERIANS OUTLAW SECT LINKED TO FATAL RIOTS," "FOR LEBANON, 'A DIRTY WAR' IN MOUNTAINS," "FOR PROMINENT TURKS, SHAVED HEADS AND JAIL GARB."

Ads: "HOW TO SURVIVE IN THE ELECTRONIC JUNGLE," "FA-   3
DEN FUR FASHION EXPLOSION!," "FACE-TO-FACE DESIGN CON-
FRONTATION BY MICHAELE VOLLBRACHT," "N.Y.'S BIGGEST AUC-
TION OUTLET STRIKES AGAIN."

Movie titles: "Creepshow," "First Blood," "Brimstone   4
& Treacle," "Dawn of the Dead," "Friday the 13th: Part 3,"
"Funeral Home," "The Slumber Party Massacre," "Conan
the Barbarian," "Alone in the Dark," "The Burning," "Hal-
loween III: Season of the Witch," "Maniac," "Jinxed,"
"Caligula," "Horror Planet," "Basket Case."

Toys: Masters of the Universe Battle Ram Mobile   5
Launcher, Masters of the Universe Skeletor Lord of Destruction, Masters of the Universe He-Man Most Powerful Man
in the Universe, Masters of the Universe Beast Man Savage
Henchman, Masters of the University Zodac Cosmic En-
forcer, Masters of the Universe Battle Cat Fighting Tiger,
Masters of the Universe Wind Raider Assault Lander, Mas-
ters of the Universe Mer-Man Ocean Warlord, Masters of
the Universe Stratos-Winged Warrior, M*A*S*H Medical Unit
Helicopter, G.I. Joe A Real American Hero Mobile Missile
System (MMS) with Removable Missiles You Elevate and
Swivel, Star Wars: The Empire Strikes Back Rebel Trans-
port Vehicle, Star Wars: The Empire Strikes Back Laser
Pistol, The Star Wars Micro Collection Hoth Turret Defense.

Games: Stay Alive, Survive!, Conspiracy, Cobra Battle   6
Game, Curse of the Cobras, Clue, Trouble, Headache.

Video games: Communist Mutants from Space, Chop-   7
per Command, Megamania, Night Stalker, Laser Blast,
Gangster Alley, Suicide Mission, Sub Hunt, Rip Off, Ber-
zerk, Demon Attack, Space Hawk, Star Strike, Astromash,

Space Armada, Space Battle, Armor Battle, Sea Battle, Space Spartans, B-17 TM Bomber, Bomb Squad.

Rock groups called Cheap Trick, The Boomtown Rats, 8 Missing Persons, The Clash, George Thorogood and the Destroyers.

Records called "Screaming for Vengeance," "Bad 9 Boy/Having a Party," "Children of the Grave," "Famous Last Words," "Combat Rock," "Maneater," "Paranoid," "Bad to the Bone."

Television fare: "The Human Vapor," "Roots of Evil," 10 "The Ambushers," "Hear No Evil," "Cape Fear," "Peeping Tom," "Someone Behind the Door," "Murder on Lenox Avenue," Escape from Alcatraz," "An Eye for an Eye," "The Gun," "Destroyer," "Shark Bait," "The Border Menace," "Terror in the Wax Museum," "Juggernaut," "White Line Fever," "The Howling."

We sought cover by turning on the new "Saturday Night 11 Live," and there we heard the guest host, seven-year-old Drew Barrymore, of the movie "E.T.," deliver these lines written for her: "I'm a Barrymore. Get me a drink. And make it a double!"

QUESTIONS

1. What point is *The New Yorker* making about the headlines, ads, movie titles and other details given? Is *The New Yorker* making the same point about each of the classes discussed?

2. Would the essay be more effective, in your view, if the article had stated this point or thesis directly?

3. Are the various classes—headlines, ads, and the like— arranged in a random order? If they are, do you see an advantage in such an arrangement?

4. The final detail—the statement of the seven-year-old girl on a television night show—has clearly been reserved for the conclusion. Why do you think *The New Yorker* saved it for the end?

5. In general, what persuasive means has the *The New Yorker* chosen to tell us about the world? Do you find these means effective?

WRITING ASSIGNMENTS

1. Make a point about the town or city you live in by presenting details about it, gathered from the media and from your own experience. Do not state the point directly. Organize your details in a way that will best persuade the reader to accept your view of this world.

2. Discuss what the names of current automobiles—Mustang, Charger, and the like—tell you about the values of the manufacturers and the consumers who buy them.

W. S. MERWIN

W. S. MERWIN *is a poet, playwright, translator, and essayist whose work appears often in* The New Yorker *magazine. He is a highly gifted writer of the short essay, as his description of unchopping a tree shows. Merwin in his essay talks to the reader in an ironic tone, as if to say, "We share a secret, something that I am hinting at, and I need not say directly." When writer and reader share an understanding of this kind, they share it about a third party—someone who does not know what they do and needs to be enlightened.*

Unchopping a Tree

Start with the leaves, the small twigs, and the nests that have 1 been shaken, ripped, or broken off by the fall; these must be gathered and attached once again to their respective places. It is not arduous work, unless major limbs have been smashed or mutilated. If the fall was carefully and correctly planned, the chances of anything of the kind happening will have been reduced. Again, much depends upon the size, age, shape, and species of the tree. Still, you will be lucky if you can get through this stage without having to use machinery. Even in the best of circumstances it is a labor that will make you wish often that you had won the favor of the universe of ants, the empire of mice, or at least a local tribe of squirrels, and could enlist their labors and their talents. But no, they leave you to it. They have learned, with time. This is men's work. It goes without saying that if the tree was hollow in whole or in part, and contained old nests of bird or mammal or insect, or hoards of nuts or such structures as wasps or bees build for their survival, the contents will have to be repaired where necessary, and reassembled, insofar as possible, in their original order, including the shells of nuts already opened. With spiders' webs you must simply do the best you can. We do not have the spider's weaving equipment, nor any substitute for the leaf's living bond with its point of attachment and nourishment. It is even harder to simulate the latter than the leaves have once become dry—as they are bound to do, for this is not the labor of a moment. Also it hardly needs saying that this is the time for repairing any neighboring trees or bushes or other growth that may have been damaged by the fall. The same rules apply. Where neighboring trees were of the same species it is difficult not to waste time conveying a detached leaf back to the wrong tree. Practice, practice. Put your hope in that.

Now the tackle must be put into place or the scaffolding, 2 depending on the surroundings and the dimensions of the tree. It is ticklish work. Almost always it involves, in itself, further damage to the area, which will have to be corrected later. But as you've heard, it can't be helped. And care now is likely to save you considerable trouble later. Be careful to grind nothing into the ground.

At last the time comes for the erecting of the trunk. By 3 now it will scarcely be necessary to remind you of the delicacy of this huge skeleton. Every motion of the tackle, every slight upward heave of the trunk, the branches, their elaborately reassembled panoply of leaves (now dead) will draw

from you an involuntary gasp. You will watch for a leaf or a
twig to be snapped off yet again. You will listen for the nuts
to shift in the hollow limb and you will hear whether they
are indeed falling into place or are spilling in disorder—in
which case, or in the event of anything else of the kind—
operations will have to cease, of course, while you correct
the matter. The raising itself is no small enterprise, from the
moment when the chains tighten around the old bandages
until the bole hangs vertical above the stump, splinter above
splinter. Now the final straightening of the splinters themselves can take place (the preliminary work is best done
while the wood is still green and soft, but at times when the
splinters are not badly twisted most of the straightening is
left until now, when the torn ends are face to face with each
other). When the splinters are perfectly complementary the
appropriate fixture is applied. Again we have no duplicate
of the original substance. Ours is extremely strong, but it is
rigid. It is limited to surfaces, and there is no play in it.
However the core is not the part of the trunk that conducted
life from the roots up into the branches and back again. It
was relatively inert. The fixative for this part is not the same
as the one for the outer layers and the bark, and if either of
these is involved in the splintered section they must receive
applications of the appropriate adhesives. Apart from
being incorrect and probably ineffective, the core fixative
would leave a scar on the bark.

When all is ready the splintered trunk is lowered onto   4
the splinters of the stump. This, one might say, is only the
skeleton of the resurrection. Now the chips must be
gathered, and the sawdust, and returned to their former
positions. The fixative for the wood layers will be applied to
chips and sawdust consisting only of wood. Chips and sawdust consisting of several substances will receive applications of the correct adhesives. It is as well, where possible, to
shelter the materials from the elements while working.
Weathering makes it harder to identify the smaller frag-
ments. Bark sawdust in particular the earth lays claim to
very quickly. You must find your own ways of coping with

this problem. There is a certain beauty, you will notice at moments, in the pattern of the chips as they are fitted back into place. You will wonder to what extent it should be described as natural, to what extent manmade. It will lead you on to speculations about the parentage of beauty itself, to which you will return.

The adhesive for the chips is translucent, and not so 5 rigid as that for the splinters. That for bark and its sub-cutaneous layers is transparent and runs into the fibers on either side, partially dissolving them into each other. It does not set the sap flowing again but it does pay a kind of tribute to the preoccupations of the ancient thoroughfares. You could not roll an egg over the joints but some of the mine-shafts would still be passable, no doubt. For the first explor-ing insect who raises its head in the tight echoless passages. The day comes when it is all restored, even to the moss (now dead) over the wound. You will sleep badly, thinking of the removal of the scaffolding that must begin the next morn-ing. How you will hope for sun and a still day!

The removal of the scaffolding or tackle is not so dan- 6 gerous, perhaps, to the surroundings, as its installation, but it presents problems. It should be taken from the spot piece by piece as it is detached, and stored at a distance. You have come to accept it there, around the tree. The sky begins to look naked as the chains and struts one by one vacate their positions. Finally the moment arrives when the last sustain-ing piece is removed and the tree stands again on its own. It is as though its weight for a moment stood on your heart. You listen for a thud of settlement, a warning creak deep in the intricate joinery. You cannot believe it will hold. How like something dreamed it is, standing there all by itself. How long will it stand there now? The first breeze that touches its dead leaves all seems to flow into your mouth. You are afraid the motion of the clouds will be enough to push it over. What more can you do? What more can you do?

But there is nothing more you can do. 7

Others are waiting. 8

Everything is going to have to be put back. 9

QUESTIONS

1. What are the chief indications of Merwin's purpose in this essay? Does he state that purpose directly?

2. Examine the following statement from paragraph 4 carefully: "You will wonder to what extent it should be described as natural, to what extent man-made. It will lead you on to speculations about the parentage of beauty itself, to which you will return." What is the tone of the statement—that is, what seems to be the writer's attitude toward his reader as well as toward the act of unchopping a tree? Is an attitude *implied* in the whole essay that no single statement expresses? Could you accept such an implication as embodying the thesis?

3. The writer has chosen a strategy to deal with his idea—that is, he approaches his reader in a particular way to achieve a particular effect. What does he want his reader to think and feel at the end of the essay, and what is his strategy in realizing these aims?

4. The essay ends with three single-sentence paragraphs. To what effect? What is Merwin saying?

WRITING ASSIGNMENT

Write an essay on a similar topic, for example, undoing an insult. Be consistent in conveying a tone and in building to your conclusion. Do not state your thesis directly; let the reader discover it in your tone and details.

BARBARA WARD

BARBARA WARD *(1914–1981) was a British economist, teacher, and journalist, who wrote much about the growing gap between rich and poor nations and the growing scarcity of food and natural resources. Her famous books include* Faith and Freedom *(1954),* Spaceship Earth *(1966) and* The Home of Man *(1976). The*

*term "triage" refers in general to a selection we make
on the basis of quality, and in the early 1970s became a
term for the allocation of food to people considered
worthy of it. Ward in her essay—published in* The New
York Times *on November 15, 1976—is responding to
those arguing that a policy of "triage" is needed and
inevitable, given the enormous rise of population, particularly in poor countries.*

"Triage"

Now that the House of Representatives has bravely passed 1
its resolution on the "right to food"—the basic human right
without which, indeed, all other rights are meaningless—it
is perhaps a good moment to try to clear up one or two
points of confusion that appear to have been troubling the
American mind on the question of food supplies, hunger,
and America's moral obligation, particularly to those who
are not America's own citizens.

The United States, with Canada and marginal help 2
from Australia, are the only producers of surplus grain. It
follows that if any part of the world comes up short or
approaches starvation, there is at present only one remedy
and it is in Americans' hands. Either they do the emergency
feeding or people starve.

It is a heavy moral responsibility. Is it one that has to be 3
accepted?

This is where the moral confusions begin. A strong 4
school of thought argues that it is the flood tide of babies,
irresponsibly produced in Asia, Africa, and Latin America,
that is creating the certainty of malnutrition and risk of
famine. If these countries insist on having babies, they must
feed them themselves. If hard times set in, food aid from
North America—if any—must go strictly to those who can
prove they are reducing the baby flood. Otherwise, the
responsible suffer. The poor go on increasing.

This is a distinctly Victorian replay of Malthus.* He first 5
suggested that population would go on rising to absorb all
available supplies and that the poor must be left to starve if
they would be incontinent. The British Poor Law was based
on this principle. It has now been given a new descriptive
analogy in America. The planet is compared to a battlefield.
There are not enough medical skills and supplies to go
round. So what must the doctors do? Obviously, concentrate
on those who can hope to recover. The rest must die. This is
the meaning of "triage."

Abandon the unsavable and by so doing concentrate 6
the supplies—in the battlefield, medical skills; in the world
at large, surplus food—on those who still have a chance to
survive.

Thus the people with stable or stabilizing populations 7
will be able to hold on. The human experiment will continue.

It is a very simple argument. It has been persuasively 8
supported by noted business leaders, trade-unionists, aca-
demics and presumed Presidential advisers. But "triage" is,
in fact, so shot through with half truths as to be almost a lie,
and so irrelevant to real world issues as to be not much more
than an aberration.

Take the half truths first. In the last ten years, at least 9
one-third of the increased world demand for food has come
from North Americans, Europeans and Russians eating
steadily more high-protein food. Grain is fed to animals and
poultry, and eaten as steak and eggs.

In real energy terms, this is about five times more 10
wasteful than eating grain itself. The result is an average
American diet of nearly 2,000 pounds of grain a year—and
epidemics of cardiac trouble—and 400 pounds for the average Indian.

It follows that for those worrying about available 11

---

*Thomas Malthus (1766–1834), in his *Essay on the Principle of Population* (1798),
argued that population growth would have to be controlled, because population
increases faster than the food supply. He opposed relief for the poor and higher
wages on the ground that these encouraged idleness and early marriage. Ed.

supplies on the "Battlefield," one American equals five Indians in the claims on basic food. And this figure masks the fact that much of the North American eating—and drinking—is pure waste. For instance, the American Medical Association would like to see meat-eating cut by a third to produce a healthier nation.

The second distortion is to suggest that direct food aid 12 is what the world is chiefly seeking from the United States. True, if there were a failed monsoon and the normal Soviet agricultural muddle next year, the need for an actual transfer of grain would have to be faced.

That is why the world food plan, worked out at Secre- 13 tary of State Henry A. Kissinger's earlier prompting, asks for a modest reserve of grain to be set aside—on the old biblical plan of Joseph's "fat years" being used to prepare for the "lean."

But no conceivable American surplus could deal with 14 the third world's food needs of the 1980's and 1990's. They can be met only by a sustained advance in food production where productivity is still so low that quadrupling and quintupling of crops is possible, provided investments begin now.

A recent Japanese study has shown that rice responds 15 with copybook reliability to higher irrigation and improved seed. This is why the same world food plan is stressing a steady capital input of $30 billion a year in third-world farms, with perhaps $5 billion contributed by the old rich and the "oil" rich.

(What irony that this figure is barely a third of what 16 West Germany has to spend each year to offset the health effects of overeating and overdrinking.)

To exclaim and complain about the impossibility of 17 giving away enough American surplus grain (which could not be rice anyway), when the real issue is a sustained effort by all the nations in long-term agricultural investment, simply takes the citizens' minds off the real issue—where they can be of certain assistance—and impresses on them a nonissue that confuses them and helps nobody else.

Happily, the House's food resolution puts long-term 18
international investment in food production firmly back into
the center of the picture.

And this investment in the long run is the true answer 19
to the stabilizing of family size. People do not learn restraint
from "give-aways." (The arms industry's bribes are proof
enough of that.) But the whole experience of the last century
is that if parents are given work, responsibility, enough food
and safe water, they have the sense to see they do not need
endless children as insurance against calamity.

Because of food from the Great Plains and the reform 20
of sanitation, Malthusian fears vanished as an issue in
Europe and North America in the 1880's. China is below 2
percent population growth today on the basis of intensive
agriculture and popular health measures.

Go to the root of the matter—investment in people, in 21
food, in water—and the Malthus myth will fade in the third
world as it has done already in many parts of it and entirely
in the so-called first and second worlds.

It may be that this positive strategy of stabilizing popu- 22
lation by sustained, skilled and well-directed investment in
food production and in clean water suggests less drama
than the hair-raising images of inexorably rising tides of
children eating like locusts the core out of the whole world's
food supplies.

But perhaps we should be wise to prefer relevance to 23
drama. In "triage," there is, after all, a suggestion of the
battlefield. If this is how we see the world, are we absolutely
certain who deserves to win—the minority of guzzlers who
eat 2,000 pounds of grain, or the majority of despairing men
of hunger who eat 400 pounds?

History gives uncomfortable answers. No doubt as they 24
left their hot baths and massage parlors for the joys of
dining, vomiting and redining, Roman senators must have
muttered and complained about the "awkwardness of the
barbarians." But the barbarians won. Is this the battlefield
we want? And who will "triage" whom?

QUESTIONS

1. The general issue of Ward's essay is the feeding of the poor throughout the world: the point at issue is stated in paragraph 3: "It is a heavy responsibility. Is it one that has to be accepted?" What are the real issues that Ward identifies later, in dealing with the point at issue?

2. What background or narration does Ward provide? How does she use this narration to state the assumptions of those who argue for triage?

3. What assumptions does she present in opposition to those she is criticizing? How does she explain these assumptions?

4. Notice that Ward has put a deductive argument to the use of persuasion: this is why she must explain and defend her own assumptions. In doing so, what appeal to experience does she make, particularly in the concluding paragraph?

5. In the course of the essay, Ward poses a dilemma: either we select certain people to feed, or we all eventually starve and die. How does she deal with this dilemma?

WRITING ASSIGNMENT

Discuss the extent of your agreement with Ward's assumptions and conclusions. If you agree with her conclusion for different reasons, explain what these are, and defend them.

JONATHAN SWIFT

JONATHAN SWIFT *(1667–1745), the son of English Protestant parents, was born and educated in Ireland. In
1688 he went to England to seek a career in literature.
Swift wrote satirical poems, essays, pamphlets, and
tracts on the major issues of the day and became involved in many of its political and religious controver-
sies. In 1713 he became Dean of St. Patrick's Cathedral*

*in Dublin and in the succeeding years wrote widely on
various questions bearing on Ireland and England. His
most famous satirical work,* Gulliver's Travels, *was published in 1726. Swift was deeply concerned about the
sufferings that he had observed in his country from
boyhood. Ireland, under the control of the British government, was an impoverished country—restricted in
selling its goods and incapable of producing enough
food to feed the population. Most of the poor were
Catholic, a point that Swift emphasizes in his "modest
proposal"—written in 1729 to suggest a remedy for the
widespread starvation and misery of the country. Swift
writes as a disinterested observer, anxious to perform a
service to both the English and the Irish with his proposal. The persuasive means that Swift uses deserves the
closest study.*

A Modest Proposal

For Preventing the Children of Poor People in
Ireland from Being a Burden to Their Parents or
Country, and for Making Them Beneficial to the
Public

It is a melancholy object to those who walk through this   1
great town, or travel in the country, when they see the
streets, the roads, and cabin-doors crowded with beggars of
the female sex, followed by three, four, or six children, all in
rags, and importuning every passenger for an alms. These
mothers, instead of being able to work for their honest
livelihood, are forced to employ all their time in strolling to
beg sustenance for their helpless infants: who, as they grow
up, either turn thieves for want of work, or leave their dear
native country to fight for the Pretender in Spain, or sell
themselves to the Barbadoes.

I think it is agreed by all parties, that this prodigious   2
number of children in the arms, or on the backs, or at the

heels of their mothers, and frequently of their fathers, is in the present deplorable state of the kingdom, a very great additional grievance; and, therefore, whoever could find out a fair, cheap, and easy method of making these children sound and useful members of the commonwealth, would deserve so well of the public, as to have his statue set up for a preserver of the nation.

But my intention is very far from being confined to provide only for the children of professed beggars; it is of a much greater extent, and shall take in the whole number of infants at a certain age, who are born of parents in effect as little able to support them as those who demand our charity in the streets.

As to my own part, having turned my thoughts for many years upon this important subject, and maturely weighed the several schemes of other projectors, I have always found them grossly mistaken in their computation. It is true, a child, just dropped from its dam, may be supported by her milk for a solar year with little other nourishment; at most, not above the value of two shillings, which the mother may certainly get, or the value in scraps, by her lawful occupation of begging; and it is exactly at one year old that I propose to provide for them in such a manner, as, instead of being a charge upon their parents or the parish, or wanting food and raiment for the rest of their lives, they shall, on the contrary, contribute to the feeding, and partly to the clothing, of many thousands.

There is likewise another great advantage in my scheme, that it will prevent those voluntary abortions, and that horrid practice of women murdering their bastard children, alas, too frequent among us, sacrificing the poor innocent babes, I doubt more to avoid the expense than the shame, which would move tears and pity in the most savage and inhuman breast.

The number of souls in this kingdom being usually reckoned one million and a half, of these I calculate there may be about two hundred thousand couple whose wives are breeders; from which number I subtract thirty thousand couple, who are able to maintain their own children (although I apprehend there cannot be so many, under the present distresses of the kingdom); but this being granted, there will remain an hundred and seventy thousand breeders. I again subtract fifty thousand for those women who miscarry, or whose children die by accident or disease within the year. There only remain a hundred and twenty thousand children of poor parents annually born. The question therefore is how this number shall be reared and provided for? which, as I have already said, under the present situation of affairs, is utterly impossible by all the methods hitherto proposed. For we can neither employ them in handicraft or agriculture; we neither build houses (I mean in the country) nor cultivate land: they can very seldom pick up a livelihood by stealing until they arrive at six years old, except where they are of towardly parts; although I confess they learn the rudiments much earlier; during which time they can, however, be properly looked upon only as probationers; as I have been informed by a principal gentleman in the county of Cavan, who protested to me, that he never knew above one or two instances under the age of six, even in a part of the kingdom so renowned for the quickest proficiency in that art.

I am assured by our merchants that a boy or a girl 7 before twelve years old is no salable commodity; and even when they come to this age they will not yield above three pounds or three pounds and half-a-crown at most, on the exchange; which cannot turn to account either to the parents or kingdom, the charge of nutriment and rags having been at least four times that value.

I shall now, therefore, humbly propose my own 8 thoughts, which I hope will not be liable to the least objection.

I have been assured by a very knowing American of my 9 acquaintance in London, that a young healthy child, well nursed, is, at a year old, a most delicious, nourishing, and wholesome food, whether stewed, roasted, baked, or boiled; and I make no doubt that it will equally serve in a fricassee or a ragout.

I do therefore humbly offer it to public consideration, 10 that of the hundred and twenty thousand children already computed, twenty thousand may be reserved for breed, whereof only one-fourth part to be males; which is more than we allow to sheep, black cattle, or swine; and my reason is, that these children are seldom the fruits of marriage, a circumstance not much regarded by our savages, therefore one male will be sufficient to serve four females. That the remaining hundred thousand may, at a year old, be offered in sale to the persons of quality and fortune through the kingdom; always advising the mother to let them suck plentifully in the last month, so as to render them plump and fat for a good table. A child will make two dishes at an entertainment for friends; and when the family dines alone, the fore or hind quarter will make a reasonable dish, and, seasoned with a little pepper or salt, will be very good boiled on the fourth day, especially in winter.

I have reckoned, upon a medium, that a child just born 11 will weigh twelve pounds, and in a solar year, if tolerably nursed, increaseth to twenty-eight pounds.

I grant this food will be somewhat dear, and therefore 12 very proper for landlords, who, as they have already devoured most of the parents, seem to have the best title to the children.

Infants' flesh will be in season throughout the year, but 13 more plentifully in March, and a little before and after: for we are told by a grave author, an eminent French physician, that fish being a prolific diet, there are more children born in Roman Catholic countries about nine months after Lent than at any other season; therefore, reckoning a year after Lent, the markets will be more glutted than usual, because the number of popish infants is at least three to one in this kingdom; and therefore, it will have one other collateral advantage, by lessening the number of papists among us.

I have already computed the charge of nursing a beg- 14

gar's child (in which list I reckon all cottagers, labourers, and four-fifths of the farmers) to be about two shillings per annum, rags included; and I believe no gentleman would repine to give ten shillings for the carcass of a good fat child, which, as I have said, will make four dishes of excellent nutritive meat, when he has only some particular friend, or his own family, to dine with him. Thus, the squire will learn to be a good landlord, and grow popular among his tenants; the mother will have eight shillings net profit, and be fit for work till she produces another child.

Those who are more thrifty (as I must confess the times 15 require) may flay the carcass; the skin of which artificially dressed, will make admirable gloves for ladies, and summer-boots for fine gentlemen.

As to our city of Dublin, shambles[1] may be appointed 16 for this purpose in the most convenient parts of it, and butchers we may be assured will not be wanting; although I rather recommend buying the children alive, and dressing them hot from the knife, as we do roasting pigs.

A very worthy person, a true lover of his country, and 17 whose virtues I highly esteem, was lately pleased, in discoursing on this matter, to offer a refinement upon my scheme. He said, that many gentlemen of this kingdom, having of late destroyed their deer, he conceived that the want of venison might be well supplied by the bodies of young lads and maidens, not exceeding fourteen years of age, nor under twelve; so great a number of both sexes in every country being now ready to starve for want of work and service; and these to be disposed of by their parents, if alive, or otherwise by their nearest relations. But, with due deference to so excellent a friend, and so deserving a patriot, I cannot be altogether in his sentiments; for as to the males, my American acquaintance assured me from frequent experience, that their flesh was generally tough and lean, like that of our schoolboys, by continual exercise, and their taste disagreeable; and to fatten them would not an-

---

[1]Butcher shops. (All notes in this selection are the editor's.)

swer the charge. Then as to the females, it would, I think,
with humble submission, be a loss to the public, because
they soon would become breeders themselves: and besides,
it is not improbable that some scrupulous people might be
apt to censure such a practice (although indeed very un-
justly) as a little bordering upon cruelty; which, I confess
hath always been with me the strongest objection against
any project, how well soever intended.

But in order to justify my friend, he confessed that this 18
expedient was put into his head by the famous Psalmanazar,[2] a native of the island Formosa, who came from
thence to London above twenty years ago; and in conversation told my friend, that in his country, when any young
person happened to be put to death, the executioner sold
the carcass to persons of quality as a prime dainty; and that
in his time the body of a plump girl of fifteen, who was
crucified for an attempt to poison the emperor, was sold to
his Imperial Majesty's prime minister of state, and other
great mandarins of the court, in joints from the gibbet, at
four hundred crowns. Neither indeed can I deny, that if the
same use were made of several plump young girls in this
town, who, without one single groat to their fortunes, cannot
stir abroad without a chair, and appear at playhouse and
assemblies in foreign fineries which they never will pay for,
the kingdom would not be the worse.

Some persons of a desponding spirit are in great con- 19
cern about that vast number of poor people who are aged,
diseased, or maimed; and I have been desired to employ my
thoughts what course may be taken to ease the nation of so
grievous an encumbrance. But I am not in the least pain
upon that matter, because it is very well known, that they
are every day dying, and rotting, by cold and famine, and
filth and vermin, as fast as can be reasonably expected. And
so to the younger labourers, they are now in almost as
hopeful a condition: they cannot get work, and consequently

[2]A French writer, George Psalmanazar, who posed as a native of Formosa in a
fake book he published about that country in 1704, in England.

pine away for want of nourishment, to a degree, that if at any time they are accidentally hired to common labour, they have not strength to perform it; and thus the country and themselves are happily delivered from the evils to come.

I have too long digressed, and therefore shall return to 20 my subject. I think the advantages by the proposal which I have made are obvious and many, as well as of the highest importance.

For first, as I have already observed, it would greatly 21 lessen the number of papists, with whom we are yearly overrun, being the principal breeders of the nation as well as our most dangerous enemies; and who stay at home on purpose with a design to deliver the kingdom to the Pretender, hoping to take their advantage by the absence of so many good Protestants, who have chosen rather to leave their country than stay at home and pay tithes against their conscience to an idolatrous Episcopal curate.[3]

Secondly, the poorer tenants will have something valu- 22 able of their own, which by law may be made liable to distress, and help to pay their landlord's rent; their corn and cattle being already seized, and money a thing unknown.

Thirdly, whereas the maintenance of an hundred thou- 23 sand children, from two years old and upwards, cannot be computed at less than ten shillings a piece per annum, the nation's stock will be thereby increased fifty thousand pounds per annum; besides the profit of a new dish introduced to the tables of all gentlemen of fortune in the kingdom who have any refinement in taste. And the money will circulate among ourselves, the goods being entirely of our own growth and manufacture.

Fourthly, the constant breeders, besides the gain of 24 eight shillings sterling per annum by the sale of their children, will be rid of the charge of maintaining them after the first year.

---

[3]Swift is attacking the prejudice against Irish Catholics in his time, and also the motives of a number of Protestant dissenters from the Church of England.

Fifthly, this food would otherwise bring great custom to 25 taverns; where the vintners will certainly be so prudent as to procure the best receipts for dressing it to perfection, and, consequently, have their houses frequented by all the fine gentlemen, who justly value themselves upon their knowledge in good eating: and a skillful cook, who understands how to oblige his guests, will contrive to make it as expensive as they please.

Sixthly, this would be a great inducement to marriage, 26 which all wise nations have either encouraged by rewards, or enforced by laws and penalties. It would increase the care and tenderness of mothers towards their children, when they were sure of a settlement for life to the poor babes, provided in some sort by the public, to their annual profit instead of expense. We should soon see an honest emulation among the married women, which of them could bring the fattest child to the market. Men would become as fond of their wives during the time of their pregnancy, as they are now of their mares in foal, their cows in calf, or sows when they are ready to farrow; nor offer to beat or kick them (as is too frequent a practice) for fear of a miscarriage.

Many other advantages might be enumerated. For in- 27 stance, the addition of some thousand carcasses in our exportation of barrelled beef; the propagation of swine's flesh, and improvement in the art of making good bacon, so much wanted among us by the great destruction of pigs, too frequent at our tables, which are no way comparable in taste or magnificence to a well-grown, fat yearling child, which, roasted whole, will make a considerable figure at a Lord Mayor's feast, or any other public entertainment. But this, and many others, I omit, being studious of brevity.

Supposing that one thousand families in this city would 28 be constant customers for infants' flesh, besides others who might have it at merry meetings, particularly weddings and christenings, I compute that Dublin would take off annually about twenty thousand carcasses; and the rest of the kingdom (where probably they will be sold somewhat cheaper) the remaining eighty thousand.

I can think of no one objection that will possibly be 29
raised against this proposal, unless it should be urged, that
the number of people will be thereby much lessened in the
kingdom. This I freely own, and it was indeed one principal
design in offering it to the world. I desire the reader will
observe that I calculate my remedy for this one individual
kingdom of Ireland, and for no other that ever was, is, or I
think ever can be, upon earth. Therefore let no man talk to
me of other expedients: of taxing our absentees at five
shillings a pound: of using neither clothes nor household-
furniture except what is of our own growth and manufacture: of utterly rejecting the materials and instruments that
promote foreign luxury: of curing the expensiveness of
pride, vanity, idleness, and gaming in our women; of introducing a vein of parsimony, prudence, and temperance: of
learning to love our country, wherein we differ even from
Laplanders, and the inhabitants of Topinamboo:[4] of quit-
ting our animosities and factions, nor act any longer like the
Jews, who were murdering one another at the very moment
their city was taken:[5] of being a little cautious not to sell our
country and consciences for nothing: of teaching landlords
to have at least one degree of mercy towards their tenants:
lastly, of putting a spirit of honesty, industry, and skill into
our shopkeepers; who, if a resolution could now be taken to
buy only our native goods, would immediately unite to cheat
and exact upon us in the price, the measure, and the goodness, nor could ever yet be brought to make one fair proposal of just dealing, though often and earnestly invited to it.

Therefore I repeat, let no man talk to me of these and 30
the like expedients, till he hath at least some glimpse of hope
that there will ever be some hearty and sincere attempt to
put them in practice.

But, as to myself, having been wearied out for many 31
years with offering vain, idle, visionary thoughts, and at
length utterly despairing of success, I fortunately fell upon

[4]A district of Brazil notorious for its barbarism and ignorance.
[5]Swift is referring to the fall of Jerusalem to the Babylonians.

this proposal; which, as it is wholly new, so it hath something solid and real, of no expense and little trouble, full in
our own power, and whereby we can incur no danger in
disobliging England. For this kind of commodity will not .
bear exportation, the flesh being of too tender a consistence
to admit a long continuance in salt, although perhaps I could
name a country which would be glad to eat up our whole
nation without it.

After all, I am not so violently bent upon my own 32
opinion as to reject any offer proposed by wise men which
shall be found equally innocent, cheap, easy, and effectual.
But before something of that kind shall be advanced in
contradiction to my scheme, and offering a better, I desire
the author, or authors, will be pleased maturely to consider
two points. First, as things now stand, how they will be able
to find food and raiment for a hundred thousand useless
mouths and backs? And, secondly, there being a round
million of creatures in human figure throughout this kingdom, whose whole subsistence put into a common stock
would leave them in debt two millions of pounds sterling,
adding those who are beggars by profession, to the bulk of
farmers, cottagers, and labourers, with the wives and children who are beggars in effect; I desire those politicians
who dislike my overture, and may perhaps be so bold as to
attempt an answer, that they will first ask the parents of
these mortals, whether they would not at this day think it a
great happiness to have been sold for food at a year old, in
the manner I prescribe, and thereby have avoided such a
perpetual scene of misfortunes as they have since gone
through, by the oppression of landlords, the impossibility of
paying rent without money or trade, the want of common
sustenance, with neither house nor clothes to cover them
from the inclemencies of weather, and the most inevitable
prospect of entailing the like, or greater miseries, upon their
breed for ever.

I profess, in the sincerity of my heart, that I have not the 33
least personal interest in endeavouring to promote this necessary work, having no other motive than the public good of

my country, by advancing our trade, providing for infants, relieving the poor, and giving some pleasure to the rich. I have no children by which I can propose to get a single penny; the youngest being nine years old, and my wife past child-bearing.

QUESTIONS

1. How does Swift establish the basic character and motives of this observer in the opening paragraphs of the proposal?

2. How does Swift reveal his attitude toward the writer of the proposal? Is he in accord with his general views of English motives? Are those motives stated directly or instead implied?

3. Is the proposer—and perhaps Swift himself—critical of the Irish poor, or does he exonerate them entirely?

4. Short of adopting the actual "modest proposal," is there another way of remedying the evils exposed in the course of the essay? In other words, does Swift suggest other policies that would reduce poverty and starvation in Ireland?

5. In general, what strategy does Swift employ to deal with English policies and motives and perhaps Irish attitudes too?

6. How persuasive do you find the essay? Is it an essay of historical interest or literary interest only, or does it have something to say to people today?

WRITING ASSIGNMENTS

1. Write your own "modest proposal" for dealing with a current social or political evil. You may wish to write as yourself or, like Swift, impersonate someone who wishes to make a modest proposal. Maintain a consistent tone throughout your essay, or at least make any shifts in tone consistent with the character of your speaker and his or her motives in writing.

2. Contrast Swift's attack on the English with Ward's attack on the idea of "triage." Distinguish the various persuasive means that they employ.

BARBARA BROWN

At the time she wrote her essay about the situation of poor people in a time of economic hardship, BARBARA BROWN *was assistant to the dean of the theology school at Emory University, in Atlanta. Her powerful statement employs satirical devices different from those employed by Merwin and Swift, and her approach to the question of dealing with poverty is completely different from that of Ward.*

All the Poor Patriots

Never has it been so apparent that the poor bear the burden 1 of the future. This past summer, President Carter invoked faith to combat the energy crisis and presented practical guidelines for living out that faith: consume less, conserve more, consider the good of the world community in all things. Where I live, at least, there has been no sign of cooperation, except on the part of the ever-visible poor.

The poor do not seem particularly conscious of their 2 patriotism. One old man has been pushing a grocery cart up and down Peachtree Street for years, collecting bottles and aluminum cans for the few dollars they will bring him at a recycling center. He lives off the trash of the city, and has never heard of ecology. He does not own an automobile and does not make unnecessary trips out of town. His only experience with an air conditioner is in the doughnut shop where he waits out the nights. He is a model conservationist. He has no choice.

When Atlanta opened the first six miles of its new mass 3 transit system in July, the stations were for a while crowded with curious citizens from every neighborhood in town. Now that almost everyone has enjoyed the ride at least once, the trains, like the city buses before them, serve a predominantly black and poor working class. These people use public transportation, loyally—not because the president asked them to, but because it is how they get to work on time.

Those of us who continue our commutes to the office in 4 automobiles we cannot yet give up lament an energy crisis that is in fact a crisis of life style, of individual privacy and freedom. For as long as I drive my own car, I go where I want when I want, without asking permission or waiting for anyone. I can even tune in some music or adjust the climate to my comfort. It is a small thing to visit friends across town, and if the city begins to wear me down, I can always throw a suitcase into the trunk and head for the lake.

Such freedom is beyond the experience of whole popu- 5 lations, and it is this freedom that the energy crisis threatens to repeal. Because we cannot talk about the price of the way we live our lives, we talk about the price of gasoline. Because we cannot face the global compromise that is our only real hope for the future, we turn our backs, turn into reactionaries, who appeal with sudden fervor to the constitutional promise of liberty for all, which we misunderstand as license for each.

Even the church disappoints. In a July pastoral letter, 6 the bishops of the Episcopal Church outlined their concern for world hunger and proposed that September 14, Holy Cross Day, be a day of fasting and prayer. For this exercise in self-denial, they suggested that "two light meals are appropriate and one meal eliminated altogether." Two light meals? Since when did two meals constitute a fast? If this is the church's institutional response to the world's hunger, one can only blush and apologize. The peasants of Nicaragua have not seen two meals a day since May.

The crisis is not one of energy but one of mortality. 7 Cash has always purchased a mighty bulwark against the inevitabilities of discomfort and death, but the national economy has robbed more than a few of that privileged defense. Retirement savings are worth less now than when they were socked away years ago, and careful investments have shriveled under the hot sun of inflation. The old defenses are not working any more, and our human limits are cropping up all around us—cropping up from where they have been rooted all along.

Despite increased security, Atlanta's murder rate is 8 double what it was last year, but what most of Walter Cronkite's audience does not know is that the majority of the killings happen in the poor parts of town, in the black and transient neighborhoods where the future is beginning to happen. Death is no stranger there, and everyone knows that money only hastens its appearance, as blood attracts a shark. The idea is to keep to yourself, mind your own business, and stay away from the door after dark.

But on those blocks where neighbors get together and 9 make commitments to one another, where they agree to watch each other's houses and keep track of each other's kids, the murders decrease, move on to other sections of town where people are not yet talking, are not yet pooling their resources. Their crisis is the real energy crisis, because whether the current issue is fuel or food or air to breathe, the fundamental crisis is what energy it takes to be human, and to survive on the planet with other humans—and not merely to survive but to live together in a way that defines integrity once and for all.

It is an ancient lesson. Why are we so slow to learn? We 10 are one body. If any part of the body suffers or sickens, so will the whole, sooner or later. If I have more than enough, it is because someone else has less than enough, and that is no platitude but physics. Our lives impinge upon one another. It is no longer possible to pretend that we are not related, that we exist independent of one another. Our fortunes are linked at head, heart and gut—and the poor command the crystal ball.

I do not wish to sentimentalize the poor. Poverty is no 11 tonic for character; it may in fact murder character, but what it guarantees is a severe simplification, a forced distillation of what is necessary for life and what is damnable luxury. This knowledge of the essences is the wisdom of poverty, and with just such unelected clarity do the poor bear the future into the present.

Consuming less, conserving more, they are the good 12 citizens of this country, but not by their own choice. They are patriots by necessity, because the expensive choices have already been made, and those of us still naive to the power of their witness would be well—would do mortally well—to fear their rebuke.

QUESTIONS

1. The tone of this essay changes as Brown moves from her response to President Carter's appeal to her final statement of what constitutes a good society. What is the tone of her comments in paragraphs 1–3?

2. How does her tone change as she turns to the situation of the privileged in American society and to the response of the bishops (paragraphs 4–5)? What is the tone of the paragraphs that follow?

3. What is Brown's thesis, and what strategy has she chosen to persuade her readers of it? What satirical devices of Swift's does she also use?

4. In her concluding paragraphs she returns to the point of her opening paragraphs. How effective do you find this return? How effective is the rhetoric of the whole essay?

WRITING ASSIGNMENT

Compare the rhetoric of "A Modest Proposal" with the rhetoric of "All the Poor Patriots," noting similarities and differences in strategy and devices of persuasion. Comment on the relative effectiveness of these devices.

THEMATIC
TABLE OF CONTENTS

Issues of Justice

War

The author wishes to thank the copyright holders of the selections in this book, which are listed below in order of their appearance:

INDEX